Haiti & the Dominican Republic

THE ISLAND OF HISPANIOLA

The Bradt Story

In 1974, my former husband George Bradt and I spent three days sitting on a river barge in Bolivia writing our first guide for like-minded travellers: *Backpacking along Ancient Ways in Peru and Bolivia*. The 'little yellow book', as it became known, is now in its sixth edition and continues to sell to travellers throughout the world.

Since 1980, with the establishment of Bradt Publications, I have continued to publish guides for the discerning traveller, covering more than 100 countries and all six continents; in 1997 we won *The Sunday Times* Small Publisher of the Year Award. *Haiti and the Dominican Republic* is the 149th Bradt title or new edition to be published.

The company continues to develop new titles and new series, but in the forefront of my mind there remains our original ethos – responsible travel with an emphasis on the culture and natural history of the region. I hope that you will get the most out of your trip, and perhaps have the opportunity to give something in return.

Travel guides are by their nature continuously evolving. If you experience anything which you would like to share with us, or if you have any amendments to make to this guide, please write; all your letters are read and passed on to the author. Most importantly, do remember to travel with an open mind and to respect the customs of your hosts – it will add immeasurably to your enjoyment.

Happy travelling!

Hilary Bradt

41 Nortoft Road, Chalfont St Peter, Bucks SL9 0LA, England
Tel/fax: 01494 873478 Email: bradtpublications@compuserve.com

Haiti & the
Dominican Republic

THE ISLAND OF HISPANIOLA

Ross Velton

Bradt Publications, UK
The Globe Pequot Press Inc, USA

First published in 1999 by Bradt Publications,
41 Nortoft Road, Chalfont St Peter, Bucks SL9 0LA, England
Published in the USA by The Globe Pequot Press Inc,
6 Business Park Road, PO Box 833, Old Saybrook, Connecticut 06475-0833

The author and publishers have made every effort to ensure the accuracy of the
information in this book at the time of going to press. However, the publishers
cannot accept any responsibility for any loss, injury or inconvenience resulting
from the use of information contained in this guide.

British Library Cataloguing in Publication Data
A catalogue record for this book is available from the British Library
ISBN 1 898323 82 8

Library of Congress Cataloging-in-Publication Data
Velton, Ross.
  Haiti & the Dominican Republic : the island of Hispaniola / Ross
    Velton.
    p. cm.
  Includes index.
  ISBN 1-898323-82-8
  1. Haiti–Guidebooks. 2. Dominican Republic–Guidebooks. 3.
    Haiti–Description and travel. I. title. II. Title: Haiti and the
    Dominican Republic.
  F1915.5.V45 1999
  917.29304'54 DC21   08-37511
                                                          CIP

Photographs
Cover: Rio San Juan, Dominican Republic (John MacPherson/Woodfall Wild Images)
Text: Peter Baker/Photobank (PB), Ross Velton (RV)

Illustrations Carole Vincer
Maps Steve Munns

Typeset from the author's disc by Wakewing, High Wycombe
Printed and bound in Italy by LEGO, Vicenza

Author

Ross Velton was trained as a lawyer. He took his first degree at the University of Durham and then went on to complete a Master's Degree in European Law at the prestigious College of Europe in Bruges, Belgium.

However, Ross' real passion is for travel. He was barely 18 when he made his first independent trip and since then he has travelled extensively in Asia, Africa and Latin America. At the same time he moved away from academic writing and started to earn his living as a travel writer.

These days he concentrates on writing and travel photography, supplementing his income with occasional acting and presenting work.

Ross spent the early years of his childhood in the West Indies where he became fascinated with the island of Hispaniola. He returns there in adulthood to write the first guide of its kind to give equal coverage to Haiti and the Dominican Republic.

STOP PRESS...HURRICANE GEORGES

In October 1998 Hurricane Georges swept across the island of Hispaniola, causing considerable damage and loss of life. The southeastern part of the Dominican Republic was badly affected, and most of the 260 who died and the 180,000 who lost their homes came from the shanty towns of Santo Domingo and the villages along the south and east coasts. The hotels and resorts in this area were also hit, but not as badly as the local people whose fragile homes were blown away like tents in a stiff breeze. The villages in Haiti were even less able to resist the winds, and once Georges had finished with Hispaniola and was en route to the southern states of the USA, a further 150 people had died and 300,000 were homeless.

This local tragedy has not been fatal for the tourist industry in Hispaniola. For a start, the north of the island, one of the most popular parts for tourism, was virtually unaffected by Georges, and even the tourist areas bearing the brunt of the damage – Santo Domingo, the Costa Caribe, Punta Cana and Bávaro – were quickly back on the road to recovery. Several resorts were forced to close in the immediate aftermath, but by December 1998 most of them, including the most important, Casa de Campo, had re-opened.

The story is somewhat different for the thousands of people left destitute by this disaster. Please remember this when you visit Hispaniola: travel with a responsible attitude, and give generously to your hosts.

Contents

Introduction

'*Dèyè mòn gin mòn*'
Beyond mountains there are more mountains
Haitian proverb

I opened my map of Hispaniola and saw two countries on one island. The one on the left was about half the size of the one on the right, but apart from that there seemed to be no difference between them. The roads did not stop at the border and each side had a generous helping of multicoloured squares, circles and squiggly lines. Then I studied the legend explaining what all these shapes and colours meant. I looked carefully and at the bottom in tiny print I saw the words: 'A 4WD car is necessary for many roads in Haiti.' This innocuous sentence fascinated me. 'How bad,' I asked myself, 'could Haiti be?' This was, after all, the Caribbean; and nowhere in the Caribbean is really poor, is it? The thought of roads bad enough to necessitate 4WD were anathema to the dreamy notions of a West Indian holiday, full as they usually are of rum punches by the pool, pretty colonial towns and an easy pace of life. My map had hinted that Haiti was going to be a little special.

Since most of the roads – so mischievously represented by my map as principal highways – are, in fact, no more than dirt tracks, 4WD certainly appears to be necessary in Haiti. Yet this is by no means the only way in which the western one-third of the island of Hispaniola differs from the eastern two-thirds that is the Dominican Republic. In stark contrast to the luxurious resorts and the fun-in-the-sun atmosphere of its neighbour, in Haiti the sun beats down on the harsh realities of life in the western hemisphere's poorest nation. The difference is most shocking when you cross the border between the two countries. Walking from Dajabón on the Dominican side to Quanaminthe on the Haitian side is like walking back in time. Paved streets turn to rubble; electricity pylons are held up at immigration; and lush vegetation is replaced by bare rock – a sign that even the trees have forsaken the poor, dry land of Haiti.

In recent years the tourists have followed suit and have kept away from Haiti. The halcyon days of the early 1950s when tourism boomed and Port-au-Prince enjoyed the company of Graham Greene, Noel Coward and Irving Berlin are dim and distant memories today. Fresher in people's minds are the atrocities of the Duvalier years, the dreaded Tontons Macoute with their red scarves and dark glasses, the mass exodus of the 'boat people' and the political oppression and violence that has plagued the lives of a generation. Gloomy newspaper headlines and UN statistics have become the tourist brochure for Haiti. In this climate, even the country's greatest attractions have gained notoriety. Voodoo, for example, is no longer a harmless show for the tourists, but an evil ritual involving sinister dolls, black magic and zombies. In short, Haiti needs a new image.

The departure of the UN soldiers in December 1997 was a good start, even if, in the words of the chief of the UN mission, 'Haiti is still a country that has not left the intensive care ward'. Hopefully, it has entered a period of stability where the fledgling Haitian National Police can effectively maintain law and order. If a fear for your safety is making you reluctant to visit Haiti, you really have nothing to worry about. In fact, I can say without exaggeration that I have never been to a country where I have felt safer. Put this down to the misleading media image of Haiti as a crime-ridden black spot of the Caribbean, or the essential honesty of the Haitian people, but so long as you take all the precautions you would normally take anywhere else in the Caribbean, security need not be a major concern.

At the same time remember that you are not just anywhere in the Caribbean – you are in Haiti, which is different. There are some interesting things to see, including the most extraordinary building in the West Indies – the Citadelle La Ferrière. But I must say that Haiti is not so much seen as experienced. Uncompromising poverty and a dilapidated infrastructure mean that travel is often hard work. However, if you come with an open mind and expect nothing, but be ready for anything, you will never forget this place.

How ironic that troubled Haiti should share an island with the most popular tourist destination in the Caribbean. Thousands of people flock to the Dominican Republic, almost all of them on pre-paid packages at an all-inclusive resort. This surprises me, not because the Dominican Republic is popular, but because so many people can visit a country with so much to offer, yet be content to spend the whole of their time sitting on the same stretch of beach, eating at the same restaurant and watching the same sunset day in and day out. Of course, the beaches can be idyllic, the food quite tasty and the sunsets breathtaking, but even so the Dominican Republic is underselling itself, or someone is underselling the Dominican Republic.

How many people know that this country has the three highest mountains in the West Indies, a saltwater lake 40m below sea level and the oldest city in the New World? Perhaps slightly more than those who know that a good hotel room can be had for US$15 and a bus ticket to anywhere in the country rarely costs more than US$5. In short, the Dominican Republic is tailor-made for independent travel.

So you see, both of the countries on this island have been misunderstood. Haiti is not hell on earth; and there is more to the Dominican Republic than meets the eye. This, of course, is why I have written this guide. Hispaniola is a compelling island which is still waiting to be discovered (or rediscovered), not by another tour operator or international aid organisation, but by you – the independent traveller.

About this book

I hope that I have followed the many Bradt authors before me who have given their readers well-balanced and thought-provoking background information to the countries they are about to visit. I also hope that I have produced a practical and user-friendly guide that will save you time and perhaps a little money. I have written it for travellers who are serious about exploring this island independently, using public transport and staying away from the all-inclusive resorts. This guide is not simply a listing of all the hotels and restaurants in Hispaniola, nor is it by any means comprehensive. I have tried to point you in the right direction by giving you a few ideas and supplying what I think is useful information. The actual exploring and discovering is up to you.

The guide itself treats Haiti and the Dominican Republic separately. Each country is divided into regions, which are then divided into towns and other places of interest. When I travel, I find that one of the most time-consuming and frustrating things can be finding out how to get from A to B. With this in mind, I have tried to make the *Getting there and away* section for each town as detailed and specific as possible. Where there is no map, I hope that my directions are clear and simple. Accommodation is another important consideration when travelling. At the very least, it should be safe and preferably clean. Since the first-time visitor has no way of knowing whether or not this is the case, I have placed a strong emphasis on the *Where to stay* sections. I have tried to include a broad range of places, although the resort-type hotels have been given short shrift.

Prices

One of the biggest drawbacks of a guidebook is how quickly it dates. This is especially true where prices are concerned. It might be that by the time you visit Hispaniola few of the prices are as I have quoted them in this guide. Nonetheless, I have chosen to be as specific as possible about the price of things. Even if they are not spot on when you arrive, they will give you a good idea how to plan your holiday budget. I have written the prices in the currency in which they were quoted to me. In Haiti this could be in US dollars (US$), Haitian dollars (H$) or *gourdes* (Gde). In the Dominican Republic it is either US dollars or *pesos* (RD$). Both countries have relatively stable currencies that are unlikely to fluctuate much vis à vis the US dollar, so you can be quite accurate about the exchange rates. Initially, this might be a little confusing and mind-boggling. But after a few days in Hispaniola you'll be thinking in the local currency; and I think that a guide book which constantly refers back to US dollars is ultimately unhelpful.

Acknowledgements

Dedicated to our hosts:
The people of Haiti
and the Dominican Republic

I have depended on the support of a lot of people to write this book.

One of my greatest debts of gratitude is to my father who put up with me for much longer than I had any right to expect while I eked out the words of this guide. I thank him and his wife for their hospitality and all-round support.

Another big thank you goes to Jacqualine Labrom and her chauffeur/husband, Tony. They provided me with the perfect introduction to Haiti and were always there when I needed them. I would also like to thank the following people in Haiti: Nicolas Bussenius, Madam Madsen, Eric Johnson, Suzanne Seitz, Paul Paryski and Patrique de la Torre. In the Dominican Republic, I greatly appreciate the help of José Ramón Martínez Batlle, Luis Santiago, Dennis Carroll Smith, Christian Vierheilig, Ali and, in particular, Julius Geier.

When travellers are on the road exploring unfamiliar places, they are ultimately dependent on the help and generosity of the local people. I thank everyone in Haiti and the Dominican Republic for their advice, friendship and hospitality.

The team at Bradt Publications should also be acknowledged – not only for publishing this original guide, but also for having the courage to commission it in the first place.

Moral support was given in different ways by Allan Foenander, Hilary Gagan, Christopher Townley, the McNamara brothers, Peter Curran and, of course, my mother. Thanks to them all.

Part One

General Information

Poinciana 'flame tree'

2

Key to Chapters

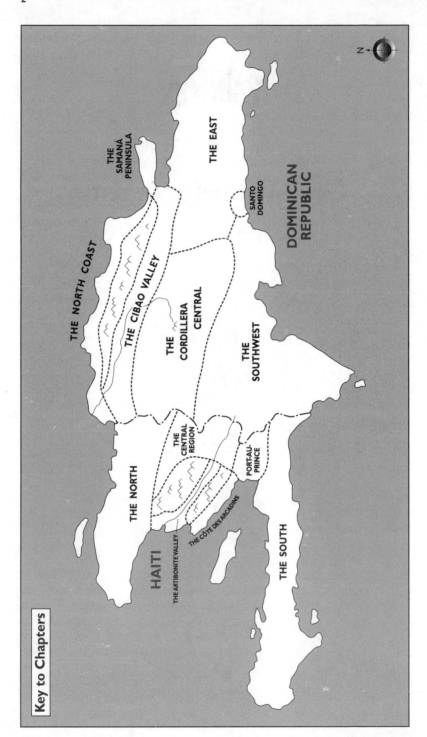

Introducing Hispaniola

EARLY HISTORY
Before Columbus

The pre-Columbian populations of the West Indies can be divided into three distinct chronological groups. The first wave of migration occurred between about 5000 and 2000BC. These people, known as the Paleo-Indians, probably came from Central America, crossing the now submerged mid-Caribbean islands that stretched from the coast of Honduras and Nicaragua to the Greater Antilles. The second group, the Meso-Indians, started to arrive from about 1000BC. They came from the coast of South America in large, dugout canoes and reached as far as the Greater Antilles. The remnants of these people have been labelled the Ciboney. The third wave of migration started around 300BC, once again from the South American mainland. These people were known as the Neo-Indians. First, the Arawak spread to the Lesser and Greater Antilles; and then, after AD1000, the more aggressive Caribs started to arrive in the Lesser Antilles, driving the Arawak out as they came.

By the time Columbus arrived in Hispaniola in 1492, there were approximately six million Indians in the Caribbean, divided into three distinct groups: the Ciboney, the Arawak and the Carib.

The Ciboney

By 1492, the Ciboney had been driven to the western parts of Hispaniola (Haiti) and Cuba by their more powerful Arawak neighbours. They were the most primitive of the three groups, surviving by collecting shellfish and fruit and living in caves and rock shelters along the coast (indeed, Ciboney is the Arawak name for cave dweller). The Haitian Ciboney used implements made from chipped stone, while the Cuban Ciboney based their technology on shells.

The Arawak

The Arawak, who occupied the Greater Antilles and Trinidad, were more advanced than the Ciboney. As well as hunting and gathering, they developed other techniques of subsistence. The most important was a system of cultivation known as *conuco*, whereby an area of land was cleared and the soil heaped into mounds about 12m high. Various plants rich in starch and sugar were then planted in the mounds. The most important was cassava, which was used to make cassava bread, one of the Arawak's main foods. But the Arawak were also quite advanced in other areas, making pottery and baskets, weaving simple cotton clothing and wearing gold rings and necklaces.

The Carib

Caribs were great seafaring people – the Caribbean Sea is named after them – and they had already driven the Arawak out of the Lesser Antilles, overrun Puerto Rico and reached the eastern tip of Hispaniola by the time of first European contact. Unlike the Arawak, Caribs fought efforts to enslave them and gained the reputation for being bloodthirsty savages. In fact, the English word 'cannibal' is derived from the Carib's Arawak name *caribal*. Their culture was certainly more warlike than the other Indians in the Caribbean; but whether or not they were quite as bad as the Europeans made out is debatable.

Taino culture

As the Arawak developed their culture, they became known as the Taino, meaning 'noble' or 'prudent'. These were the people that Columbus encountered when he arrived in Hispaniola, whom he described as 'loveable, tractable, peaceable and praiseworthy'.

There were many Taino villages on the island, normally with populations of between 1,000 and 2,000. Each village had a *cacique* (chief), and he or she (there was no gender discrimination) was responsible for organising the daily activities of the village, storing surplus commodities and acting as host when the village received visitors. Meanwhile, district *caciques* would oversee a group of villages, while regional *caciques* would oversee the district *caciques*. When Columbus arrived, there were about five regional *caciques* in Hispaniola.

Houses were generally made of wood with palm thatched roofs. They were cone-shaped and arranged around a central open space, in the middle of which stood the *cacique's* square-shaped house.

As a rule, Tainos went naked, although unmarried women would wear a headband and married women a short skirt. Gold jewellery and other ornaments were popular (fatally so when the Spaniards saw them), as was flattening the forehead by binding hard objects against it during childhood.

The Taino worshipped deities known as *zemis*, and religious ceremonies and rituals were presided over by a *shaman*, whose other function was as the village doctor. It was also possible for individual Tainos to commune with their *zemis*. All they had to do was poke a stick down their throat to induce vomiting, thereby emptying the stomach and purifying it. Crushed seeds from the piptadenia tree were then swallowed, causing hallucinations through which the *zemi* would appear. The most important deities were Yucahu, the lord of cassava and the sea, and his mother, Atabey, goddess of fresh water and fertility.

Entertainment was an important part of Taino culture. One of the most popular pastimes was a game called *batey*, which was played with a rubber ball that was passed back and forth across a court between two teams of 20 or 30 people. The basic idea, if not the execution, was similar to tennis.

The Taino, like the Carib, were great seafaring people – they had, after all, sailed over open sea from South America to get to Hispaniola. They travelled in canoes of hollowed-out logs, sometimes large enough to carry 150 people and not dissimilar to the long boats found in Polynesia.

Despite the agricultural techniques developed by the Arawak, hunting and fishing were still important. Tainos supplemented their cassava bread diets with iguanas, pigeons, doves, parrots, shellfish, crabs and many types of waterfowl.

Christopher Columbus

On December 6 1492, the three ships of Columbus' first voyage to the New World – the *Piña*, the *Niña* and the *Santa María* – dropped anchor in a bay on the northwestern peninsula of an island Columbus later named La Isla Española. A few days later, on Christmas Eve, the Santa María ran aground in a bay a little further along the north coast. A Taino *cacique* called Guacanagari met Columbus and helped him to strip the boards from the *Santa María* and use them to construct La Navidad. This was the first European settlement in the New World. On January 16 1493, Columbus left for Spain with his remaining ships, leaving 39 Spaniards behind in La Navidad.

When Columbus returned to Hispaniola in November 1493 he came with 17 ships loaded with priests and criminals – the former to teach Christianity to the Taino, the latter to colonise the island. In his absence, however, La Navidad had been destroyed and all the Spaniards killed (allegedly by the Indians). The site chosen for the new settlement, La Isabela, was further east along the coast. Even though it had few prospects (it was unprotected, hot and a breeding ground for disease), according to Spanish thinking this was the gold-bearing region of the island. Columbus erroneously believed that the Yacque del Norte River and the Cibao Valley contained huge gold reserves that would make fortunes. In anticipation of these riches, Columbus set about pacifying the Indians. This was achieved in March 1495 when the Spaniards routed the Taino in a battle in the valley of La Vega. After this, the Taino were little more than serfs, their lives reduced to serving the Spanish and working in the gold mines. This was the situation when Columbus returned to Spain on March 10 1446, leaving his brothers, Bartolomé and Diego, in charge of Hispaniola.

Just as La Navidad had been unable to survive Colombus' first period of absence, when he returned to Hispaniola for the third time, in 1498, La Isabela had been abandoned and the colony was being run from a new site called Santo Domingo on the southern coast. (Santo Domingo was also the name given at this time to the whole colony.) Columbus returned to an atmosphere of resentment. His brothers had not been popular and a rebellion, led by the mayor of La Isabela, Francisco Roldán, had flared up on the island. This prompted the Spanish Crown to send someone to investigate. In August 1500, the Spanish chief justice, Francisco de Bobadilla, arrived in Santo Domingo, arrested all three of the Columbus brothers and sent them back to Spain. This marked the end of Christopher Columbus' association with Hispaniola, and although he won back the favour of his royal patrons in Spain and was sent on a fourth voyage, he was not trusted enough to be allowed to return to Hispaniola. Meanwhile, de Bobadilla had failed to restore order in Santo Domingo and was replaced as governor in 1502 by

Nicolás de Ovando. On de Bobadilla's return voyage to Spain, his ship and all aboard were destroyed by a hurricane.

Spanish Rule

Nicolás de Ovando presided over an era of prosperity for Santo Domingo and the Spanish, during which the Taino population was virtually obliterated. Santo Domingo was the centre of the New World, its lands were rich and its gold mines, while not as bountiful as Columbus had hoped, were certainly not insignificant.

In order to meet the demand created by a good economy, Ovando introduced the *ecomienda*. This was a system whereby land was granted by the crown to a conquistador, who had the right to demand an *ecomendero* from the Indians living within a certain area. In return for this tribute – which could be paid in gold, in labour, or in kind – the conquistador was obliged to protect the Indians and instruct them in the Christian faith. This part of the bargain was rarely fulfilled and the *encomienda* was effectively a system of forced labour. However, it was still not enough, as the Taino population was declining at an alarming rate and more labour was needed to work the mines. It was at this time that the first slaves were brought over from Africa.

The genocide of the Taino Indians was one of the greatest crimes of Spanish rule in Hispaniola. Many died through overwork, many more were simply slaughtered, and the rest perished from diseases brought over by the Europeans. In 1492 there were between 300,000 and one million Tainos on the island. This number had fallen to 60,000 in 1508, and by 1548 there were fewer than 500. A whole civilisation wiped out in little over 50 years.

Nothing much changed when Diego Columbus, Christopher's only legitimate son, replaced Ovando as governor in 1509 (although the gold reserves were dwindling almost as much as the Taino population). Diego spent most of his time trying to regain his father's former privileges and preserve his own, which had been threatened when an *audencia* (royal court) was established in Santo Domingo with jurisdiction over civil, criminal and military matters. By the time Diego Columbus left Santo Domingo in 1524, it was already in decline.

Little gold was produced after 1515, and almost none after 1519. In any case, the conquests of Mexico and Peru meant that gold was now more readily available on the Spanish Main.

The writing was on the wall for the Spanish in Hispaniola, and in 1564 an earthquake which destroyed the important towns of Santiago and La Vega did nothing to improve their fortune. Back in Europe, Spain was at war with England, and in 1586 Sir Francis Drake sacked Santo Domingo on behalf of his queen. In 1655, the English (then ruled by Oliver Cromwell) attempted another invasion of Hispaniola, which this time was unsuccessful. Meanwhile, in the western part of the island the French were causing trouble. By the 1630s French pirates had settled on the off-shore island of Tortuga and were gradually moving over to the mainland where they started to establish farms and plantations. Eventually, in 1664, the French West India Company, with support from the

English, took possession of the western end of Hispaniola for France.

It was clear that the Spanish could no longer exercise proper control over Hispaniola. War in Europe preoccupied the crown and Santo Domingo was a low priority. Indeed, it was perhaps with some relief that the Spanish formally ceded the western third of Hispaniola to France in the Treaty of Ryswick (1697). From then on the history of Hispaniola became the history of two colonies – the French in Saint Domingue and the Spanish in Santo Domingo – now two independent nations: Haiti and the Dominican Republic.

THE NATURAL WORLD
Vegetation
The array of plant life is understandably impressive on an island with the highest and lowest points in the West Indies, as well as places where it never rains and others where it never stops raining. Despite the extensive deforestation in Haiti, which has deprived the country of all but 3% of its forest cover, there is still a great diversity of flora in Hispaniola.

The most common type of life zone is subtropical forest, which is found in lowland areas and on the floors and slopes of most valleys. This is the lush, green, exotic and eminently healthy landscape usually associated with the Caribbean. It is characterised by royal palms, coconut palms, Hispaniolan mahogany, West Indian cedar, wild olive, American muskwood and others.

Meanwhile, the Hispaniolan coastline has its fair share of red, white and button mangroves – although not as many as some Caribbean countries due to the numerous cliffs around the island's coast. As you go up into the highland regions, you start to see mountain forests with palms, pines (the Creolean pine is the most common), ferns and hundreds of different species of orchid. In stark contrast, the desert regions – for example in the southwest of the Dominican Republic – have arid landscapes where multi-shaped cacti predominate.

Wildlife
Birds
The considerable bird population in Hispaniola is made up of indigenous species and wintering birds from the North American mainland. The deforestation in Haiti notwithstanding, Hispaniola is still a bird-watchers' paradise.

Look out for species like the Hispaniolan parrot, the Hispaniolan woodpecker, the rarer Hispaniolan trogon and Hispaniolan parakeet, the palmchat (which nests in the royal palms on the coastal plains) and several types of owl and pigeon, including the endangered white-crowned pigeon. Around the coast plenty of shorebirds can be seen. Great egrets, American frigate birds, brown pelicans, blue herons, glossy ibis, ruddy ducks and flamingos are all relatively common – especially on the off-shore islands of the Dominican Republic and around the numerous lakes and lagoons on the mainland. In the mountains there are yet more species like the Antillean siskin, the white-necked crow, the green-tailed warbler and numerous types of butterfly and hummingbird. This is just the tip of the iceberg. It remains to be seen what other species exist in the hitherto unexplored parts of the island.

HAITI'S ENVIRONMENTAL DISASTER

Deforestation is one of Haiti's most critical problems. Currently, all but 3% of the country's forest cover has been destroyed and 15,000 hectares of arable land is being lost each year.

Poverty and a growing population are at the root of the deforestation problem. For many Haitians, survival depends on felling trees and planting every piece of available land. The trees are burnt into charcoal – the preferred fuel of the majority – and the cleared land is planted with subsistence crops. However, these crops seldom thrive and, ironically, deforestation has led to food shortages. Given the mountainous terrain and the many fast-flowing streams in Haiti, tree roots are vital to anchor the soil. Deprived of forest cover, the precious topsoil, which makes the land fertile and productive, is washed into the sea at a staggering rate. A vicious circle has developed. More land is being cleared to feed a growing population, yet as the trees fall so does the productivity of the soil, meaning that more land has to be farmed to produce enough food for the people. If this continues, experts predict that Haiti could be a desert by the middle of the 21st century.

In 1994 a Ministry of the Environment was created, and more recently a National Environmental Action Plan is being developed with the help of international organisations such as the United Nations Development Project (UNDP). Solving the problem is another matter. For instance, in an attempt to wean the Haitian peasantry off charcoal, schemes were introduced to promote the more sustainable use of gas. However, as soon as the gas cylinders arrived in the villages (where there were no gas stoves to use them in any case) they were sold to buy charcoal and the wood of younger trees, which has recently become as popular as charcoal as a burning fuel. Re-education is undoubtedly the way forward, although it is easier said than done in a country where even short-term survival is a struggle.

Land mammals

The Caribbean in general doesn't have many land species, and Hispaniola is no exception. Most of the mammals you see on the island today – dogs, cats, pigs, boars, horses, rats and mice – were introduced by the Europeans. In fact, there are only two endemic land mammals in Hispaniola. The **solenodon** is an insectivore not dissimilar to a rat, but nicer. It has a long snout, lives in caves and hollow tree trunks and feeds on insects and worms. The **hutia** is another small rodent which, like the solenodon, lives in caves and tree trunks. The chances of spotting either of these animals on your travels are slim: firstly, because they are nocturnal creatures, and secondly, because some believe that they might already be extinct.

Marine mammals

The **West Indian manatee** is an endangered marine mammal. They can sometimes be seen in the coastal areas of the national parks or in Samaná Bay, but hunting and the increase in boat traffic has caused a decline in their numbers. Nicknamed the 'sea cow', manatees can grow to over 3.5m in length and they 'graze' on aquatic plants on the ocean floor.

One of the principal breeding grounds in the world for **humpback whales** is on the Silver and Navidad banks off the north coast of the Dominican Republic. Each winter, some 3,000 whales migrate from their feeding grounds in the North Atlantic and congregate here to reproduce in shallow waters protected by coral reefs and free of boats and other distractions. Nearer to the mainland, Samaná Bay is also a popular spot for whale watching, which has become an important tourist activity during the months of January, February and March.

The humpback is one of the larger species of whale, measuring from 12–15m and weighing up to 60 tons. Adult humpbacks are dark grey, while their calves are a lighter colour. Although their name would suggest otherwise, humpbacks do not actually have a humped back. It only looks as though they do when they jump out of the water with arched backs. Other distinguishing features are their knobbly heads, long, white flippers and large tails. Moreover, unlike all other toothed whales, the humpback has two blowholes rather than one.

Humpbacks do not eat during their stay in Hispaniolan waters. Instead, they live off the 15–20cm of fat accumulated during the feeding season by eating about a ton of food a day. Most of this turns to fat and is the equivalent of a human daily diet of 8,000 hamburgers. The humpback's preference, however, is small fish and crustaceans called krill (about 6cm long and resembling shrimps). While adult humpbacks reproduce and diet, the newly born calves drink 50 gallons of milk a day. This milk, produced by the mother, is about 50% fat, allowing the calves to grow big enough to survive the journey back to the feeding grounds in the north.

Amphibians and reptiles

Reptiles and amphibians are not particularly abundant in Hispaniola. The lizards outnumber the snakes and frogs, but other species unique to the island are invariably under threat.

The **rhinoceros iguana** is an endangered species endemic to Hispaniola. They like dry, rocky ground with cacti and thorny bushes and are most commonly found in the Enriquillo basin. The males, in particular, look like fearsome creatures with three small horns on their snout, a pad like a helmet on top of their head and a large throat pouch (the females have neither helmet nor horns). However, they are actually very shy animals who prefer flight to fight. Their size (often over 1m in length) and their uniform grey colour explains why they are called rhinoceros iguana. They live on plants and berries and are active only by day. The other species of iguana found in Hispaniola is the **ricord iguana**.

The four main types of **turtle** living off the Hispaniolan coast are the leatherback (the largest living turtle), the loggerhead (found in lagoons and coastal bays), the hawksbill (prized for its beautiful shell) and the green sea turtle (hunted for *calipee*, a glutinous yellow substance used to make soup).

The **American crocodile** is the most widely distributed of the four crocodile species present in the New World. On its travels it has managed to colonise most of Central America, South America as far as Peru and much of the Caribbean. In Hispaniola, the American crocodile is so well established that it represents one of the largest wildlife crocodile populations in the world. Its favourite haunts are the brackish waters of Lake Enriquillo in the Dominican Republic and Étang Saumâtre in Haiti. However, while the adults can survive in hyper-saline conditions by way of a salt gland in their mouth and by taking advantage of fresh water in the environment (rainfall, for example), hatchlings cannot, so the water must not be too salty. Lake Enriquillo is now four times saltier than the sea – due in large part to the diversion of streams feeding into the lake for irrigation purposes – which has put the younger crocodile population under real threat.

Take my word for it that any crocodiles you see will be American crocodiles. If you don't believe me, get as close as you dare and look for the fourth tooth protruding above the level of the upper jaw. American crocodiles also have an olive-brown shade and an obvious swelling on the snout in front of the eye sockets. An average length for a female is 2.5m, but males can grow to about 4m.

Although they are reputed to be a threat to man, attacks are rare and American crocodiles stick to their normal diet of fish, turtles and the occasional dog or goat. They often hunt at night and spend the hottest parts of the day in deeper areas of water. The best time to see them on land is during the early morning or late afternoon when they emerge from the water to raise their body temperature under the sun's rays.

The coral reef
With so many coral reefs around the island, diving and snorkelling are two of the most popular activities on a trip to Hispaniola. Before you put on your flippers or tank, bear in mind a few general rules, which are all part and parcel of being a responsible tourist. Do not stand on the reef, touch it, remove pieces from it, or otherwise interfere with what you see.

Types of coral reef
One of the discoveries made by Charles Darwin during his voyages on the *Beagle* was that there are three kinds of reef. The first is known as the fringing reef, which is what you see if you go snorkelling just off the shore. The fringing reef is always connected to the mainland, but can extend quite far out to sea. It has a variety of coral types and species and for the uninitiated it's a great place to see some underwater life. Beyond the fringing reef across the lagoon – an area of shallow water with a floor of coral sand and debris – you'll come to the barrier reef or, as is more common in Caribbean and tropical Atlantic waters, the bank/barrier reef. The difference between the two is their size: the barrier reef, found mainly in the Pacific, is larger than the

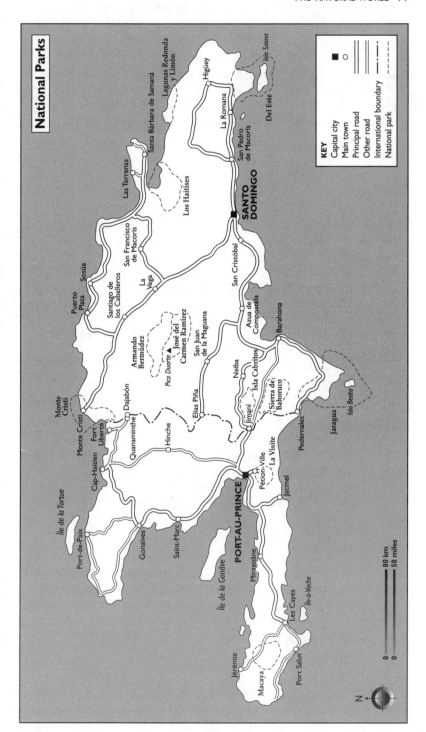

National Parks

KEY
- ■ Capital city
- ○ Main town
- Principal road
- Other road
- International boundary
- National park

Isla Saona

Higüey

Lagunas Redonda y Limón

Santa Bárbara de Samaná

La Romana

San Pedro de Macorís

Del Este

Las Terrenas

Los Haitises

San Francisco de Macorís

SANTO DOMINGO

Sosúa

Puerto Plata

Santiago de los Caballeros

La Vega

San Cristóbal

Azua de Compostela

Barahona

Armando Bermúdez

José del Carmen Ramírez

Pico Duarte ▲

San Juan de la Maguana

Neiba

Isla Cabritos

Sierra de Bahoruco

Isla Beata

Jaragua

Monte Cristi

Dajabón

Elías Piña

Jimaní

Pedernales

Cap-Haïtien

Fort Liberté

Ouanaminthe

Hinche

Île de la Tortue

Port-de-Paix

Gonaïves

Saint-Marc

La Visite

Pétion-Ville

PORT-AU-PRINCE

Jacmel

Île de la Gonâve

Miragoâne

Jérémie

Macaya

Les Cayes

Port Salut

Île-à-Vache

N

0   80 km
0   50 miles

bank/barrier reef and is separated by lagoons thousands of metres wide, rather than the hundreds that separate the bank/barrier reef from the mainland. This type of reef is home to more species than the fringing reef, but you'll need a boat to get out to it. The third type of reef is the atoll – an incomplete ring of sandy islands built up on coral reefs surrounding a submerged volcano. They are usually found far from any continent or large island and are rare in the Caribbean. The closest atoll to Hispaniola lies off the coast of Belize.

Species of the coral reef

There are hundreds of species in both the fringing reef and the bank/barrier reef. These include corals, sponges, worms, molluscs, crabs, lobsters and fish.

There are basically two types of coral. Both photosynthesise the energy of the sun and excrete limestone from the calcium carbonate in the water. In the case of hard corals, this limestone creates a skeleton which encloses the animal altogether – a build-up of which in turn creates the reef. Soft corals, meanwhile, have no such skeleton and resemble plants. However, the creation and maintenance of the reef depends on more than just the hard coral. Instead, it's a team effort. Several types of algae also help to bind and solidify the reef's frame, while molluscs, crustacea, sea urchins, starfish and sponges all anchor to the reef, thereby helping to line and protect it. At the same time, other species dependent on the reef for their survival like the fireworm, the coral snail, the green reef crab and, most notoriously, the parrot fish are ironically doing their best to destroy it by living off the coral tissue. It is estimated that for every acre of reef, one ton of solid coral skeleton is converted into fine sand every year. The major culprit is the parrot fish.

NATIONAL PARKS

A network of national parks protects the flora and fauna of Hispaniola. Sadly, the vast majority of them are in the Dominican Republic, where nearly 10% of the total land area is protected. In theory you can visit all of these parks, including the two in Haiti, but in practice few of them are easily accessible and in most cases you'll definitely need your own transport. For more information about the national parks in the Dominican Republic contact the Dirección Nacional de Parques, 2478 Avenida Máximo Gómez, Santo Domingo; tel: 472 3911. There is currently no equivalent body in Haiti.

Before You Go

HEALTH
Written in collaboration with Dr Jane Wilson-Howarth
Inoculations
Polio, tetanus, diphtheria, typhoid and hepatitis A are all a risk in undeveloped tropical areas where sanitation is sometimes primitive.

Most people are immunised against **polio**, **tetanus** and **diphtheria** in infancy. However, you need a booster every ten years, so make sure that you're up to date.

Typhoid is a nasty gut infection which is caught through the consumption of contaminated food or water. There are occasional outbreaks in Hispaniola – most recently in the Dominican Republic – so in addition to observing the normal, common sense rules of hygiene, you should also be immunised against the disease. You can either have an injection, which provides protection for three years, or a course of three oral capsules, which lasts for one year.

Hepatitis A, a viral disease which attacks the liver and usually causes jaundice, is also caught by consuming contaminated food or water. Moreover, something as innocuous as not washing your hands after visiting a public lavatory can put you at risk, since the virus is spread from person to person, usually from dirty hand to mouth. Once again, hygiene and common sense are the keywords. Apart from hygiene, there are two ways to protect yourself against hepatitis A. The best, although more expensive, option is the Havrix vaccine. The initial injection provides protection for about a year; the second of the course covers you for ten years. Havrix needs ten days to become effective. If your stay in Hispaniola is only going to be short, a shot of immunoglobulin (gamma globulin) is cheaper. It helps reduce – not eliminate – the risk for about three months. With this in mind, have the gamma globulin dose as close to your departure as possible.

Travel clinics
United Kingdom
Berkeley Travel Clinic, 32 Berkeley St, London W1X 5FA, tel: 0171 629 6233.

British Airways Clinics These are now situated in 30 towns in the UK and three in South Africa (UK tel: 01276 685040 for the nearest). They provide inoculations, malaria prophylaxis and they sell a variety of health-related travel goods including bed net treatment kits.

Fleet Street Travel Clinic, 29 Fleet St, London EC4Y 1AA, tel: 0171 353 5678.

MASTA (Medical Advisory Service for Travellers Abroad), London School of Hygiene and Tropical Medicine, Keppel St, London WC1 7HT, tel: 0906 8 224100. This is a premium line number.

Nomad Travellers' Store and Medical Centre, 3–4 Wellington Terrace, Turnpike Lane, London N8 0PX, tel: 0181 889 7014.

Trailfinders Immunisation Clinic, 194 Kensington High St, London W8 7RG, tel: 0171 938 3999.

Tropical Medicine Bureau This Irish-run organisation has a useful website specific to tropical destinations: www.tmb.le.

USA

Centers for Disease Control This Atlanta-based organisation is the central source of travel health information in North America, with a touch-tone phone line and fax service. Travelers' Hot Line: (404) 332 4559. Each summer they publish the invaluable *Health Information for International Travel* which is available from the Center for Prevention Services, Division of Quarantine, Atlanta, GA 30333.

IAMAT (International Association for Medical Assistance to Travellers), 736 Center St, Lewiston, NY 14092, USA. Tel: 716 754 4883. Also at Gotthardstrasse 17, 6300 Zug, Switzerland. A non-profit organisation which provides health information and lists of English-speaking doctors abroad.

Australia

TMVC has 20 clinics in Australia, New Zealand and Thailand. For the nearest clinic, phone 1300 65 88 44, or try their website: http://www.tmvc.com.au.

Brisbane, Dr Deborah Mills, Qantas Domestic Building, 6th floor, 247 Adelaide St, Brisbane, QLD 4000 (tel: 7 3221 9066; fax: 7 3221 7076).

Melbourne, Dr Sonny Lau, 393 Little Bourke St, 2nd floor, Melbourne, VIC 3000 (tel: 3 9602 5788; fax: 3 9670 8394).

Sydney, Dr Mandy Hu, Dymocks Building, 7th floor, 428 George St, Sydney, NSW 2000 (tel: 2 221 7133; fax: 2 221 8401).

Malaria

Malaria is now almost non-existent in the Caribbean, but there is a limited risk in Haiti where the malignant *falciparum* form exists throughout the year below 300m in suburban and rural areas. For this reason, some form of prophylactic is recommended. Chloroquine is the preferred antimalarial for visits to Haiti. It has proven to be safe to use, has minimal side effects and only involves taking one pill a week – as opposed to the alternative, Paludrine, which must be taken twice a day every day. Start your course one week before leaving for Haiti and continue taking the pills for four weeks after your return (because there is normally a delayed reaction of a few weeks between catching malaria and displaying the symptoms).

Don't let your bottle of malaria pills lull you into a false sense of security. You must also take precautions not to be bitten by mosquitoes, the insects responsible for transmitting malaria. The Anopheles mosquito, which carries the disease, comes out at dusk. At this time cover up your arms and legs and wear socks. You should also use a good insect repellent, preferably one containing diethyltoluamide or DEET. Some hotels in Hispaniola have mosquito nets, while most can provide mosquito coils. Nets give good protection while you're asleep and coils reduce the amount you are bitten.

With a combination of malaria tablets, insect repellent, net or coils, and common sense, you should have nothing to worry about on the malaria front. Even without these protective measures the risk is minimal. Nevertheless, if you start to get headaches, aches and pains, fevers and chills, you should assume the worst and consult a doctor immediately.

Rabies
Rabies does exist on Hispaniola and you might consider having the highly effective (but also expensive) immunisation against the disease. Much will depend on the nature of your trip. If you intend to have a lot of contact with animals, it is worth having the vaccine. Rabies is carried by mammals – usually dogs – and is passed on to man through a bite, a scratch or a lick of an open wound. If you know or think that a rabid animal has assaulted you, go to a doctor without delay. In the interim, scrub the wound thoroughly with soap under running water for five minutes, then pour on a strong iodine or alcohol solution. You might not eradicate the risk of rabies, but you will guard against wound infection and the very real risk of catching tetanus (if you haven't had your booster).

AIDS
The bottom fell out of the Haitian tourist industry in 1981 when the US Center for Disease Control defined Haitians as a 'high risk group' for AIDS. People started to refer to the four H's: heroine addicts, haemophiliacs, homosexuals and Haitians. Paranoia spread and soon it was widely believed that AIDS in the region had originated in Haiti. Subsequent research has told a different story.

The sad irony of the AIDS problem and its disastrous effects on the country's population and economy is that it was probably imported to Haiti from abroad. The most likely importers were the American homosexuals who visited Haiti in droves during the 1970s. The disease was initially confined to urban areas – specifically the red-light districts of Port-au-Prince where the sex tourists used to go for their kicks. It has since spread all over the country and nowadays AIDS claims as many victims in the countryside as it does in the towns. The extent of the disease is hard to gauge, but there is no doubt that the problem is immense.

The importance of practising safe sex is self-evident. This means wearing a condom, or perhaps a femidom, especially if you have sex with a prostitute. The same rule applies if you want to reduce the risk of catching other sexually transmitted diseases.

Diarrhoea

Diarrhoea (not to be confused with 'faggot's diarrhoea', one of the expressions used to describe AIDS in Haiti) is always a risk when travelling in the tropics. For some reason travellers delight in sharing their experiences in this area; and every cure known to man must have been debated around the camp-fire. Diarrhoea is the way the body flushes out noxious bugs, and rest, relaxation and a little abstinence is recommended. If you do feel hungry, opt for bland foods like bread, rice and plantains. Most importantly, you should drink plenty of fluids to avoid dehydration, the most serious complication of diarrhoea and a particular danger in hot countries. Not only will you be losing a lot of fluid from your bottom end, but you will also be sweating a lot in the heat and humidity of Hispaniola. Try to drink after each bowel movement – preferably two glasses of water with a pinch of salt and some sugar added. Diarrhoea tablets such as Imodium and Lomotil are called 'blockers' and they keep the poisons in your body, causing the diarrhoea to last longer than it would if left to run its natural course. Only use them if you have to.

Prevention is best. The majority of travellers succumb to diarrhoea after eating contaminated food or drinking dirty water. In Haiti and the Dominican Republic hygiene is a very important part of the culture and most places you go will be clean. However, these are also developing countries competing with a climate in which bacteria love to breed, so you should take sensible precautions. Ironically, street food served fresh and hot is safer than the reheated buffet food you get in expensive restaurants. Other things to avoid, or at least be wary of, are salads, unpeeled fruit, ice and ice-cream – all of which are potential carriers of bacteria. The only way to be sure that water is completely clean is to bring it to the boil. Obviously, this will not always be practical. Since bottled water and sachets of purified water are so readily available in both Haiti and the Dominican Republic, I would recommend not taking your chances with the tap water. If you do, purify it first. Iodine is the favoured method; chlorine-based water purification tablets are slightly less effective, but are also fine.

If you do get a bout of diarrhoea, unpleasant as it is, it should not last more than about 36 hours. If it persists, you should see a doctor.

Sunburn and heatstroke

Of all the potential health risks, the sun is the most dangerous you'll face in Hispaniola. Even with the best of intentions, it's easy to burn. This is especially true if you travel a lot in Haiti, where hours spent in an open-backed *camion* during the hottest part of the day invites sunburn and, in the worst cases, heatstroke – where the body overheats like a car engine with sometimes fatal results. Over-exposure to the ultraviolet rays of the sun can also cause skin cancer. Wear a good sun-block to protect your skin from these rays and a pair of sunglasses to protect your eyes. If travelling in an open-backed vehicle or on a motorbike, wear a shirt. Use a wide-brimmed hat, cover up as much as is possible and practical in the heat and avoid being out in the midday sun from 12.00 to 15.00. Finally, don't be suckered into thinking that you'll be OK when it's cool and overcast, since on these days 80% of the ultraviolet radiation can still be present.

Medical kit

A small medical kit might be a good idea, but don't go over the top. Remember that pharmacies abound in Haiti and the Dominican Republic, and you could probably put together a better medical kit there than you could at home. Nevertheless, for peace of mind I recommend the following:

- malaria pills (Chloroquine)
- plasters (Band Aids)
- scissors or a knife
- antiseptic
- calamine lotion to ease the discomfort of sunburn and over-scratched mosquito bites
- good sun-block lotion
- mosquito repellent
- supply of condoms (or femidoms)

TRAVEL INSURANCE

Having spent a small fortune on an airline ticket, there is a temptation to bypass travel insurance. Don't. This is not to say that you can't economise. Buying travel insurance is no different to buying a new pair of shoes: shop around and opt for the one that best fits your needs. Don't be pressured into buying the comprehensive policy offered by most travel agents when you book your ticket. £2,000 to compensate you for the inconvenience of being hijacked might sound impressive, but do you really need it?

Some degree of health cover is obviously essential. The exact amount is up to you, but most policies offer at least £1,000,000 in emergency medical expenses (note that often you pay the first £50 or so). The rest, in my opinion, is optional.

Your most difficult decision will probably be whether or not to insure your baggage and personal belongings. This really bumps up the cost of travel insurance, so estimate first if the amount of cover offered would reimburse the amount you stand to lose. It rarely does, in which case you would be better off saving your money – or leaving the camera at home.

Most of the travel agencies specialising in independent travel also sell travel insurance (see page 22 for addresses and telephone numbers). The advantage here is that these policies are tailored to the needs of the independent traveller and are slightly cheaper than the norm. For specialist travel insurance companies, see page 164.

WHAT TO TAKE

The golden rule is to travel light. If you are serious about travelling around this island by public transport, arriving in towns and finding your own place to stay and being on the move a good deal of the time, you can ill afford to have a heavy and cumbersome bag (or bags). Quite apart from the hassle and discomfort, there are sound financial reasons for keeping your luggage to a minimum. Particularly in Haiti, the buses, *camions* and pick-up trucks that provide the local means of transport get so crowded that large bags often cost extra. If a woman carrying her mangoes to market has to pay, so will a *blanc* carrying a backpack the size of a small child. So, bearing this important proviso in mind, what should you take?

Backpack

The travellers' debate about backpacks is right up there with malaria pills and cures for diarrhoea in the controversy league: most people like them, but some don't. I must admit that a good backpack has its advantages. So long as it's well packed and worn properly, even a heavy pack can be carried for hours with little discomfort. Your hands, meanwhile, are left free to consult this guide. Try to centre most of the pack's weight on the hip belt and minimise the pressure on your shoulders. If not, it will tend to drag you down. The durability of a good pack is also important on an island where luggage is rarely handled with care.

These days most backpackers opt for internal frames, which tend to be better for active travel and keep the load closer to your own centre of gravity. However, if you're going to be doing a lot of hiking in hot weather, or are carrying a large load (see my reservations above), you might consider an external frame, which is stronger and allows air to circulate between your body and the backpack. The purchase of a new backpack can eat up a lot of your holiday money, so make sure you choose one that will last. Check the material, the stitching, the zips and the straps before you hand over your hard-earned cash.

You could, of course, choose to carry your worldly possessions in something other than a backpack – a small suitcase, for instance. Naturally, much will depend on the type of trip you have planned. If you were going to spend most of your time hiking in the mountains, for example, you would be wise to carry a backpack. However, for general travel between towns, a small suitcase certainly shouldn't be ruled out. Its main advantage over the backpack is on the crowded *tap-taps* of Haiti and, to a lesser extent, the *gua-guas* of the Dominican Republic. When space is at a premium, a slim suitcase is a lot easier to slip between your legs than a bulky backpack, which will probably be thrown on to the roof where anything could happen to it. A backpack which converts into a hand-held bag is another alternative, although it is still bulkier than a conventional suitcase.

Clothing

Selecting your wardrobe for a trip to the tropics should be an exercise in common sense. Cool, light, cotton clothing is good for the day, while in the evening trousers and a long-sleeved shirt will help fend off mosquitoes. Warmer clothes might be an idea for the higher mountains in the Dominican Republic, but don't overdo it. A comfortable pair of shoes is obviously very important.

Money

Ideally, you should take a combination of cash, travellers' cheques and plastic.
In Hispaniola the US dollar is king. This doesn't mean that other currencies

are useless – just that with US dollars you'll be able to change money anywhere without many problems. Carry your currency in small denominations, avoiding the US$100 bill, which is occasionally treated with suspicion due to the number of counterfeit notes in circulation.

Having travellers' cheques in small denominations is also a good idea. Obviously there's a limit to the number of US$10 cheques you can stuff into your money belt. But having them means that you can avoid buying more of the local currency than you need at the time. Once again, US dollars are best and American Express travellers' cheques are known and accepted in most places.

A credit card (or debit card) is useful in case of emergencies and, with all the ATM machines in the Dominican Republic, you could use it instead of cash and travellers' cheques. Note, however, that in Haiti the facilities for credit card users are not as developed.

Necessities and luxuries

Only you know exactly what you'll need for a trip to Hispaniola. The following are what I consider to be necessities – items you should not be without – and luxuries – items to make your life more comfortable.

Necessities
- passport
- airline ticket
- insurance policy
- photocopies of passport, airline ticket and insurance policy
- travellers' cheques and/or credit card
- money belt to store the above – you should always wear it underneath your clothing
- medical kit (see page 17)
- spare glasses (losing your glasses or tearing a contact lens can really ruin a trip)

Luxuries
- penknife
- torch and batteries (worth their weight in gold during the frequent power cuts in Haiti)
- matches to light gas lamps and mosquito coils
- insect repellent
- washing powder to wash your clothes as you dirty them (a 'wash-and-wear' approach means that you can reduce the number of clothes you pack in the first place; also remember that the more powder you use, the lighter your bag becomes)
- map – detailed and recent
- calculator for currency conversion
- camera with some spare film, which can be difficult to find in Haiti (see page 20–1)

MAKING THE BEST OF YOUR TRAVEL PHOTOGRAPHS
Subject, composition and lighting

If it doesn't look good through the viewfinder, it will never look good as a picture. Don't take photographs for the sake of taking them; film is far too expensive. Be patient and wait until the image looks right.

People

There's nothing like a wonderful face to stimulate interest. Travelling to remote corners of the world provides the opportunity for exotic photographs of colourful people and intriguing lifestyles which capture the very essence of a culture. A superb photograph should be capable of saying more than a thousand words.

Photographing people is never easy and more often than not it requires a fair share of luck plus sharp instinct, a conditioned photographic eye and the ability to handle light both aesthetically and technically.

- If you want to take a portrait shot, always ask first. Often the offer to send a copy of the photograph to the subject will break the ice – but do remember to send it!
- Focus on the eyes of your subject.
- The best portraits are obtained in early morning and late evening light. In harsh light, photograph without flash in the shadows.
- Respect people's wishes and customs. Remember that, in some countries, infringement can lead to serious trouble.
- Never photograph military subjects unless you have definite permission.
- Be prepared for the unexpected.

Wildlife

There is no mystique to good wildlife photography. The secret is getting into the right place at the right time and then knowing what to do when you are there. Look for striking poses, aspects of behaviour and distinctive features. Try to illustrate the species within the context of its environment. Alternatively, focus in close on a characteristic which can be emphasised.

- The eyes are all-important. Make sure they are sharp and try to ensure they contain a highlight.
- Get the surroundings right – there is nothing worse than a distracting twig or highlighted leaf lurking in the background.
- A powerful flashgun can transform a dreary picture by lifting the subject out of its surroundings and putting the all-important highlights into the eyes. Artificial light is no substitute for natural light, so use judiciously.
- Getting close to the subject correspondingly reduces the depth of field; for distances of less than a metre, apertures between f16 and f32 are necessary. This means using flash to provide enough light – build your own bracket and use one or two small flashguns to illuminate the subject from the side.

Landscapes

Landscapes are forever changing; good landscape photography is all about light and mood. Generally the first and last two hours of daylight are best, or when peculiar climatic conditions add drama or emphasise distinctive features.

- Never place the horizon in the centre – in your mind's eye divide the frame into thirds and exaggerate either the land or the sky.

Cameras

Keep things simple: light, reliable and simple cameras will reduce hassle. High humidity in tropical places can play havoc with electronics.

- For keen photographers, a single-lens reflex (SLR) camera should be at the heart of your outfit. Look for a model with the option of a range of different lenses and other accessories.
- Totally mechanical cameras which do not rely on batteries work even under extreme conditions. Combined with an exposure meter which doesn't require batteries, you have the perfect match. One of the best and most indestructible cameras available is the FM2 Nikon.

- Compact cameras are generally excellent, but because of restricted focal ranges they have severe limitations for wildlife.
- Automatic cameras are often noisy when winding on, and loading film.
- Flashy camera bags can draw unwelcome attention to your kit.

Lenses
The lens is the most important part of the camera, with the greatest influence on the final result. Choose the best you can afford – the type will be dictated by the subject and type of photograph you wish to take.

For people
- The lens should ideally should have a focal length of 90 or 105mm.
- If you are not intimidated by getting in close, buy one with a macro facility which will allow close focusing. For candid photographs, a 70–210 zoom lens is ideal.
- A fast lens (with a maximum aperture of around f2.8) will allow faster shutter speeds which will mean sharper photographs. Distracting backgrounds will be thrown out of focus, improving the images' aesthetic appeal.

For wildlife
- Choose a lens of at least 300mm for a reasonable image size.
- For birds, lenses of 400mm or 500mm may be needed. They should be held on a tripod, or a beanbag if shooting from a vehicle.
- Macro lenses of 55mm and 105mm cover most subjects, creating images up to half life size. To enlarge further, extension tubes are required.
- In low light, lenses with very fast apertures help.

For landscapes
- Wide-angle lenses (35mm or less) are ideal for tight habitat shots (eg: forests) and are an excellent alternative for close ups, as you can shoot the subject within the context of its environment.
- For other landscapes, use a medium telephoto lens (100–300mm) to pick out interesting aspects of a vista and compress the perspective.

Film
Two types of film are available: prints (negatives) and transparencies (colour reversal). Prints are instantly accessible, ideal for showing to friends and putting into albums. However, if you want to share your experiences with a wider audience, through lectures or in publication, then the extra quality offered by transparency film is necessary.

Film speed (ISO number) indicates the sensitivity of the film to light. The lower the number, the less sensitive the film, but the better quality the final image. For general print film and if you are using transparencies just for lectures, ISO 100 or 200 are ideal. However, if you want to get your work published, the superior quality of ISO 25 to 100 film is best.
- Film bought in developing countries may be outdated or badly stored.
- Try to keep your film cool. Never leave it in direct sunlight.
- Do not allow fast film (ISO 800 or more) to pass through X-ray machines.
- Under weak light conditions use a faster film (ISO 200 or 400).
- For accurate people shots use Kodachrome 64 for its warmth, mellowness and gentle gradation of contrast. Reliable skin tones can also be recorded with Fuji Astia 100.
- To jazz up your portraits, use Fuji Velvia (50 ISO) or Provia (100 ISO).
- If cost is your priority, use process-paid Fuji films such as Sensia 11.
- For black-and-white people shots take Kodax T Max or Fuji Neopan.
- For natural subjects, where greens are a feature, use Fujicolour Reala (prints) and Fujichrome Velvia and Provia (transparencies).

Nick Garbutt is a professional photographer, writer, artist and expedition leader, specialising in natural history. He is co-author of 'Madagascar Wildlife' (Bradt Publications), and a winner in the BBC Wildlife Photographer of the Year Competition. John R Jones is a professional travel photographer specialising in minority people, and author of the Bradt guides to 'Vietnam' and 'Laos and Cambodia'.

TOUR OPERATORS
The list below represents a small fraction of the travel agencies around at the moment. They are all well established and most tend to specialise in independent travel. Note that in many cases these agencies also sell travel insurance and have travel clinics.

In the UK
Bridge The World 47 Chalkfarm Road, London NW1 8AN; tel: 0171 911 0900
British Airways Travel Shop 156 Regent Street, London W1R 6LB;
tel: 0171 434 4700
Campus Travel 52 Grosvenor Gardens, London SW1W 0AG; tel: 0171 730 8111;
web site: http://www.campus-travel.co.uk
Council Travel 28A Poland Street, W1V 3DB; tel: 0171 437 7767
Journey Latin America 16 Devonshire Road, London, W4; tel: 0181 747 3108
STA Travel 117 Euston Road, London, NW1; tel: 0171 361 6262
Trailfinders 194 Kensington High Street, London, W8 7RG; tel: 0171 938 3939
Travel Cuts 295a Regent Street, London, W1R 7YA; tel: 0171 255 2082

In the US
Council Travel tel: 1 800 226 8624; web site: HYPERLINK http://www.ciee.org/cts/ctshome.htm
STA Travel 6560 Scottsdale Road, F100, Scottsdale, AZ 85253; tel: 1 800 777 0112;
web site: HYPERLINK http://www.sta-travel.com

RESEARCH
What you get out of your trip will depend on what you put in. I refer not only to a healthy approach while on the road, but also to the research you do before you go. Try to do a bit of further reading (some suggestions are listed in Appendix 2). Even if you only read the background sections of this book, any prior knowledge you have will be useful when you land on the island and start the lengthy process of trying to understand its different cultures and people. Research is really all part of being a responsible tourist.

RESPONSIBLE TOURISM
'Responsible tourism' is a wonderful expression. It describes all of our obligations as tourists, without really describing any. The ambiguity of the word 'responsible' is perfect. Picking up your rubbish and taking your hat off in church is, of course, responsible behaviour; but so is speaking a little of the local language and paying a fair price for things at the market. Responsible tourism means more than just obeying rules of social etiquette and being on your best behaviour. You must be proactive as well as reactive. In a nutshell, try to give something back to the country you are visiting. Speaking a little Creole, French or Spanish (even just 'hello' and 'thank you') is respectful and demonstrates a willingness to adapt to the local culture, which might in turn help you to make some friends. Remember that Haiti and the Dominican Republic are developing countries where life

can be hard and very little is taken for granted. Think twice before haggling for an hour over the price of a mango or a bunch of bananas. Even if you have to pay a tourist price, you'll be contributing to the local economy — in other words, to the street vendors and hawkers in the market who are normally the last to see the benefits of mass tourism. As an independent traveller you are in the privileged position of being able to give something back directly to the people because you are in constant contact with them. Our ultimate responsibility then, is to make sure that we don't waste this opportunity.

Cultural sensitivity

A responsible tourist is a culturally aware tourist who is willing to adapt to and respect the local customs. I have already mentioned learning a bit of the language, which I think is an easy and enjoyable thing to do. The point about bargaining is as much about respecting the local way of life as not taking advantage of other people's poverty. In a similar vein, ask before you take photographs of people and be aware that your camera probably costs more than your subject's yearly wage. I'm not saying don't do it – just be humble about the way you do it. Sometimes when I take out my camera in Haiti, the vitriolic words of Diacoute, a poem by Félix Morisseau-Leroy, persuade me to put it away again. The final verse reads:

> 'Tourist, don't take my picture.
> You don't understand my pose.
> You don't understand a thing.
> It's none of your business, I say.
> Gimme five cents, tourist,
> And then – be on your way.'

Low-impact tourism

This, of course, is all part and parcel of being a responsible tourist. Once again, it means different things to different people, but so much of it is really just common sense. It hardly needs saying that you should pick up your litter (or not throw it in the first place), refrain from uprooting plants, flowers and coral and use energy resources like water and electricity – so precious in Hispaniola – efficiently. Less obvious, but equally important aspects of low-impact tourism include not washing in lakes, collecting shells or getting to close to the wildlife – all of which act to the detriment of the natural world in some form or another.

Local charities

Making a donation to a local charity is one of the most obvious ways in which you can give something back. Apart from the programmes run by the United Nations and other international organisations, most services to the poor and needy are provided by religious groups. These are normally autonomous Catholic groups.

Hispaniola is a poor island and, naturally, there are many charities. Sadly, some of them are set up as money-making schemes by unscrupulous opportunists, but the majority are worthwhile and deserving of your support. Hopefully, on your travels you'll come across good causes that merit a small donation or help in some other form. Before you start to make your own discoveries, here are a few of my own:-

The Ecole Saint Trinité (tel: 22 0340), next to the Cathédrale Sainte Trinité in Port-au-Prince, is a school for the grossly disadvantaged children of the shanty towns of the Haitian capital. These children live, eat and are educated at the school during the week and return to their other lives at the weekends. You can sponsor a child for H$310 (US$92) a year. Contact Madam Coty. The Fermathe Mountain Maid Mission is run by a conservative group of US Baptists in the foothills behind Port-au-Prince. The mission has projects relating to education, health care and sustainable agricultural development, where the emphasis is on self-help rather than dependence. See Chapter 6, page 91 for more information.

In the Dominican Republic each Catholic diocese has its own service organisation called Caritas which provides services to the poor. More specifically there is a group of Canadian Catholic nuns called the Sisters of the Immaculate Conception running non-denominational schools for the poor in Consuelo, a sugarcane region in the east where Dominicans and Haitian immigrants are in close contact with each other. You can contact them in Santo Domingo at PO Box 3180; tel: 553 7292.

Back at home

Try to be an ambassador in your own country. Keep in touch with the people you met on your travels and share your experiences with others back home. This is especially important in the case of Haiti, which suffers from such a bad reputation even though it must be one of the most rewarding countries in the world for travellers. Consider joining groups through which you can continue to contribute to the countries you have just visited.

The Haiti Support Group (tel: 0181 201 9878) regularly holds meetings in London. Its name is self-explanatory and if you have an opportunity, get along to some of the meetings. On the subject of responsible tourism in general, Tourism Concern (tel: 0171 753 3330) are well established and know what they're talking about. Call them for one of their information packs. There are also plenty of environmental organisations and conservation projects that you can get involved with. Some of the larger ones are Earthwatch (tel: 01865 311 600 in the UK, or 617 926 8200 in the US), Greenpeace (tel: 0171 865 8100) and the United Nations Environmental Program (UNEP). Many international charities have projects in Hispaniola. You can't go far wrong with Oxfam (tel: 0171 240 7873), while several United Nations organisations, such as UNESCO and UNICEF, are particularly active in Haiti. Finally, you might like to adopt a child. The great thing about doing this is that you get to see at first hand the difference that your contribution is making to someone's life. Try contacting Plan International (tel: 0171 485 6612) who have programmes in Hispaniola.

Cruise-Ship Passengers

One way of visiting Hispaniola is on a cruise. While the island is not as popular as some on the Caribbean cruise circuit, it does receive its fair share of ships. Ironically, most of them drop anchor off the coast of unfashionable Haiti at Labadie. The majority of the others call at Santo Domingo, with a few stopping at Puerto Plata in the Dominican Republic and at Cap-Haïtien on the north coast of Haiti.

As a cruise-ship passenger you only get a few hours of shore leave and there is a limit to what you can do in this time; this chapter is designed to allow you to take full advantage of these few hours. It should be read in conjunction with the chapters on the relevant towns in the main part of the guide. See pages 70 and 170 for guidelines on the exchange rate.

LABADIE

Three times a week at about 08.00 the *Grandeur of the Seas*, the *Majesty of the Seas* and the *Splendour of the Seas* – all part of the fleet of the **Royal Caribbean** cruise line – drop anchor in Labadie Bay. Small boats are on hand to ferry you across the bay to Labadie Beach, where you can play volleyball, participate in limbo contests and overeat on a stretch of sand instead of on the deck of your floating hotel. Before you disembark, you'll be told that Labadie is a private island for the exclusive use of Royal Caribbean guests. True enough perhaps, but it's also on the north coast of the most fascinating country in the Caribbean and a mere 45 minutes away from its second-largest town, Cap-Haïtien. You have about eight hours before your ship sets sail – ample time to have a real look at Haiti.

Getting to Cap-Haïtien

When you land at the small dock at Labadie, make your way to the Artisan's market, which is at the entrance to the 'private island' Royal Caribbean are so proud to call their own. Leave the complex and wait for a *tap-tap* to Cap-Haïtien (see page 121), which costs H$2 and takes 45 minutes. You can exchange money at the shops in Labadie, or buy something at the market in US dollars and ask for the change in Haitian dollars or *gourdes*, which are, in fact, the same currency.

The ride to Cap-Haïtien is a spectacular one. The *tap-tap* bumps along a rocky path cutting across cliffs that plunge straight into the ocean at certain points – a typical feature of the Hispaniolan coastline. About 15 minutes from

Labadie you'll see a stretch of white sand, **Cormier Plage**, where there's a nice hotel noted for its excellent seafood. On the approach to Cap-Haïtien, you pass through a number of villages as the *tap-tap* edges down the hill towards the town centre. These villages are common all over Haiti: rustic and poor, yet full of life, colour and spirit. The *tap-tap* will leave you at Rue 20 Q (ie at the end of Rue 20 where it intersects with Rue Q).

For help getting around Cap-Haitien, what to see and where to eat, see Chapter 9, *Haiti: The North*. The town is a pleasure to walk around, and although it's Haiti's second most important town after the capital, Port-au-Prince, it has a relaxed pace of life. You can quite easily see the town in a couple of hours and be back at Labadie for the final of the limbo contest.

To return to Labadie, go back to the end of Rue 20 Q and wait for a *tap-tap*. Their frequency is hard to predict, but on average there seems to be about one every 30 minutes. However, give yourself plenty of time to budget for the vagaries of life in Haiti.

Nearby creeks

Although my first recommendation is an excursion to Cap-Haïtien, there are some nice creeks near Labadie Beach. This time, wait at the dock for another boat to take you across the bay to Labadie town, from where local fishermen will take you across to the creeks. Negotiate a fair price.

Alternatively, ask for directions to a hotel called **Habitation Labadie** on **Beli Beach** (next to Labadie Beach), where you can hire boats to the creeks. The asking price is about H$30. As well as the creeks, you can see **Rivière Glacé** and the **Baie de l'Acul**, where Christopher Columbus dropped anchor during his first voyage to the New World in December 1492.

CAP-HAÏTIEN

Every now and then a ship will turn up in Cap-Haïtien harbour, which is close to the centre of town. When you exit the harbour, turn right and walk up Boulevard de Mer until you come to Rue 24. This is where you'll find the **tourist office**, which only seems to open when a cruise ship comes to town.

Depending on how long you have in the Cap, you should really try to see the **Sans-Souci Palace** and the **Citadelle La Ferrière** (see page 129) – the two most remarkable sights in the whole of the West Indies. These excursions will take the best part of a day if you do them independently, so bear this in mind if you only have a few hours of shore leave. *Tap-taps* to **Milot**, the nearest town, can be caught at the end of Rue 2, over the footbridge known as **Pont Neuf**. The journey takes about 45 minutes and costs H$1.

SANTO DOMINGO

The most popular cruise-ship destination in the Dominican Republic is Santo Domingo, on the Caribbean coast. Major companies like **First Choice Cruises**, **Holland America Line** and **Carnival** all go there. Some cruises end in Santo Domingo and include a week or so at a beach resort. If you're on this type of holiday, you'll have ample time to explore the capital. Others only stop for a few hours in a city that really needs several days to see properly. Nonetheless, plenty of sights can be covered in just a few hours if you put your mind to it.

Arriving at Puerto Sans Souci

Cruise ships arrive in Santo Domingo at Puerto Sans Souci on the eastern side of the Ozama River. Many of the things to see in Santo Domingo, including the beautiful Colonial District, are on the other side of the river.

The wharf at Puerto Sans Souci is dedicated to cruise ships and their passengers. A large building that looks like an airport terminal houses several useful facilities: a post office, international telephones, a bank and a tourist information stand. These should all be open when you arrive. In addition, there are gift shops, boutiques and a good restaurant overlooking the harbour.

The Colonial District

Santo Domingo is a large city and some of the things to see, like the Botanical Gardens and the zoo, are really too far from Sans Souci to be practical. The museums at the Plaza de la Cultura (see page 187) are closer, but none of these attractions compare to the Colonial District (see map page 178). Fortunately, this fascinating 'city within a city' is just on the other side of the Ozama River. A taxi or a *motoconcho* (a motorcycle taxi) will take about 10 minutes, or you could walk there in about 30 minutes. Go to the main road, turn left and continue along it until you come to the first of the two bridges across the river (the Mella Bridge). Cross the bridge and you're on the northern outskirts of the Colonial District.

The two tours suggested below each take about an hour at a relaxed pace. They are designed so that you don't retrace your steps and have no respect for the historical chronology or continuity of the sights. I have used El Conde, the Colonial District's main thoroughfare, as the starting point for both.

Walking tour 1: North of El Conde

Walking east along El Conde eventually leads to a staircase (**La Victoria staircase**), at the bottom of which is the Ozama River and the port of Santo Domingo. Turn left in front of this staircase and walk up **Calle Las Damas**, the first stone-laid street in the Western Hemisphere. Dubbed the 'Street of the Ladies', legend has it that this is where Maria de Toledo, wife of Viceroy Diego Columbus, and the ladies of her court used to stroll in the afternoons. Some guides, not content with the romantic impression created by this story, claim that these afternoon strolls had the express purpose of finding husbands. Whatever you choose to believe, Calle Las Damas is one of the most charming places in the Colonial District.

It is perhaps appropriate that the first building of note on this tour should be the house of the founder of Santo Domingo, Nicolás de Ovando. **Hostal Nicolás de Ovando** is opposite the French Embassy and normally operates as one of the Colonial District's most distinguished hotels. At the time of writing it was closed due to restoration work. Nevertheless, you can still enjoy the impressive Elizabethan doorway, which is the only one in the New World. Next door, **Casa de Dávila** is considered to be one of the most complete colonial houses in the old city. A little further up on Calle Las Damas is the **Panteón Nacional** (National Pantheon), originally a Jesuit convent, but now used as the final resting place for many of the nation's heroes. The Pantheon's two most interesting features, apart from the unflinching soldier guarding the entrance, both have rather sombre connections. The bronze chandelier hanging from the domed roof was a gift from the Spanish dictator, General Franco, to his Dominican counterpart, General Trujillo; and the iron gates inside are said to have belonged to a Nazi prison. If you look closely, you can still see the swastikas. Next to the Pantheon is the **Casa de los Jesuítas**, where the convent priests used to reside. It was also used as a college, and in 1747 the University of Santiago La Paz was founded there. In the same complex of buildings, the **Casa de las Gárgolas** contains the gargoyles that once adorned the cathedral. Opposite the Pantheon is the **Capilla de los Remedios** (Chapel of Our Lady of Remedies), the private chapel of the eminent Dávila family, whose house is a few doors down the street.

Arguably the most important museum after those at the Plaza de la Cultura is the **Museo de las Casas Reales** (Museum of the Royal Houses) on the corner of calles Las Damas and Las Mercedes. The museum occupies the restored palace of the Royal Court, created in 1511 by King Ferdinand of Spain, which had jurisdiction over the entire New World. Along with its interesting displays relating to all aspects of colonial life, there is also a large collection of weapons and armour. Opening hours are from 09.00 to 17.30 (closed Mondays) and the entrance fee is RD$15. Just in front of the museum, the **Reloj del Sol** (Sundial), built in 1753, apparently still gives the exact time.

The Sundial overlooks the Plaza de España and leading down to the right is **Puerta de San Diego** (San Diego Gate), the original point of access to the old walled city. At the southern end of Plaza de España stands the **Alcázar de Don Diego Colón** (Castle of Don Diego Colombus). Don Diego Columbus was Christopher's son and Viceroy of Santo Domingo from 1509 to 1523. Work started on the Alcázar in 1510 with 1,500 Indians under the direction of architects brought from Spain. Four years later an elegant castle, combining Gothic and Moorish styles with Spanish and Italian Renaissance, had been built using only saws, chisels, hammers and not a single nail (mahogany bolts were used instead). You can visit the Alcázar every day from 09.00 to 17.00. Entrance costs RD$20 and inside, the various colonial relics, not all of them dating from Don Diego's time, have been well restored.

A staircase immediately to the left of the Alcázar leads down to the **Puerta de la Atarazana** (Shipyard Gate). Opposite this is the **Museo de las Atarazanas Reales** (Royal Shipyard Museum), which displays various items salvaged from the more famous shipwrecks along the Dominican coast. You are now on a street called La Atarazana, the main shipbuilding street in the first trading centre of the New World. La Atarazana stretches round the Plaza de

España and ends up on the northern side of the square, where a number of bars and cafés now occupy the shipbuilding warehouses of the 16th century.

Beside these bars, Calle Emiliano Tejera leads off the main square. Walk down this street and turn left onto Calle Isabel La Católica where you'll see the Banco Popular Dominicano, which now occupies the **Casa del Cordón** (House of the Cord). One of the oldest stone buildings in the Americas, it was occupied by Don Diego and his wife for a while, and two of his children were born here in 1510 and 1511. Visit during the bank's normal opening hours (08.00-16.00 Monday-Friday). There are one or two other interesting things to see north along Calle Isabel La Católica. The birthplace of Juan Pablo Duarte (see page 146) is one block from the Casa del Cordón. The **Museo de Juan Pablo Duarte** commemorates the event (on January 26 1813) with a small selection of the great man's personal belongings. Duarte was baptized further up the road at the **Iglesia y Fuerte de Santa Bábara** (Santa Barbara Church and Fort), which is an eclectic mix of Gothic and baroque styles. The quarry upon which the church and fort are built supplied the materials used to construct most of the other buildings in the Colonial District.

Returning back towards El Conde, this time along Calle Arzobispo Meriño, turn right at Calle Emiliano Tejera. In front of you are the ruins of **Monasterio de San Francisco** (San Francisco Monastery). I could tell you that Maria de Toledo had a chapel here, but I challenge you to distinguish it from the other stones and rubble. You can find more ruins further south on Calle Hostos. **Hospital San Nicolás de Bari** was constructed by order of Governor Nicolás Ovando in the early 16th century, and continued to care for the sick and poor until the beginning of this century, when it was ironically deemed to be a hazard to the public and torn down. Next to the ruins is the **Iglesia de La Altagracia** (Church of Our Lady of Higher Grace). Both San Francisco and San Nicolás are actually very impressive ruins, but the great appeal of this part of the Colonial District is the neighbourhood itself. At times the old city can seem like a colonial version of Disneyland: everything is so perfect and impossibly romantic.

Neighbourhoods such as San Miguel and Jobo Bonito serve as a reminder that life here goes on as it would anywhere else in the Dominican Republic. Lest we forget, the Colonial District is not just a tourist attraction. You'll see what I mean when you walk from the ruins of San Nicolás along Calle Las Mercedes to the **Iglesia de Las Mercedes** (Church of Our Lady of Mercy). This large 16th-century church is apparently where the Spanish writer, Tirso de Molina, wrote his famous *Don Juan*.

You could finish this particular tour by continuing along Calle Las Mercedes and turning right up Calle Santome until you reach Avenida Mella. This is the principal shopping street on the northern edge of the Colonial District. The **Mercado Modelo**, which should be opposite you, is the city's main arts and crafts centre. This is a melting pot of woodcarvings, amber jewellery, carnival masks, Haitian paintings, oversized cigars and other tourist trinkets, and is either a good place to come for souvenirs at the end of your trip, or a place to avoid like the plague.

Walking tour 2: South of El Conde

For this alternative tour, walk east along El Conde and stop at the bronze statue of Christopher Columbus in **Parque Colón** (Columbus Park). This is one of my favourite parts of the Colonial District. You can sit here for hours, especially at night when ornate lamps illuminate the square, enjoying the tranquillity and antiquity of this area. Standing at the base of the statue, to your left, on the corner of the square, is a building with a large tower known as '**El Vivaque**' (The Bivouac). This was once the original city hall. To your right is **Palacio de Borgella**, a 19th-century building also used for administration purposes, and today housing a small post office and tourist information office.

Behind you is the oldest cathedral in the Americas, **Catedral Basílica Menor de Santa María de Encarnation**. Don Diego Columbus laid the first stone in 1513 and on its completion in 1546, Pope Paul III gave it the status of Primate Cathedral of the Indies. During the traumatic history of its construction, the cathedral's original architect, Alonso de Rodríguez, quit halfway through to build the cathedral in Mexico City; and to this day the cathedral's bell tower has still not been finished. The style is basically late-Gothic with certain Renaissance, Romanesque and Mudejar features. The entrance facing Parque Colon is Gothic. Inside there is a mahogany altar, 14 chapels, stained-glass windows designed by the Dominican artist, Rincon Mora and, until they were transferred to the Faro a Colón, the mortal remains of Christopher Columbus, stored in a mausoleum built in 1898. When visiting the cathedral, note that it closes in the mid-afternoon and you won't be allowed in if you're wearing shorts.

Next, walk to the south side of the cathedral, along Calle Isabel La Católica, and turn left down a small alley called **Callejón de los Nichos** (Alley of Niches). This is where the archbishop and many of Santo Domingo's most prominent families had their homes. Look for **Casa de Diego Caballero** and **Casa del Sacramento**, while round the corner on Calle Las Damas, **Casa de Bastidas** is open to the public.

Southbound on a quieter stretch of Calle Las Damas (if that's possible) is **Fortaleza Ozama** (Ozama Fortress). It was built by Governor Nicolás Ovando in 1502 and overlooks the Ozama River and Caribbean Sea. The grounds of this large, military complex are dominated by the **Torre del Homenaje** (Tower of Homage) and a statue of Gonzalo Fernández de Oviedo, governor of the fortress from 1533 to 1557 and author of *Historía Natural y General de Indias*. The Tower of Homage looks a bit like a medieval castle and was the first residence of Don Diego Columbus and Maria de Toledo when they arrived in Santo Domingo. The Ozama Fortress is open from 09.00 to 19.00 and entrance costs RD$10. An informative pamphlet is available at the gate or you could take a guide.

You are now in the southeastern corner of the Colonial District. Walk down Calle Las Damas until you get to the sea. Across the Malecón, looking out over the Caribbean Sea, is an impressive statue of **Fray Antonio de Montesino**, one of the celebrated defenders of the Taino Indians (see page 4).

Turn back towards El Conde and go up Calle Arzobispo Meriño. At the intersection with Calle Padre Billini is **Casa de Tostado**, one of the most beautiful of the early colonial homes. It was owned by Francisco de Tostado, the first native-born professor at the University of Santiago La Paz and one of the many people killed when Sir Francis Drake sacked the city in 1586. The **Museo de la Familia Dominicana** (Museum of the Dominican Family) is inside the house. It is open from 09.00 to 12.00 and contains artefacts from the 19th and 20th centuries. Next to Casa de Tostado and just behind the cathedral, **Callejón de las Curas** (Alley of the Priests) is worth a look. This is one of the best-preserved parts of the Colonial District and there are some interesting sculptures on the entrance gate to the cathedral cloister.

The final part of this tour takes in one or two of the more interesting churches south of El Conde. Come out of Casa de Tostado and proceed west along Calle Padre Billini. The first church you come to is the **Iglesia y Convento de los Dominicos** (Dominican Church and Convent), built in the early part of the 16th century in the shape of a Latin cross. Next door is the **Capilla de la Tercera Orden** (Chapel of the Third Order), and a couple of blocks further down is the **Iglesia de la Regina Angelorum**, which contains the remains of Father Billini. If you turn right here and go up Calle José Reyes, you'll pass the **Museo de la Porcelana** (Porcelain Museum). This is one of Santo Domingo's more unusual museums and you might find the respite from churches, forts and palaces quite refreshing. On leaving the Porcelain Museum, continue up Calle José Reyes and turn left at Calle Arzobispo Nouel. Go west along this street, passing the **Iglesia del Carmen** (Church of Our Lady of Carmen) and the site opposite where *La Trinitaria* – the society dedicated to fighting for Dominican independence from Haiti – was founded (a marble plaque marks the spot).

Calle Arzobispo Nouel eventually leads to **Parque Independencia** (Independence Park). You are now at the westernmost end of El Conde. Directly in front of you, across the busy Calle Palo Hincado is the **Puerta El Conde** (Count's Gate). Through this gate, in the middle of the park, is the **Altar de la Patria** (Altar of the Nation). The remains of the three Founding Fathers – Duarte, Sanchez and Mella – are interred here beneath an eternal flame, which itself is set underground. Behind the Altar are the ruins of the **Fuerte de la Concepción** (Fortress of the Conception), which used to guard the old city wall and now marks the northwestern boundary of the Colonial District.

Other sights

There are several more interesting sights to see without having to cross the Ozama River. The **Faro a Colón** (Columbus Lighthouse) is relatively close to Puerto Sans Souci (see page 188). Go to the main road, cross it and continue up Avenida del Este for about 10 minutes. The lighthouse is at the end. **Parque Mirador del Este** (see page 189) and **Parque de los Tres Ojos** (see page 189) are both near by. Alternatively, turn right when you get to the main road and a couple of kilometres further on you'll arrive at the **National Aquarium** (see page 189).

PUERTO PLATA

As a cruise-ship passenger, you might dock on the north coast of the Dominican Republic at Puerto Plata. The port is at the western end of town, close to the **San Felipe Fortress** and the other attractions in the centre. However, the best thing to do in Puerto Plata is to go up to the top of **Mount Isabel de Torres**, the tallest of the peaks overlooking the town. You might have a look at the map and fancy a trip to **La Isabela**, the first settlement in the New World, which doesn't seem too far away. However, public transport to this town is time-consuming and there's not a lot to see when you get there. See Chapter 16, *Dominican Republic: The North Coast* for further information on the places suggested above.

Part Two

Haiti

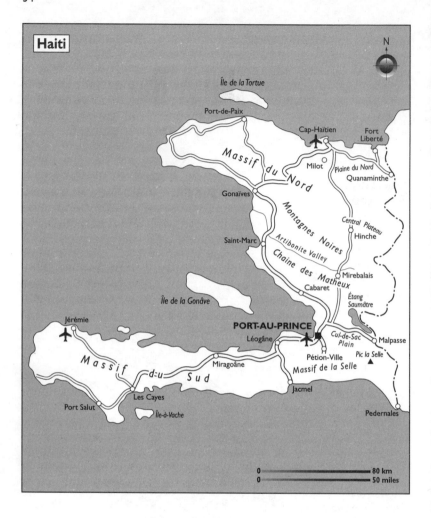

Haiti: Background 4

GEOGRAPHY
Size and location
Haiti occupies the western third of the island of Hispaniola. It has an area of 27,750km², which is about the same size as the US State of Maryland and a little smaller than Belgium. Haiti's coastline stretches for 1,369km, while its border with the Dominican Republic is 311km long. The country has two peninsulas in the north and south separated by the Gulf of Gonâve. In the middle of the Gulf is the island of La Gonâve, conveniently placed for those who like to describe Haiti as a crab's claw about to clamp a morsel of food.

Apart from the Dominican Republic, Haiti's closest neighbour is Cuba, which lies 90km to the northwest across a stretch of sea called the Windward Passage. Jamaica is 180km to the southwest across the Jamaica Channel, while the southeastern tip of Florida is 900km away.

Topography
'Haiti' was the original Arawak word for 'mountainous land' and about 75% of the country can be considered mountainous, or at least hilly. The remainder consists of lowland plains, on which most of Haiti's agricultural production takes place.

Highlands
The mountains in Haiti occupy 21,000km² and can be crudely divided into four regions. The **Massif du Nord** runs across the northern peninsula and into the Dominican Republic. Its counterpart in the south, the **Massif du Sud**, occupies the southern peninsula and is sometimes referred to as the Massif de la Hotte. The Massif de la Selle is the easterly continuation of the Massif du Sud and the range in which Haiti's tallest peak, Pic La Selle (2,674m), is found. The other highland area is in the centre, where the **Montagnes Noires** and the **Chaine des Matheux** rise either side of the Artibonite River.

Lowlands
The chief lowland areas can also be divided into four. The most important as far as the economy is concerned is the **Plaine du Nord**, the land around Cap-Haïtien – the centre of the old French colony where the soil is the richest in Haiti. In terms of size, the **Central Plateau**, between the Massif du Nord and the Montagnes Noires, is the most significant lowland region. Grassland

predominates here and it's mainly used for cattle grazing. Large areas of swampy land are found in the **Artibonite Valley**, sandwiched between the Montagnes Noires and the Chaine des Matheux. Finally, the **Cul-de-Sac Plain** runs eastward from Port-au-Prince into the Dominican Republic.

Islands

Of the islands that surround Hispaniola, four of them belong to Haiti. The two most significant are **La Gonâve**, in the Gulf of Gonâve, and **La Tortue** (Tortuga), off Port-de-Paix in the Atlantic Ocean. The two smaller islands, both densely populated, are **Île-à-Vache** (Cow Island), lying off Les Cayes, and **Grande Cayemite**, just off the north coast of the southern peninsula.

Rivers and lakes

The main river in Haiti is the **Artibonite River**, which runs through the Artibonite Valley for some 280km before emptying into the Gulf of Gonâve. Other rivers of note include the Grande Anse, which drains most of the southern peninsula, and Trois Rivières, which drains into the Atlantic Ocean near Port-de-Paix.

Although it doesn't rival Lake Enriquillo in the Dominican Republic, **Étang Saumâtre** in the Cul-de-Sac Plain, close to the Dominican border, is quite large (170km²). It has slightly salty waters and a significant number of crocodiles, iguanas, flamingos and other bird life. Lake Miragoâne is another salty lake close to the town of the same name. Haiti's largest freshwater lake – Lake Péligre – is in fact man made, created in the 1950s when a dam was built on the upper Artibonite River.

CLIMATE

Because most of Haiti is well above sea level, the temperatures are often cooler than other tropical lands in the Caribbean. Nevertheless, you can still expect an average temperature of 24°C in winter (January and February) and 28°C in summer (July and August). The average temperature in Port-au-Prince is a sticky 27°C.

The **rainy season** varies according to where you are in Haiti. In the south it tends to be from April to October, while in the north most of the rain falls between November and March. Port-au-Prince has two wet seasons: April to June and August to November.

Meanwhile, the **hurricane season** starts in August, peaks in September and October, and has normally blown itself out by November.

HISTORY
Saint Domingue

When the eastern third of the island was ceded to France in 1697 it became known as Saint Domingue. For the next 94 years it was to be the most prosperous colony in the New World, providing sugar, coffee, cocoa, indigo and cotton to all of Europe. In a good year the French might have sent 700 ships to Saint Domingue. Many of them arrived at Cap-Français (now Cap-

Haïtien), to where the plantations in the fertile Plaine du Nord sent their produce for export. This town with its beautiful, colonial architecture was called the 'Paris of the Antilles', and it was considered quite something in Paris to be 'as rich as a Dominguan'. By 1789 Saint Domingue had a population of 556,000, of which 500,000 were black slaves imported from West Africa to work on the plantations.

Toussaint Louverture and the slave revolt
Early insurrections had been organised in the 1750s by Makandal, a legendary black slave who was eventually broken on the wheel in 1758. Then, in August 1791, stimulated by the French Revolution and the granting of political rights to the *gens de couleur* in France, the slaves in Saint Domingue revolted. The uprising was plotted at a voodoo ceremony in the Plaine du Nord and subsequent stories of whites being sawn in half and the glow from burning plantations being seen from as far away as Bermuda were not uncommon. In its early stages, the slave revolt was passionate, disorganised and indiscriminate. Once the pent-up resentment had been released, the insurrection needed good leadership if it was going to succeed. Toussaint Louverture emerged as the man for the job.

Toussaint was born in 1743 in Breda, a village near Cap-Haïtien. He was the son of an educated slave and was legally freed himself in 1777. After helping his former master to escape the ravages of the insurrection in 1791, he joined the black forces and soon became their leader.

By 1794 the colonists were almost defeated. Toussaint had taken advantage of the state of war between France and Spain to join forces with the Spaniards in Santo Domingo; the British had invaded the coastal areas; and the mulattos were doing well against the French in the south. To retrieve the situation, the French National Convention officially abolished slavery in the French colonies in February 1794. This was enough for Toussaint. He reverted back to the French side, was appointed lieutenant-governor by the colonial governor, Étienne Laveaux, and fought for France against the British, who had taken Port-au-Prince in June 1794. The British were forced to leave in 1798 and the following year Toussaint's army, led at the time by a young black general, Jean-Jacques Dessalines, defeated the mulattos in the south. By 1801 Toussaint controlled the whole colony, notwithstanding the colonial governors who had come and gone with great regularity during his lieutenant-governorship.

At this point the 'Gilded African', as Napoleon called him, could have declared the independence of the colony. Instead, he invaded Santo Domingo, emancipated the slaves and declared himself governor for life of the whole island. Meanwhile, back in France, Napoleon took no comfort from Toussaint's repeated declarations of loyalty. The emperor wanted to restore slavery in Saint Domingue and rid himself of the troublesome blacks. These tasks were appointed to an expeditionary force led by General Leclerc (Napoleon's brother-in-law), which was sent to the island in January 1802. Toussaint had anticipated this move and a large black army, led by Dessalines and Henri Christophe, awaited their arrival. Fierce fighting ensued for the next five months, with the French dominating. Toussaint and Leclerc came to an agreement in May: the blacks would lay down their arms in return for a French promise not to restore slavery. However, Leclerc reneged on the deal, arrested Toussaint and packed him off to France, where he was imprisoned in Fort-de-Joux in the Jura Mountains. He never saw his homeland again and died in prison in April 1803.

Independence

The leadership torch was passed to Jean-Jacques Dessalines to continue the struggle. After a meeting between him and Alexandre Pétion, the leader of the mulattos in the south, it was agreed that Dessalines should be the commander-in-chief of a united black and mulatto force against the French. With the aid of the British and yellow fever, which had decimated the French ranks and taken Leclerc's life in November 1802, the expeditionary force was finally defeated at the Battle of Vertières in November 1803. On January 1 1804, Dessalines completed the work started by Toussaint by declaring the independence of the whole island, which he renamed with its original Arawak name: Haiti.

Later that same year Dessalines proclaimed himself emperor and ruled as Jacques I. Even though he continued many of Toussaint's policies (such as the system of forced labour on plantations to maintain the nation's economic output), Dessalines was a bitter man. A slave himself, he could not forget or forgive what the whites had done. He confiscated their property and conducted a campaign of extermination, ensuring that whites would never again return to the island to rule over the blacks (perhaps this is why he is revered so much by the Haitian people today). Dessalines also discriminated against the mulatto elitists in the south, causing them to revolt under Pétion's leadership. In 1806 Dessalines was assassinated while trying to restore order.

North-south divide

Barely three years after independence, Haiti had already been split in two. Pétion ruled in the mulatto-dominated south, while Henri Christophe had established control in the north, after a failed attempt to seize the whole of the country in 1807.

Details of Christophe's early life are uncertain. According to most accounts he was born in Grenada and came to Haiti sometime during his teens. As a boy he went to Savannah to fight in the War of Independence, and later he became a general in the armies of Toussaint and Dessalines. Christophe will be remembered for many things, both good and bad. In March 1811 he crowned himself King Henri, renamed Cap-Haïtien 'Cap-Henri' and ruled as an absolute monarch for the next nine years. This period was marked by great economic prosperity (Christophe was another fan of forced labour), the establishment of a judicial system, a navy, a printing press and schools following the latest English system. Indeed, King Henri had a great love of all things English. He dressed in imitation of his 'dear brother' King George III, went about in a carriage imported from London and even spelt his name with a 'y'. The two great monuments built during his rule – the Sans-Souci Palace and the Citadelle La Ferrière – were designed to rival the best Europe had to offer. They were intended to show that Haitians were as cultured and civilised as anyone else in the world. As the years wore on, the good work done by Christophe was in danger of being cancelled out by his increasing tyranny. Opposition grew, his army started deserting to Pétion and in October 1802 the king suffered a paralytic stroke. Soon after he shot himself with a silver bullet.

Alexandre Pétion has been described as 'Haiti's best-loved ruler and the architect of her economic ruin'. Educated in France, Pétion was full of French notions of liberalism when he took control in the south. Unlike the situation in the north, where land was owned by the state and labour was controlled by strict discipline, in the south the plantations were divided into small lots and given away to the people. This created a peasant class that only produced enough to meet its own needs, thus reducing Haiti's once formidable agricultural production to a subsistence economy.

Haiti's dark age

Jean-Pierre Boyer, another mulatto, replaced Pétion on his death in 1818, and became the president of the whole country when Henri Christophe died in 1820. Boyer tried to halt the economic decline of the Pétion years by forcing peasants to work on the plantations and denying them access to the towns. The *Code Rural*, as this policy was known, was largely unsuccessful and the Haitian economy stagnated. Matters were not helped in 1825 when Boyer agreed to pay France an indemnity of 150 million francs a year in return for French recognition of Haiti and as compensation for the massacre of the colonists during the slave revolt. In 1822 Boyer renewed the conflict with Santo Domingo when he invaded and occupied that part of the island. He abolished slavery, confiscated church land and packed the ruling class with Haitians. In 1844 Juan Pablo Duarte and his supporters forced the Haitians out and declared the independence of the Dominican Republic.

A succession of rulers, some less tyrannical than others, resided at the national palace from 1843 to 1915 – a period sometimes called Haiti's 'dark age'. Faustin Soulouque, who became president in 1847, was more colourful, and certainly more tyrannical than most. A former slave who fought in the 1791 revolt, Soulouque was named president by a group of mulattos who had intended for him to be no more than a puppet ruler. Soulouque, however, had different ideas. He turned on his backers in 1849 and by 1852 had crowned himself Emperor Faustin I. He ruled with pomp and despotism – the *zinglins*, his secret police, were an early incarnation of the Tontons Macoute (see page 41) – and he was ridiculed in Europe as 'Monsieur Garibaldi-Robespierre-Napoleon Soulouque'. Nonetheless, he was quite an astute politician, who realised the potential threat of the newly created independent Dominican Republic. Thus, until 1858, when he was deposed by General Fabre Geffrard, most of Soulouque's time was spent trying to conquer the eastern part of the island.

US occupation

In 1912 the Haitian American Sugar Company was formed to organise the production and sale of sugar in Haiti and the United States. This was one of a number of recent measures that had increased US financial interests in Haiti. At the same time, Haiti's presidents were getting overthrown (sometimes quite violently) at an alarming rate: six in three years. President Woodrow Wilson, fearing for US interests, invoked the Monroe Doctrine and sent US marines to Haiti on July 28 1915 on 'humanitarian grounds'. The Haitians initial reception was indifference, as they had grown tired of political turmoil, and the arrival of the Americans at least brought stability, along with new roads, schools, telephones, hospitals and sanitation programmes. However, it did not take long for opposition to grow. The improvements to the infrastructure instigated by the Americans depended on a system of forced labour not seen since Henri Christophe's time. This revived memories of slavery and resulted in guerrilla groups, known as *cacos*, forming in the countryside to fight the marines. Order was restored in 1919 when their leader, Charlemagne Peralte, was captured and executed in Grand-Rivière du Nord, his body nailed to a door as a warning.

The Americans eventually withdrew in August 1935, leaving the mulatto elite firmly in control of the government. Sténio Vincent, whose generally solid presidency was marred by the massacre in the Dominican Republic of some 30,000 migrant Haitian workers in October 1937, was replaced by another mulatto, Élie Lescot, in 1941. He lasted until 1946, when he was deposed by the military and replaced by Dumarsais Estimé, the first black to hold the presidency since before the US intervention. The years of mulatto domination and the associated American influence had fostered feelings of black nationalism. These sentiments were expressed, albeit with reserve, by the Estimé administration. For instance, foreign ownership of land in Haiti was made more difficult and voodoo was given semi-official status. However, in 1950 a mulatto, Paul E Magloire, took up the leadership. Friendly relations were restored with the United States and the black nationalists were left to brood in the background.

In 1956 Magloire felt confident enough to go against the constitution and extend his six-year term as president. However, crops were failing, Hurricane Hazel had wreaked havoc in October 1954 and the people were in no mood to accept Magloire's political liberties. He was forced into exile, leaving a power vacuum in his wake. The mulattos lined up on one side, the blacks on the other. Estimé's presidency had put black nationalism on the political agenda for the first time since the revolution, and now it was up to a myopic country doctor to finish what Estimé had started.

Papa Doc and Baby Doc

Dr François Duvalier first made a name for himself in 1943 when he was appointed to direct a rural clinic near Port-au-Prince. Under his leadership the clinic had great success in combating yaws – a nasty disease once common in Haiti – and overnight he became Papa Doc: the great country doctor. Duvalier's work in the field earned him posts in the ministries of Public

Health and Labour under Estimé. But when Magloire took over, Duvalier disappeared from public life. Keeping a low profile and gathering his supporters around him, he bided his time until the people had tired of Magloire. In 1957 he emerged, promoting himself as the natural successor to Estimé and proclaiming an unsubtle philosophy devoted to seizing power from the mulatto elite and returning it to the black masses. On September 22 1957 Papa Doc was elected president.

Within months, the general theme of Duvalier's presidency had been set: prominent opposition figures were arrested, much of the independent press was banned, and trade union activity was curtailed. Duvalier did not rely on the army to cement his authority, but instead restructured the *cagoulards* (a band of thugs who had silenced opposition to Papa Doc in the lead-up to the election) into an armed civilian militia. Officially called the Volunteers of National Security, it was more infamously known as the Tontons Macoute. In Haitian nursery stories, Tonton Macoute (literally translated as Uncle Knapsack) is a bogeyman who creeps up on naughty children in the night and kidnaps them in his *macoute* (shoulder satchel). The rank and file of the Tontons Macoute was drawn from the existing *cagoulards* and increased by peasants, non-mulatto traders in Port-au-Prince and other towns, disaffected members of the army, and even voodoo priests. Their uniform, in keeping with their hierarchical structure, was informal and unpredictable. Many wore the blue denim and red scarves of the *caco* guerrilla as well as dark glasses, a trend that Graham Greene attempted to explain in *The Comedians*, his novel about Haiti under Papa Doc.

> 'I could understand why it was that these men wore dark glasses –
> they were human, but they mustn't show fear: it might be the end of
> terror in others.'

The greatest threat to Duvalier's absolute power came in two forms. Firstly there was his ailing health. His first heart attack was in May 1959 and even his own physician conceded (at some risk to his own life) that Duvalier was prone to lapses into insanity. Secondly there were the frequent, albeit largely abortive, invasion attempts by the anti-Duvalierists who had been driven into exile when François had come to power. The first of these was easily suppressed in July 1958. In the same month the legislature authorised Duvalier to do what had always come naturally – rule by decree – and he was not shy to use this new power. By April 1961, his authority was so complete that even the constitution, expressly forbidding a president succeeding himself, could not prevent an election result of 1.3 million for and none against a second term for Duvalier. Nor could it prevent an election with ballot papers that only carried François Duvalier's name.

In April 1963, Duvalier's men surrounded the Dominican Embassy because the perpetrator of a shooting at a Port-au-Prince college had taken refuge inside. Juan Bosch, the Dominican president, ordered the withdrawal of Duvalier's men and mobilised his own troops on the Haitian border to show that he meant business. Duvalier booked seats on a Pan-Am flight to Paris and was ready to leave Haiti when, at the eleventh hour, Bosch's army failed to follow orders and the threat of war was diverted. Duvalier had ridden his luck and won, making his power and authority absolute. In June 1964, 2.8 million people voted 'oui' in a referendum and, although there were actually fewer than 2 million eligible voters in Haiti, Duvalier became president for life.

The remaining years of his regime were a resounding success – from his point of view at least. The highlight was perhaps in 1966 when Haile Selassie, the Ethiopian emperor, was Duvalier's guest at the National Palace. At the time, schools all over Haiti were reciting a new version of the Lord's prayer: 'Our Doc, who art in the National Palace for life, hallowed be Thy name by the present and future generations. Thy will be done in Port-au-Prince as it is in the provinces. Give us this day our new Haiti and forgive not the trespasses of those anti-patriots who daily spit upon our country …' But Duvalier's health was failing fast, and in February 1971 a referendum was held on whether or not Haiti would accept Papa Doc's son, Jean-Claude, as his successor for life. The people were asked: 'Does this choice respond to your aspirations? Do you ratify it? Answer: Yes'. All 2.4 million who voted answered 'yes'. On April 21 1971, François Duvalier died.

Jean-Claude Duvalier was only 19 when he became president on April 22 1971. Moreover, he seemed to lack the leadership qualities of his father, even though he had inherited the same thirst for power. A struggle for influence in the new government developed between those who wanted to modernise the practice of Duvalierism and those who wanted Baby Doc to continue where Papa Doc had left off.

During the rest of the 1970s, the priority of Jean-Claude's regime was to restore and maintain good relations with the United States. Haiti was in economic ruin, there was famine in the northwest and US aid was needed desperately. Since the election of President Jimmy Carter in 1976, aid to Haiti had become dependent on a respect for human rights. This prompted Jean-Claude to instigate a number of liberalising measures. A certain amount of independence returned to the media, some political prisoners were released and trade unions began to function again in a limited way. However, these reforms were symbolic and cosmetic, initiated only to get international aid, and once it was received, the true colours of Jean-Claude's regime shone through. In December 1980, for example, US$16 million of the US$22 million granted to Haiti by the IMF had found its way into Jean-Claude's personal accounts, and the state was baptised a 'kleptocracy'.

By 1980, the brief period of liberalisation was over. It was thought that President Reagan would be less exacting about human rights than Carter, and in addition Jean-Claude had married the mulatto, Michele Bennett in May 1980. This brought him increasingly under the influence of the mulatto elite and the business classes, who persuaded him that economic modernisation was much more important than political reform. A new constitution in 1983 restated the maxim of Duvalierism – namely the absolute power of the president for life – and rendered meaningless any subsequent reforms, like the referendum in July 1985 which theoretically allowed other political parties.

There were signs that the people were nearing breaking point. Dissident voices in the church and media were becoming more outspoken and in 1984 and 1985 protests flared up in Cap-Haïtien and Gonaïves. In January 1986 there was another wave of rebellion, this time involving thousands of people all over the country. Jean-Claude's response was instinctive: he declared a state of siege, suspended citizens' normal rights and gave the Tontons Macoute free reign to arrest and detain. This sparked protests in Port-au-Prince for the first time in 29 years. Jean-Claude had lost control. After 19 years of the Duvaliers, the people had finally had enough. On February 7 1986, Jean-Claude Duvalier and his wife fled Haiti for France.

'Haiti libérée'

On February 8 1986 a provisional military council, led by General Henri Namphy, assumed control of the country. The following days were marked by a violence and thirst for revenge not seen since the slave revolt. The Tontons Macoute were set upon by the crowd and the houses of prominent Duvalierists were looted and burned. This period was known as the *dechoukaj*, a Creole word meaning literally 'to uproot a tree'. The most symbolic act in this process of uprooting Duvalierism and all its evils was when an enraged crowd scaled the walls of the National Cemetery and dismantled the grave of Papa Doc. The dictator's body was missing from within.

While the people were taking the law into their own hands, the military council talked of 'reconciliation', sometimes rescuing Tontons Macoutes from the angry crowd and taking them to prison under police protection. Some were later allowed to leave the country. This apparent leniency, interpreted by many as complicity with the Duvalierists, did not win the trust of the people. Namphy promised presidential elections and reforms, but continued to rule by decree. The most significant reform came in the shape of a new constitution in 1987, which was ratified by 99.81% of the people in March. Presidential elections, meanwhile, were promised for January 17 1988, and were won by Leslie Manigat. However, by June 1988 Namphy had deposed Manigat in a military coup, abolished the constitution and was once again ruling by decree – this time as president of a military government. He continued to rule until September, when he was ousted by his rivals and replaced by General Prosper Avril. During 1989 Avril survived two coup attempts, but was forced to resign as president of the military council in March 1990.

Aristide

Since the departure of Jean-Claude, a power vacuum had existed in Haiti. Few people trusted the military, whose ties with the Duvalierists were too close, while the leaders of other political parties were suspected of opportunism and self-improvement. This combination pushed the Catholic Church to the forefront of Haitian politics.

In the early 1980s dissident voices in the church had joined others in speaking out against Baby Doc. One of the most outspoken had been Father

Jean-Bertrand Aristide, a liberation theologian who encouraged the people – basically Haiti's poor – to rise up against a corrupt generation. He listed the government, the military, the Americans and even the church as enemies of the people. This made him unpopular with many sections of society, but universally revered by the masses. While military juntas ruled post-Duvalier Haiti, Aristide was the focal point of opposition. He was the great hope for the people and in December 1990 he put himself forward in the first fully free presidential elections in Haiti's history. He won by a landslide. The next month a coup attempt by Roger Lafontant, an interior minister under Baby Doc, was foiled; and on February 7 1991 Aristide was inaugurated as president.

One of his first moves was to curtail the powers of the military. He retired six of the country's eight generals and turned Fort Dimanche, the prison made notorious as a house of torture under Papa Doc, into a museum. Then he set about forming his government; René Préval, a close friend, was appointed prime minister and, ominously, an up-and-coming mulatto officer, Raoul Cédras, was made the army's chief of staff. The new president also formed what was variously described as 'a small security force' or a 'private army'. This, along with the other restrictions imposed on their power, was too much for the army. On September 30 1991 Aristide was deposed by the military under the leadership of Cédras. He fled to the United States and the junta took control.

Embargoes, 'boat people' and the United Nations

International pressure to make the military regime to step down was applied immediately. In October 1991 the Organisation of American States (OAS) proposed an oil and trade embargo, with which the Americans complied in November. These sanctions were to remain in force for the next three years. During this time smuggling across the Dominican border increased and the Haitian people, though not the ruling class, experienced almost constant electricity blackouts and food shortages. To make matters worse, the Cédras regime was conducting a violent campaign against Aristide's numerous supporters. These appalling conditions led thousands to make the dangerous trip on crowded and unseaworthy boats to a new life in the United States and the Bahamas. Many never made it.

Meanwhile, the Haitian issue had become an important part of President Clinton's foreign policy. He frequently met with Aristide and negotiated, along with the OAS and the United Nations, for his return. On June 23 1993, the UN Security Council extended the existing OAS embargo to a worldwide ban on the sale of oil and arms to Haiti. This proved to be a catalyst for talks between the army and Aristide on Governors Island, Rhode Island, at the end of June. On July 3 an accord was signed, Cédras agreed to step down on October 15 and Aristide was to make his triumphant return by October 30. However, none of this happened. October 15 came and went, General Cédras remained in power, the violence continued and the 'boat people' increased in number. By the middle of 1994 negotiations had almost run their course, and in July the UN Security Council authorised a US invasion to restore Aristide. In a final attempt to avert military intervention, a US peace mission led by former president Jimmy Carter was sent to Haiti on September 18 1994. A compromise was reached in which Cédras once again agreed to step down in October. This time the Americans were taking no chances and the following day 20,000 US troops began landing in Haiti. Their original brief was to work alongside the Haitian military, but soon they were authorised to intervene to stop the violence against civilians. By October 15 the Americans had established control, Cédras had fled to Panama and the path was clear for Father Aristide to return, just over three years after he had been forced to leave.

He returned to a country with no trained police force and no justice system. The people had been pushed to near breaking point by the economic sanctions, crime continued unabated and there were still 'boat people'. It was clear that Aristide needed help, and in January 1995 a US$1-billion aid package was approved, while a 6,000-strong United Nations force replaced the Americans, who had remained to see Aristide through the early days of his return. In the summer of 1995 the president's *Lavalas* party swept the board in elections for the Chamber of Deputies and the Senate. Although the economic and security situations remained precarious, Aristide was still the people's choice. Despite this, he decided to retire from office at the end of 1995.

Elections were held in December 1995 and Aristide's handpicked successor, his former prime minister René Préval, was elected with 87% of the vote (although there was only a 25% turnout). He appointed Rosny Smarth as his prime minister and set about tackling the country's problems. Prime among them was the security situation. It was agreed that a UN force (albeit a much smaller one) would remain until the fledgling Haitian National Police were established enough to take control, which came to pass in December 1997. Although some UN personnel remain in an advisory capacity, there are no longer any soldiers in Haiti.

In 1996 Prime Minister Rosny Smarth's main task was to negotiate the economic reforms required by the International Monetary Fund (IMF) if additional foreign aid was to be granted. In May 1996 an agreement was reached which involved cuts in government spending and a certain amount of privatisation. This exacerbated the already dire economic situation and there were strikes, demonstrations and calls for Smarth's resignation. He resigned in June 1997 and a replacement has yet to be found.

ECONOMY

Agriculture is the mainstay of the Haitian economy. It accounts for over half of the land, two-thirds of the labour force and one-third of the gross domestic product. However, gone are the days when Saint Domingue used to provide sugar for the whole of Europe. Nowadays, coffee is the largest export crop and an important source of cash and hard currency. The best-quality arabica coffee is used to make 'Haitian Blue' – a brand reserved exclusively for export – which is being well received in the international marketplace.

Sugarcane remains an important cash crop, although since the late 1970s Haiti has become a net importer of sugar. If it isn't being chewed on the streets, most sugarcane these days is distilled to produce low-quality rum called *clairin*. Cacao, rice, mangoes, bananas and sisal – a fibre used in making rope – are other exports, but none of them bring in huge amounts of revenue. Haiti is noted for the aromatic plants grown in the south that provide the essential oils used to make perfume. Most of these export crops are produced by a few large plantations. Otherwise, the land is divided into small plots and used to grow subsistence crops like corn, rice, beans, sweet potatoes, peanuts, fruits and vegetables.

These plots are owned by 79% of the people, who cultivate them primarily to meet their own needs. However, unlike their self-sufficient neighbours, food production in Haiti has not kept up with demand. This is largely due to the infertility of the soil caused by widespread deforestation. The problem has been compounded by other events, like the outbreak of swine fever in the early 1980s which led to the total eradication of the Creole pig in Haiti. The food shortage has led to increased smuggling, and contraband makes up 20% of the country's food consumption.

The small domestic market means that most of Haitian **industry** is dedicated to producing light consumer items such as clothes, baseballs and electronic components for export. Few of Haiti's natural resources are commercially exploited today. The country's gold reserves were exhausted in the 16th century; bauxite has been mined in the south since the 1950s, but world demand has declined; and the country's other resources – silver, copper, manganese and coal – are not extensive enough to merit commercial exploitation. Oil is rumoured to lie off the coast of Haiti, but it requires a huge investment in order to be developed.

Two-thirds of Haiti's **trade** is with the United States. The rest is with the Caribbean (petroleum from the Netherlands Antilles, for example), Europe and Japan. Haiti's chief imports are food, machinery and oil. The major port is Port-au-Prince, while Cap-Haïtien has recently been upgraded. For contraband traffic, the ports at Miragoâne, Petit Goâve, Saint-Marc, Gonaïves and Port-de-Paix are quite lively.

TOURISM

Believe it or not, the tourist industry once thrived in Haiti. President Dumarsais Estimé was the first to recognise the huge potential of tourism, and in 1949 he spent US$6 million cleaning up Port-au-Prince, even going as far as passing laws requiring peasants to wear shoes in town and merchants to display neon signs outside their shops. Improvements to the tourist infrastructure continued under the Magloire regime and gradually foreigners (principally from the United States) started to visit Haiti. Soon Port-au-Prince was a popular gathering place for the art and literary world, attracting the likes of Noel Coward, Graham Greene and Irving Berlin. The initial shock of Papa Doc's regime brought about a decline in tourism, but by the late 1960s, with relations between Haiti and the United States improving, the tourists started to return. By the early 1980s there was a veritable tourist boom. However, this was brought to an abrupt end by the climatic events of 1986 and the political instability that followed. The fear of AIDS in Haiti was also a major factor in keeping the tourists away. In 1980 it was recorded that 332,000 tourists had visited Haiti, but by 1993 the number had fallen to 77,000.

Although the Secretary of State for Tourism is making a concerted effort to bring the tourists back, the current situation is not much better. Other than Port-au-Prince, three areas have been selected for intensive development: Cap-Haïtien, Jacmel and the Côte des Arcadins. Cruise ships occasionally visit Cap-Haïtien (many stop at nearby Labadie) and Jacmel is earmarked as a future port-of-call. The Côte des Arcadins – the stretch of coast north of the capital – already has a few all-inclusive resorts, with more planned for the future. These are money-spinning projects designed principally for package tourists.

Ecotourism
Despite the huge problems of deforestation and over-farming, Haiti remains one of the most naturally beautiful and ecologically diverse countries in the West Indies. In the mountains there are dense pine forests, waterfalls, cave systems and cloud forests to explore, while around the coast are some excellent beaches and coral reef systems. Added to these are desert landscapes with several types of unusual cacti: Haiti certainly seems to have potential when it comes to ecotourism. There are 6,000 species of plants – 35% of which are endemic – and as many as 600 different species of orchid. The 220 species of birds include the beautiful and rare Hispaniolan trogon and the vervain hummingbird – the smallest bird in the world.

Unlike the Dominican Republic, with its system of national parks and scientific reserves, ecotourism in Haiti is in its embryonic stages. The Secretary of State for Tourism has acknowledged the tourist potential of the country's natural history and seems keen to develop what it describes as *tourisme d'aventure* (adventure tourism). Currently you can go hiking in Parc La Visite in the Massif de la Selle, although Parc Macaya in the Massif de la Hotte is less accessible. Plans for the future include developing scuba diving sites around the island of La Gonâve and Pestel on the north coast of the southwestern peninsula, as well as improving the accessibility of the country's waterfalls, lakes, caves and grottoes. The island of Tortuga, with its rugged mountains, beautiful beaches, grottoes and Arawak artefacts, has been singled out as a particularly promising site for ecotourism, and a development plan has been formulated by the United Nations Development Project (UNDP).

On your travels you might hear about **Route 2004**. This is the largest of the numerous government tourist initiatives. Funded by UNDP and UNESCO, Route 2004 aims to preserve the historical, cultural and natural resources of the country. What this means in practice is the restoration of some of the principal historical sites in Haiti, mainly in the north in Cap-Haïtien, Milot, Fort-Liberté and Môle Saint-Nicolas. Sans Souci Palace and the Citadelle La Ferrière were the first to receive attention; and it is hoped that all the restoration work will be completed by 2004, the bicentennial of Haiti's independence.

THE TRIALS AND TRIBULATIONS OF THE CREOLE PIG

Descended from pigs imported by European settlers centuries earlier, the Creole pig is small and black with long legs and a long snout. They are hardy animals requiring no special care, they eat anything from mango skins to human excrement, need little water and live tied to trees.

The Creole pig, which always fetches a good price at market, is of great economic value to the Haitian peasant, since it provides the means to pay for major expenses such as school fees, weddings, funerals and the occasional trip to Port-au-Prince. The black pig also has a religious importance, being the favoured animal for voodoo sacrifices. Indeed, so important is the role of the Creole pig in Haitian rural life, that an outbreak of African Swine Fever (ASF) in 1981 spelt the beginning of the end for Jean-Claude Duvalier and his regime.

ASF originated in Africa and, like AIDS, the virus is highly infectious and incurable. It is transmitted by ticks, contaminated food or direct contact, attacks the pig's respiratory apparatus and kills within 48 hours. ASF was first detected in the Caribbean in Cuba in 1971; it had spread to the Dominican Republic by 1978, and in 1979 cases were reported in Haiti.

By 1981, ASF had taken root in Haiti, and Jean-Claude Duvalier was put under pressure by the United States to take appropriate action, as they feared the spread of the disease to North American herds. The chosen solution was the Program for the Eradication of Porcine Swine Fever and

PEOPLE

There are two main groups in Haitian society: the blacks and the mulattos. The blacks constitute 95% of Haiti's 7 million people, while the remainder is predominantly mulatto. The differences between these two groups go beyond mere skin colour, leading the anthropologist J G Leyburn, author of *The Haitian People* (1941), to describe them as 'castes'.

According to a Haitian proverb, 'a rich black is a mulatto; a poor mulatto is a black'. Spend some time in the hills behind Port-au-Prince – for example in Pétion-Ville and Boutilliers – and you'll see a fair sprinkling of million-dollar homes. Some of them are owned by blacks, but most of them belong to mulattos. Then go into the countryside, where the Haitian peasant scratches a living on small plots of land, and almost all the faces are black. This division between the rich urban elite – a disproportionate number of which are mulatto – and the black Haitian peasantry has persisted since the times of slavery. Moreover, after independence, apart from a few notable and often notorious exceptions, the traditional ruling class has also been mulatto.

But the difference between the blacks and the mulattos is cultural as well as material. Under white rule, the mulattos or *gens de couleur* were basically free people who had African blood. Louis XIV's *Code Noir* allowed them to become French citizens, and for many of them Paris was more of a home than Haiti.

Development (PEPPADEP), funded by America, Canada and Mexico, whose objective was the slaughter of the 1.2 million native Creole pigs in Haiti. Pig-owners were paid a few dollars for their pigs and by way of compensation were given a brand new 'white' American pig. The eradication programme began in May 1982 and by December 1983 the Creole pig was extinct in Haiti.

From an American point of view, PEPPADEP was a great success, but for the Haitian peasant its effects were disastrous and a cause of much resentment towards the man held responsible – the pig-killer, Baby Doc Duvalier. The peasants' main bone of contention was that the American pigs offered as replacements for their native Creole pigs were totally unsuited to the harsh conditions of rural life in Haiti. When the new pig arrived (and it often never did) it had to be fed with expensive cereal feed enriched with proteins and vitamins, it drank like a fish and needed housing in a specially constructed concrete sty because it was unused to Haitian soil. In short, the peasant was expected to raise his pigs more comfortably than his own family.

When Duvalier fled Haiti in 1986, a petition signed by 160,000 people demanding the reintroduction of the Creole pig was handed to the new government. The French, eager to score diplomatic points, announced that they would assist the government in reintroducing the small, black Creole pig to the countryside. Today, it is once again a common feature of the Haitian landscape.

This association with Europe, or disassociation with Haiti, continued after independence, and the mulatto elite sent their children to school in France and spoke French rather than their native Creole language. In short, their values were more European than African. The opposite was true for the Negro majority, who took considerable pride in the fact that they were descendants of the revolting slaves who had won Haiti her freedom. This culture celebrated its African roots; Creole was the spoken language and voodoo was the most important religion. On several occasions in early Haitian history, the tension between these two cultures led to civil war. Nowadays, it bubbles under the surface.

Blancs

The white man's relationship with Haiti – a relationship characterised by exploitation, slavery, interference and occupation – makes his position in the country today ambivalent, which is perfectly expressed by the term 'blanc'. The word, of course, is French for 'white', but it's actually used to describe anyone who is not black, and on your travels around Haiti, you'll hear it often. Because of its literal meaning, the word might seem like a term of abuse with overtly racist connotations, but in fact it serves simply to describe white people and there is rarely any malice attached.

Women in Haiti

Life is especially hard for women in Haiti, who seem to carry a disproportionate load of the work. They must bear and look after children, work on the peasant smallholdings, carry produce to market and sell it. In spite of these hardships, they have a tremendous sense of humour and a resolve that earns them universal respect. Without the women, Haitian society would surely collapse.

Haitians abroad

There are approximately 3 million Haitians living abroad. About 2 million are in the United States, the majority concentrated in New York and Miami. Elsewhere, 10% of the population of the Bahamas and most of the sugar-cane cutters in the Dominican Republic are Haitian; there are also significant communities in Canada, Cuba and France.

There are two types of exile. The first is the poverty-stricken, illiterate peasant who is desperate to leave the drought, famine and infertile soils of Haiti for a more prosperous life in North America or elsewhere in the Caribbean. These are the desperados, otherwise known as the 'boat people'. The second category is the intelligentsia and professional elite – doctors, lawyers, engineers and architects – who have left Haiti for a more profitable life in North America or Europe. This group constitutes Haiti's 'brain drain'.

The mass exodus of people from Haiti started during Papa Doc's regime and continued when Baby Doc took over. There was a brief respite after the fall of Duvalierism, but the 'boat people' emerged again during Aristide's exile in the early 1990s.

LANGUAGE

French is the official language in Haiti, but only about 10% of the people are comfortable speaking it. Instead, **Creole** is the language widely spoken. In 1979, Jean-Claude Duvalier decreed that Creole should be used in schools, and in the 1987 constitution, the language was given official recognition.

The origins of Creole are debatable. Some say that it existed on the island long before the slaves arrived, while others contend that it emerged as a language of convenience to facilitate communication between the slaves and the French. Indeed, Creole does contain strong French and African elements: approximately 80% of the words are derived from French and the pronunciation and sentence structure is very African. It also has several words of English and Spanish derivation.

If you know French, and as long as the speaker takes it slowly, you might understand a bit of Creole. Although Creole sounds quite French, there are some important differences. French-derived words in the Creole vocabulary have often broadened their meaning. For example, '*blan*' is derived from the French word '*blanc*', meaning 'white', but in Creole it also means any foreigner who is not black. Similarly, '*nèg*' (derived from the French word '*nègre*', meaning 'negro') is the word for 'man'. Creole words can also appear in a slightly different form from their French ancestors; for instance, '*ti*' (Creole) and '*petit*' (French) both mean 'little'. When Baby Doc decreed that Creole should be spoken in schools, philologists from the United States came up with a phonetic system of orthography that made good use of the letter 'k'. This makes many Creole words look a bit strange. But if you say what you see, you can sometimes work out what they mean. To give you an idea: '*kado*' comes from '*cadeau*' meaning 'gift'; '*kanpagn*' comes from '*campagne*' meaning 'countryside'; and '*ke*' comes from '*cœur*' meaning 'heart'.

The basic rules of Creole grammar and pronunciation are listed in *Appendix 1*, along with a few useful expressions and words.

RELIGION

Officially about 80% of Haiti's population is Roman Catholic and 20% are Protestant. Unofficially, most people have some involvement with voodoo.

You get the impression that the church plays an important role in Haitian life when you see the crowds outside who can't get a seat in church during mass, the children dressed in their Sunday best, and *tap-taps* (see page 65) called *Angel of God, Living Christ* and *Immaculate*. In the early 1980s this role became political as well as social. Pope Jean Paul II visited Haiti in March 1983 and delivered a homily attacking injustice and oppression. 'Things have got to change' he said. From this moment on the Catholic Church started to speak up for the poorest sections of Haitian society, culminating in the election of Father Aristide as president in 1990.

Protestantism is equally as strong as Catholicism, but lacks the mass appeal. You'll find Methodists, Presbyterians and Episcopalians, as well as Baptists, Mormons, Seventh-Day Adventists and Jehovah's Witnesses, who all came to Haiti during and after the US occupation.

Voodoo

Before I came to Haiti and learned a little more about this fascinating religion, scenes from *The Night of the Living Dead* were stuck firmly in my mind. I had expected a land full of zombies and black magic, but instead I discovered that voodoo, far from being the evil cult of some Hollywood director's imagination, is the lifeblood of this nation and taken very seriously by its followers.

This is as true today as it was when Haiti was Saint Domingue and its people toiled under the yoke of slavery. During those hard times, voodoo functioned as a survival mechanism – a way of preserving some African culture in a world dominated by Europeans (voodoo derives from the West African *Yoruba* religion). Naturally, the Catholic settlers were not prepared to tolerate 'barbaric' African cults, so the slaves learned how to integrate elements of Catholicism into their own religion in order to make it acceptable to their masters. Christian saints, symbols and rituals came to be identified with their African counterparts, giving birth to voodoo – a religion described in the textbooks as 'syncretic' (evolving from a mixture of beliefs). Ever since the slave revolt – appropriately plotted at a voodoo ceremony at Bois-Cayman – voodoo has been one of the defining features of the nation's culture.

Voodoo beliefs

Voodoo, in common with many other African religions, is based on the concept of a life spirit which is found in all living things. As in Catholicism, there is a Supreme Being. However, unlike Catholicism, this Supreme Being – the Gran Maître – is too remote to be contacted directly by the material world. Instead, mere mortals must serve the voodoo spirits or *loas*. The aim of a voodoo ceremony is to get in touch with this spiritual world.

A devotee of voodoo will tell you that in The Beginning the earth was created by Damballah, the *loa* of life. He slithered over the earth in the form of a serpent, creating hills and valleys on his journey. When he had finished, he shed his skin in the sun and released all waters over the land. The sun shone on the water and a rainbow appeared. Damballah saw the rainbow, fell in love, and made her his wife, Aida-Wedo.

As far as death is concerned, things get a little more complex. The mortal flesh is not particularly relevant, since it rots away after death, but what happens to the two parts of the soul is vital. If they are not banished from the earth by death rituals, they have the potential to do harm to others. The *gros-bon-ange* (great good angel) is the part of the soul that passes into the human being at conception. It comes from the spiritual world and charges the body during life. On death, the *gros-bon-ange* is sent to Ginen, Creole word for Guinée (Africa) and the spiritual homeland of all voodooists. There it resides with the other *loas* and is worshipped as one itself. The journey to Ginen is facilitated by a death ritual called *dessounin*. The *houngan* or voodoo priest becomes possessed by a *loa* and is reborn as the *gros-bon-ange* that belonged to the dead person as it passes through on its way to Ginen. The other part of the soul is the *ti-bon-ange* (little good angel). This is an accumulation of a person's

TEN HAITIAN PROVERBS

The Haitians are a philosophical bunch and their language is packed with proverbs on all subjects. Here are ten of my favourites:

- *Dèyè mòn gin mòn* – Beyond mountains there are more mountains
- *Déveinn cé pian* – Bad luck is a disease
- *Mauvé nouvèl toujou vré* – Bad news is always true
- *Papillon caressé lamp, li fait ronn li, et cé ladan li mouri* – The moth flirts with the lamp, circles around it, and then is killed by it
- *Zorier cé bon conséyé* – The night is a good counsellor
- *Boi pouri min paròl pa pouri* – Wood rots, but words do not
- *Bondié di: 'Tout ti moun yo, couché', Couleuvre di: 'Moin a tè a déja'* – God says: 'You who are my children lie down'. The snake replies: 'I am already on the ground'
- *Ou toujou songé sa ou té vlé bliyé* – You always remember what you want to forget
- *Nan poin lajan nan poin fanm* – No money, no woman
- *Cé lesprit kò ki condui kò* – It's the spirit that leads the body

experience and knowledge and determines character, personality and will. After death, the *ti-bon-ange* hovers over the dead body for a period of nine days, during which time the *houngan* must perform a death ritual called 'nine night' to banish the spirit to the land of the dead. Failure to do this leaves the *ti-bon-ange* free to wander the earth and cause harm to others.

The loas

The *loas* inhabit all living things: they are the life spirits around which voodoo is based and all voodoo worshippers want to make contact with them. There are hundreds of *loas* in the voodoo pantheon, but basically they can be split into two categories: the *Rada loas* and the *Petro loas*.

The **Rada loas** are gentle and benevolent, associated with life and creation. They are white in colour and ceremonies in their honour are characterised by drumming with a good and consistent beat and rhythmic dancing. *Rada loas* have modest appetites and are satisfied with a chicken or pigeon as a sacrifice. Damballah and Aida-Wedo are the two main *Rada* spirits. Others include Ogou, the warrior *loa*, who as Ogou Ferraille is also associated with metalwork, order and stability, and Loco, the *loa* of vegetation and spirit of the earth, for whom the trees are sacred.

The **Petro loas** are darker and more aggressive than their *Rada* counterparts. They are associated with death and vengence and their colour is red. At *Petro* ceremonies, the drumming is off-beat and sharp, with dancing to match. The sacrificial menu includes hogs, goats, sheep, cows, dogs and the occasional dead body from a tomb. The *Petro loas* are generally more powerful than the peace-loving *Rada*, and probably the most powerful of all is Papa Legba. As the guardian of the gate between the spiritual world and the material world, no *loa* can join a voodoo possession ceremony without Legba's permission. In some of his other forms, he is master of the crossroads and *loa* of wisdom and medicine. During slavery, when voodoo had to hide behind a veneer of Catholicism, Papa Legba was identified with St Peter, and his wife, Erzulie, was associated with the Virgin Mary. She is the *loa* of love and beauty and in her pure and virginal state she represents the moon. However, her range is diverse and in other forms she represents Venus, a bull, a serpent and an old, grief-stricken woman. Baron Samedi is *loa* of the dead and, as Baron Cimetière, *loa* of the cemetery. While other *loas* enjoy association with famous Christian saints, Baron Samedi has been identified with Papa Doc. Legend has it that he used to hold conversations with the heads of his executed enemies and enjoy blood rites and sacrifices, which led many to believe that Baron Samedi himself was living in the National Palace. The last of the principal *Petro loas*, Guedé, is a group of spirits related to the theme of death. Baron Samedi, for instance, is a Guedé, as are *loas* representing gravediggers, lightning bolts and the suffering Christ.

Possession

The *loas* control the affairs of man by 'mounting the horse' – in other words, taking possesion of a human's body during a voodoo ceremony. While possessed, the horse will display the characteristics of the *loa* in possession. So if a devotee starts slithering around on the floor, although it looks like he's gone mad, he's probably just been possessed by Damballah, the sky-serpent *loa*. Assuming the gait of an old man on crutches signifies the presence of Papa Legba; a vain and flaunting attitude is the trademark of Erzulie; and a devotee who insists on telling dirty jokes, wearing dark glasses, eating, drinking and smoking to excess and perhaps even cross-dressing, is usually under the influence of Baron Samedi.

To achieve possession, the *loas* must be 'called' in the proper way. This is the point of a voodoo ceremony. It takes place in the *hounfor* (temple) or, if it's a public ceremony or *Petro loas* are being invoked, an open-sided building adjacent to the *hounfor* called the *peristyle*. All ceremonies are presided over by either a *houngan* (priest) or a *mambo* (priestess).

Proceedings begin with an invocation to Papa Legba to open the gate and let the *loas* pass from the spiritual world to the material world. Legba is the keeper of the centre-post in the *peristyle* – the *poteau-mitan* – down which the spirits must come if they want to take possession of a devotee. To entice them down the *houngan* draws *vévés* – elaborate designs symbolising the different *loas* – on the beaten earth floor of the *peristyle*. Meanwhile, the community of worshippers known as a *société* has begun a series of chants accompanied by frenetic drumming and dancing. Offerings are then made and possession takes place partly so that the *loa* can receive the sacrifice.

Black magic and zombies

Balancing the forces of good and evil is very important in voodoo belief. This is why all *houngans* also know how to practise black magic, although few ever do. The exceptions are called *bokors*, or 'those who serve the *loa* with both hands'. Their specialities are using the dead to do evil acts and creating zombies.

While the soul is hovering over its dead body, it can be turned into a *zombie astral* – a soul without a body – commanded by the *bokor* to do harm to others. Alternatively, the *bokor* has the power to create a zombie – a dead body without a soul. A powerful zombie poison is administered to the victim, causing paralysis and coma. A few days later a second drug with hallucinogenic qualities (the 'zombies cucumber') revives the now speechless, senseless and soulless body. The zombie is then used as the *bokor's* slave. To my knowledge it neither eats human brains nor shuffles about with outstretched arms.

MUSIC

Music is a vital part of Haitian culture and you hear it everywhere. Even when there is no power (which is often) Haiti is rarely quiet. Pass a church and you'll hear the most beautiful evangelical singing; and when a crowded *camion* bursts into spontaneous song, all of it in perfect tune, you'll find it hard not to shed a tear at the poignancy of it all.

The popular music is **compas**, which, in common with most other Caribbean music, is a composition of several musical styles. Typically, it contains elements of salsa, soca, zouk, calypso and, fundamentally, Haitian *méringue*, which is slower than its Dominican counterpart, with guitars instead of accordions. The two great orchestras of Haiti, **Septentrional** and **Tropicana**, play traditional *compas*: sedate, smooth and swinging. They are both from Cap-Haïtien and continue to release albums and give live performances – in Septent's case, more than 50 years after its formation.

The evolution of modern *compas* can be traced back to the 1960s when jazz and funk started to influence the music. A range of new instruments such as electric guitars, saxophones and bass were used by **'mini-jazz' bands** who played a faster, punchier style of *compas*. Large Haitian communities had grown in New York and Miami during the Papa Doc years, and groups like Tabou Combo and Skah Shah were putting *compas* on the international stage.

At the same time, *compas* was being exposed to new influences like North American rap, French Antillean zouk, reggae and, more recently, ragga. The **Nouvel Jenerayshun** (New Generation) of Haitian bands, many of them based in North America, use synthesisers and other electronic sounds to produce a *compas*-style of dance music. Look out for names like the System Band, Sakud and Top Vice – a group based in Miami who combine rap with *compas*.

Meanwhile, back in Haiti a more traditional style of music persists. Coupé Cloué are one of the few surviving mini-jazz bands who play guitar-led *compas* with a dreamy quality, far removed from the high-speed sounds of the US-based groups. Other bands, like Boukman Eksperyans, have drawn on Haiti's voodoo roots to produce music with ra-ra rhythms played on a variety of percussion instruments and bamboo trumpets. In addition to this Afro-Haitian religious music, evangelical songs – like those sung by Lochard Remy – are very popular.

HAITIAN ART

Haiti is a small nation and international recognition (not to be confused with notoriety) in any field is a major achievement. In the field of art, Haiti has deservedly become world famous. In the country itself, where most people are illiterate, paintings of colourful scenes from everyday life – weddings, funerals, market days, beautiful girls, political events and the voodoo religion – are the novels, poems, newspapers and religious texts of the masses. Given such a responsibility, Haitian art has to be good.

Art historians trace the history of art in Haiti back to the Taino Indians who used to paint the walls of their huts and caves. However, for our purposes let's start in 1944 when Dewitt Peters, an American English teacher, established the **Centre d'Art** in Port-au-Prince, with the aim of providing a suitable environment for native painters with talent but no formal training to develop their skills and exhibit their work. The Centre d'Art opened its doors to peasants, taxi drivers and voodoo priests – all of them ignorant of the finer points of the rules governing perspective and composition, but with the ability to express themselves with passion, colour, emotion and a childlike innocence. These painters became known as 'primitive' or 'naïve'. Some of the most famous are Hector Hyppolite, Philomé Obin, Castera Bazile, Rigaud Beniot and Wilson Bigaud.

The 'primitive' painters were the pioneers of Haitian art and from them sprang different schools in towns like Port-au-Prince and Cap-Haïtien. The general trend was towards a more sophisticated style, where greater attention is paid to realism and the aesthetic quality of the picture. In the 1950s *La Realisme de Cruauté* (Realism of Cruelty) came to the fore with artists like Dieudonné Cédor and Néhémy Jean Paquot – both of whom have painted murals at Port-au-Prince International Airport. In the 1960s *L'Esthétique de la Beauté* (School of Beauty) attempted to capture beauty, elegance and grace in their paintings. The work of Bernard Séjourné provides some good examples.

The majority of contemporary artists have maintained a sophisticated approach to their work, while some continue to paint with the simple lines and bold, primary colours of the 'primitive' style. New styles and methods have also been developed, so that nowadays there are such things as Haitian abstracts and expressionism, as well as pictures painted with pallet knives and beeswax. Love it or loathe it, Haitian art is certainly different.

LITERATURE

Haiti's writers and poets have not quite managed to capture the life and soul of Haiti and put it down on paper the way the nation's painters have on canvas. This is not to say that Haitian literature is bland. Read some of the indigenous writers – those who write about Haiti and its roots – like Jacques Romain or the poet, Félix Morisseau-Leroy, and their attempts to evoke the native African culture of Haiti are certainly powerful. Romain's most famous novel, *Gouverneurs de la Rosée* (Masters of the Dew), describes in aggressive language the hard life of the Haitian peasant. However, I often find that in literature there's something missing. When I pick up a Haitian novel or poem I expect to read about what I've seen painted with so much passion and feeling by the artists. But maybe I am expecting too much. After all, it was only at the turn of this century that Haitian literature was starting to be written in Creole. Even then, the writers came from the sophisticated élite – educated in Europe, living in the swanky suburbs of Port-au-Prince, yet writing about Haiti's slum-dwellers and peasants. Perhaps it's no wonder that their work can sometimes seem detached, soulless and aloof.

You might see some of the following names in the bookshops: Dr Jean Price-Mars, one of the pioneers of indigenous writing who tried to elevate negro pride in their African heritage and was a great influence on Papa Doc; Dr Jean Chrysostome Dorsainville, another political writer who dedicated his work to the political and social aspects of Haitian culture, especially voodoo; the historian, Thomas Madiou, known for the several volumes of his *Histoire d'Haiti*, which charts the nation's history since 1492; and Oswald Durand, the 'Shakespeare of Haiti', who wrote on all aspects of Haitian life. His most famous work is *Choucoune*, a poem set to music about the beauty of a Haitian woman.

SPORT

Sport is very important to Haitians, perhaps because it provides a distraction from the hardships of daily life, or an outlet for pent-up aggression.

Soccer is the national obsession. The Haitian national team reached the World Cup finals in 1974, where it lost all three of its games to Poland, Argentina and Italy, conceding a total of 14 goals. Nowadays, teams from Guadeloupe and Martinique give them a good run for their money. This doesn't matter all that much, since the national team *in absentia* is Brazil. During the most recent World Cup the country ground to a halt for a month, Électricité d'Haiti put advertisements in *Le Nouvelliste* promising power during the matches, and there was crying in the streets when Brazil lost in the final.

Basketball is the next most popular sport. The American NBA is followed closely and the game is often played in the street, where basketball hoops are a more common sight than street lamps. The other 'sport' with mass appeal is **cockfighting**, which takes place everywhere.

FOOD AND DRINK
Traditional dishes

With every Haitian meal comes the *viv*. Derived from the French verb 'vivre' meaning 'to live', *viv* is the starchy, life-giving food that is so important in the Haitian diet. It is served with the meat and sauce and might consist of *bananes* (green plantains), *patates* (sweet potatoes) and yams, but not rice, which is normally served as a separate dish after the *viv*. Haitian-style rice – rice mixed with other ingredients – is some of the best in the Caribbean, although it can be a little greasy. The national rice, the one you'll be able to eat practically everywhere is *diri kole* (rice mixed with red kidney beans). A variation of this is *diri ak sos pwa* (plain rice with a kidney bean sauce). *Diri djon djon* (rice cooked with dry, black mushrooms and congo peas) is another favourite, although this is slightly more up-market, and therefore less widely available.

Griots are possibly Haiti's favourite food. Depending on where you go, these are either tasty chunks of pork, boiled then fried and served with a spicy *ti malice* sauce, or balls of fat and gristle. *Ti malice sauce* is added to other meat dishes and can also feature with spaghetti, rice or anything else that needs spicing up. It is made with sour orange and lime juice, peppers, shallots and salt. In this way, *poule* (chicken) with a *ti malice sauce* becomes *poule creole*, another Haitian favourite. Of the other meats on offer, *cabri* (goat) is worth trying. It can either be fried in chunks like *griots*, or served with a sauce as *cabri creole*. *Tassot* is any meat (often goat or turkey) which has been dried under the sun, marinated and grilled. Beef is less common than the other meats, but it can be found as a *tassot* or a *salaise* (dried beef served with avocado and plantain).

Lambi creole (conch meat, either grilled or served in a stew) is seldom absent from Haitian restaurant menus. However, the coastal towns are your best bet for other seafood. *Poisson gros sel* is fish (usually snapper or seabass) cooked with coarse salt, while *homard* (lobster) is particularly good on the south coast.

These typical Haitian dishes are spicy and filling, but they can tend to get a little repetitive. To break the monotony of your chicken, goat and conch diet, try some Haitian soup. *Bouillon* is, in fact, more like a thin stew with plantains, sweet potatoes, vegetables and meat. *Soup joromou* is a similar type of thing, but with pumpkin.

Street food

As good as all these traditional dishes sound, the fact is that restaurants often don't have the ingredients to make them. If you draw a blank at Chez Claude, the world of Haitian street food awaits you. Most of it is fried. The golden discs of fried plantain you see heaped on many a street vendor's cart are called *bananes pesées*. *Croquettes véritables* are the breadfruit equivalent and *patates* are the same with sweet potato. *Griots*, fried chicken, hot dogs, brochettes and corn-on-the-cob are also widely available. There really are no bounds to what you can pick up on the street. My best advice is to try anything you think you might like. The bread, by the way, can be particularly good.

Fruits and vegetables

Tropical fruits are plentiful in Haiti. Mangoes, pineapples, papayas, bananas, melons, oranges and *chadéques* (like grapefruits, but not as sharp) are sold everywhere, while in the supermarkets you can normally find imported apples, pears and grapes. One of the great joys of Haiti are mangoes. If, like me, you love them, try to plan your visit around May or June – the mango season. Haiti is famous in the Caribbean for the size of her mangoes. The *fransique* is the largest variety, but there are all sorts of others.

Bananas are especially popular at breakfast. Note that if you want a yellow banana, as opposed to a green plantain, you should ask for a *banane figue*.

Apart from the starchy root vegetables, beans, tomatoes, onions and one or two others, vegetables are not the most important part of the Haitian diet.

Desserts

Most of the desserts you find in smarter restaurants have a strong French influence. *Zoeuf-au-lait* (burnt caramel custard) is one of the most popular, while *pain patate* is a traditional Haitian pudding made with sweet potatoes, coconut and raisins. On the street you'll find various cakes, pastries and tablets (sticky squares of candy often containing peanuts). However, *the* choice of the sweet-toothed Haitian is a stick of sugarcane. They tear the flesh off with their teeth, chomp on it for a while and then spit the pulp out. Not attractive, but effective!

Drinks

Coke, Pepsi, Sprite, Fanta and Miranda come in thirst-quenching half-litre bottles, and Couronne is the local competition. It is very sweet and described as 'fruit champagne'. With all the tropical fruit around, juices are a good alternative to fizzy drinks. If you can't get them fresh, look out for bottled varieties like Tampico and Tropic. Larco is a Haitian brand which is less sweet.

Culligan purified water is an institution in Haiti and a traveller's godsend. It comes in small sachets, large enough to take the edge off a thirst or to brush your teeth with – you can find it almost anywhere.

Rum is the preferred liquor in Haiti and Barbancourt is the preferred brand. This locally produced rum, made from sugarcane, is truly one of the best in the world. It comes in three classes: three star, *Réserve Spéciale* or five star, and *Réserve du Domaine*, the 15-year-old variety. You hardly ever see the last of these, which apparently tastes like a fine cognac. The five star is about twice the price of the three star, which just about reflects the difference in quality. Barbancourt also do a selection of rum liqueurs under their Barlin label. They come in a variety of flavours like mint, papaya, orange and banana. *Crémasse* is a typical Haitian drink, popular during holidays. It is usually made with condensed milk, coconut and rum. At the other end of the scale, *clairin* or *tafia* is white brut rum distilled from raw sugarcane: the local firewater. Beer joins rum as the other favourite tipple. A range of imported beers is available, along with the well-regarded local offering, Prestige.

60

Sans Souci Palace, Milot, Haiti

Haiti: Practicalities

RED TAPE AND IMMIGRATION
General requirements
For UK, US and Canadian citizens, the entry requirements for Haiti are simple and unexacting: only a valid passport is required for a stay of up to 90 days. Note that in theory US and Canadian nationals only need proof of their citizenship (such as a birth certificate), but due to the constantly changing political situation, especially between Haiti and the United States, it is always best to carry a passport. Currently nationals from Germany, Austria, Luxembourg, Denmark, Sweden, Norway and Switzerland are allowed to stay for up to 90 days without a visa. Other nationals might require a visa. Be prepared to submit two photographs and about US$20 with your application for a visa for a stay of up to 90 days and valid for three months.

There is an airport departure tax of US$25 for foreigners, payable only in US dollars. Add to this a Gde10 security tax. There is no departure tax when you cross the land border, although when you enter Haiti from the Dominican Republic you may or may not be asked to pay a US$10 bank tax and a Gde25 immigration tax.

Embassies and consulates
Haitian representation abroad
Canada: 112 Rue Kent Suite 1308, Place de Ville, Tour B, Ontario K1P 5P2; tel: 613 238 2986; Consulate in Montreal (tel: 514 499 1919)
Dominican Republic: 33 Avenida Juan Sanchez Ramirez, Santo Domingo; tel: 809 686 5778
France: 10 rue Théodule Ribot, 75017 Paris; tel: 01 47 63 47 78; Consulate: 35 avenue de Villiers, 75017 Paris; tel: 01 42 12 70 50
USA: 2311 Massachusetts Avenue, Washington DC 20008; tel: 202 332 4090; Consulates in New York (tel: 212 697 9767), Miami (tel: 305 859 2003) and Boston (tel: 617 266 3660)

Foreign representation in Port-au-Prince
The following countries have embassies in Port-au-Prince:

Canada: Delmas 18; tel: 23 2358
Dominican Republic: Rue Pan-americaine, Pétion-Ville: tel: 57 0568
France: 20 Rue Manoir des Lauriers, Champ de Mars; tel: 45 6212

Netherlands: Shodecosa; tel: 23 5146
Spain: 11 Rue Oscar Deprez; tel: 45 4411
USA: Boulevard Harry Truman; tel: 23 0202

The following countries have consulates in Port-au-Prince:

Italy: 12 Rue Louverture, Pétion-Ville; tel: 57 3968
Netherlands: 26 Shodecosa; tel: 22 0955
Switzerland: Building Villedrouin, Pétion Ville; tel: 57 0503
UK: Rue Cardozo, Hotel Montana; tel: 23 7011

GETTING THERE AND AWAY
By air
Europe

The only direct flight from Europe to Port-au-Prince is with Air France from Paris. There is one a week and, not surprisingly, it is normally full. This means that most visitors from Europe are obliged to go via North America or the few other countries in the Caribbean and Latin America that have direct flights to Haiti.

Without doubt the cheapest way of getting to Haiti is via Santo Domingo on one of the many charter airlines flying to the Dominican Republic at the moment. The main problem with this option is that if you want to stay longer than the one or two weeks normally allowed by the charter companies, you'll have to buy another return ticket. This can be expensive in the Caribbean. Also remember that in order to buy a ticket on a charter flight, you may have to book a hotel package in the Dominican Republic – obviously not much good if you're spending the bulk of your time in Haiti.

North America

The gateway cities for scheduled airlines to Port-au-Prince from North America are New York, Montreal and Miami. American Airlines has one flight a day to Port-au-Prince from New York and Air Canada fly from Montreal. From Miami, American Airlines fly to Port-au-Prince twice a day and Air France three times a week. An alternative to the larger carriers is ALM Antillean Airlines. They have flights from Miami to Curaçao via Port-au-Prince. All of these airlines have toll-free numbers in the US: **American Airlines** (tel: 1-800-433-7300); **Air Canada** (tel: 1-800-776-3000); **Air France** (tel:1-800-237-2747); **ALM** (tel: 1-800-327-7230). A couple of charter airlines (Canada 3000 and Air Transit) also have services from Montreal.

If you want to start your trip in Cap-Haïtien, try **Lynx Air International** (tel: 1-888-5969-247), who fly there four times a week from Fort Lauderdale in Florida.

Caribbean and Latin America

Details of travel from the Caribbean and Latin America can be found in Chapter 21.

By sea

(See Chapter 20 for more information about getting to Haiti by sea.) Other than arriving by cruise ship, you might be able to secure a berth on a private yacht or a cargo ship. Look around in places like New York and Miami if this appeals to you. To my knowledge there are no international ferry services to Haiti.

By land

Crossing the border from the Dominican Republic to Haiti and vice versa is easy. In the north there are immigration facilities at Dajabón and Quanaminthe, and at Jimaní and Malpasse in the south. Currently there is just one direct bus service linking the two countries. This is called the **Terra Bus** (tel: 23 7882) and it travels between Santo Domingo and Port-au-Prince six days a week. The fare is the same regardless of the direction in which you are going: US$45 single, US$75 return. The trip takes six hours and uses the Jimaní-Malpasse border crossing. From Santo Domingo, the bus leaves from the Plaza Criolla at 06.00 on Wednesday, Thursday and Friday and 12.00 on Saturday, Sunday and Monday. From Port-au-Prince, the bus leaves from the Steak-Inn Restaurant at 37 Rue Magny, Pétion-Ville at 14.00 on Tuesday, Wednesday, Thursday, Friday and Sunday and at 20.00 on Monday. To buy a ticket in Port-au-Prince go to Agence Chatelain (tel: 23 2400) at the top of Rue Pavée.

GETTING AROUND
By air

The number of aeroplane symbols on recent maps of Haiti would seem to suggest that internal air travel is a common thing. This is unfortunately not the case. Most of the so-called airports are, in fact, tiny airfields not capable of accommodating even the smallest of commercial planes.

Caribintair operate the only domestic flights in Haiti, connecting Port-au-Prince, Cap-Haïtien and Jérémie. (The ten-minute flight from Port-au-Prince to Jacmel was recently suspended due to lack of interest.) The plane arrives in Port-au-Prince each morning from Santo Domingo, and makes two return journeys to the Cap and one to Jérémie before returning to Santo Domingo in the evening. I have given the times and prices of these flights in the *Getting there and away* section of the relevant towns. You should bear in mind that Caribintair use small planes and flights fill up quickly. This is especially true on the Port-au-Prince – Jérémie – Port-au Prince flight. Book early to avoid disappointment.

By sea

You should exercise caution before deciding to travel by boat in Haiti. A bus crowded to three times its capacity is one thing, a boat with a similar load is quite another. In September 1997 an overloaded ferry coming from La Gonâve capsized as it tried to dock at Montrouis. It sank in 35m of water, drowning more than 170 people. Only about 60 survived.

Haiti's three main islands – La Gonâve, Tortuga and Île-à-Vache – are well populated and can be reached by boat. For La Gonâve and Tortuga you should be able to go out in the morning and return to the mainland in the afternoon, leaving you a few hours to look around. For Île-à-Vache you might have to stay overnight.

The one boat a week that sails along the north coast of the southwestern peninsula between Port-au-Prince and Jérémie is always overcrowded and even less appealing than the 12-hour bus trip.

Of course, you always have the option of hiring a boat privately. This generally works best if there is a group of you, since fishermen will always base their price on the boat, not the number of people.

Travelling by sea really comes into its own on the two peninsulas where the road network is least developed. For example, consider sailing from Port Salut to Jérémie around the tip of the southwestern peninsula instead of negotiating the rocky road across the mountains (although this will also appeal to the adventurous).

By road

If the map slightly embellishes the number of airports available to the visitor in Haiti, it downright misleads when it comes to the country's roads. Judging by all the lines criss-crossing Haiti, it seems that you can get anywhere easily and quickly. Let me assure you that this is not the case.

Before the US intervention in 1915 there were no roads in Haiti. Now there are 3,688 km of roads – but only one-fifth are paved. The best route links Port-au-Prince to the Dominican border at Malpasse. The two main roads (generously described as highways by the cartographers) are **Route Nationale One**, going north from Port-au-Prince to Cap-Haïtien, and **Route Nationale Two**, also known as the 'Great Southern Highway'. This title, now used with tongue firmly in cheek, was supposed to provide an express highway between Port-au-Prince and Les Cayes when it was planned during the US occupation. Nowadays, Route Nationale Two is paved from Port-au-Prince to Les Cayes, but it's ridden with potholes and slow-going. Apart from a few small stretches here and there, the rest of Haiti's roads are really no more than dirt tracks.

Hiring a vehicle

If money is no object and you are up to driving on the roads, hiring your own vehicle is the best way to see Haiti. Of course, you miss out on the unique experience of travelling on the *tap-taps*, but there are other advantages. Provided you opt for 4WD, you'll be able to go where the *tap-taps* don't or can't. Some of Haiti's most beautiful and remote places, like Dame Marie and Môle Saint-Nicolas, become a distinct possibility. All car-hire companies in Haiti have a range of 4WD vehicles. As a rough guide, budget for about US$60 a day for a small car and US$75 and up for 4WD. **Hertz** (tel: 46 0700), **Avis** (tel: 46 4161), **Budget** (tel: 46 0554) and a number of smaller companies all have desks at Port-au-Prince International Airport.

Tap-taps

A *tap-tap* can be anything from a pick-up truck, sagging under the weight of five times its normal load, to a gaily painted, American-style school bus bearing a God-fearing name like *Dieu Qui Decide* (God Who Decides), *L'Ange de Dieu* (The Angel of God) or *Christ Vivant* (Living Christ). Originally derived from the tapping sound made by the engines as they laboured over hills, 'tap-tap' is an appropriate word to describe almost all of the various types of public transportation on offer in Haiti. The one exception is the *camion* (from the French word meaning 'lorry' or 'truck'). I describe this as a *camion* rather than a *tap-tap* because this is precisely what it is: an open-backed truck, more used to carrying cattle than people. A short piece of rope dangles from the back so that people can haul themselves up, while more rope is strapped across bars in the back to provide something to hang on to while on the move. Not that many people need it. The Haitians seem to have a remarkable sense of balance, a fact you should remember before claiming one of the sought-after seats on top of the driver's cabin. There are no timetables and generally *tap-taps* and *camions* go when they are full.

One tip is to do your travelling in the morning. The frequency starts to taper off in the afternoons and by about 18.00 you'll be lucky to find anything.

It is an accepted fact of life in Haiti that travel is hard and uncomfortable. Nonetheless, if you want to witness the spirit and camaraderie of the Haitian people at its strongest and most poignant you should use the *tap-taps* and *camions*.

Hitchhiking

Getting a ride in Haiti is not a great problem. Getting a free ride, however, is another proposition. The international organisations are your best bet if you don't want to pay. When a private vehicle stops, the driver is probably expecting some money. Even if he isn't, you should offer to pay in any case. Running a car is not cheap in Haiti and you are, after all, travelling in comparative luxury.

Around town

All Haitian towns, with the possible exception of Port-au-Prince, are small enough to cover on foot. In fact, other than in the capital, you will probably not have the option of taking a taxi or a *tap-tap* around town. Even in Port-au-Prince, you can walk to most of the places of interest. If you do have recourse to a *tap-tap*, most of them run to the suburbs and slum areas of the capital – such as Carrefour, Delmas, Canapé Vert, Pétion-Ville and Cité Soleil. Try to get on where they originate, which is often, but not always, on Grand Rue.

While the *tap-taps* serving Port-au-Prince are normally painted in bright colours and stick out like sore thumbs, the taxis, or *publiques*, are less conspicuous. If you see a red ribbon hanging from the rear-view mirror, two zeros on the bonnet, or a number-plate with 'taxi' written on it, there's a good chance it's a *publique*. These are, in fact, shared taxis that ply a certain route, picking up and dropping off passengers along the way. Conventional taxis that carry you, and only you, to a pre-selected destination are also available. You'll find them outside the large hotels and at the airport.

ACCOMMODATION

Relatively few towns in Haiti have hotels. In fact, outside of the towns covered in this guide, you'll be taking a chance expecting to find a place to stay.

These days few of the hotels in Haiti are dedicated to tourists. There are some along the Côte des Arcadins and in Cap-Haïtien and Jacmel, but the majority of the more up-market establishments serve the United Nations, journalists and businessmen. This is certainly true in Pétion-Ville, where comfortable but unspectacular accommodation rarely costs under US$50 a night. Also note that you pay for the room and not per person, which can penalise the single traveller quite severely.

In the provinces you can generally count on there being one hotel in the larger towns which has, or purports to have, facilities for the tourist. This means air conditioning, a swimming pool, a restaurant and prices in US dollars. These hotels are normally used to accommodate the United Nations personnel based in the provinces.

This leaves the budget hotels. Generally speaking, you should have no reservations about staying at the cheaper hotels and guesthouses in Haiti. They are usually equipped with the bare essentials like a fan, a bathroom and a lock for the door; I rarely had to buy a bar of soap or use the towel that I'd packed; and I never stayed in a place where I feared for my safety or the safety of my belongings. Of course, there are bad places in Haiti just as there are bad places all over the world.

Bear in mind a few points when looking for a place to stay:

* Does it have a generator? Even if it does, it won't be on all the time, but at least you'll get some power. A hotel without a generator is at the mercy of Electricité d'Haiti, which in most towns means no power for most of the time.
* Does it have water? Running water is not really necessary as long as buckets are available.
* Does it charge by the hour? This type of place is known as a *suivant* – from the French word meaning 'next'. If you see somewhere open 24 hours a day inviting you to '*passer un bon moment*', you should probably leave it alone!

TOURIST INFORMATION

The **Ministry of Tourism** is in Port-au-Prince at 8 Rue Légitime, Champs de Mars; tel: 23 5631. They will be happy to provide you with all the information they have. The other tourist office in Cap-Haïtien only seems to open on the rare occasions when a cruise ship docks in the town's harbour.

Public holidays

Christmas Day, New Year's Day (which is also Independence Day) and Easter are all public holidays in Haiti. **Carnival** normally takes place sometime in February. After carnival, the **Ra-Ra bands** play at the weekends leading up to Easter. The Ra-Ra contains voodoo and Christian elements, and the reason for the wild singing and dancing is to keep Baron Samedi – the voodoo *loa* of the dead who holds the keys to heaven – awake until Easter so that he can unlock the gates and allow Jesus to pass into heaven (see page 51 for more on voodoo). Most businesses and shops are closed on public holidays.

January 1	Independence Day, New Year's Day
January 2	Ancestor's Day (Heroes of Independence Day)
February	Carnival
March/April	Easter
April 14	Pan American Day
May 1	Agriculture and Labour Day
May 18	Flag and University Day
October 17	Death of Dessalines
October 24	United Nations Day
November 1	All Saints' Day
November 2	Day of the Dead
November 18	Vertières Day (the decisive battle in the War of Independence)
December 5	Discovery Day
December 25	Christmas Day

Tour operators
There are plenty of travel agents selling airline tickets in Port-au-Prince. Many of them can be found in the Cité de l'Exposition. Three of the bigger ones are **Cap Travel Service**, 15 Avenue Marie Jeanne; tel: 22 3150; **Chatelain Tours**, at the top of Rue Pavée; tel: 22 0130; and **Omni Tours**, 34 Rue des Casernes; tel: 23 8870. However, the place for tours is **Agence Citadelle**, 35 Place du Marron Inconnu; tel: 22 5900. The same is true if you go into one of the few travel agents in Cap-Haïtien. They can do nothing without the approval of Agence Citadelle.

My recommendation if you only have a few days in Haiti and want a brief introduction to the country is to contact **Voyages Lumière**, BP 15010, Pétion-Ville; tel: 57 4005; fax: 57 3973/74. They also have an agent in the UK: **Interchange**, 27 Stafford Road, Croydon, Surrey, CR0 4NG; tel: 0181 681 3612. Run by an English lady who lives in Haiti, Voyages Lumière offer tours to the major sights in and around Port-au-Prince and Cap-Haïtien, including the Citadelle La Ferrière and Sans-Souci Palace. They are informative and fun and conducted by someone who obviously has a great passion for Haiti and its people.

COMMUNICATIONS AND MEDIA
Post
You should have no fears about sending post in Haiti. In fact, the quality of this particular service is actually underrated. It costs Gde5 to send a postcard

or a small letter to Europe, Gde3 for the same to the United States and Canada. Count on it taking about a week to ten days to Europe, a little less to North America. Post offices generally open at 08.00 and most are closed by about 15.00 from Monday to Friday. On Saturday they are open from 08.00 to 12.00.

One small criticism is the difficulty in finding some of the post offices. The prize for the best hidden and most intimate must go to the post office at Hinche, which is literally in the front room of a private house, as far as you can get from the centre of town without leaving Hinche altogether. There are several more that are nearly as obscure.

If you want to **receive post** while you're in Haiti, my best advice is to have it sent to the American Express (AMEX) office in Port-au-Prince, 35 Place du Marron Inconnu; tel: 22 5900; fax: 22 1792; email: citagen@haitiworld.com. This service is open to all AMEX customers – if you've never had any dealings with AMEX, just say you have. You can also receive faxes and emails.

Telephone

Local calls in Haiti are free. (In Port-au-Prince this includes Pétion-Ville and Delmas.) However, there are no public call boxes. Your best hope of finding a phone is at hotels, banks, government offices, and some shops and restaurants, but don't automatically assume that it will work.

Given the scarcity and unreliability of the telephones, people have got used to using Teleco, the Haitian equivalent to British Telecom or AT&T. In fact, if you want to make an international call, or even a call to another town in Haiti, you are obliged to go to a Teleco office. They are in almost every town, open for about 14 hours a day and usually busy. Register your call at the counter, then sit with the masses until the number of your booth is announced. If you are travelling around the whole island, try to save your calls for the Dominican Republic. In Haiti they are prohibitively expensive (about Gde126 a minute to Europe or North America). Phone cards for international calls are available, but they won't save you much.

Media

The most widely read newspaper in Haiti is *Le Nouvelliste*. The news content isn't bad and it contains information about what's going on in Port-au-Prince. However, most of the articles are in French. Other papers, also in French, include *Le Matin*, *Haiti en Marche* and *Haiti Progrès*. The paper for English-speakers, *Haiti Observateur*, is published in New York. About half of its articles are in English and it's arguably more political than the rest. The paper in Cap-Haïtien is called the *Cap Express*.

MONEY

If you weren't any good at maths before this trip, you certainly will be after a few weeks in Haiti. The official currency is the *gourde* (Gde) which comes in the following notes: 500, 250, 100, 50, 25, 10, 5, 2 and 1. You also see gold coins worth Gde5, particularly in Port-au-Prince. There are 100 *centimes* to the *gourde*, in denominations of 50, 20, 10 and 5. Although the *gourde* is the official name of the currency, most prices will be quoted to you in Haitian dollars (H$). One Haitian dollar is equivalent to Gde5. At current exchange rates you can get about Gde17 to the US dollar and Gde25 to the British pound sterling. Thus:

- H$1 = Gde5 = 30¢ = 20p
- H$5 = Gde25 = US$1.50 = £1

Therefore, as long as the exchange rate hasn't fluctuated dramatically by the time you arrive in Haiti, bear in mind that H$5 is roughly equivalent to US$1.50 or £1 and do your calculations in multiples of five until you become a dab hand.

Exchanging money
Banking hours vary. The official times are 09.00 to 13.00, Monday to Friday, but in practice many banks stay open later (perhaps to about 15.00) and sometimes also on Saturdays (in Pétion-Ville, for instance). The main Haitian banks are Banque Nationale de Crédit, Banque de l'Union Haitienne, Banque Intercontinentale, Sogebank, Socabank and Promobank. Some international banks like Citibank and Scotiabank also operate in Port-au-Prince.

Most of the main towns have at least one bank, and there is a reasonable chance that it changes travellers' cheques as well as cash. You should, however, carry your travellers' cheques in US$, since other currencies might not be accepted. Carrying your cash in other major currencies is certainly feasible, although US$ are still preferred, especially in the provinces. Credit cards are quite useful in the capital and other tourist areas, but don't count on them off the beaten track.

There is a **black market** in Haiti. It is illegal and the rate offered is not much different to the banks. I wouldn't take the risk of being sold a wad of forged notes or getting caught by the police.

HEALTH AND SAFETY
Doctors and pharmacies
Medical facilities in Haiti are fairly good. Not surprisingly, the standard is highest in Port-au-Prince, where there are English-speaking doctors and plenty of well-stocked pharmacies. If you need a doctor, you should go initially to the good hotels. Most of them have designated doctors who can speak English and are used to dealing with common tourist maladies. The quantity and quality of the pharmacies in Haiti is impressive. Most towns have at least one where you can find all the component parts of a good medical kit. You'll need a prescription from a doctor to get hold of certain medication. You might have to pay a US$10 consultation fee, but once you have the prescription you can use it as many times as you like. (For further information on health see Chapter 2, *Before You Go*.)

Security and the Haitian National Police

For many travellers the question of security is an important one when considering a trip to Haiti. No-one can deny that the country has had its problems in this respect; and since the departure of the United Nations peacekeeping force in December 1997, the Haitian National Police have been struggling to restore law and order. However, this doesn't mean that Haiti is in a state of anarchy. Of course, crime exists, as it does all over the world, but the visitor would be unlucky if he or she became a victim. In my opinion, you are as safe in Haiti as you are in the Dominican Republic. This is as true for women as it is for men.

DANGER: TOURISTS

Tourism need not be a destructive force for tribal people but unfortunately it frequently is. We at Bradt Publications totally support the initiative of the charity Survival in protecting the rights of tribal peoples:

Recognise land rights
Obtain permission to enter
Pay properly
Behave as if on private property

Respect tribal peoples
Don't demean, degrade, insult or patronise

Don't bring in disease
Diseases such as colds can kill tribal peoples
AIDS is a killer

Survival (11–15 Emerald Street, London WCIN 3QL, England; tel: 0171 242 1441; fax: 0171 242 1771; email: survival@gn.apc.org) is a worldwide organisation supporting tribal peoples. It stands for their right to decide their own future and helps them protect their lives, lands and human rights.

Port-au-Prince

When you come out at Port-au-Prince International Airport, the taxi drivers give you two options. You can either go to Pétion-Ville, the residential suburb overlooking the capital, or simply 'la ville', meaning downtown Port-au-Prince. The majority of new arrivals opt for the comfortable hotels and quality restaurants of Pétion-Ville, choosing to sample Port-au-Prince in small, digestible chunks, perhaps by making the odd trip down the hill. In many ways this decision is understandable. For all the improvements made since 1864, when a European historian came to Port-au-Prince and left describing it as 'the most ridiculous caricature of civilisation in the whole world' and a 'Paris of the gutter', it remains the dirtiest and most overcrowded city in the Caribbean. Yet despite the congestion, pollution, slum areas and open sewers, I like Port-au-Prince a lot. Maybe this is because it lives up to expectations. Haiti is a Third World country and Port-au-Prince is an uncompromising Third World capital. People, noise, heat, sweat and smells are what Port-au-Prince is all about. There are no compromises here and either you go with the flow or retreat to the hills. Admittedly, it takes some time to get used to, but even if you do spend most of your time in Pétion-Ville, consider staying a few days in the capital. It will certainly prepare you for anything the rest of Haiti has to offer.

If you include the surrounding residential districts and slums, Port-au-Prince is home to some 2 million of Haiti's 7 million population. Even for the rest of the Haitians (with the possible exception of fiercely independent Cap-Haïtien), Port-au-Prince is regarded as the focal point of life and the place to go to make some money. Thus migration to the capital from the provinces continues to increase, placing a further burden on the city's sagging infrastructure and swelling the shantytowns of Cité Soleil and La Saline in the northern part of the city. The steady expansion of Port-au-Prince to include these areas in the north, Carrefour in the south and Pétion-Ville has made it one of the largest cities in the West Indies. Originally occupying a prime spot in a bay in the Gulf of Gonâve, Port-au-Prince now spreads across the Cul-de-Sac Plain and into the foothills of the Massif de la Selle.

Port-au-Prince has been the capital of Haiti, or at least a part of Haiti, ever since it was founded in 1749 and named after a French vessel, *Le Prince*, which had dropped anchor in its harbour in the early 18th century. In the years during and after the War of Independence, Port-au-Prince was the stronghold of the

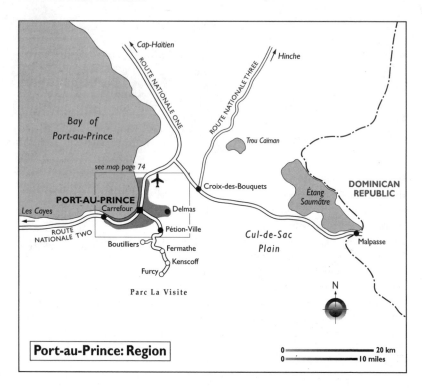

Port-au-Prince: Region

mulatto-dominated south. In 1806 Dessalines was assassinated at Pont Rouge at the northern entrance to the town as he tried to suppress the mulattos and bring Port-au-Prince under black control. In 1812 a similar attempt, this time by King Henri Christophe and an army of 25,000, also failed. When Jean-Pierre Boyer reunited the country in 1820, Port-au Prince became the undisputed capital and has remained so ever since. Practically all the great, and not so great, moments of Haiti's history since 1820 have had something to do with Port-au-Prince, leading cynics to talk about the 'Republic of Port-au-Prince'. Statistics from the mid-1980s illustrate how great the divide between capital and province actually is. The capital accounts for 40% of GDP, 90% of industry, 98% of energy consumption, 83% of state expenditure, 85% of medical services and 80% of secondary education facilities. Meanwhile, 70% of the country's population live outside Port-au-Prince, but as long as the city receives such preferential treatment, it will continue to attract migration from the provinces. This will further bloat an already over-crowded city, adding to its thousands of homeless, while the provinces will continue to fester, deprived now of a labour force as well as government attention.

ORIENTATION
Metropolitan Port-au-Prince
The city of Port-au-Prince looks out onto the Bay of Port-au-Prince in the Gulf of Gonâve. Going north along its main thoroughfare, Boulevard Jean-

Jacques Dessalines, you pass the slums of La Saline and Cité Soleil before the road eventually becomes Route Nationale One, the main highway to Cap-Haïtien (see page 121). Going south, Boulevard Jean-Jaques Dessalines bends around the bay, passes through the suburb of Carrefour and then becomes Route Nationale Two, the main highway to Les Cayes (see page 99). The Cul-de-Sac Plain stretches all the way to the Dominican border in the east, while the foothills of the Massif de la Selle rise in the southeast.

About 6km up into these hills lies the town of Pétion-Ville, included in this guide as part of Port-au-Prince. Pétion-Ville is linked to the downtown area by three main roads: Avenue John Brown, Route de Delmas and Route du Canapé Vert. Avenue John Brown (also known as Lalue) is the most useful of these roads since it leads down into the centre of Port-au-Prince, passing through the residential suburbs and finishing at the Champs de Mars. Route de Delmas skirts around the northern edge of the city, linking Pétion-Ville with the commercial zones in the north of the downtown area. Route de Canapé Vert runs roughly parallel to Lalue and is popular with commuters in the morning. However, for the tourist it is of limited interest since most *tap-taps* go along Lalue. About half way between Pétion-Ville and downtown Port-au-Prince, Avenue Martin Luther King cuts across these three main roads. After crossing Route de Delmas it becomes Avenue H Selassie, which is the road to the airport if you're coming from the centre of Port-au-Prince.

Downtown and neighbourhoods

Port-au-Prince is easy enough to navigate. Your point of reference should always be Boulevard Jean-Jacques Dessalines, or Grand Rue as it's more commonly known. If you get lost, return to Grand Rue (which isn't hard since it runs north to south through the heart of downtown) and walk along it until you find the street you want. At the northern end of Grand Rue, *tap-taps* to the north and the Central Plateau depart from various service stations. At the southern end near the cemetery, *tap-taps* leave for the south from Portail Léogâne. Many of Port-au-Prince's sights are on Grand Rue, or not far from it.

The other main area of interest for the visitor is the Champs de Mars – a large area of uncluttered space where parks, statues, museums, art galleries and the National Palace can be found. This is east of Grand Rue. West of Grand Rue and running parallel to it along the coast is the city's other main thoroughfare, Boulevard Henry Truman, also known as Bicentenaire. This road passes through the Cité de l'Exposition – another relatively uncluttered space on the waterfront – and by the port in the northern part of town.

Around the downtown area and stretching all the way up to Pétion-Ville are the residential neighbourhoods of Port-au-Prince. The most interesting from the visitor's point of view are Bois Verna and Pacot to the north and northeast of the Champs de Mars respectively. This is where much of the capital's gingerbread architecture can be found (see page 87). Other important neighbourhoods that you might come across, but not necessarily have cause to visit, are Turgeau, Nazon, Canapé Vert, Bourdon and Delmas. All of them lie between Port-au-Prince and Pétion-Ville.

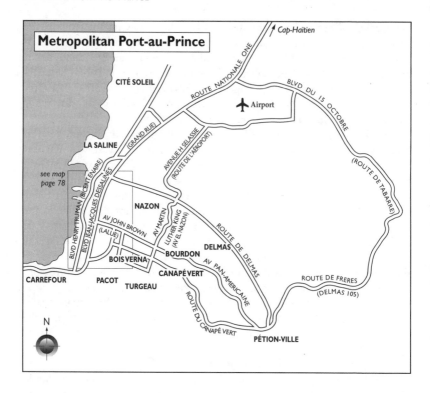

Street names

Throughout Haiti, the name given to a road on a map or on a street sign is not necessarily the name in common usage. Port-au-Prince is littered with examples. In this guide I have tried to use the local street names. The most important name changes in Port-au-Prince are as follows.

Boulevard Jean-Jacques Dessalines = Grand Rue
Boulevard Henry Truman = Bicentenaire
Avenue John Brown = Lalue
Avenue Martin Luther King = Avenue El Nazon
Avenue H Selassie = Route de l'Aéroport
Boulevard du 15 Octobre = Route de Tabarre

GETTING THERE AND AWAY
By air

(For international arrivals and departures see *Getting there and away* in Chapter 4.) Caribintair (tel: 46 0737) provides the only domestic air service in Haiti and all flights leave from Port-au-Prince. There are two flights a day to Cap-Haïtien leaving at 09.00 and 14.00. A single is US$40 and a return US$70. The only other destination served by Caribintair is Jérémie. It leaves Port-au-Prince at 10.30, costs US$55 for a single and is very popular.

Port-au-Prince International Airport

When you arrive at Port-au-Prince International Airport and clear immigration (a simple procedure), you come to a crowded baggage hall with colourful murals on the walls, but not much else in the way of tourist facilities. Apparently, a Monsieur Poux is in charge of the Office de Tourisme at the airport, but there was no sight or sound of him when I arrived. In fact, all the airport facilities, except the car rental companies, which are to your left as you exit the airport, and the elusive tourist office, are in the departures hall. These include a post office, a Teleco office, a couple of snack bars and a small gift shop.

When you leave the airport terminal, you become fair game for the taxi drivers waiting outside. There are two official taxi companies and you shouldn't bother with anyone else. Those dressed in yellow shirts and black trousers belong to the Association des Chauffeurs Indépendants pour le Développement du Tourisme (ACIDT), while those in white shirts and green trousers are members of the Association des Chauffeurs Guides d'Haiti (ACGH). Both charge US$20 to downtown Port-au-Prince and US$30 to Pétion-Ville. You can catch a *tap-tap* to Port-au-Prince (Gde2) by leaving the airport, walking across the arrivals car park and waiting beside the main road. If you want to go up to Pétion-Ville, take the same *tap-tap* and get off when you reach Route de Delmas (Carrefour d'Aeroport).

By sea

One boat a week a week leaves from Port-au-Prince to Jérémie on the northern tip of the southern peninsula. The voyage is usually done at night (currently Tuesday) and you arrive the next morning. It costs roughly the same as the *tap-tap* (H$20) and is equally crowded. I don't particularly recommend it.

By land

You can get to anywhere in the country from three main points in Port-au-Prince, all of them along Grand Rue.

For all points south, walk along Grand Rue until you get to the cemetery. This is the Portail Léogâne. Here you can get *tap-taps* to Jacmel (3 hours, H$5), Les Cayes (6 hours, H$7) and Léogâne (1 hour, Gde4). They leave at regular intervals during the day, tapering off as it starts to get dark. There is one *tap-tap* a day to Jérémie. This leaves at 14.00 from opposite a large, white building, called the Lido, on Grand Rue. It takes between 10 and 12 hours and costs H$20. Buy your ticket before you get on the bus.

For all points north, walk along Grand Rue until you get to the *marché en fer*. Directly opposite, you can get *tap-taps* to Mirebalais in the Central Plateau; and a little further on opposite the Marché Tête Bœuf *tap-taps* leave for Malpasse on the Dominican border (1½ hours, H$10). The main stations for the other towns in the north are beyond the intersection of Grand Rue and Route de Delmas. For Hinche (6–10 hours, H$15) and Port-de-Paix (6 hours H$20), turn left at Route de Delmas and walk down to Boulevard La Saline. *Tap-taps* and *camions* leave from the Texaco service station on your right. Further on, where Boulevard La Saline rejoins Grand Rue, there is a Shell service station. This is the departure point for *tap-taps* to Cap-Haïtien (5 hours, H$20), Gonaïves (2 hours, H$5) and Saint-Marc (1½ hours, H$3).

GETTING AROUND

I recommend exploring Port-au-Prince on foot. Unless you want to go to Pétion-Ville or some way up Route de Delmas, walking around the downtown area and to the nearby neighbourhoods is certainly the way to go. Other options are basically twofold:

You can take a *tap-tap* to various points within the city. They follow certain routes, so ask where it's going before you board. Grand Rue is a good place to catch *tap-taps*, as is the Cathédrale Notre-Dame and the cemetery. The other way of getting around town is by *publique*. These shared taxis stop if they have room and cost a bit more than the *tap-taps*.

Port-au-Prince to Pétion-Ville

You will most likely use a *tap-tap* to make the trip up to Pétion-Ville. The most common and convenient route if you're in the centre of downtown is along Lalue. It remains a mystery to me where the *tap-taps* plying this route originate. Therefore, I stand along with many others at the service station at the end of Rue Pavée and the beginning of Lalue and wait for one bound for Pétion-Ville. Note that some will already be full (avoid the early evenings to maximise your chances of getting a place) and many stop at the intermediate neighbourhood of Bourdon (these will be marked 'Christ Roi'). Another option, convenient if you end the day in the northern part of town, is along Route de Delmas. The *tap-taps* are as full as the ones along Lalue, but there are more of them. Grand Rue is probably the best place to catch them; they are marked 'Delmas'. The standard fare to Pétion-Ville is Gde2.5 regardless of the route taken. This can vary slightly depending on the condition of the *tap-tap* and the demand.

WHERE TO STAY

The problem with staying in Port-au-Prince is that there are very few hotels that can be described as moderate – both in terms of price and quality. The choice is between hotels where the rates have been inflated to take advantage of the inexhaustible coffers of the United Nations, or insalubrious doss-houses. Budget hotels – simple rooms with a fan and perhaps a bathroom for US$10 or US$15 – are few and far between in the capital.

Downtown and neighbourhoods

The cheapest accommodation is available in the downtown area of Port-au-Prince, while in the surrounding residential neighbourhoods there are a couple of more up-market options.

Hotel Oloffson (tel: 23 4000) is not the most expensive, but it's certainly the most famous hotel in town. This old gingerbread house in the Pacot neighbourhood, not far from the cemetery, was a hospital during the US occupation (the convalescents' rocking chairs still sit on the veranda outside each room). As a hotel, it became a favourite gathering place for journalists, writers and rock stars; it was immortalised in Graham Greene's *The Comedians* as the Hotel Trianon. Nowadays, like so much of Haiti, this place is not what it was. The garden is a little overgrown and the house could do with sprucing up. Nonetheless, this remains *the* place to stay in Port-au-Prince. It trades a lot on its reputation, but it does have tremendous character. A standard room is US$65 for a single and US$75 for a double, which is not good value – but that's not the point.

The **Prince Hotel** (tel: 45 2764) is quite close to the Oloffson. Go up Rue 3 and it's at the top on Avenue N. The hotel itself is quite tatty, but the rooms have a cosy feel and the views of Port-au-Prince are excellent. However, with prices starting at US$50 and being so far from the centre of town, I wouldn't particularly recommend it.

For a prime location in the centre of town, the hotels on the Champs de Mars are hard to beat. **Hotel Excelsior International** (tel: 23 4055) is on Rue Légitime next to the Secretary of State for Tourism. It's not particularly good value at H$120 for a standard room, but it is very central. **Le Plaza Holiday Inn** (tel: 23 7232) is on Rue Capois overlooking the Champs de Mars. It offers what you'd expect from a Holiday Inn: characterless, air-conditioned rooms with large beds and a TV for the handsome price of US$75 for a single and US$90 for a double. Much more interesting is **Le Palace Hotel** (tel: 22 3344), a few doors down the street in the white mansion on the corner of the Champs de Mars. The rather grand exterior belies an interior where wooden boards partition off some 72 rooms, most of which are simple and quite comfortable. This is a popular place with Haitian businessmen and the prices are quoted in Haitian dollars. A single costs H$70, a double H$80 and a triple H$90. This is the only moderate hotel in the downtown area. After this you start to scrape the barrel a bit.

The cheap hotels are at either end of Grand Rue. Starting in the south, there is a cluster of flophouses and *suivants* (see page 66) next to the Portail Léogâne from where the *tap-taps* depart to the south. Walking along Grand Rue towards the centre, the first reasonable place that doesn't charge by the hour is the **Building Hotel** (tel: 21 3628) on the corner of Rue Champs de Mars. In fact, this hotel is quite impressive, with rooms in the H$40, H$50 and H$60 range, their own generator and, so I'm told, air conditioning to be installed after the 1998 World Cup. As if all this wasn't enough, there's a lively bar and restaurant on the first floor. Almost directly opposite is the modest **Hotel Chalet d'Or**, where simple rooms are only H$30. **Hotel C'Est Mon Etoile** (tel: 21 1973) is just past Rue Champs de Mars on the same side as the Building Hotel. This is a typical budget hotel, with a corridor of box-like rooms each with fan and primitive bathroom. After the Building Hotel, however, it seems to be the best in the area. Single rooms are good value at H$30. For some reason, the **Akropolis Guest House** (tel: 23 1871), on the other side of Grand Rue, charges more than twice as much as the C'Est Mon Etoile. The rooms are virtually no different and I can only imagine that the difference in price is because of the (dirty) swimming pool on the roof.

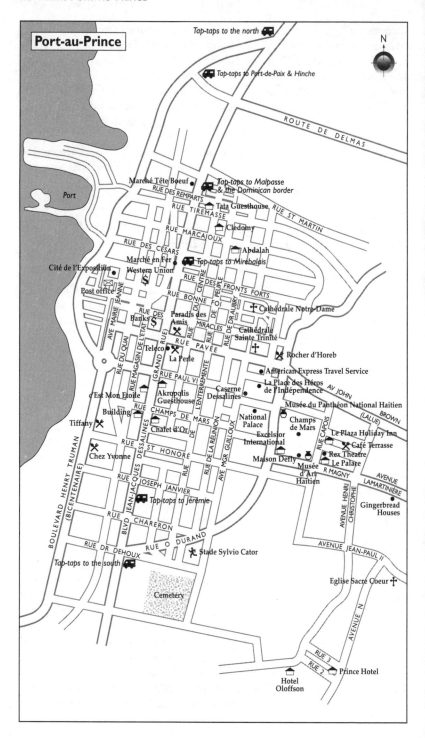

Port-au-Prince

Tap-taps to the north

Tap-taps to Port-de-Paix & Hinche

ROUTE DE DELMAS

Port

Marché Tête Boeuf
RUE DES REMPARTS
Tap-taps to Malpasse
& the Dominican border

RUE TIREMASSE
Tata Guesthouse
RUE ST MARTIN

RUE MARCAJOUX
Cledomy

RUE DES CÉSARS
Abdalah

Marché en Fer
Cité de l'Exposition
Western Union
Tap-taps to Mirebalais

Post office
RUE DE DR AUBRY
Cathédrale Notre Dame

RUE BONNE FOI
RUE DES
RUE MARIE JEANNE
Banks
Paradis des
Amis
Cathédrale
Sainte Trinité

Teleco
La Perle
RUE PAVÉE
Rocher d'Horeb

RUE MAGASIN DE L'ÉTAT
RUE DU QUAI
GRAND RUE
RUE PAUL VI
American Express Travel Service
La Place des Héros
de l'Indépendence
AV JOHN

c'Est Mon Etoile
Akropolis
Guesthouse
Caserne
Dessalines
Musée du Panthéon National Haitien
BROWN
(LALUE)

Building
CHAMPS DE MARS
Tiffany
National
Palace
Champs
de Mars
Le Plaza Holiday Inn

Chalet d'Or
RUE ST HONORÉ
Excelsior
International
Café Terrasse
Rex Theatre
Le Palace

Chez Yvonne
RUE DE LA RÉUNION
AVE MGR GUILLOU
Maison Defly
Musée
d'Art
Haitien
R MAGNY

RUE JOSEPH JANVIER
JEAN-JACQUES DESSALINES
Tap-taps to Jérémie
AVENUE
LAMARTINIÈRE

RUE CHARERON
BLVD CHARERON
Gingerbread
Houses

BOULEVARD HENRY TRUMAN
(BICENTENAIRE)
RUE DR DEHOUX
RUE O DURAND
AVENUE JEAN-PAUL II

Tap-taps to the south
Stade Sylvio Cator
AVENUE HENRI CHRISTOPHE

Cemetery
AVENUE N

Eglise Sacré Coeur

RUE 3
RUE 2
Prince Hotel

Hotel
Oloffson

At the other end of Grand Rue, several cheap hotels are located near the Marché en Fer and further north near Marché Tête Boeuf. The best is probably the **Tata Guest House** (tel: 22 1417) on Rue des Remparts opposite Marché Tête Boeuf. This place only opened in 1998 and the rooms with bathroom are clean and cheap (H\$30). Near to the Tata, on Rue du Centre, is the **Cledomy Hotel** another of the better options in this area, although you have to share a bathroom. Even so, the rooms come with a fan and a bedpan and only cost H\$25. **Hotel Abdalah** is a large, noisy hotel on Rue Marcajoux, where rooms go for H\$35. Also on Marcajoux, the **Hudson Hotel** charges H\$25, but it's essentially a brothel. On Grand Rue itself between the two markets, the **Chaly Hotel** (tel: 23 6056) has grotty rooms for H\$30. Other places to look out for – but not necessarily patronise – include the **Atlantic Hotel** on the corner of Rue des Remparts and Grand Rue, **Hotel Familial** on Rue Tiremasse and the **Chez Salnave Speciale Hotel** on Rue Marcajoux, just off Grand Rue towards the port.

Pétion-Ville

There are no budget hotels in Pétion-Ville and most places cost over US\$50 a night. However, this is the charge for the room, so if you're travelling with someone, staying in Pétion-Ville isn't necessarily expensive.

Probably the cheapest of all is **La Belle Etoile Hotel** (tel: 57 7305) on Rue C Peralte behind the St Jean de Bosco church. It was erected very quickly during the blockade and the rooms are simple and clean. The manager is very friendly and will probably let you stay for around US\$25 after a bit of haggling. It might get on your nerves after a while, but the singing during evening and very early morning mass at the church is beautiful.

On Rue Gregoire at the intersection with Villate is the **Ifé** (tel: 57 0737), named after a Nigerian deity which brings luck. The Ifé is a good choice if there are three of you, as triples here cost US\$75. Doubles cost US\$65 and singles US\$45, with a large breakfast included.

On the right side of the Place St Pierre at the start of Route de Kenscoff is the **Kinam** (tel: 57 0462). A room here will set you back about US\$65 for a single and US\$75 for a double. If you have to part with this much for a bed for the night, you might as well do it here. The air-conditioned rooms are nice enough and the restaurant overlooking the hotel's small pool has a huge selection of French and Creole dishes, But the Kinam's greatest appeal is the hotel itself – a beautifully restored and irresistibly charming green and white gingerbread house.

The **Tamarin** (tel: 57 9521) is a short walk up Route de Kenscoff, but as the 14 rooms here are in high demand, it's best to make a reservation. Expect to pay about US\$50 for a single, US\$75 for a double. Because this is a small hotel, the approach aims to be personal. For instance, as long as they have the ingredients, you can order whatever you like for dinner. Another feature of the Tamarin is art and craft. The restaurant doubles as an art gallery (as the medieval iron plates set at the tables will testify) and the hotel sponsors upcoming artists and organises exhibitions of their work.

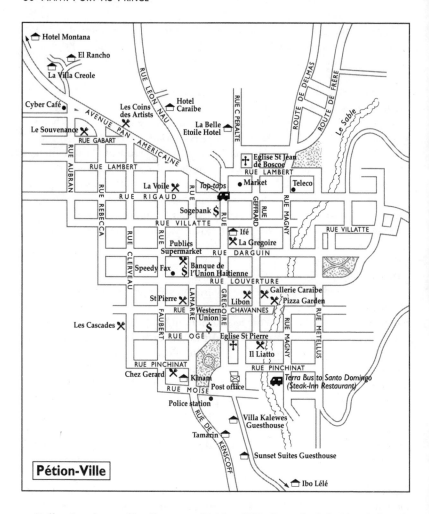

Pétion-Ville

Following the road leading out of Pétion-Ville from the left side of Place St Pierre, you'll eventually arrive at the **Ibo Lélé** (tel: 57 5668). A large proportion of the Ibo's clientele are UN, a fact revealed in the high prices: US$70 for a single, US$100 for a double. The great views of the Cul-de-Sac Plain and, for the homesick, bathtubs in most rooms, go some way towards giving value for money. It is also a long way out of town. A bit closer, still on Route Ibo Lélé, is the **Sunset Suites Guest House** (tel: 57 0553). If you can put up with the lime-green bedspreads, this place offers special rates for long stays – US$1,000 for a month. Otherwise they charge US$50 or US$65. They also pick you up and drop you off at the airport.

Continuing back down the hill to Place St Pierre, the **Villa Kalewes Guest House** (tel: 57 0817) is on your left. This brown-and-white gingerbread house is the antithesis of the Kinam. While the latter is quaint and charming, the Villa Kalewes is like something out of a horror movie. The house is slightly dilapidated, and inside, the dark, wooden furniture makes it gloomy and a bit sinister. The manager shuffles about speaking garbled French and the garden is overgrown. You either love this place or you hate it. I loved it. The rates are relatively low and the single traveller is not penalised quite so much as at other hotels. It costs Gde400 (about US$27) for a single, twice that for a double. Nightmares are included.

There are several hotels just off Avenue Pan-Americaine on the way to Port-au-Prince. The first is the small **Hotel Caraibe** (tel: 57 2524) on Rue Leon Nau. Singles start at US$50 and doubles are US$75. The most luxurious hotel in Pétion-Ville is **El Rancho** (tel: 57 2080), the turning for which is opposite the Elf service station next to the Dominican Republic embassy. Described as a 'palatial private estate', El Rancho has all the amenities you would expect in a first-class hotel: two swimming pools, two restaurants, three bars, a casino, gym, sauna etc. Rates start at US$85 and go up to US$240. Competing with El Rancho at the top of the price league is **La Villa Creole** (tel: 57 1570) next door. With similar facilities on offer, prices are slightly higher than at El Rancho. Further down Avenue Pan-Americaine another turning, marked by a small and barely visible sign, takes you to **Hotel Montana** (tel: 23 6221). It was hard to judge this place fairly when I was there since they were in the process of building 12 new rooms, a restaurant and a lift. The work should be finished by the end of 1998. A single costs about US$75, a double US$90. The views of Port-au-Prince are fantastic.

A few more hotels further along Avenue Pan-Americaine (which has by this time become Avenue John Brown or Lalue) are **Hotel Christophe** (tel: 45 6124) and the **Villa St Louis Hotel** (tel: 45 6241), both in a neighbourhood called Bourdon, half way between Pétion-Ville and Port-au-Prince. Neither of them are cheap and their inconvenient location weighs against them. Meanwhile, the **Visa Lodge** (tel: 46 2662) is a business hotel out by the airport.

Carrefour

Despite its decline as a tourist attraction, there are still one or two hotels in Carrefour, such as **Auberge de Quebec** (not far from the Shell service station), **Hotel Plage** (Archeon 32) and the **Bamboulinas Hotel** (on Côte Plage). However, the scene nowadays is rather depressing. The large **Royal Haitian Hotel** (tel: 34 3003) is the closest to Port-au-Prince.

WHERE TO EAT

For fine dining, go to Pétion-Ville. There are some excellent French and Creole restaurants, as well as Italian, Chinese, Lebanese and other international cuisines. Downtown Port-au-Prince is not such a culinary delight, although there are some good places, especially for lunch.

Downtown

If you go by reputation, the **Tiffany Restaurant** on Boulevard Henry Truman just past the roundabout is meant to be one of the best restaurants in Port-au-

Prince. They serve steaks and seafood in air-conditioned comfort. Much more genuine is **Chez Yvonne**, a few doors further down Boulevard Harry Truman. The waiters might wear black bow ties, but this place reminded me of an American diner, serving good, honest Creole cooking instead of greasy burgers and fries. **La Terrace** at Le Plaza Holiday Inn (see page 77) is also one of the better restaurants in Port-au-Prince. The highlight here is the Creole buffet where you'll find most of the main Haitian dishes represented. The restaurant at **Hotel Oloffson** (see page 76) is worth a visit, if only for its lovely terrace overlooking the garden. Back in the centre of town, **Restaurant Rocher d'Horeb** at the top of Rue Pavée is air-conditioned, serves ice-cream and seems to be open for breakfast, lunch and dinner – worth a try perhaps.

Port-au-Prince really comes into its own at lunchtime, when a number of good restaurants and cafés knock out tasty lunches for the capital's workforce. A favourite with *blancs* is **Café Terrasse** in a side street off Rue Capois next to the Air France office. Open until about 16.00, they do great steaks and sandwiches. Other good places for lunch can be found on Rue Pavée. **Restaurant Paradis des Amis**, between Grand Rue and Rue du Centre, offers a wide selection of Creole food (try the soup), as well as fruit juices, milkshakes and ice-cream. You'll be lucky to get a table if you come during the lunch hour, but they are open until midnight. Over the road, **La Perle Restaurant** is also good, although not quite as popular as the Paradis des Amis. They have daily lunch menus which include a drink and a dessert for H$12 and, unlike the Paradis, air conditioning – quite a lure in the suffocating early afternoon heat of Port-au-Prince. Not surprisingly, several lunchtime cafés can be found around Rue des Miracles and Grand Rue, where most of the city's banks are located. One of the most popular is **La Pause** between Banque Intercontinentale and Sogebel. Chicken and rice, lasagne, hamburgers and the like are served until 16.00. There is another **La Pause** in the Delimart Plaza on Route de Delmas, open until 21.00. The **Bec Fin**, also on Rue des Miracles, is a good example of the many small cafés selling fast food that can be found in downtown Port-au-Prince. Look along Rue Pavée and Rue Bonne Foi for others.

Pétion-Ville

Opinions differ as to which is the best restaurant in Pétion-Ville. It seems, however, that most of the main candidates have a strong bias towards French cuisine, with a few well-chosen Creole dishes thrown in to add balance to the menu. Restaurants like **La Voile** on Rue Rigaud, between Lamarre and Faubert (the entrance is hidden by trees); **Le Souvenance** on Rue Gabart, between Rebecca and Aubaen; **Les Cascades** on Rue Clerveau and Ogé; and **La Plantation** on Rue Borno not far from the Ibo Lélé all offer similar menus, with main dishes starting at around H$30. **Chez Gerard** on Rue Pinchinat is another restaurant with a reputation, but for some reason it charges about H$10 more than the rest (perhaps this is due to the plush leather chairs and the gentleman's club atmosphere).

There are plenty of other options, particularly along rues Gregoire, Geffrard and Lamarre and along Avenue Pan-Americaine. For Chinese, Thai, Cambodian and Vietnamese dishes, try **La Gregoire** on the road of the same name; while the **China Garden** on Rue Villate serves generous portions of reasonable Chinese food. On Rue Geffrard, the small restaurant at **Gallerie Caraibe** is good value, with a small selection of Haitian dishes for around H$15. The **Libon**, opposite Gallerie Caraibe, has Lebanese food, as does the **Beyroth** on Rue Villate and **La Bouffe** on Rue Rigaud. On Lamarre, **St Pierre** has a cosmopolitan menu which includes couscous and *casse-croûte* (snacks). Along Avenue Pan-Americaine good seafood can be had at **Les Coins des Artists**; pizza and ice-cream is a speciality at **Harry's**; and if you're near **El Rancho** on a Sunday, treat yourself to their afternoon barbecue by the pool (Gdes150). Of course, virtually all of the hotels in Pétion-Ville have restaurants, one of my favourites being the **Kinam**, with its vast menu and charming atmosphere (see page 79).

Pizza is not hard to find in Pétion-Ville. The **Pizza Palace** on Rue Faubert probably has the largest selection, but the nicest atmosphere is at the **Pizza Garden**, in a quiet, shady side street off Rue Geffrard. Pizza, pasta and a panoply of other Italian dishes are available at the Italian-run **Il Liatto** on Rue Ogé. If you want your pizza delivered, call **Fabrizio Pizza** (tel: 46 3558) who are at Delmas 56.

In stark contrast to downtown Port-au-Prince, where there are none, Pétion-Ville is bulging with supermarkets and grocery stores. The largest in the centre of town is the **Publics Supermarket** on the corner of Rue Lamarre and Darguin. (**Mona's Café** is in the same plaza and is a reasonable place for coffee and a snack.) The **Caribbean Supermarket** at Delmas 95 has a larger selection and is the most popular with the many *blancs* who live in and around Pétion-Ville.

NIGHTLIFE

The bar scene is well and truly concentrated in Pétion-Ville. For rum punches, reggae music and all the local gossip, try the **Sunset Bar** on Rue Gregoire and the **Roots Bar** on Rue Rigaud (which has live bands on Saturday nights). Other popular hangouts attracting an eclectic crowd of locals, the military, international organisations and the UN are **Cheers** on Rue Villate and Clerveaux, and **Le Boléro** on Rue Louverture. **Café Cubano** on Rue Lamarre is open 24 hours for those who want to dance into the early hours. The **Café des Arts** – the *brasserie française* – is more sedate and refined, attracting an artistic crowd of red-wine drinkers.

Away from the bars, nightlife in Port-au-Prince seems to follow rather a predictable pattern. Every Thursday night RAM, a popular Haitian group, play at the **Hotel Oloffson**, while on Fridays there's Latin American dancing at **Hotel El Rancho**. However, this *is* the capital and every Haitian group wants to play here. As a result, many discotheques – many of them in Carrefour – often play host to some of the biggest names in Haitian music. The upcoming concerts appear on billboards around town, so keep your eyes open. Some of the bigger nightclubs in town include the **Versailles** (complete with swimming pool), **Mango's** (at El Rancho), the **Distinction**, the **Lambé**, the **Paladium** and the **Domaine Ideale**, all of which continue to cling on to past glories out at Carrefour.

ENTERTAINMENT

Every now and then Port-au-Prince is treated to a slice of culture in the form of ballet, theatre, opera or classical dance. If you are lucky enough to be in town at the same time – and if you can get hold of a ticket – these events normally take place at the **Rex Theatre** on Rue Capois on the Champs de Mars.

At other times the Rex is a **cinema**. Another good one, on nearby Rue Lamarre, is the Capitol, which shows quite recent films dubbed into French. The best cinema – not just in Haiti, but in the whole of Hispaniola – has to be the Imperial Cinema at Delmas 19. The dubbed films are recent, the auditoriums are air conditioned and the screens are the largest I have ever seen.

TOURIST INFORMATION
Communications and media

The main **post office** in Port-au-Prince is on Rue Bonne Foi in the Cité de l'Exposition. The other one is in Pétion-Ville on Place St Pierre.

The main **Teleco** office is on Grand Rue where it intersects with Rue Pavée (there is another one further up Grand Rue opposite the Marché Tête Bœuf). The Teleco office in Pétion-Ville is on Rue Rigaud, but there are other places where you can make international calls quicker and with less hassle. One of the more efficient ones is **Speedy Fax** on Rue Louverture. The **Cyber Café** is on Avenue Pan-Americaine near the turn-off for Hotel El Rancho. You can access the Internet here for H$15 an hour.

Money

Almost all of the large **banks** in the downtown area are on Rue des Miracles (Banque Nationale de Crédit, Banque Populaire Haitienne, Sogebank, Citibank etc). Most of these are also represented in Pétion-Ville. Note, however, that not all of them change travellers' cheques. Sogebank on Rue Gregoire and Banque Intercontinentale do, but Banque de l'Union Haitienne on Rue Lamarre does not.

The Pétion-Ville **moneychangers** are on Rue Gregoire by the market. They offer more-or-less the same rates as the banks, but should be given a wide berth. A simple 'non merci' is usually enough to shrug them off.

In case of emergencies, **Western Union** has offices in Port-au-Prince (Rue Bonne Foi between Rue du Quai and Magasin de l'Etat) and Pétion-Ville (in the Big Star Market on Place St Pierre). The **American Express Travel Service** is in the same building as Agence Citadelle, behind the statue of the Marron Inconnu.

Health and safety

If you get really sick, go to one of the expensive hotels, all of which have **doctors** who can speak English and know what they're talking about. This might not be the cheapest option, but that's where the travel insurance comes in. **Pharmacies** are a dime a dozen in both Port-au-Prince and Pétion-Ville and you should have no trouble getting medicines for minor ailments.

Previous page
Fruit vendor, Cabarete,
Dominican Republic (PB)

Above Houses in Haiti (RV)

Right The En Joy Your Self
Hotel, Port-de-Paix, Haiti (RV)

Opposite page
Hotel pool, Confresi,
Dominican Republic (PB)

Above Street art,
Boutilliers, Haiti (RV)

Right Haitian roulette wheel,
Saint-Marc, Haiti (RV)

Below A *tap-tap* in
Port-au-Prince, Haiti (RV)

The main police station – the headquarters of the fledgling Haitian National Police – is opposite the National Palace. The police station in Pétion-Ville is on Place St Pierre.

WHAT TO SEE
La Place des Héros de l'Indépendence

You have to walk single file down most streets in Port-au-Prince as they are so cluttered and given over to commerce. Perhaps this makes the cleared space of the Place des Héros de l'Indépendence, right in the centre of Port-au-Prince, more impressive than it actually is. Or perhaps it's the historical resonance.

On one side of the square, the statue to the **Marron Inconnu** (Unknown Slave) reminds us of the slave uprising. The figure represented is a slave, broken chain around his ankle and sword in hand, blowing through an empty conch shell to call his compatriots to revolt.

On the other side of the square, the **National Palace** reminds us of the dictators and tyrants that have ruled Haiti since its independence. The existing structure – surely the most well-cared for building in Haiti – was built in 1918 after revolutions had destroyed the previous two in 1869 and 1912. Rumour has it that this is where Papa Doc used to hold conversations with the heads of his dead enemies. Just in front of the National Palace, the **Caserne Dessalines** (Dessalines Barracks) – equally notorious as a Tontons Macoute torture house – is now the headquarters of the fledgling Haitian National Police.

In the middle of the square, between the Marron Inconnu and the National Palace, statues of the heroes of the War of Independence – Louverture, Dessalines and Pétion – remind us of what Haiti could have been and can still be.

To tie all these memories together, the **Place de Martyr** (Martyr's Square) was built beside the Marron Inconnu in 1994. The statue in the middle is of a man with outstretched arms freeing a dove with a mass of people writhing at his feet. The monument is dedicated to all the victims in the struggle for democracy.

Champs de Mars

Some include the Place des Héros de l'Indépendence when they talk of the Champs de Mars, another area of open space between the National Palace and Rue Capois, with trees, parks, bandstands, more monuments and the obligatory street vendors.

The **Musée du Panthéon National Haitien** is on the Champs de Mars across the road from the National Palace. This is Haiti's national museum, but you might be disappointed if you're expecting something on the same scale as the museums in Santo Domingo. This place is small and well presented, although a little disconcerting. Many of the exhibits – and certainly the most prominent ones – relate to the horrendous suffering endured by the blacks during slavery. At most times of the day school children file past the iron manacles, branding irons, chains, muzzles, pokers and other instruments of torture, lest they grow up not knowing the real truth about their past. There is also a small art gallery in a corridor behind the main part of the museum with a painting by the greatest of all Haitian painters, Hector Hyppolite. The museum is open from 08.00 to 16.00,

Monday to Thursday, until 18.00 on Friday, and from 14.00 to 18.00 at weekends. It costs Gde40 for foreigners and Gde10 for Haitians.

The **Musée d'Art Haitien** is at the other end of the Champs de Mars next to Rue Capois opposite the Rex Theatre. Opening hours are 10.00 to 16.00, Monday to Saturday and the price of admission is Gde10. Behind the museum, take a look at the **Maison Defly** (Defly House). You see prettier gingerbread houses elsewhere (such as Bois Verna), but this one has been restored and is furnished as it would have been when the Deflys were in residence.

Cité de l'Exposition

There is nothing really to see in the Cité de l'Exposition, but it does have merit as another open space in a town where there are few respites from the noise and chaos. This area at the end of Rue de Miracle, more or less in front of the port, was cleared during the Estimé presidency when tourism was important to Haiti and the waterfront slums were something of an embarrassment. However, nothing was built in the Cité and now it feels rather deserted and incongruous in a town fighting for all the space it can get. The post office and plenty of travel agencies are here, but not much else.

Markets

The market in Port-au-Prince stretches from Cathédrale Notre-Dame to the port, bound on one side by Rue Pavée and on the other by Route de Delmas. In other words, half of Port-au-Prince is a market. Go up to the cathedral and look down from its slight elevation to the port and you'll see what I mean. Thousands of *marchands*, often three-deep along the streets, sell everything you could imagine. A pitch along Grand Rue is the most sought after in town.

Starting at Rue Pavée and walking north, you pass *marchands* selling suitcases, pots and pans, perfume, music, crackers, soap, Culligan water, Barbancourt rum and so on, until you reach the **marché en fer** (iron market) where you can buy it all under one roof at a special tourist price. Rumor has it that President Hippolyte (whose name is inscribed on the clock tower) bought the marché en fer from a French factory that had originally built it for the Turkish government. Indeed, it does look a bit like a mosque, albeit a steel one painted in red and green.

Looking around – let alone shopping – in the marché en fer can be quite an ordeal; I have heard gruesome accounts of tourists being physically dragged into shops. To avoid this, my advice is to walk around with purpose and confidence. If you see something you like, breeze right past it and come back for a second look when the vendors have got used to your face and the fact that you are 'just looking'.

As you enter the market, the tourist trinkets are to your right, and even in these days of tourist drought there is plenty to choose from. Paintings, woodwork, ironwork, leatherwork, straw hats and baskets, pottery, voodoo rattles and dolls are all for sale. Haggle, but don't be too stingy. **Marché Tête Boeuf** is a couple of blocks further north on Grand Rue, offering mainly clothes and shoes.

Churches

The main Catholic church in Port-au-Prince is the **Cathédrale Notre-Dame**. Completed in 1915, this pink and white church in the Romanesque style, with twin towers that look like Islamic minarets, is impressive from the outside; but when you go inside it's rather disappointing.

This is not the case at the **Cathédrale Sainte Trinité**, off Rue Pavée not far from the National Palace, as the interior here is decorated with the famous **Saint Trinité murals**. Painted in 1949 by four of the best 'primitive' painters of the time – Castera Bazile, Rigaud Benoit, Wilson Bigaud and Philomé Obin – these murals use scenes from everyday Haitian life to illustrate stories from the Bible. For instance, Obin shows Calvary (the hill where Christ was crucified) as a town street in Haiti, while Bigaud's version of the wedding feast at Cana (where Christ performed his first miracle) shows guests seated in Haitian-style rocking chairs.

Another church worth a look is the pretty **Eglise Sacre Cœur** situated in the neighbourhood famous for its gingerbread houses, Bois Verna.

Gingerbread houses

Gingerbread houses are basically tropicalised versions of Victorian architecture. They first started to appear in Port-au-Prince in the 1890s and the best remaining examples tend to be in the neighbourhoods of Turgeau, Paco and Bois Verna – at one time the aristocratic quarters of the capital, and now full of colleges, lawyers and doctors. There are some beautifully restored houses, particularly along Avenue Lamartinière, as well as many more dilapidated ones, not only in these neighbourhoods, but all over Port-au-Prince and Haiti. **Maison Cordasco** and **Maison Peabody**, both in Pacot, are two of the most frequently visited houses. Wander around and you'll find your own favourite.

The cemetery

The cemetery is at the southern end of town by Portail Léogâne, next to the **Stade Sylvio Cator**, where soccer matches and music concerts are held. The main reason people visit the cemetery is to see what is left of Papa Doc's grave. When Baby Doc fled the country in 1986 and the process of 'uprooting' the evils of Duvalierism began, François Duvalier's tomb was razed to the ground by the angry crowd. Rubble and memories are all that are left today. Be prepared for two things when you try to get in to the cemetery: firstly, the opportunists who insist that you pay them an admission fee; and secondly, that you have some form of identification to show the officials at the entrance.

PÉTION-VILLE

Although I speak of Pétion-Ville in the same breath as Port-au-Prince, ever since it was founded in 1831 by President Boyer in honour of his predecessor, Alexandre Pétion, this town has always had its own identity. Pétion-Ville is, in fact, the alter-ego of Port-au-Prince. While the capital is vibrant, bustling, dirty and poor, Pétion-Ville seems to pride itself on a more rarefied atmosphere. For a start, it's about 6km up in the foothills of the Massif de la Selle, which makes it slightly cooler and less oppressive than downtown. It also lacks the crowds, although the market is certainly busy enough to have the usual Haitian character. But what really sets Pétion-Ville apart is its strong emphasis on elegant and sophisticated living. Up here you'll only find expensive hotels and restaurants that would sit well in Paris. Art galleries, jewellery shops and perfumeries almost outnumber the street vendors, while French competes with Creole for status as the majority language. This way of life is a result of the fact that Pétion-Ville has always been the home of the Haitian elite – the ones with the European education and all the money. These days it also tends to be where the majority of foreigners working for international organisations choose to live, which means that you'll see more *blancs* here than in the rest of Haiti put together.

Orientation and what to see
If you're coming up Route de Delmas, Pétion-Ville officially starts at Delmas 66. On Lalue, it's where Avenue John Brown becomes Avenue Pan-Americaine. Pétion-Ville is easy and pleasant to tour on foot. *Tap-taps* from Port-au-Prince will deposit you next to the market and not far from **Eglise St Jean de Boscoe**, the town's most popular church. Come here early in the morning or evening, or stay at the nearby La Belle Etoile Hotel, and you'll hear beautiful singing and witness the crowds standing outside because there's no room inside the church during mass. Pétion-Ville's other church is the yellow-brick **Eglise St Pierre** on the town's main square, **Place St Pierre**. There is a **statue of Alexandre Pétion** in the middle of the park and the post office and police station are on the square. Continue up the hill along Route de Kenscoff for Boutilliers, Fermathe, Fort Jacques, Kenscoff and Furcy (see *Excursions from Port-au-Prince* on page 89).

DELMAS
Delmas is, in fact, a large urban district with a population of over 250,000. For the tourist, however, it has little to offer apart from a few shops, restaurants and other amenities. These are all found along Route de Delmas. To make life easier, all of the side roads leading off the main road are given a number. Delmas 1 is in Port-au-Prince, while Delmas 103 is in Pétion-Ville. Therefore, I have given the precise location of anything of interest along Route de Delmas by referring to the side road to which it is nearest. For example, the Caribbean Supermarket is at Delmas 95 because it's on the corner of Route de Delmas and Delmas 95.

CARREFOUR
In the days when Haiti had a tourist industry, Carrefour was *the* place to go for bars, restaurants and nightclubs, and Côte Plage was a popular beach resort. Nowadays, Côte des Arcadins has taken over from Côte Plage and few people make the effort to trek out to Carrefour for a night on the town. At the height of its popularity in the 1970s and early 1980s Carrefour was

also notorious for its prostitution, attracting tourists who came to Haiti expressly for sex. The prostitutes – many of them young Dominican girls – still work the hotels and nightclubs today, although apparently business is not as good as it was.

CITÉ SOLEIL

Just beyond the sugar warehouses and factories on the northern outskirts of Port-au Prince lies Cité Soleil, built on landfill at the harbour's edge. This shantytown was constructed on the orders of Papa Doc, who wanted to sanitise the streets of Port-au-Prince, but had nowhere to put all the beggars. Cité Soleil, or rather Cité Simone as it was originally called (after Papa Doc's wife), was the solution. It was, and still is, the most desperate slum in the West Indies. Suffice it to say that most residents of Cité Soleil are unemployed, and of the few that do work, many are employed on a casual basis off-loading the ships that arrive at the port immediately next to the slum. An armed guard now escorts the loaded trucks from the wharf to the warehouse, since in the past they have been held up and forced to turn down the road leading straight into the heart of Cité Soleil, never to be seen again.

EXCURSIONS FROM PORT-AU-PRINCE
Boutilliers

There are many great views of Port-au-Prince from the hills behind the city, but none are as good as those 1,000m up at Boutilliers, the cool retreat of Haiti's rich and infamous. Million dollar homes are not uncommon up here, and many of them are built on the side of the mountain to take advantage of the view. Fortunately, the tourists and the young couples who come up to Boutilliers are also provided for. There is a viewing platform, and in better times there was a café serving light refreshments. Hawkers selling primitive art are still here, even if the café is no more.

Boutilliers is about half an hour from Pétion-Ville and an hour from downtown Port-au-Prince. Take a *tap-tap* from Pétion-Ville bound for Fermathe or Kenscoff and get off at Laboule 12. From here you have to walk up the hill to Boutilliers. It takes about 15 minutes and is not all that hard going.

Before you start your ascent, you might like to stop off at the **Barbancourt Rum Distillery**. This imitation castle at the foot of the Boutilliers hill is not a distillery at all, but rather a place where the tourists can taste some Barbancourt rum and perhaps buy a few bottles after the experience. You might also get the chance to meet Jane Barbancourt, the founder of the famous name, who is sometimes in residence. The distillery normally opens only when a group of tourists is in town, however, so don't be surprised if it is shut.

The Fermathe Mountain Maid Mission

There are so many worthwhile charities in Haiti that it's hard to choose which ones deserve a mention. The mission at Fermathe, about 45 minutes by *tap-tap* from Pétion-Ville, is certainly one of them.

Run by a conservative Baptist church from the United States, the Mountain Maid Mission has the motto 'self-help, not dependence'. With this in mind, around the nucleus of the church there is a hospital, a tuberculosis sanatorium, a school, a reforestation nursery, greenhouses, workshops, fish and irrigation ponds, livestock pens and chicken coops. Education is the key here and most of what is produced is sold to visitors, with the profits going back to the mission's new projects. The food shop sells fresh fruit, bread, brownies, jam and hot pepper marmalade, the souvenir shop various arts and crafts, and the Mountain Maid Tea Terrace – especially popular with Americans – has hot dogs, hamburgers, doughnuts and ice-creams. There is also a small museum with various artefacts gathered by the mission. Note that everything is closed on Sundays.

Fort Jacques and Fort Alexandre
The turn-off for Fort Jacques and Fort Alexandre is just beyond the mission at Fermathe. After a good walk up the hill (tap-taps rarely make the trip) you arrive at Fort Jacques. Inevitably, young boys will offer their services as guides, but you really don't need one. Fort Jacques was built in 1804 on the orders of Dessalines, who feared French reprisals after their defeat in the War of Independence. Fort Alexandre was an afterthought, built to protect Jacques' southeastern flank, but never finished. The two forts are apparently linked by a tunnel, although visual evidence is unavailable. In fact, there's not a lot to see inside Fort Jacques either – just a couple of cisterns and rusty cannons – and the greatest reward for hiking up the hill is probably the fantastic view you get of Port-au-Prince and the Cul-de-Sac Plain.

Kenscoff
Kenscoff is a small market town 15km from Port-au-Prince. Tap-taps leave regularly from Pétion-Ville: it takes about an hour and costs less than Gde10. There is nothing to see as such, except the market and a small church, but at 1,300m Kenscoff is considerably cooler than the capital. Bring a picnic up here or shop at the market where you can find good lettuces, tomatoes and even raspberries.

Although it's a long trek down to Port-au-Prince each day, you might consider basing yourself in Kenscoff. The one hotel in town is the American-run **Le Florville** (tel: 45 2092). There are two rooms, each costing H$100 with TV, hot water and breakfast included. Kenscoff also has a bar, the **Neneete Bar**, and a coffee shop, **La Patisserie**.

Parc National La Visite
The road up into the foothills of the Massif de la Selle ends at the small town of **Furcy**. This is the departure point for a trek across the high trails of La Visite National Park, leading eventually to Jacmel on the Caribbean coast. While this route is not exactly well trodden, it can be done with relative ease in two days. The trail leads through pine forests, alpine meadows and a waterfall at **Seguin**, providing one of the few opportunities in Haiti to see bird- and plantlife, especially orchids.

If you are interested in doing this trek, you should try to speak to an Italian chap called Enrico. He lives about 15 minutes from Jacmel, or a 10-minute walk from Cyvadier Beach (see *Jacmel* on page 93), in a house called *Villa Détente*. He is well known in the area and most people can tell you where he can be found. Enrico owns several horses and a cabin up in the mountains and is well versed in the practicalities of trekking in Parc La Visite. If you can't get to Enrico, ask around in Pétion-Ville (Roots Bar is a good place to start) for the condition of the trail and the practicalities of making the trip. Remember that things change quickly in Haiti.

MALPASSE AND THE DOMINICAN BORDER

The best road in the whole of Haiti links Port-au-Prince to the Dominican border at Malpasse. It cuts through the Cul-de-Sac Plain and allows the *tap-taps* to show what they can do on a well-paved, pot-hole-free road. The 50km or so can be covered in as little as an hour.

As you approach the border, the waters of **Étang Saumâtre** – the largest lake in Haiti – can be seen from the road. Like Lake Enriquillo a few kilometres across the border, Étang Saumâtre is a brackish lake that plays host to colonies of American crocodiles, iguanas and flamingos. However, while the Dominican lake has been given national park status and is regularly visited by tourists, Étang Saumâtre is virtually inaccessible.

Malpasse seems to be no more than a border checkpoint, where *tap-taps* arrive and leave from the immigration office. You have to pay two taxes when entering Haiti – an immigration tax of Gde25 and a bank tax of US$10. I don't know why they are imposed, but I do know that you have to pay them. If for some reason you don't, you might have problems at the police checkpoint further down the road at Fond Parisien.

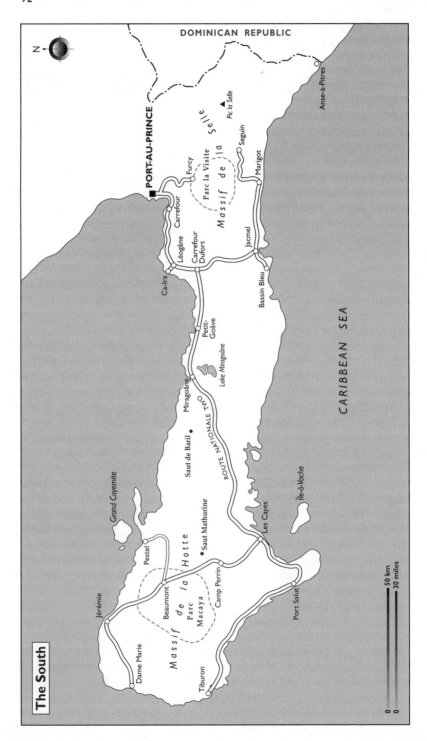

The South

DOMINICAN REPUBLIC

N

CARIBBEAN SEA

Anse-à-Pitres

PORT-AU-PRINCE

Pic la Selle

Seguin

Marigot

Jacmel

Furcy

Parc la Visite

Massif de la Selle

Carrefour

Léogâne

Carrefour Dufort

Ca-Ira

Bassin Bleu

Petit-Goâve

Lake Miragoâne

Miragoâne

Saut de Baril

ROUTE NATIONALE TWO

Les Cayes

Île-à-Vache

Grand Cayemite

Pestel

Saut Mathurine

Beaumont

Parc Macaya

Massif de la Hotte

Camp Perrin

Port Salut

Jérémie

Dame Marie

Tiburon

50 km

30 miles

0

0

The South

The land south of Port-au-Prince is almost entirely mountainous. The Massif de la Hotte dominates the western end of the peninsula, while in the east there is the Massif de la Selle and Haiti's highest mountain, Pic La Selle. The terrain obviously dictates which parts of the region are accessible by public transport. Thanks to Route Nationale Two, the southern peninsula is more accessible than its northern counterpart, even if the road is in poor shape and travel is slow.

JACMEL

As far as tourism is concerned, Jacmel is the most important town in southern Haiti. A relatively easy drive from Port-au-Prince, good beaches and a selection of hotels and restaurants, have made Jacmel a popular place to come for weekend breaks away from the capital. On a grander scale, there are plans to improve the road between Jacmel and Mariget (where the beaches are found) and to develop the town's small port so that it can receive cruise ships. Until they arrive and tourism makes Jacmel rich once again, it must live off memories of a time when it was a cosmopolitan colonial port doing a roaring trade in coffee.

During its heyday, Jacmel exported 25,000 sacks of coffee to England per year and had a lucrative sideline in cotton and orange peel. Some of the coffee houses, with their huge, iron doors and imposing balconies, are still in use today, but most of them are empty. The same is true for the brightly painted, wooden houses, some dating back to 1896 when Jacmel was rebuilt with prefabricated houses from Germany. The overall effect is charming, romantic and a little sad.

Getting there and away
By air
Daily flights to Jacmel by Caribintair have recently been discontinued, but could be reinstated at any time. Don't expect a meal, or even a drink and a packet of peanuts, as the flight only takes about 10 minutes.

By road
The **bus station** is on Avenue de la Liberté. *Tap-taps* to Port-au-Prince leave at regular intervals during the day and take about three hours. Expect to pay H$5.

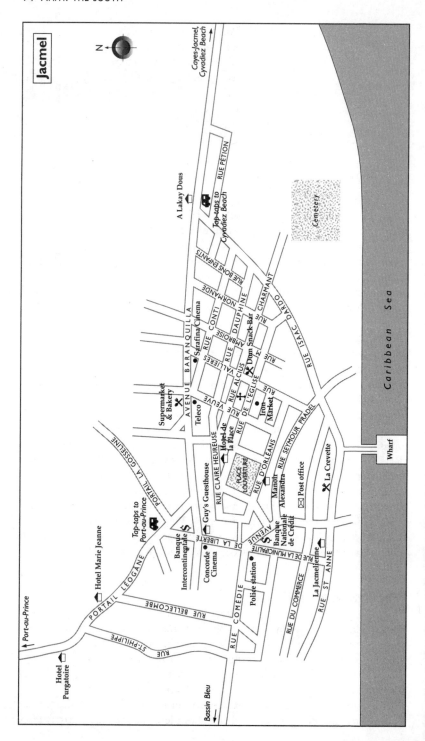

If you want to go to Les Cayes, Port Salut, Jérémie, or anywhere else on the southern peninsula, you'll have to get another *tap-tap* at Carrefour Dufort. This is where the road across the Massif de la Selle to Jacmel joins Route Nationale Two. Stand by the Texaco service station and flag down a *tap-tap* going in your direction. You might have trouble stopping the faster buses from Port-au-Prince, but the *camions* will be only too happy to bump you along the Great Southern Highway to Les Cayes or Miragoâne for a few *gourdes*. Whatever your mode of transport, Carrefour Dufort to Les Cayes should not take more than five hours.

Where to stay

If you stay only one night in Jacmel, try to spend it at **Manoir Alexandra** (tel: 88 2711). Rooms cost H$20 per person including breakfast. You have to share a bathroom and the electricity and water are unreliable, but the veranda overlooking Jacmel and the Caribbean should tip the balance. Try to get room 3 or room 5, both of which have direct access to the balcony.

There are hotels in Jacmel to suit all types of budget. The most expensive is **Hotel Cyvadiez** (tel: 88 3323), a few kilometres east of Jacmel on Cyradiez beach. Quite apart from being so far out of town, this place is overpriced (US$50 for a single, US$70 for a double) and characterless. In Jacmel itself, top of the range is **La Jacmelienne** (tel: 88 3451) on the coast near the wharf. It charges nearly as much as Hotel Cyradiez. The conveniently located **Hotel de la Place** (tel: 88 2832) is the pick of the mid-range hotels, charging Gde400 for a single and Gde450 for a double. Further from the centre, and with only three rooms, is **A Lakay Dous** (tel: 88 2148), meaning Home Sweet Home. This small guesthouse is run by a Canadian who has lived in Jacmel for a number of years. If you get the chance, pick his brains for any useful information. Rates are H$45 per person with breakfast included.

Jacmel's budget hotels are all found on the road to Port-au-Prince. The cleanest, best-value and closest to the centre is **Guy's Guest House** (tel: 88 3421) on Avenue de la Liberté. It costs H$34 for a single, H$61.50 for a double and there's also a small restaurant. Past the bus station is **Hotel Marie Jeanne** (tel: 88 2385) for a similar price; and a little further down is **Hotel Purgatoire** which, as its name suggests, should be avoided. However, if for your sins you feel forced to spend some time in purgatory, snoop around the back of the hotel where you'll find a fully operational *peristyle* for voodoo ceremonies.

Where to eat

The most popular place to eat, especially with *blancs* who have come from Port-au-Prince for the weekend, is the restaurant at Hotel de la Place. The menu is extensive and the range of drinks particularly impressive. A live band plays here on Saturday night. Further down on Rue de l'Eglise, in the square occupied by the church and the iron market, is the unpretentious **Dom Snack Bar**. A generous helping of *griots* will set you back H$15. If seafood is what you're looking for, try **La Crevette** on the beach next to the wharf. This is also a good place to sip a cool drink while watching the modest activity in Jacmel's small port. Walking along the beach away from the wharf, you pass a shipwreck and come to **La Jacmelienne**, where set menus in the restaurant start at H$25. **A Lakay Dous** also does a set dinner for H$30. **Hotel Cyradiez** has a restaurant if you're staying there and don't want to come into town.

A good **supermarket** and **bakery** can be found opposite the Teleco office on Avenue Baranquilla.

Nightlife and entertainment

If the cruise ships ever come to Jacmel, there'll no doubt be more to say, but as things stand at the moment, a quiet cocktail on the veranda of **Manoir Alexandra** and the live Saturday band at **Hotel de la Place** seem to be the highlights of Jacmel's nightlife. Of course, I am not counting the Jackie Chan film that was showing at the **Sarafina Ciné** on Rue Vallieres during my visit. There is another cinema, the **Concorde**, opposite Guy's Guest House, and if you overheat during the day and can't be bothered to trek out to one of the beaches, Gde25 will give you access to the **freshwater pool** at La Jacmelienne.

Tourist information

There is no danger of just stumbling across the **post office** in Jacmel. No signs lead you to it and the building itself isn't even marked. In fact, it's on Rue du Commerce. Turn right off Avenue de la Liberté and look for the second building on your left with the grey doors. The **Teleco** office is more obviously placed on Avenue Baranquilla.

The two **banks** are on Avenue de la Liberté. Banque Nationale de Crédit is next to the Alliance Française, while Banque Intercontinentale is near the bus station.

The **police station** is situated on Rue Comédie at a crossroads with a signpost in the middle directing you to various far-flung destinations such as Miami, Panama and Amsterdam.

What to see

Apart from its **architecture**, Jacmel is a town where the atmosphere is paramount and you could do a lot worse than just wander the streets soaking it up. There is an **iron market** next to **Place Louverture** and the town's main church, **Eglise St Jacques et St Philippe**, is directly opposite. One of the most interesting things to see, however, is **Hotel Manoir Alexandra**. This pretty green-and-white house is also near Place Louverture. Walk up the steps on Avenue de la Liberté opposite the Alliance Française and turn right just before you get to the top. This place was immortalised by one of Haiti's best-known writers, René Depestre. In his novel *Hadriana dans tous mes reves* (Hadriana in all my dreams) he tells of a young woman from Jacmel called Hadriana who died on her wedding day and was turned into a zombie. The house where she used to live became a hotel and was named Hotel Hadriana. However, this upset the townspeople so much that the hotel owner was forced to change its name to Alexandra. Nowadays, Manoir Alexander is also renowned for its cocktails – an interesting mixture of rum, Cointreau, cocoa and egg white. Try one on the sloping veranda, which has lovely views of the Bay of Jacmel.

Excursions from Jacmel
Beaches
The beaches within striking distance of Jacmel are on the road leading to Cayes-Jacmel and Marigot. The closest and smallest is **Cyvadiez** beach, about 30 minutes by *tap-tap* from Jacmel. This small strip of sand, in a bay where the water is more green than blue, looks more Mediterranean than Caribbean. For beaches more classically West Indian, with white sand, palm trees and blue sea, you must go further down the road to **Raymond Les Bains** and **Ti Mouillage**.

The best place to catch a *tap-tap* to any of these beaches is opposite A Lakay Dous on Avenue Baranquilla.

Bassin Bleu
The brilliant blue waters of Bassin Bleu – a pool in the middle of the jungle with a waterfall spilling into it – are well known around these parts. So much so, in fact, that visitors regularly make the two-hour trek through some quite dense jungle to see them. The numerous guides along the route are also testament to Bassin Bleu's popularity.

Unfortunately, on the day I made the trip recent rainfall had made Bassin Bleu disappointingly green and murky, but getting there was fun. Whether you go on foot or in a 4WD vehicle, you should leave Jacmel via Rue Comédie. When you are out of town, cross the river (it's only knee deep) and rejoin the path that continues up a small hill. You can drive for another kilometre or two, before you have to leave your vehicle and continue on foot through the jungle. This is where the guides latch on to you, although the path itself is not too hazardous or difficult to make out. The scenery here is impressive. It's very green, very lush and very fertile – not words normally associated with Haiti. After about half an hour you reach Bassin Bleu, which actually consists of three pools. The first two are easy enough to see unaided, but for the third and most stunning you must be lowered down into the Bassin by a rope tied around your waist. Let the guides know if you want to do this before you set off, as they have to bring the rope with them.

ALONG THE GREAT SOUTHERN HIGHWAY
The main road, in fact, the only road serving the south – if road is taken to mean more than just a dirt track – is Route Nationale Two. When this road was built during the US occupation, it was called the Great Southern Highway. It never really deserved this grand title and today the route is littered with potholes. However, it is more-or-less paved as far as Les Cayes, so perhaps we should count our blessings.

The Great Southern Highway starts in Port-au-Prince as Boulevard Jean-Jacques Dessalines and continues as such until it reaches Carrefour, where the urban sprawl of the capital ends rather abruptly. After this, fields, cows and mountains start to appear on one side of the road, while the sea is never far away on the other. Less than an hour from Carrefour the highway passes the town of Léogâne.

LÉOGÂNE

Barely 20km from Port-au-Prince, Léogâne is very far removed from the capital, for this is rural Haiti where nothing much happens except life itself. Two rusty cannons set a little way back from the highway signal your arrival at Léogâne, and this is about as dramatic as it gets. Walk down Grand Rue, turn left at the first opportunity and you're in the centre of town. An austere cathedral and the market opposite are the highlights.

If you decide to stop off at Léogâne, you should walk the short distance to **Ca-Ira**. Continue walking away from the highway down Grand Rue, which has become a relatively busy dirt track frequently used by buffalo-drawn carts – the trade link between Léogâne and the coastal hamlet of Ca-Ira. Apart from a few fishing boats and a small mangrove swamp, Ca-Ira's claim to fame is its conch shells. Come at the right time (there seems to be no telling when) and you'll see thousands of them piled up on the beach in what the postcards describe as 'nature's most beautiful rubbish tip'.

The **Continental Hotel** – locally known as the St Yves Hotel – is on the buffalo track, a little closer to Ca-Ira than to Léogâne. If you want to stay a day or two to soak up the atmosphere, for in truth Léogâne has little else to offer, a basic room with fan and bathroom will cost H$50, which is not great value.

Tap-taps to Port-au-Prince leave from the top of Grand Rue on the main road and only cost Gde4. To continue along the Great Southern Highway, flag down a *tap-tap* or *camion* going in the opposite direction.

A few kilometres further along Route Nationale Two, you come to a Texaco service station and the turn-off for Jacmel. This crossroads is known as **Carrefour Dufort**. Continuing along the main road, you pass through the small town of Grand-Goâve and the considerably larger one of Petit-Goâve before arriving at yet another Texaco service station. This is a sure sign that you've arrived at a crossroads. Turn left for Les Cayes and go straight on for the lively town of Miragoâne.

MIRAGOÂNE

The bustling little port of Miragoâne is bursting at its seams. Rumour has it that a large company is going to base itself in the town, bringing investment and expansion. From Miragoane's point of view, this leap of faith has come not a moment too soon. As it is, almost every inch of the town's streets is devoted to selling something or other; and as quickly as the *marchands* can sell it, new stock is being dragged from ships at the wharf. If time permits, stop off at Miragoâne, as it epitomises the energy and great potential of Haiti and the Haitians.

Getting there and away

Tap-taps bound for Les Cayes or Port-au-Prince will leave you at the crossroads called Carrefour Dessineaux if you want to stop at Miragoâne. From here it's a short *tap-tap* ride or a 15-minute walk to town. The road leading from Carrefour Dessineaux eventually becomes Miragoâne's Grand Rue. Leaving Miragoâne, retrace your steps to Carrefour Dessineaux (the walk is uphill this time) and catch a *tap-tap* going to either Port-au-Prince or Les Cayes.

Where to stay and eat
There seem to be three hotels in Miragoâne, all of a similar price and quality. First choice, especially if you get a room overlooking the Hotel de Ville and port, is **Hotel Paradis de Amis**, where rooms cost H$25 per person. **Hotel Bella Mar** is at the end of Grand Rue – when I arrived at midday, the manager was drinking Barbancourt five star and the hotel bar was full of rough, seafaring types. I found the cute bedspreads with pictures of racing cars on them rather incongruous in such a setting. Anyway, beds cost H$30. Next door at **Hotel Excelsior**, it's H$40 for pretty much the same thing.

In a place like Miragoâne, where everything is sold on the streets, you really should try some of the various delicacies offered by the *marchands*. In any case, there is not a great deal in the way of restaurants. The Bella Mar has a restaurant, otherwise look on and around Grand Rue.

Tourist information
The **post office** is in the Hotel de Ville, just in front of the port. The town's **bank** (Banque Nationale du Crédit) is on Grand Rue. The **police station** is next to the Bella Mar, which is surely no coincidence.

Due west of Miragoâne a road continues along the coast to Petit-Trou-des-Nippes. In between, Petite Rivière de Nippes is the stopping-off point for **Saut de Baril**, one of Haiti's four great waterfalls. Returning to the Great Southern Highway, the road turns south at Miragoâne and passes through towns such as St Michel de Sud, Fonds des Nègres, Virgile, Aquin, Saint-Louis du Sud and Cavaillon before arriving at Les Cayes.

LES CAYES
Les Cayes was destroyed by two great fires in 1885 and 1911, so perhaps it can be forgiven for looking a bit tatty today. However, while other tatty towns have retained their charm, if not their riches (Jacmel springs to mind), Les Cayes has not. Nor does it seem particularly concerned about aesthetic beauty. So long as it enjoys relative prosperity (this is the commercial centre of the south), what do unpaved roads, desecrated statues and a dirty beach matter? All this, combined with the scarcity of good hotels and restaurants, makes Les Cayes the big disappointment of the south.

Getting there and away
Tap-taps leave for Port-au-Prince, Port Salut and Camp Perrin from Carrefour des Quatre Chemins. Those going to Port-au-Prince and Port Salut congregate on the road leading off to the left as you approach the crossroads from Les Cayes. There are frequent departures to both of these destinations

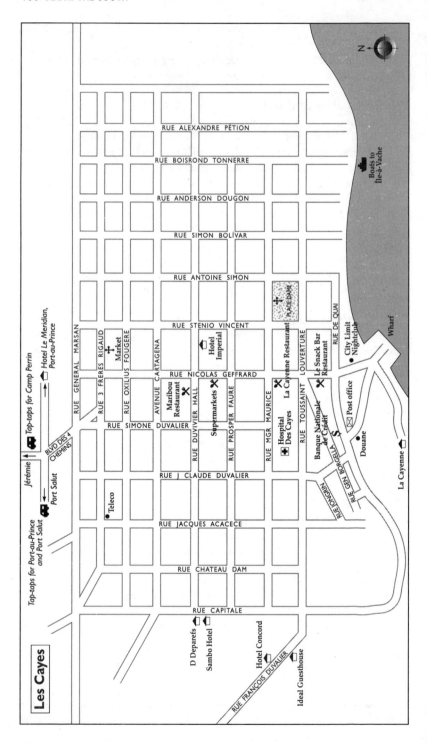

Les Cayes

Tap-taps for Port-au-Prince and Port Salut

Tap-taps for Camp Perrin

Hotel Le Meridian, Port-au-Prince

Jérémie

Port Salut

BLVD DES 4 CHEMINS

RUE GENERAL MARSAN

RUE ALEXANDRE PÉTION

RUE BOISROND TONNERRE

RUE ANDERSON DOUGON

RUE SIMON BOLÍVAR

RUE ANTOINE SIMON

RUE STENIO VINCENT

RUE NICOLAS GEFFRARD

RUE SIMONE DUVALIER

RUE J CLAUDE DUVALIER

RUE JACQUES ACACECE

RUE CHATEAU DAM

RUE CAPITALE

RUE 3 FRERES RIGAUD

RUE OXILIUS FOUGERE

AVENUE CARTAGENA

RUE DUVIVIER HALL

RUE PROSPER FAURE

RUE MGR MAURICE

RUE TOUSSAINT LOUVERTURE

RUE DE QUAI

RUE GEN BORGELLA

RUE ONGNIN

RUE FRANCOIS DUVALIER

Market

Hotel Imperial

Maribou Restaurant

Supermarkets

La Cayenne Restaurant

Le Snack Bar Restaurant

PLACE D'ARMES

Hospital Des Cayes

Banque Nationale de Crédit

Post office

Douane

City Limit Nightclub

Wharf

La Cayenne

Boats to Île-à-Vache

Teleco

D Deparefs

Sambo Hotel

Hotel Concord

Ideal Guesthouse

N

OK LES CAYES!

'OK' is probably the most the most frequently used slang expression in the English language. Did you know that according to legend it owes its existence to Les Cayes? Legend has it that when rum was exported from Les Cayes in the 18th century, it was put in crates marked with the words 'Aux Cayes', indicating that it came from Les Cayes. At that time all the crates arriving in New York were opened and inspected as they came off the ships. However, when the stevedores saw crates emblazoned with 'Aux Cayes', they let them go uninspected knowing that they contained nothing but the finest rum. In this way, 'Aux Cayes' became a general term of approval. It was abbreviated and pronounced as 'OK' in English.

during the day. The journey to Port Salut is a dusty one in the back of a *camion*. It takes between one and two hours, depending on the state of the road and the number of wheel changes en route.

In theory you can get a *tap-tap* direct to Jérémie from Les Cayes. In practice, however, this means squeezing into (or on top of) the daily bus from Port-au-Prince. Another way of getting to Jérémie is to take a *tap-tap* to Camp Perrin (about an hour) then a *camion* to Beaumont (about three hours) where you wait for the daily bus from Port-au-Prince which passes through at 22.00. Swings and roundabouts!

Where to stay

Les Cayes is not a town noted for its tourist attractions, a fact reflected in the meagre offering of hotels, restaurants and other amenities for visitors.

One person who has either failed to notice that there are no tourists in Les Cayes, or is hopefully predicting an imminent boom, is the owner of **La Cayenne** (tel: 86 0379), a beach hotel with tennis, volleyball and basketball courts – but no guests – where rooms cost H$150. There is also a nightclub next door and a restaurant in town, both called La Cayenne. To get there, turn right at the end of the wharf and follow the beach until you see a large, thatched roof behind a blue wall. Fortunately, there are other places to spend the night in Les Cayes; in my opinion, the best is **Hotel Imperial**, right in the centre of town. The name conjures up images of very grand and rather stuffy rooms, but nothing could be further from the truth. The lady who runs the hotel is a motherly type and each of the rooms (priced at H$50) has a very cosy feel. The communal bathroom is also the best I've seen in Haiti: sparkling clean, flowers all over the place and a generous supply of soaps and other toiletries. On the roof there is a hose and a bucket of water for washing clothes.

Most of the other hotels are on the western edge of town. Rue Capitale is the place to go for the budget options. Probably the best value is **Sambo Hotel** (tel: 86 0045) which has rooms for H$20 and H$30, although the first thing I noticed when I put my bag down was a cockroach. Next door is the more expensive, but air conditioned, **D Deparefs** (tel: 86 0523). Over the road are a couple of places 'ouvert 24/24', so I'll leave you to make up your own mind about them. If you follow Rue Toussaint Louventure past Rue Capitale, the expensive **Ideal Guest House** is on the left and **Hotel Concord** on the right.

Finally, if you have an early *tap-tap* to catch, **Le Meridian** is at Carrefour Quatre Chemins on the road to Port-au-Prince.

Where to eat

If you're staying at **Hotel Imperial** you could do worse than eat at their restaurant, but let them know a bit in advance. If you're staying at **La Cayenne**, the manager will frog march you to his restaurant on Rue Nicolas Geffrard, which is adequate, but nothing special. A good place for breakfast is the **Maribou** restaurant on Rue Duvivier Hall. They also have a reasonable dinner menu and, if you're contemplating a stay of a month or more, you could try their guesthouse. **Le Snack Bar Restaurant** on Rue Nicolas Geffard, down by the wharf, serves sandwiches, hamburgers, hot dogs and, after 18.00, ice-cream.

If the dearth of good restaurants is getting you down, there are one or two good supermarkets on Rue Nicolas Geffard. One is called the **Star Supermarket**, and there's another a few doors down towards the sea.

Nightlife and entertainment

Having enjoyed a spot of tennis and a meal at the restaurant, it's now time to continue the 'La Cayenne Experience' at the nightclub next door to the hotel. In fact, **La Cayenne Nightclub** is quite good and occasionally plays host to some fairly big names in Haitian music. They have *soirées* about once a week and the entrance fee is between H$15 and 20. More down-to-earth and certainly cheaper at H$2 is City Limit, in the side-alley leading down to the wharf. They play *compas*, *merengue*, zouk and salsa every evening except Monday.

Tourist information

The **post office** is on Rue de Quai, almost opposite the Douane. The **Teleco** office is inconveniently located on Rue 3 Frères Rigaud where it intersects with Rue Jacques Acacece. There is a **bank** on the same road (Banque Nationale de Crédit), while Banque de l'Union Haitienne is on Rue Nicolas Geffrard.

Orientation and what to see

Tap-taps will leave you at Carrefour des Quatre Chemins, a crossroads dominated by an arch in honour of Alexandre Pétion. The centre of town is about a kilometre away and you can either walk or take a motorbike down Boulevard des Quatre Chemins. Les Cayes is not a difficult town to work out, as the streets criss-cross each other and are well marked by signposts.

Unlike some other towns in the south, like Jérémie and Jacmel, Les Cayes is flat and the streets are generally wide and uncluttered, which makes cycling a good way of getting around. Ask the bicycle vendors in the market if you can rent a bike for the day. Alternatively you can buy one for a little over US$100.

The **market** and the town's largest and smartest church, **Eglise Sacre Cœur**, are at the end of Boulevard des Quatre Chemins. This is at the northern edge of town where most of the activity takes place. As you walk down the main thoroughfare, Rue Nicolas Geffrard, towards the sea, the town gets steadily more depressing. **Place Dam**e, a couple of streets before the beach, is the main square. A **cathedral**, completed in 1908 and severely damaged by Hurricane Allen in 1980, and a derelict statue of **Boisrond Tonnerre**, the author of Haiti's Act of Independence, are the attractions here. Rue Nicolas Geffrard eventually becomes the wharf, and from here you can look across the Canal de l'Est to **Île-à-Vache**. From the same place on April 10 1816, **Simón Bolívar** set sail with an expedition, armed and funded largely by Pétion, to liberate Venezuela. There is a memorial to commemorate the event, but like the statue of Tonnerre, it has seen better days.

ÎLE-À-VACHE

Measuring about 32km long and 6.5km wide, Île-à-Vache is Haiti's third largest island and the last piece of land before you get to the South American mainland. You don't have to be a genius to work out that Île-à-Vache (Cow Island) got its name from the healthy presence of beef cattle on the island. Nowadays there are more people than cows – some of them descendants of the first concerted attempt to populate the island in the 19th century.

In 1862, Abraham Lincoln signed a contract with Bernard Koch, an entrepreneur from New Orleans, to settle 5,000 emancipated slaves on Île-à-Vache. Eventually 500 negroes were sent to the island under the Negro Deportation Plan, where Koch was supposed to make provisions for their well-being. However, no houses were provided, sanitation was non-existent and food was in short supply. The freed slaves began to die one after the other and in 1864 the Haitian government ordered Koch and the negroes to leave the island. Most left, but some fled to the hills and were never found.

Île-à-Vache is rich in Indian remains and there are some nice beaches, particularly on the Caribbean side around the main town, La Hatte. Most boats leave from the mainland (at the end of Rue Bernard Tonnerre) to Madam Bernard or Ca Côq, on the Les Cayes side of the island. Be warned that there is only one boat per day, which brings people to the mainland in the morning and returns them to Île-à-Vache in the afternoon. This means that you will have wait until morning to catch a boat back to the mainland. The crossing takes about an hour and costs H$2. You might find a hotel at Ca Côq, but at Madam Bernard you are dependent on the hospitality of the missionaries who live on the island. Alternatively, you can fix a price with a fisherman to take you back to Les Cayes on the same day. I was quoted between H$100 and H$300.

PORT SALUT

The town of Port Salut is two hours southwest of Les Cayes, provided that wheel changes and punctures are kept to a minimum, and the excellent beach in this peaceful town is the ideal place to unwind.

If you restrict yourself to the beach (Macaya Beach) and the few restaurants along the coast, Port Salut seems a very small town, but in fact it extends up into the hills and has a population of about 50,000.

Getting there and away

There are many *tap-taps* from Les Cayes to Port Salut. Unless they are continuing along the coast to Chandonnieres and Les Anglais (which is seldom the case) you will be left about 2kms from the beach in downtown Port Salut. Brace yourself for the walk as traffic is thin along this road, which runs parallel to the coast. Going in the other direction towards Les Cayes, *tap-taps* will pick you up at Hotel Village if you tell the manager at what time you intend to leave. The road continues west along the coast as far as Tiburon.

If you want to explore the rest of the western tip of the peninsula, you might be able to find boats at Port Salut prepared to take you to places like Anse d'Hainault and Dame Marie. Negotiate the price yourself.

Where to stay and eat

The one hotel by the beach is **Hotel Village**. They have several bungalows and prices start at H$55 plus 10% tax. The only other hotel in Port Salut is the **Arada-Inn**, which is close to where the *tap-taps* from Les Cayes stop. They have nice rooms for H$35 (single) and H$50 (double), but it suffers from not being on the beach.

The manager of Hotel Village has a brother who runs the only real restaurant in Port Salut, the **Reposoire**. You can eat on the beach at the hotel, but the food comes from the restaurant. The *homard* (lobster) is very good. Other eating options can be found if you walk along the beach past the small island which lies just offshore. **Chez Imene** and **Chez Denise** are on the beach; **Chez Marie** and **Chez Colina** are on the other side of the beach road. All of these places have fresh seafood and other dishes, but you must tell them in advance what you want, as they have to buy the food.

If you want to do some self-catering, the nearest market is at Carpentiers, about a 30-minute walk from Hotel Village.

JÉRÉMIE

Isolated on the northern tip of the southern peninsula, 12 hours away from Port-au-Prince by either sea or road, there is something different about Jérémie. The abandoned coffee warehouses and decayed gingerbread mansions you find today don't quite tell the story of a town once described as the 'shop window of France'. At the turn of the century, Jérémie was a prosperous and cosmopolitan port, full of rich mulatto families who drank French claret and sent their children to school in Paris. It was a refined place, the home of many of Haiti's most famous poets, where the culture was more European than

African, in contrast to the rest of the country. Indeed, until Papa Doc came to power, the social segregation between the dominant mulattos and the minority blacks in the town had been vaguely akin to apartheid, with mulatto-only clubs, residential areas and marriages. This all changed in the summer of 1964 when 13 expatriates (12 of them mulattos from Jérémie) landed at Dame Marie, a few kilometres away, hoping to incite a rebellion against Papa Doc. This gave Duvalier, the arch black nationalist, the excuse he needed to wipe out the mulattos. He closed Jérémie's busy port and, while the insurgents held out in the surrounding hills, the Tontons Macoute ran amuck in the town, randomly slaughtering mulattos on the grounds that they were involved with the rebels. The number who died in the massacres of 1964 is uncertain, but many of the victims were buried in shallow graves in a wooded plain behind the airport called Numéro Deux. Jérémie has never been the same since.

The town suffered badly during the embargo, and shortages (primarily of electricity) are still common today. Walking around Jérémie can be a little depressing. For some reason, perhaps because the town used to pride itself on being a centre of culture and sophistication, the streets and buildings look more dilapidated and the people seem more bitter than elsewhere. This is the attraction of Jérémie. The town is rather like a road accident: you know shouldn't look, yet for some perverse reason you are compelled to.

Getting there and away
By air
Flying to Jérémie is as spectacular as getting there by road. It takes 45 minutes from Port-au-Prince with Caribintair and the current cost is US$55. Currently the plane leaves Jérémie at 11.40. They fly every day except Sunday, but since the plane only has 17 seats, flights are booked up well in advance. The airport at Jérémie is about seven miles out of town and about two miles beyond Anse d'Azur. Men on motorbikes will transport you to and from town for an arranged fee.

By sea
Every Wednesday evening at about 18.00 a boat leaves the wharf at Jérémie for Port-au-Prince. The cost and length of the journey are about the same as the bus (see below). If you opt to go by sea, don't expect a Caribbean cruise – it's standing room only and they really pack you in. I think the safer option is by road – and that's saying something.

By road
The trip from Port-au-Prince to Jérémie by road must rank as both one of the most spectacular and tiring in the West Indies. The distance between the two towns is considerable, but not really long enough to justify a journey of some 12 hours. Half of this is along the relative comfort of the paved and partially paved surface of The Great Southern Highway, and even the hour or so from Les Cayes to Camp Perrin is bearable, but after Camp Perrin the road winds up into the mountains of the Massif de la Hotte and you creep along for about

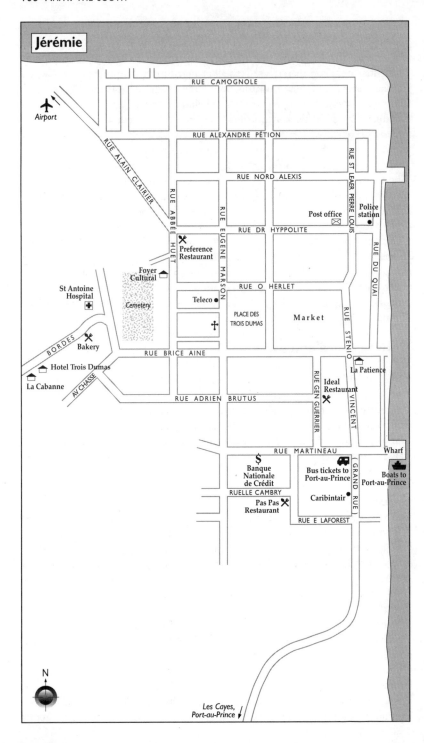

three hours at little more than walking pace. At this time, when the journey is starting to get slightly on your nerves, you probably don't need me telling you that the view is great; but it is. Haiti's largest waterfall, **Saut Mathurine**, is not far from Camp Perrin; and along the route small rivers and waterfalls can be spotted at the bottom of cliffs hundreds of metres high. At one spot, called *Gouffre Effrayant* (Terrifying Abyss), the road is only just wide enough to accommodate the American-style school buses that ply the route. I am reliably informed that accidents are rare, although not much evidence would remain if a *tap-tap* did go over the edge. A lot of work has apparently been done on the road from Beaumont to Jérémie and the pace, if not the comfort, picks up a little from here on in.

You pay H$20 for the privilege of making this journey. There is one *tap-tap* a day from Port-au-Prince, but from Jérémie you have more choice. You must buy your ticket in advance from the various companies on Grand Rue, where it intersects with Rue D Martineau. Most of them leave in the morning and there is one night service a week. All of these *tap-taps* leave from beyond the bridge on the road to Port-au-Prince. To get there, either walk south along Grand Rue for about 20 minutes, or take a motorbike from where you bought your ticket.

Here are some companies and their times.

L'Ange de Dieu:	Tue, Thur, Fri – 09.00
Dieu Qui Decide:	Tue, Thur, Sun – 11.00
Esperance:	Mon, Wed, Fri – 20.00
Immaculée:	Tue, Thur, Fri, Sat – 10.00

To get anywhere else other than Port-au-Prince and the towns en route is difficult. There are few, if any, *tap-taps* going between Jérémie and Dame Marie, so you'll probably have to arrange a private lift or have your own transport. The same is true for Anse du Clerc.

Where to stay

Given Jérémie's isolation and the difficulty in getting there, it is perhaps no surprise that hotels are thin on the ground, even by Haitian standards. The **Foyer Cultural** has 15 rooms with or without bathroom for H$25. You can also eat at their restaurant if you let them know in advance – worth considering because restaurants are harder to find than hotels. The largest of the hotels is **La Cabanne** (tel: 84 5128), up the hill in Bordes. Rooms are H$60 for a single and H$120 for a double. Breakfast and dinner are included in this price, but you must tell them that you want dinner otherwise you'll miss out. Next door to La Cabanne is **Hotel Trois Dumas** (tel: 84 5153). The H$30 rooms are simple and the chicken with *diri kole* in the restaurant is good, honest fare. Once again, order in advance. If all the rooms at the Foyer Cultural are full, you could try **La Patience** (tel: 84 6290) on Grand Rue, behind an ironmonger, where rooms cost H$30. Ask for a room overlooking the sea and a stepladder to get up to the bed, which was, in my room at least, over a metre high.

Where to eat

If you have forgotten to order your meal at the hotel restaurant, or you want to sample the culinary delights of Jérémie, you could be disappointed. The **Preference Restaurant** opposite the Foyer Cultural is a possibility, as is the **Pas Pas Restaurant** on Rue E Laforest. I was enticed into the latter of these by a menu boasting a full range of Haiti's favourite dishes. However, when I tried to order they only had chicken. You might have a similar experience at the **Ideal Restaurant** on Rue General Guerrier.

With its lack of restaurants, it is only fair that Jérémie has one of the best bakeries that I have come across in Haiti. It's opposite the St Antoine Hospital and they make bread, pizzas and cakes to order. Alternatively, turn up on Monday or Thursday and you can buy bread that has come straight out of the oven. If there is no one at the bakery, knock on the house with green shutters on the other side of the road.

Nightlife and entertainment

Nightlife in Jérémie is restricted by the shortage of electricity. The town is lucky if it gets power two days a week; and during the embargo it didn't get any at all. Head to the Foyer Cultural to let your hair down in the evening. They have the occasional live performance in their 500-seat theatre, and at other times a huge movie screen is lowered over the stage and films are shown.

Tourist information

The **post office** and the **police station** are both on Rue Hippolite, not far from the fishermen's jetty. The **Teleco** office is in Place des Trois Dumas, as are a number of **pharmacies**. There is a **bank** (Banque National de Crédit) on Rue D Martineau.

Orientation and what to see

The majority of the hotels in Jérémie (that is to say two) are on a hill overlooking the town in an area known as **Bordes**. To get to the centre, walk down the hill past St Antoine Hospital, the cemetery and Alliance Française and you'll eventually come to Rue Brice Aine. If you take the first turning on the left and continue along Rue Abbée Huet, you'll notice a modern-looking, pink building, the **Foyer Cultural**. Amongst other things, the Foyer Cultural has exhibitions of Haitian arts and crafts and an excellent library with a few books in English. The second turning on the left off Rue Brice Aine leads to the town's main square, Place des Trois Dumas. The first Dumas refers to General Alexandre Dumas, the French mulatto general who was born in Jérémie. The second is his son, Alexandre Dumas the Elder, author of *The Count of Monte Cristo*, and the third is his grandson, Alexandre Dumas the Younger, author of *The Lady of the Camelias*.

The cathedral is on one side of the square and opposite it a sign with iron lettering announces: 'Jérémie la Cité des Poèts'. On the other side of the square is the **market**, which extends down towards the sea, where there are two small jetties. The main one is the **wharf** at the end of Rue D Martineau, and the smaller, busier one, where fishing boats are built and repaired, is at the end of Rue N Alexis. The waters around Jérémie are rough, and waves crash against the shore, unlike the calm sea around Les Cayes on the Caribbean side of the peninsula.

The town's Grand Rue, Stenio Vincent, runs along the coast. If you follow it south, it leads away from the sea up into the hills, on the way to Les Cayes and Port-au-Prince. The other road out of Jérémie is Rue Alain Clairier, which leads to the beach at Anse d'Azur and the airport.

Excursions from Jérémie
Beaches
Jérémie is very proud of its beach at **Anse d'Azur**, about five miles out of town, and it's easy enough to get there on a motorbike from Grand Rue. Less accessible are the beaches further along the coast at **Anse du Clerc** and **Abricot**. Try arranging a lift, hitchhiking or hiring your own vehicle. The road, it goes without saying, is not all that good. Rumour has it that a hotel is going to open in Anse du Clerc, so watch this space.

Latibolière: birthplace of Dumas
Latibolière is where Jérémie's most famous son, General Alexandre Dumas, was born. There is not much to see at the old plantation house known as *L'Habitation Madère*, but if you want to go, make your way to the crossroads for Port-au-Prince, ignore the turning for the capital, and continue down the other road for about 30 minutes. Once again, a motorbike on Grand Rue might be persuaded to take you for the right price.

EAST AND WEST OF JÉRÉMIE
Between Jérémie and Beaumont another road goes east to the towns of **Corail** and **Pestel**. There is a French fort near Pestel and the town itself is the jumping-off point for the island of Grande Cayemite.

Apart from the coastal road to Anse d'Azur, another route west of Jérémie cuts inland and leads to **Dame Marie** on the tip of the peninsula. *Tap-taps* are inconsistent and you might have to arrange a ride yourself. Alternatively, you could try hiring a boat in Jérémie or Port Salut on the southern coast of the peninsula. If you can get to Dame Marie, you'll have arrived in Haiti's richest and most fertile land. For instance, this is one of the few places in the country where mahogany reserves can still be found. As things stand, Dame Marie's nearest hotel is in Jérémie.

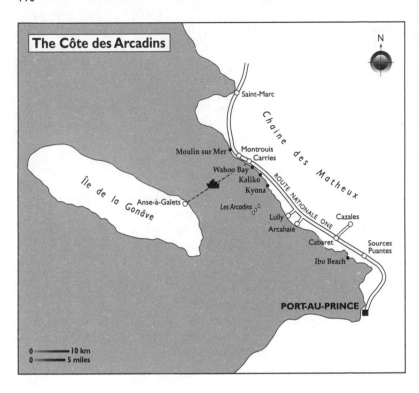

The Côte des Arcadins

The Côtes des Arcadins

The area known as the Côte des Arcadins stretches from
Sources Puantes to the town of Saint-Marc on the fringe of
the Artibonite Valley. The coast is on one side and the
mountain range called the Chaîne des Matheux is on
the other. While the area around Cabaret is a fertile,
well-irrigated plain, where plantains, bananas,
tomatoes and other vegetables are produced, the rest of
the region consists of arid, deforested foothills and low-lying mountains. The
Côte des Arcadins, along with Cap-Haïtien and Jacmel, is being targeted as an
area for tourist development. Much work has still to be done and at the
moment only really the coastal attractions have been set up for tourists. Several
beach resorts offer all-inclusive packages, watersports and excursions to the
island of La Gonâve, the three islets called Les Arcadins and the surrounding
mountains.

CABARET

The first town of any note along Route Nationale One and the largest town
on the Côte des Arcadins is Cabaret, once called Duvalierville. This
nondescript place is Papa Doc's legacy to Haiti. Graham Greene described
Duvalierville in *The Comedians* – not much has changed.

> 'On the flat shoddy plain between the hills and the sea a few white
> one-room boxes had been constructed, which among the small
> houses looked almost as impressive as the Coliseum. They stood
> together in a bowl of dust ...'

The cockfighting pit is still the main landmark of the town. In its day it was
obviously meant to be a futuristic piece of architecture: now, however, it looks
incongruous and rather pathetic.

There is one hotel in Cabaret, the **Innovation**, almost opposite the Texaco
service station on the approach to town from Port-au-Prince. The Innovation,
as much as the cockfighting pit, sums up the town, with lots of rooms, a
swimming pool, a large dance floor and even slot machines in the bar – but no
guests. It waits patiently for the time when Cabaret turns into the gleaming
metropolis it was once intended to be. Rooms cost H$40. There are one or
two restaurants, such as **Paradis Bar Restaurant** next to the cinema in the
town square and the **Yolly Restaurant** opposite the Innovation.

In the mountains behind Cabaret is a small town called **Cazales**, famous for its community of Haitians of **Polish** descent. In the summer of 1803, over 2,500 Poles sailed to Saint Domingue to help the French expeditionary force restore slavery in the colony. This was on the understanding that Napoleon would then restore independence to Poland, which at that time was a protectorate of Prussia and France. After the French were defeated and independence had been declared, Dessalines allowed the small number of Poles that remained (many had been killed by yellow fever) to stay in Haiti, provided that they lived as 'blacks'. They were granted the right to own property in Cazales, where their descendants survive to this day.

Cabaret is not automatically a place where you would consider staying for any length of time, however it could serve as a base from where to visit the beaches on the Côte des Arcadins, since the Innovation Hotel is considerably cheaper than the resort hotels along the coast.

BEACH RESORTS

There are about 800 beach hotel rooms in Haiti, and around 80% of these are on the Côte des Arcadins. This is Haiti's foray into the all-inclusive tourism so popular in the Dominican Republic. To stay at these resorts will cost in excess of US$50 a night, so what a lot of people do is visit the beaches for the day. Most of them can be reached from Port-au-Prince in an hour or two, depending on the traffic and whether or not you have your own transport. You pay a daily charge (usually about US$10) to use the beach and hotel facilities. Sometimes this amount is deducted from your bill should you decide to eat at the hotel restaurant. The resorts themselves are all pretty similar – good-quality accommodation with bars, restaurants, swimming pools and various excursions, primarily to the islands in the Gulf of Gonâve.

Ibo Beach is one of the oldest resorts on the Côte des Arcadins, situated just before Cabaret on the northern side of the Bay of Port-au-Prince. **Kyona Beach** (tel: 22 6788), **Kaliko Beach** (tel: 22 8047) and **Wahoo Bay** (tel: 23 2950) are all between the fishing village of Luly and the town of Montrouis.

Moulin Sur Mer (tel: 22 1918), north of Montrouis, is one of the best resorts along the Côte des Arcadins. The hotel itself is a cluster of apartments set in lush gardens just behind the beach, but what sets Moulin Sur Mer apart from the other developments on the Côte des Arcadins is the **Colonial Museum** at the entrance to the resort. There are so few museums in Haiti that I have to be careful not to over-exaggerate the merits of this one, but it is good. It contains a small yet well-chosen selection of artefacts, weapons and daily utensils from the colonial period, and its centrepiece is a large model of a plantation. The entrance fee is US$2 and cassettes are available to guide you around the displays. There is a **Club Med** (tel:78 6096) 5km north of Montrouis, where the lifestyle is luxurious and any integration with the world outside the gates is positively discouraged. Don't waste your time.

ÎLE DE LA GONÂVE

The island of La Gonâve, the largest of Haiti's off-shore islands, lies in the middle of the Gulf of Gonâve like a beached whale, and is about the same size as Martinique. Port-au-Prince is about 50km away and due south are the Rochelois Banks, the coral reef where the ghost-ship *Marie Celeste* foundered in January 1885. The island is densely populated, but thinly forested, and most of the mountains in the middle of the island, some of them rising to heights of about 750m, are bare. Conditions are primitive and the people often have to contend with long periods of drought. La Gonâve's '15 minutes of fame' came during the US occupation in the 1920s when a Polish-American Marine Sergeant, Faustin Wirkus, was appointed civil administrator of the island. Wirkus was so loved by the people that, believing he was the reincarnated spirit of Faustin Soulouque, they literally crowned him their king. In 1931 King Faustin published his memoires, *The White King of La Gonâve*, in which he describes how the islanders revered him like a god.

Getting to La Gonâve is hard work (as is finding a place to stay), but it is possible to get to Anse-à-Galets, the island's main settlement, by public ferry. It used to leave from Montrouis, but when an overloaded boat capsized in September 1997 the authorities were convinced that it was no longer safe to leave from Montrouis. Now, equally overloaded ferries leave from Carries, near Wahoo Beach. Boats depart at 10.00 and 11.00, but I must warn you that these times and the departure point are, to say the least, capricious. The crossing takes between one and two hours. Of course, if there is a group of you, it might make more sense to hire a boat. There are plenty of fishermen in Montrouis who are open to offers.

Hotels have not yet come to La Gonâve. Therefore, if you want to stay overnight, you'll have to depend on the hospitality of the locals. Always offer to pay a fair price for a bed for the night.

LES ARCADINS

The first of the three islands known collectively as Les Arcadins is **Ti Teal** or North Island, which lies about 7km southwest of Kaliko Beach. Further south are Lighthouse Island and South Island. All three are surrounded by extensive coral reefs, have excellent water transparency and a diverse underwater life. No surprise then that Les Arcadins is a good place to go diving. Moreover, some deep-water habitats have apparently replicated in the shallow waters of these reefs, making it possible to see deep-water species in a shallow-water environment.

If you want to do some diving, or simply take a look at these islands, it is best to enquire at the resorts along the coast. Practically all of them run excursions and one of the best is from Moulin Sur Mer.

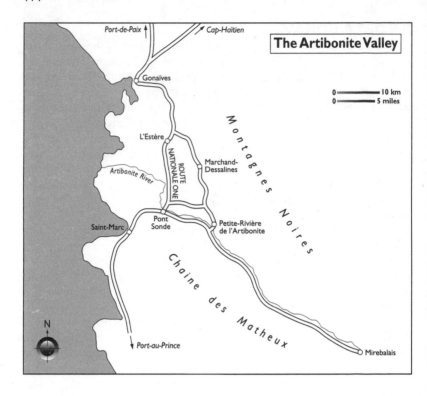

The Artibonite Valley

Port-de-Paix

Cap-Haïtien

Gonaïves

0 — 10 km
0 — 5 miles

L'Estère

Marchand-
Dessalines

Artibonite River

ROUTE NATIONALE ONE

M o n t a g n e s   N o i r e s

Saint-Marc

Pont
Sonde

Petite-Rivière
de l'Artibonite

C h a i n e   d e s   M a t h e u x

N

Port-au-Prince

Mirebalais

Haiti ground or rhinoceros iguana

The Artibonite Valley

The Artibonite Valley is one of the most fertile regions in the country. Irrigated by the Artibonite River, rice paddies are as common as coffee plantations in the heart of the valley, which is abutted on one side by the Chaîne des Matheux and on the other by the Montagnes Noires. However, the further you get from the Artibonite River, the more arid the landscape becomes. From rice paddies close to the river, cactus and thorny bush characterise the approach to Gonaïves.

SAINT-MARC

Often overlooked by tourists, Saint-Marc is a pleasant, relaxed and unassuming place with an interesting past. In 1779 the town provided most of the soldiers who went over to Savannah to fight for American independence. Among them was the 12-year-old Henri Christophe (see page 39). Ironically, during Haiti's own struggle for independence in 1802, Dessalines set fire to Saint-Marc and used the stones of its ruins to build Marchand-Dessalines (see page 116). As a colonial town, Saint-Marc enjoyed a prosperity that made it the second port of Saint Domingue, and today it continues to make a healthy contribution to the country's economy. Some of Haiti's best coffee, corn and peanut butter comes from Saint-Marc and its sugarcane mills produce syrup and *clairin* (see Chapter 4, Food and drink).

Getting there and away

Tap-taps originate in Saint-Marc for Port-au-Prince and L'Estère, the last major town before Gonaïves. The departure point is at the corner of Rue Pierre Pinchinat and Rue Geffrard in the market. To reach Port-au-Prince takes about 1½ hours and costs H$3. If you want to go to Gonaïves, you'll have to change at L'Estère.

Where to stay and eat

Saint-Marc has three hotels worth considering – one in the centre, one on the northern edge and one on the southern edge. The most central is the **Belfort Hotel**, on Rue Louverture three blocks from the main square. They have satisfactory rooms for H$40 (H$30 if you share a bathroom). **La Gou-T Hotel** (tel: 79 1497) is a 15-minute walk from the centre along the road to

Gonaïves. Opposite a lard factory, the quality and price is similar to the Belfort Hotel, although here they are friendlier. La Gou-T is also the most popular disco in town. At the other end of Saint-Marc you'll see billboards advertising **Hotel La Plage** as you drive in from Port-au-Prince. This hotel is on the beach and is more expensive than the other two.

The range of restaurants on offer is reasonable. On the main square the **Venus Restaurant** serves chicken and lobster in spacious surroundings with views of the sea. Bouillon is occasionally served at **La Détente Rose** on Rue Louverture near the Belfort Hotel, while **La Modeste Record Store**, on Rue Pierre Pinchinat in the market area, has a sideline in good-value Creole food. There is also a restaurant at **La Gou-T Hotel**.

Tourist information
The **post office** and one of the town's two **banks** (Banque National de Crédit) are on the main square. There is also a Socabank just off the main square on Rue Christophe. If both of these banks are closed, the Patou Store, next to Banque Nationale de Crédit will change money. The **Sunny Cinema** is next to Socabank.

BETWEEN SAINT-MARC AND GONAÏVES
Continuing north from Saint-Marc, Route Nationale One cuts through the heart of the Artibonite delta. Just north of **Pont Sonde** – where there is a large market twice a week on and around the bridge crossing the Artibonite River – are rice paddies.

If you turn off Route Nationale One at Pont Sonde, a bumpy, dirt road leads to the town of **Petite Rivière de l'Artibonite**. During market days (Wednesdays and Saturdays) *tap-taps* run from Pont Sonde. At other times you'll have to go to Carrefour Paille, just north of Pont Sonde on Route Nationale One, if you want to take public transport to Petit Rivière de l'Artibonite. Once there, there is a palace and a fort to inspect. The **Palace of 365 Doors** was one of Henri Christophe's provincial headquarters, and now serves as the town hall. To get there walk up the hill from the main square. Further up the hill are the ruins of **Crète-à-Pierrot Fort**. Although there is virtually nothing left, the views of the Artibonite River and the historical significance of the site make the hike up the hill worthwhile. It was here, in March 1802, that Dessalines' army was put under siege for 20 days by French forces led by Leclerc in one of the defining moments of the War of Independence.

Marchand Dessalines is north of Petit Rivière de l'Artibonite on a dirt path that joins Route Nationale One near L'Estère. There is not much to see here now; but in 1804, when Dessalines declared it the nation's capital, Marchand-Dessalines was defended by no less than five forts.

GONAÏVES
Gonaïves will always have a special spot in Haitian hearts as the place where, on January 1 1804, Dessalines declared the nation's independence. The town

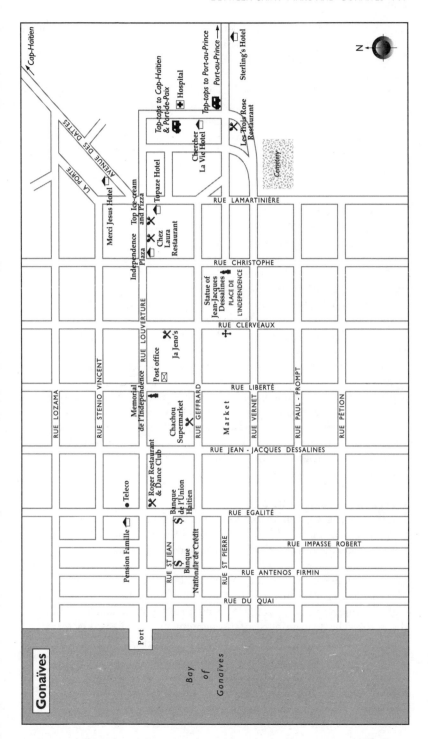

Gonaïves

has since grown to become Haiti's fourth largest conurbation, with a population of nearly 130,000. There is also a busy port which, along with those at Saint-Marc, Miragoâne, Petit-Goâve and Môle Saint-Nicolas, thrives on contraband.

More recently, Gonaïves played its part in liberating Haiti of another great evil – riots here in 1984 and 1985 sparked the series of events which led to the departure of Baby Doc and the downfall of Duvalierism.

Whether or not you like Gonaïves will probably depend on how impressed you are with towns possessing great historical resonance, but not much else besides. Gonaïves has been described as 'the ugliest place in the Antilles' and, while I can think of much uglier places, the town itself is no beauty.

Getting there and away

Gonaïves has plenty of *tap-taps* going south to Port-au-Prince and north to Cap Haïtien. American-style school buses do the trip to Port-au-Prince. They leave from next to the Texaco service station on the road leading up to the statue of Dessalines in the Place de l'Indépendence. The journey takes about two hours and costs H$5.

Pick-up trucks ply the route to Cap-Haïtien. They leave from near the hospital, not far from the Port-au-Prince departure point, and also cost H$5. Count on three hours for this trip, which involves crossing the mountains of northern Haiti.

You can also travel direct to Port-de-Paix from Gonaïves. However, you should prepare yourself for six uncomfortable and frustrating hours on a *camion* full of people transporting their worldly possessions to various villages and hamlets in the mountains. It would probably be better to do the journey in small digestible chunks via a pick-up to Gros-Morne, another one to Bassin Bleu, then a third to Port-de-Paix. This could reduce the trip by two hours. In any case, all *tap-taps* going in the direction of Port-de-Paix leave from the same place as those to Cap-Haïtien.

Orientation and what to see

Route Nationale One enters and leaves Gonaïves from the east of town. This is also where the Place de l'Indépendence is situated. Gonaïves Bay, a relatively busy port and the market are all due west of the main square.

The main sight in Gonaïves is unquestionably the **Place de l'Indépendence** or, to give it its full name, Place Dâme de Gonaïves Cité de l'Indépendence. A **monument to Dessalines** in the form of a ship's prow with the emperor at the helm and his army stretched out behind him dominates the square. The dramatic effect of this monument is emphasised by the lack of people milling around the square itself. This is perhaps an indication of the reverence given to the place where the emancipation of the Haitian people was declared. Also on the square is the town's futuristic **cathedral**. On Rue Liberté is the **Memorial de l'Indépendence** – a plaque on the wall outside contains some of the text of the Act of Independence, but inside there is nothing much to see. In any case, the caretaker is rarely there to let you in.

Gonaïves' other main attraction is its **port**. You can walk right down to the quay where ships from Belize, Honduras, New York and Miami can be seen unloading their cargo. For a moment you could be in any busy port in the West Indies. Then you see the shipwrecks in Gonaïves Bay and you know you're in Haiti.

Where to stay
The most expensive hotel in Gonaïves is **Sterling's Hotel** (tel: 74 1324), located a little out of town on the road to Port-au-Prince. It has air-conditioned rooms for H$100 per person and caters mainly for the international aid and peace-keeping organisations. The **Independence Plaza** (tel: 74 0207), on Rue Louverture in the centre of town, also has its fair share of aid workers and United Nations, but it's cheaper and better situated than Sterling's Hotel. A room with two beds, a fan and bathroom costs H$40, and free coffee is served in your room – at 06.00! The guesthouse is above a small grocery store, also called Independence Plaza. Just around the corner on Rue Lamartinière is the **Topaze Hotel** (tel: 74 0930) with slightly poorer rooms for H$30 and H$20. **Pension Famille** (tel: 74 0318), opposite Teleco on Rue Égalité, offers basic accommodation for H$25. There is no sign, so look for a set of large brown doors and you'll see the hotel behind them. The **Merci Jesus Hotel** on Avenue des Dattes is not good value at H$40 for a single and H$60 for a double; and the **Chercher La Vie Hotel** on the road where *tap-taps* leave for Cap-Haïtien offers little more than a roof over your head.

Where to eat
The **Independence Plaza** has a restaurant at the back of the grocery store serving standard Haitian dishes, and the Topaze Hotel offers **Ricky's Restaurant**. Elsewhere the choices are limited. **Les Trois Rose Restaurant**, opposite the *tap-tap* station for Port-au-Prince, looks worth a try, while the **Roger Restaurant and Dance Club**, on the corner of Rue Louverture and Égalité, rarely has more than chicken or goat. **Ja Jeno's** on Rue Clerveux is another general convenience store with a restaurant at the back. For unpretentious dining try the **Chez Laura Restaurant**, a tiny place squeezed into a gap between two buildings on Rue Louverture, near the Independence Plaza. Although the corrugated iron roof lets in the rain, the décor here would not be out of place in a café in Paris or Brussels. At Chez Laura, of course, thousands have probably not been spent on interior design. You should try their *diri kole* (beans and rice).

For generous helpings of good-quality ice-cream you should go to **Top Ice Cream and Pizza** on Rue Louverture next to Chez Laura. On the same subject, Haagen-Dazs is sold at the **Chachou Supermarket** on Rue Fabre Geffrard.

Nightlife and entertainment
Check the billboards around the Place de l'Indépendence for details of bands playing in Gonaïves. **Alliance Française** also has cultural evenings of dance,

music and cinema. Quite recent films dubbed into French are shown on a reasonably sized screen at the ubiquitous **Independence Plaza** for a small charge. They even sell popcorn in the grocery store next door.

Tourist information

The **post office** is on Rue Liberté opposite the Memorial de l'Indépendence. The **Teleco** office is on Rue Égalité – look for the satellite dishes. For **banks**, Banque de l'Union Haïtien and Banque Nationale de Crédit both have branches in Gonaïves. The former is on the corner of Rue Égalité and St Jean, while the latter is on the corner of Rue Antenos Firmin and St Jean. The **police station** is opposite the Topaze Hotel on Rue Lamartiniere and there is a good **pharmacy** at the Chachou Supermarket.

The North

Apart from the fertile Plaine du Nord around Cap-Haïtien –
the 'bread basket' of Saint Domingue in colonial times –
the land in the north of Haiti is generally poorer than in the
south. There used to be great sisal plantations around
Fort Liberté, but now all that has gone and the
northeast is almost as barren as the remote
northwestern peninsula. Historically, however, all the
great rebellions and periods of resistance to oppression have taken place in the
north. This manifests itself in forts and palaces – most notably the Sans-Souci
Palace and the Citadelle La Ferrière. You might also detect a difference in the
people. Pride is everywhere in Haiti, but it seems to be more intense and
pronounced in the north.

CAP-HAÏTIEN

The origins of Cap-Haïtien can be traced to 1670 when it was a small hamlet
called Bas-du-Cap. In 1711, the town was declared a French possession in the
New World by royal decree and renamed Cap-Français. At the start of the 18th
century, plantations were starting to appear in the fertile Plaine du Nord, and the
port at Cap-Français was used as the major outlet for the huge quantities of sugar
sent to Europe during the colonial period. As the 18th century progressed, the
Cap became the most important port in the West Indies, reaching its peak in the
1780s. After independence in 1804, Cap-Français was renamed Cap-Haïtien,
and despite the change of name the town continued to prosper, although local
oligarchies and private landowners began to administer the production and sale
of the region's produce. Coffee and wood became the principal exports.

The Cap also gained military importance due to a combination of its strategic
position and fears of a French invasion, but all this came to an abrupt end in 1842
when an earthquake levelled the town. For the next 30 years Cap-Haïtien
stagnated, and only started to get back on its feet in the second half of the 19th
century, when it started to trade seriously in cotton to meet the world demand
created by the American Civil War. Nevertheless, it never regained the
importance it enjoyed during the 18th century. Port-au-Prince was now firmly
entrenched as the country's economic and political centre, and at the start of the
century powers were centralised further in the capital, a process completed
during the US occupation from 1915 to 1934. Furthermore, regional armies were
abolished and taxes levied in Cap-Haïtien went straight to Port-au-Prince.

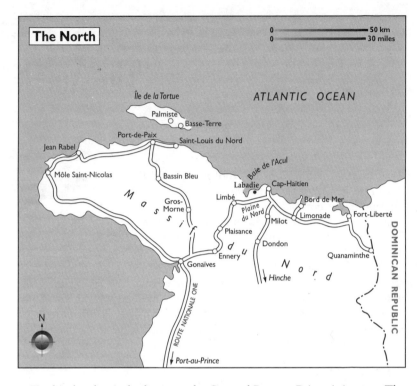

To this day the rivalry between the Cap and Port-au-Prince is intense. The Cap is fiercely jealous of the independence it fought so hard to win from the colonists and will not give it up lightly to Port-au-Prince. A recent example of the town's present-day struggle for independence saw certain members of the National Chamber of Commerce resign, protesting that it was effectively a chamber of commerce for Port-au-Prince. The dissidents, coming mainly from the Cap, have set up an independent Cap-Haïtien Chamber of Commerce.

Getting there and away
By air
Caribintair (tel: 62 2300) have two flights a day to Port-au-Prince. The first departs at 09.35 and the second at 14.35. It takes 40 minutes and costs US$40 single, US$ 70 return.

Cap-Haïtien International Airport (tel: 62 0844) is about 2km south of town. A taxi will cost H$10. Alternatively, many *tap-taps* go past the turning for the airport. Facilities are limited to a small café and a number of airline stands that are usually unmanned.

By road
For destinations south on **Route Nationale One**, *tap-taps* leave from Barrière Bouteille. The run to Port-au-Prince normally takes about five hours and

costs H$20. If you want to go to Port-de-Paix, take a *tap-tap* to Gonaïves and change there.

The other road south, known officially as **Route Nationale Three**, goes through the remote Central Plateau. The route is paved until the town of Dondon, then gets progressively worse as you approach Hinche. *Tap-taps* for Dondon, from where you can continue your journey to Hinche, leave from the end of Rue 2 on the other side of a footbridge known as Pont Neuf.

This is also the departure point for Milot (45 minutes, H$1), Fort Liberté (two hours, H$3) and Quanaminthe on the Dominican border (three hours, H$3). Only one *tap-tap* a day goes direct to Fort Liberté, but many go to Quanaminthe, passing the turning for Fort Liberté en route.

Where to stay

Cap-Haïtien has the finest selection of hotels in Haiti outside of Pétion-Ville. The best is **Hotel Mont Joli** (tel: 62 0300) up the hill on Rue B. The rooms and service are first-rate, as are the panoramic views of the Bay of Cap-Haïtien and the mountains (on a clear day you can see the Citadelle). The manager of the Mont Joli is a dynamic young man with a real passion for Haiti. He talks with enthusiasm about the independent travellers who stay at his hotel and take the time to see a bit more of his country than the package tourists who filter through on two-day excursions from Puerto Plata. Back down the hill on Rue 24 B, **Hostellerie Roi Christophe** (tel: 62 0414) is a good alternative. Built in

CAP-HAÏTIEN: 'PARIS OF THE ANTILLES'

In its heyday Cap-Haïtien was referred to as the 'Paris of the Antilles', and was famous for its beautiful architecture, mostly in the neo-Classical style, introduced by the French and continued by Henri Christophe following independence. After an earthquake destroyed most of the town in 1842, the new Haitian bourgeoisie introduced a different style of architecture known as the *architecture domestique*. Houses were no longer statements of wealth and grandeur, but simply places to live. Austere façades and large courtyards were out, while small balconies and front gardens were in. During the US occupation, yet another architectural style appeared in the form of 'gingerbread' houses built of wood in the Victorian-American style of the 19th century. Cap-Haïtien became a mixture, where the different styles didn't really complement each other, but the overall effect was charming. Nowadays things have changed. The Cap, in common with other large towns in Haiti, is overcrowded. People need somewhere to live and are not particularly concerned about the beauty of the building, so long as it keeps the rain out. Unfortunately, modern-day architecture, with its lack of uniformity and aestheticism, is gradually encroaching on the older buildings in the Cap, until one day nothing will be left to remind us that once this town was the 'Paris of the Antilles'.

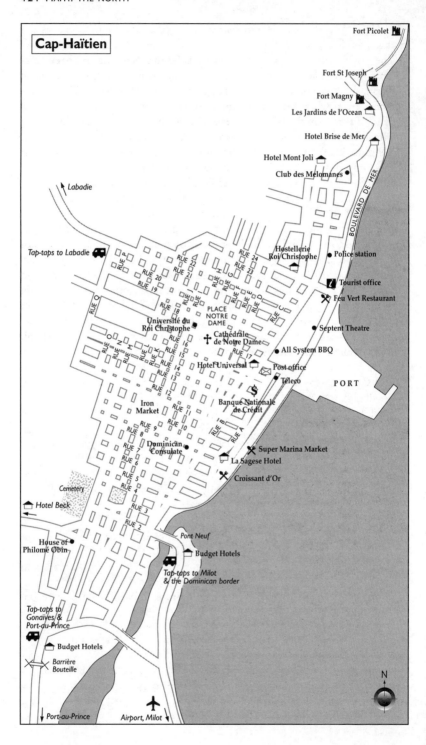

Cap-Haïtien

Fort Picolet

Fort St Joseph

Fort Magny

Les Jardins de l'Ocean

Hotel Brise de Mer

Hotel Mont Joli
Club des Mélomanes

Labadie

BOULEVARD DE MER

Tap-taps to Labadie

RUE P
RUE 22
RUE 21
RUE 24
RUE 23
RUE 20
RUE 19
RUE 18

Hostellerie
Roi Christophe

Police station

Tourist office
Feu Vert Restaurant

RUE Q
RUE H
RUE G
RUE F
RUE E
RUE D
RUE C

PLACE
NOTRE
DAME

Université du
Roi Christophe
RUE 16

Cathédrale
de Notre Dame
RUE 17

Septent Theatre

All System BBQ

RUE O
RUE N
RUE M
RUE L
RUE K
RUE J
RUE 15
RUE 14
RUE 13

Hotel Universal

Post office
Teleco

PORT

RUE 12
RUE 11

Banque Nationale
de Crédit

Iron
Market
RUE 9
RUE 10

RUE B
RUE A

RUE 8
RUE 7
RUE 6

Dominican
Consulate

Super Marina Market
La Sagese Hotel

Cemetery
RUE 5
RUE 4

Croissant d'Or

Hotel Beck
RUE 3
RUE 2

House of
Philomé Obin

Pont Neuf

Budget Hotels

Tap-taps to Milot
& the Dominican border

Tap-taps to
Gonaïves &
Port-au-Prince

Budget Hotels

Barrière
Bouteille

N

Port-au-Prince

Airport, Milot

1724 as the French Governor's palace, the house has retained its colonial character, with period furniture, a lush tropical garden and a plantation-type front porch. The third hotel in the same class as the above is **Hotel Cormier Plage** (tel: 62 0119) at Cormier Beach (see *Excursions from Cap-Haïtien* on page 128). Room rates at all of these hotels start at about US$50.

There are also some other very good places to stay in Cap-Haïtien. One of my favourites is **Les Jardins de l'Ocean** (tel: 62 2277) at the end of Boulevard de Mer. The rooms are nicely decorated and start from H$90. There are also views of the sea from the hotel's restaurant. Next to Les Jardins is **Hotel Brise de Mer** (tel: 62 0821), where the main selling point is that they have rooms for three or four people (H$264 and H$330 respectively), including breakfast and dinner. As you enter town you'll see signs for **Hotel Beck** (tel: 62 0001). This German-run hotel is in a park surrounded by trees in Bel Air. To get there from the centre of town, walk to the end of Rue 2, cross Rue L and continue up the road to the left of the cemetery. Rooms start at about US$35.

While the more luxurious hotels in Cap-Haïtien are generally good value, the budget options are disappointing. Leading the field is the **Bon Dieu Bon Hotel** (tel: 62 0740). Prices range from H$20 to H$50, with the better rooms offering air conditioning and TV. There is, of course, often no current. The Bon Dieu Bon is one of a cluster of hotels on the other side of Pont Neuf where *tap-taps* leave for Milot, Fort Liberté and Quanaminthe. These include **Hotel Peuple** and the **Bon Berger Hotel**, neither of which is as good as the Bon Dieu Bon. Barrière Bouteille is another place to look for budget hotels. **Le Flambeau** and **Hotel Chou Chou** are both very basic, charging H$20 for a single and H$40 for a double. The most centrally located hotel in Cap-Haïtien is the local brothel, **Hotel Universal** (tel: 62 0254), which is very close to the cathedral on Rue 17 B. I had been staying there two days before I noticed, with some shock, the mirror on the ceiling. The cheapest bed for the *whole* night is H$40. The hotel has its own generator, so there's usually electricity in the evenings. **La Sagese Hotel** (tel: 62 2116) on Rue 9 A is another house of ill repute. It charges roughly the same as Hotel Universal, but it's much more sleazy.

Beyond Barrière Bouteille

There are several hotels beyond Barrière Bouteille, but most are a little too far from town to be practical. **Hotel Imperial** (tel: 62 0171) and the **St Philomene Hotel** are in the Philomene district, while **Le Voyageur Hotel** (tel: 62 1009) and **La Fonda Hotel** (tel: 62 1372) are further out in Vertières. The one place I would consider is **Hotel Congo** (tel: 62 0434), just beyond Barrière Bouteille, where the H$30 rooms are clean and simple and the two young boys who seem to run the place are real entrepreneurs.

Where to eat

Most of the main hotels have good restaurants. **Les Jardins de l'Ocean** is noted for its excellent French cuisine and pizzas; the pumpkin soup at the **Mont Joli** has won awards; and many rate the seafood at **Hotel Cromier Plage** as the best in Cap-Haïtien. Good food can also be found at the **Roi**

Christophe, and **Hotel Universal** has a noisy restaurant serving Creole food.

Away from the hotels you have to look hard for a decent place to eat. The **Feu Vert Restaurant** on the corner of Boulevard de Mer and Rue 24 has a reasonable reputation and their spaghetti with *ti malice* sauce is quite good. For dessert or a mid-afternoon refresher, ice-cream is sold at one or two kiosks in Place Notre Dame.

The best place for grocery shopping is the **Super Marina Market** on Boulevard de Mer by the port. Nearby on Rue 8, an excellent bakery called **Croissant d'Or** serves freshly baked bread, croissants and pastries from 06.30 to 22.00.

Nightlife and entertainment

The best entertainment available in Cap-Haïtien centres around **music**. The town's two most famous orchestras – Septentrional and Tropicana – both have venues where they perform on various nights. Septentrional play at the **Septent Theatre** on Boulevard de Mer, while Tropicana play at the **Tropicana Nightclub**. If your visit coincides with a performance by either of these groups, fight tooth and nail to get a ticket.

A short distance beyond Barrière Bouteille is the **Caribbean Disco**. Locals boast that this is the largest disco in the West Indies and they may well be right. It's as gaudy as many of the discos in the Dominican Republic and only open at weekends. A similar experience on a lesser scale is available in the centre of town at **Club des Melomanes** (Rue 29). They play the music so loud here that the Mont Joli Hotel, some way up the hill, frequently complains. The **All System BBQ** on Rue 18 A is more a bar than a disco. Most of the tables are out in the street and the atmosphere is relaxed and easy-going.

Tourist information
Tourist office

Just before entering Cap-Haïtien, a sign at Barrière Bouteille announces the town as a 'Ville Touristique'. In accordance with this title, a tourist office can be found at the corner of Boulevard de Mer and Rue 24. However, it only tends to be open on the rare occasions when a cruise ship drops anchor at Cap-Haïtien. At other times you could try telephoning the man in charge, Monsieur Edwin Joseph on 62 1061. There is also a **tour company** called Voyage Plus on Rue 11 A. This is effectively a branch of Agence Citadelle in Port-au-Prince and all tours are arranged through them.

Communications and media

The **post office** is on Rue A between rues 16 and 17. Behind it, on an unmarked road between Rue A and Boulevard de Mer, is the **Teleco** office. The local **newspaper** is called *Cap Express* and the articles are mostly in French. There is a good **bookshop** on Rue A between rues 11 and 12 called Panoramix. They have a few books on Haiti in English and magazines like *Time* and *Newsweek*. The ubiquitous Alliance Française, with its library of French books and magazines, is on Rue B between rues 16 and 17.

Money
The major **banks** are all near the post and Teleco offices. These include Banque Nationale de Crédit and Banque de l'Union Haitienne.

Photography
Cap-Haïtien is a good place to stock up on film for your camera. Both the Super Marina Market and Panoramix bookshop stock Kodak and Fuji film.

Health and safety
Finding a **pharmacy** is not a problem in Cap-Haïtien. Also, due to the relatively high number of foreigners in town, **English-speaking doctors** are not impossible to find. Clinica Rosa Cruz (tel: 62 0740), for example, does a lot of work for the Mont Joli Hotel. Go to Rue A between rues 28 and 29. The **police station** is on Rue B just before the hill up to the Mont Joli.

Dominican consulate
The Dominican Republic has a consulate on Rue 8 E which opens at 10.00. If you want a Tourist Card, don't queue (not the most accurate word) with the crowd of Haitians applying for visas at the front gate, but go to the entrance on Rue E where you'll be let into the consulate itself. Be warned, however, that a Tourist Card here costs US$15, as opposed to the US$10 charge at Dajabón.

Orientation and what to see
Cap-Haïtien is probably the easiest town in Haiti to find your way around. The streets cross at right angles, with those running north to south given letters, and those from east to west numbers. Therefore, an address given as Rue 17 B means Rue 17 where it intersects with Rue B.

Route Nationale One terminates at **Barrière Bouteille** – three yellow sentry boxes which mark the formal entrance to the town of Cap-Haïtien.

Although the Cap is the second town of Haiti, I found it to be one of the most relaxing to walk around. In fact, for a town with a population of over 100,000, it's eerily quiet. The diverse range of **architecture** is the Cap's major attraction (see box *Paris of the Antilles* on page 123). Other features of interest include the town's famous central square and a fort overlooking the bay. The general liberation of the slaves was proclaimed on August 29 1793 in **Place Notre Dame**, formerly known as Place d'Armes du Cap-Français. These days it provides a good place to sit with an ice-cream and watch the world go by. The **Cathédrale de Notre Dame** was built in 1774 as the parish church of Cap-Français. Next to it, the **Université du Roi Christophe** is built on the ruins of the royal palace built by Henri Christophe. **Fort Picolet** – the best of the several forts in Cap-Haïtien – was built by the French in the 18th century as part of a defence network to protect the north coast from foreign enemies. It overlooks Cap-Haïtien Bay and the views are panoramic. It is situated at the end of Boulevard de Mer, along the coast, across a dirty beach and over some rocks. On the way to Fort Picolet you will pass two other forts, **Fort St Joseph** and **Fort Magny**, which is now just a row of five small cannons.

There is an **iron market** between rues 9 and 11 and rues I and K which sells mainly foodstuffs. Another market, selling clothes and shoes, is in Place Toussaint Louverture between rues 2 and 4 and rues I and K. This is the site of the former Royal Palace of Cap-Français. The house of **Philomé Obin**, Haiti's most famous painter, who was born in the Cap on July 20 1891, is on Rue L.

Excursions from Cap-Haïtien
Labadie
Labadie Beach and the town of the same name are west of Cap-Haïtien on the secluded Pointe Ste-Honoré. Most of the time this is a tranquil and idyllic spot with calm waters, white beaches and a backdrop of rolling hills. On Mondays, Tuesdays and Thursdays between 08.00 and 16.00, however, a cruise ship drops anchor in the small bay and Labadie is momentarily transformed into a vast pleasure playground. The bars, restaurants and gift shops open for business and Labadie could be any resort in the West Indies. If this isn't your scene, avoid these three days. At other times, you'll probably have the whole place to yourself. Entrance to Labadie costs H$6, even if nothing is open. Bring a picnic and spend the day.

Around this area there are a number of small creeks and a freshwater river that flows directly into the sea. Local fishermen will take you out to these creeks for an arranged fee. Enquire at Labadie Town.

Other places of interest
The **Baie d'Acul** is west of Cap-Haïtien and Labadie. On December 21 1492, during his first voyage to the New World, Columbus dropped anchor in this bay and gave it the name Port Saint Thomas. A few days later his flagship, the *Santa Maria*, foundered on a reef further along the coast. La Navidad, the first Spanish settlement in the New World, was built with the wreckage (see also Chapter 1, Early History). The site of La Navidad is not far from **Bord de Mer**, a fishing village near the town of **Limonade** on the road to Fort Liberté.

Dondon is the first town of any note on the road to Hinche. The town itself is nothing much, but in the area there are some interesting caves with Indian carvings. One is directly above Dondon and there's another to the west of town. As always, access is a problem.

Meanwhile, the first town of any note on Route Nationale One is **Limbé**. This is a fertile region that in colonial times had a high concentration of plantations. These days nothing much is left, but there is a small museum in Limbé containing Arawak artefacts.

Further down Route Nationale One and up into the mountains is the town of **Plaisance**. In 1802 Pétion and Dessalines met here to sign the pact uniting the mulattos and the newly liberated negroes (see page 38).

Vertières, is a suburb of Cap-Haïtien. This is where Dessalines defeated the French in the final battle of the War of Independence – the Battle of Butte Charrier. There's a memorial to the heroes of the liberation by the main road a few kilometres from Barrière Bouteille.

THE SANS-SOUCI PALACE AND CITADELLE LA FERRIÈRE

These two remarkable monuments – legacies of Henri Christophe – are unrivalled on the island of Hispaniola, and I can guarantee that you won't ever have seen anything quite like the Citadelle.

Sans-Souci Palace

When Henri Christophe proclaimed himself King of Haiti, he wanted to build a palace in a style to rival that of Versailles. The model was one of the castles of King Frederick II of Prussia and when it was completed in 1813 it was one of a kind in the West Indies. Fine paintings, tapestries, drapes and other furnishings were imported from Europe to decorate the polished mahogany walls and marble floors. The palace covered 8 hectares and included a mint, a hospital, a library and a church, not to mention the king's private rooms and royal stables where he stored his £700 English carriage. Sans-Souci was opulent, grand *and* state-of-the-art, boasting a network of conduits which carried cool mountain water under the floors to provide a rudimentary form of air conditioning, as well as bathrooms – a novelty at the time. This is where Christophe administered his kingdom and took his own life in October 1820, at which time the spirit of Sans-Souci also died. It never regained its past glories and in 1842 was destroyed by an earthquake.

Citadelle La Ferrière

Statistics alone don't convey the wonder that is the Citadelle La Ferrière; but they help. Between 1804 and 1817, 20,000 men built the largest fortress in the Caribbean on top of a mountain over 1,000m high. It occupies 30,000m^2 and can hold up to 10,000 men. Some of the walls are 14m thick. Eight massive cisterns, as well as reservoirs and catch-basins, were installed to hold the thousands of gallons of water that were needed to support a garrison that could hold a siege for a year. In addition, 365 cannons, some weighing more than 10 tons, were originally dragged up the mountain – not to mention the thousands of cannonballs. At this stage you might be asking yourself 'why?'. The answer is that the Citadelle was initially intended as a measure of safety, built in anticipation of an attack by Napoleon that never came. Gradually, however, it became the object of an ailing king's vanity.

On a hill beside the Citadelle is **Fort Ramier**. It is rumoured that Christophe's wife lived here, although most of the guides at the Citadelle will tell you this is not true.

Practicalities

Sans-Souci Palace is located in the town of Milot, at the foot of Bonnet à l'Evêque, on top of which sits the Citadelle. *Tap-taps* to Milot leave regularly from Cap-Haïtien, taking 45 minutes and costing H$1.

You will be left at the entrance to Sans-Souci, and if you're going up to the Citadelle as well, you must buy your ticket here. It costs H$5 and will be asked for either at the car park or the Citadelle itself. The car park is an hour-long walk at a steady pace up the mountain or 15 minutes by car. The footpath starts behind the ruins of Sans-Souci, while the road is to the left of the entrance. If you choose to walk, on the way up you'll be offered the option of hiring a donkey, both early on and again at the car park when you have only another 20 minutes to the Citadelle. It was hard going to walk the whole way, but when I reached the top I had a faint idea how much toil and suffering it must have taken to build what some call the 'Eighth Wonder of the World'. The Citadelle is supposed to open at 09.00, although the keys are only brought up when the first group of tourists arrives. Guides are always on hand to show you around for a small fee.

PORT-DE-PAIX

Port-de-Paix is the major town on the northwestern peninsula in one of the poorest parts of Haiti. On the drive over the mountains of the western section of the Massif du Nord, evidence of this poverty is not hard to find; whether it's building latrines in Gros Morne or regenerating the mango *fransique* around Bassin Bleu, international aid agencies are very active in the region.

Port-de-Paix itself is perhaps what you'd expect of a town in such a poor area. Most of the streets are unpaved, electricity and water are in short supply and people scratch a living in the market selling the odd banana or stick of charcoal. However, don't let me give you the impression that Port-de-Paix is primitive, because it's not. The amazing Haitian spirit is alive and well here. The town is proud of its past – Port-de-Paix became the first capital of Saint Domingue when the French seized control in 1664 – and optimistic for the future. Also, one of Haiti's best bands, the All Stars, comes from Port-de-Paix.

Getting there and away

Tap-taps leave regularly for Port-au-Prince (although not on Sundays) from Rue du Quai. Count on paying H$20 and the journey taking at least six hours. Gonaïves can be reached in about four hours if you take pick-ups via Bassin Bleu and Gros Morne. If you end up in a *camion*, brace yourself for a six-hour ride with lots of stopping and starting. Either way, it costs H$7 to Gonaïves. Pick-ups and *camions* leave from next to the Electricité d'Haiti building on Rue du Quai. You can also get a *tap-tap* to Jean Rabel (for Môle Saint-Nicolas) from the same place. The other main destination from Port-de-Paix is Saint-Louis du Nord. The departure point is on Rue Mgr Lebhain at the end of Rue Sylvain.

Where to stay

Port-de-Paix does in fact have two tourist-class hotels with air conditioning and a certain degree of comfort, but you need a car to get to them. **Le Plaza** and **Hotel Brise Marina** are both on the road to Saint-Louis du Nord. Le Plaza is the nearer of the two.

In the centre of town the choices are somewhat limited. The **Bienvenue Hotel** (tel: 68 5138), near the cathedral, has average rooms with bathroom for H$40, as does the **KAF Hotel** on Rue Estimé. Walking down Rue Geffrard,

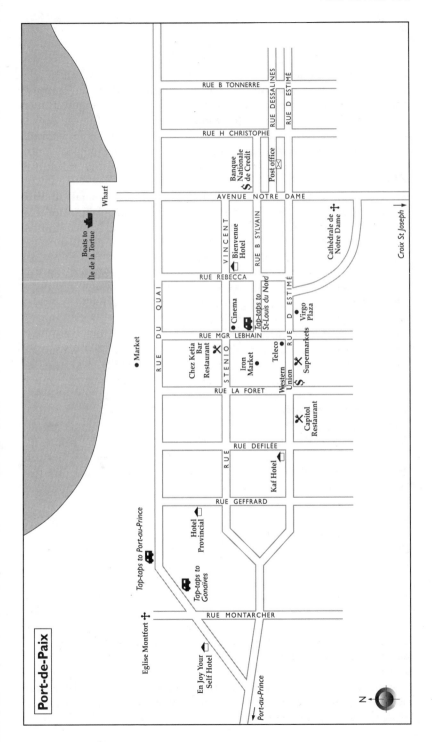

Port-de-Paix

the fluorescent-orange sign of the **Hotel Provincial** is alluring. The hotel itself rarely has electricity or running water, but the rooms are pleasant and good value at H\$20. This hotel is run by two ladies who go out of their way to make you feel comfortable. They are also devout Christians who aren't shy about asking whether or not Jesus has been accepted into your life. A negative response is like a red rag to a bull, so if you want to avoid a lengthy sermon in French, answer 'yes'. The **En Joy Your Self Hotel** is on Rue du Quai. It was probably given its name on account of the lively bar and disco on the roof, rather than the spartan rooms it rents out for the night or by the hour.

Where to eat

The **Bienvenue Hotel**, **KAF Hotel** and **Hotel Provincial** all have restaurants. It's a good idea to let them know you're coming in advance. The **Capitol Restaurant** on Rue Estimé has chicken, goat and lobster if you're lucky. Another option is **Chez Ketia Bar Restaurant** on Rue Stenio Vincent, which also has a small selection of pastries.

La **Belle Creole** and **Immaculée** are both good supermarkets on Rue Estimé opposite the iron market, and there's another one in the posh **Virgo Plaza**, also on Rue Estimé.

Nightlife and entertainment

The **All-Stars** of Port-de-Paix often play on the roof of the En Joy Your Self Hotel. Other than that, the entertainment highlight could be the cinema on the corner of Rue Stenio Vincent and Rue Mgr Lebhain.

Tourist information

The **post office** is on Rue Dessalines, a surprisingly small street off Avenue Notre Dame. **Teleco**, meanwhile, is on Rue Estimé. There is a **bank** on the same street in the Virgo Plaza (Banque l'Union Haitienne). Banque Nationale de Credit, meanwhile, is on the corner of Avenue Notre Dame and Rue Sylvain. For money transfers, a **Western Union** office can be found opposite the iron market.

Orientation and what to see

Port-de-Paix is not overloaded with things to see. The **Cathèdrale de Notre Dame** is in the main square, but the **Église Montfort**, just off Rue du Quai, with its domed roof is more interesting. The **iron market** is on Rue Estimé and an open-air market stretches along the coastal portion of Rue du Quai. This is where the **port** is situated. Whilst by no means as busy as other provincial ports such as Gonaïves or Cap-Haïtien, the port at Port-de-Paix is functional, and you get a good view of the imposing island of Tortuga from the wharf. If you walk up Avenue Notre Dame, after a few kilometres you'll arrive at **Croix St Joseph**, Port-de-Paix's equivalent of Kenscoff (see page 90). The air up here is cool and there are some good views of the coast and surrounding mountains. A short distance from Port-de-Paix there are the ruins of some **French forts**.

ÎLE DE LA TORTUE (TORTUGA)

Discovered in 1492 by Colombus, Tortuga is famous (or infamous) for being the hideout of buccaneers and filibusters in the 17th century. Under the French the island was a popular holiday resort, and in 1802 General Leclerc and his wife, Pauline Bonaparte, took refuge on Tortuga to escape the ravages of yellow fever on the mainland (a precaution which, in Leclerc's case, ultimately failed). The tourist potential of Tortuga, exploited by the colonists, has been recognised by the Secretary of State for Tourism and exciting developments lie in store. However, until the cruise ships, resort hotels and airports arrive, this island remains unspoiled. There are some lovely beaches, especially at Pointe Ouest, and Tortuga is one of the richest repositories of Arawak relics in the West Indies. The island itself is very rugged and mountainous, particularly on the Atlantic side, where people claim the coast is so precipitous that fishermen have to use ropes to get down to their boats. The main towns are **Basse-Terre**, **Cayonne** and **Palmiste**, the capital.

Getting to Tortuga is not really a problem. Boats depart in the morning from Port-de-Paix and more frequently from Saint-Louis du Nord, where the journey to Basse-Terre takes less than an hour. Staying on the island, however, poses the same problems as it does on La Gonâve and Île-à-Vache. Until the government begins to execute its plans to develop Tortuga, the island is probably best visited as a day-trip from the mainland.

WEST OF PORT-DE-PAIX

A bad road connects Port-de-Paix to the small town of Jean Rabel. Roughly halfway between the two is the **Baie des Moustiques** (Mosquito Bay). When Colombus landed here on December 7 1492, the surrounding countryside reminded him of Castille and inspired him to name the island Hispaniola (Little Spain). The previous day Columbus saw the island for the first time when he arrived at **Môle Saint-Nicolas** on the westernmost tip of the peninsula. The Môle is a rugged few hours from Jean Rabel, although you shouldn't rely on public transport, and if there's been rain, you probably won't even be able to get to Jean Rabel. The inaccessibility of Môle Saint-Nicolas is ironic, given its great strategic importance – both past and present. The ruins of French and English forts built at the end of the 18th century are evidence of the struggle between these two nations for control of the Môle and Saint Domingue. In the early 1980s, the United States bid $500m and then $780m for the Môle, which was seen as the ideal replacement for the naval base at Guantánamo. These bids were refused.

FORT-LIBERTÉ

Fort-Liberté is the most interesting town between Cap-Haïtien and the Dominican border. It also happens to be one of the sleepiest towns in Haiti, and in fact its streets are almost deserted. Quite a culture shock, although welcome, after so many crowded towns. Its other main attraction is **Fort Dauphin**.

In 1578 the Spanish founded the town of Bayaha after abandoning Puerto Real. The French took over in 1725, and in 1731 the town was renamed Fort

Dauphin in honour of Louis XV's recently born son. In the same year, Fort Dauphin was built in the extreme north of town as part of an elaborate defence system constructed by the French around the Bay of Fort-Liberté. Four other forts guard the narrow neck of the bay: Fort Labouque, Batterie de l'Anse, Fort St Charles and Fort St Frédérique. Fort-Liberté, as it became known after independence, has often been a focal point during times of revolt and insurrection. This was where the first proclamation of independence was signed on November 28 1803; and during the US occupation the town was an important *caco* stronghold. At the same time the vast sisal plantations near the town were starting to be exploited by American companies such as the Haitian American Development Corporation and the Haitian Agricultural Corporation. Indeed, up until 15 years ago, Fort-Liberté boasted some 48,000 hectares of sisal plantations. Now there is nothing.

The site at Fort Dauphin has been included in Route 2004 (see Chapter 4, page 48), but the tourists have yet to arrive. If and when they do, the **Bayaha Hotel**, the only one in town, will be heaving. It overlooks the bay next to the Douane and has a cool and breezy feel. Although the rooms are a little expensive at US$33 for a single and US$60 for a double, breakfast and dinner is included. This is quite an advantage in a town where I failed to find a restaurant. There is, in fact, another place to stay if the Bayaha is full. Turn left out of the Bayaha, walk through the market towards the sea, pass a kindergarten and look for a small, white house. There is no sign, but this hut offers beds for H$25 and is called **La Sirene**.

Tap-taps running between Cap-Haïtien and Quanaminthe will drop you at the entrance to Fort-Liberté. It's about 2km to the centre and motorbikes are on hand to take you there. It isn't necessary to retrace your steps to the main road when leaving town for Quanaminthe on the Dominican border, since pick-ups leave from the arch welcoming you to Fort-Liberté. This journey takes an hour and costs H$2.

QUANAMINTHE AND THE DOMINICAN BORDER

Quanaminthe is actually the largest town in northeast Haiti. Even so, there is little reason to come here unless you want to cross the border. Facilities are limited to a couple of basic hotels and restaurants and a **Dominican consulate**, open from 08.00 to 14.00, on the main road just past the town square. If circumstances necessitate a stay here, try the **Ideal Hotel** next to the checkpoint. **La Nuit Ragaro** and **Kag Saint-Villa** are two restaurants on the main square.

Crossing the border is an uncomplicated procedure. Walk through Quanaminthe until you come to the end of the main road. On your left you'll see a white and green building, Haitian Immigration. Get your passport stamped here and walk across the yard to a gate, on the other side of which is the Dominican Republic.

The Central Region

Although the central region of Haiti occupies a large land area, it is thinly populated. Hinche, with its population of 53,000, is by far the largest town. It lies in the Central Plateau, a lowland area between the mountains of the Massif du Nord and the Montagnes Noires. The next largest town is Mirebalais, with a population of 14,000, situated at the eastern end of the Artibonite Valley in the most fertile part of the region.

HINCHE

Even by Haitian standards, Hinche is seldom visited by tourists. It may be the most important town in the central region, but the road is bad and there is no major sight of interest at the end of it. However, Hinche is a quintessentially Haitian town where the people work hard and take nothing for granted. As elsewhere in the country, the poverty is, at times, disturbing. Nevertheless, the innate spirit and camaraderie of these people seem to rise above the hardship. I cannot recommend Hinche highly enough.

Getting there and away

Hinche lies on Route Nationale Three, almost exactly halfway between Port-au-Prince and Cap-Haïtien. The journey time to both these towns is at least six hours. Be prepared for anything up to double this if it has been raining. Parts of the road become very muddy, particularly between Hinche and Domond, and the buses and *camions* frequently get stuck. (On one occasion it took me ten hours in a *camion* from Port-au-Prince to Hinche. When we were not stuck in the mud ourselves, we were held up behind another *camion* that was.) All *tap-taps* leave from a yard just in front of the bridge over the Guayamoue River. There is a bus called *Immaculée* that runs daily to Port-au-Prince for H$15. *Camions* and pick-up trucks make the journey when there is enough demand and also charge H$15.

There are no direct *tap-taps* to Cap-Haïtien. You must first go to Pignon, then Saint-Raphaël, then Dondon, before you can finally make a connection to the Cap. The worst part of this journey is the first leg from Hinche to Pignon, where even the *tap-taps* are 4WD. The road is terrible and it takes about three hours to cover the paltry 25km. After this, the going gets smoother. The road is paved from Dondon to the Cap. Other destinations

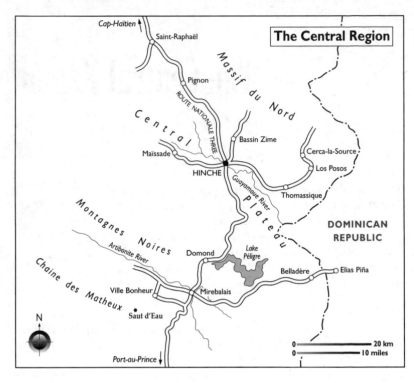

served by *tap-taps* include Cerca-la-Source (for the hot springs), Thomassique and Maïssade.

Where to stay

There are three hotels in Hinche. If you exclude the small hotel in Mirebalais, this is the sum total of the accommodation on offer in the central region of Haiti. The best of this small bunch is the **Maguana Motel** (tel: 77 0528) at the end of Rue Rivage, a small street next to the electricity generators near the entrance to town. The *cabañas* here are quite large, with a bathroom and fan, and cost H$50. The yard in which the motel is situated is dominated by mango and tamarind trees as well as chickens and turkeys. The turkeys are a refreshing addition to the omnipresent chickens, but they make one hell of a noise in the morning. If this starts to get on your nerves, you could move across town to **Hotel Prestige** (tel: 77 0646) near the bridge. The rooms are cheaper (H$40), although the standard is also one notch down. The third hotel, **Hotel El Pequeño Gigante**, is just before you cross the bridge to go north. Here you get what you pay for – namely very simple rooms for H$14.

Where to eat

When it comes to restaurants in Hinche, quality prevails over quantity. The **Lakay Bar Restaurant** is the best place in town, serving tasty Creole food accompanied by a wide selection of drinks. You'll have no problem finding

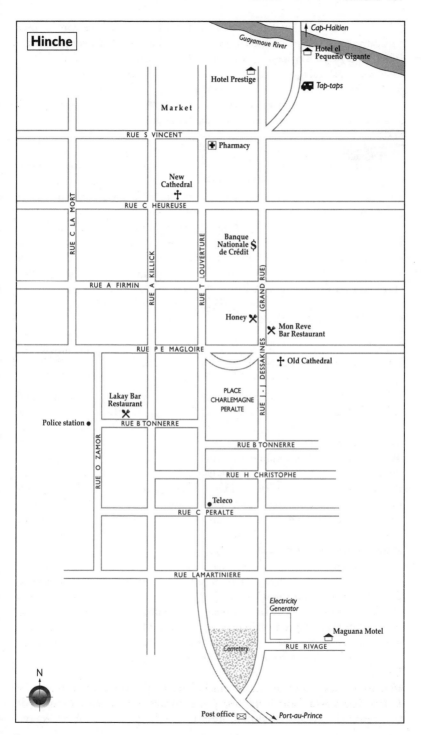

Hinche

this place after dark, since it's one of the few places in Hinche with its own generator. Go to Rue B Tonnerre and look for the lights. Another good place is the **Mon Rêve Bar Restaurant** on Grand Rue. As well as the usual Creole food, they bake cakes and pastries to order. Opposite the Mon Rêve is a small house where you can buy delicious honey.

The **market** is on and around Rue S Vincent. Market days are Wednesdays and Saturdays, although it's pretty busy at all times.

Tourist information

The **post office** is in the front room of a private house just past the arch welcoming you to Hinche. It's on the road branching off to the left and has a green door. Opening hours are 'from sunrise to sunset'. The **Teleco** office is much easier to find on Rue T Louverture.

The one **bank** in the whole of the centre of Haiti is Banque Nationale de Crédit on Grand Rue. The best **pharmacy** in town is Pharmacie du Peuple on the corner of Rue T Louverture and Rue S Vincent. This, incidentally, is one of the few places in town where you can buy Culligan water. The **police station** is at the end of Rue B Tonnerre on Rue O Zamor.

Orientation and what to see

Route Nationale Three dissects the centre of Hinche as Rue A Pétion and then Rue J J Dessalines. The entrance to town is in the south, while the bridge over the Guayamoue River marks its northern extremity. The hotels and *tap-taps* are either near the bridge or the entrance to town.

Hinche has few sights in the traditional sense of the word. The **old cathedral**, dating from the early 16th century, is on **Place Charlemagne Peralte**, the town's main square. Charlemagne Peralte, the famous leader of the resistance against the US occupation, was born in Hinche in 1886, and thus is, not surprisingly, the town's favourite son. The **new cathedral**, somewhat sterile in comparison with its predecessor, is a large, white building surrounded by a wall on Rue C Heureuse. The **Guayamoue River** is best viewed from the other side of the bridge where there is a grassy bank with plenty of trees offering shade.

Excursions from Hinche
Bassin Zime

Bassin Zime is considered by many to be Haiti's **most beautiful waterfall**. Unfortunately, there is no public transport and, at 12km from Hinche, it's a little too far to walk. If you have your own transport, turn right after the bridge and ask directions from there. The waterfall is set in lush tropical country and tips into a deep, blue basin 60m wide and 45m across. You can swim in the pool and there are also some grottoes near to the waterfall.

Grottoes

More grottoes can be found to the northwest of Hinche. **Grotte de Boucantis** and **Grotte de Bohoc** are examples, but once again access is a real problem. If you are desperate to see them, arrange transport with someone who knows the area very well.

Hot springs
The sources *chaudes* (hot springs) at Cerca-la-Source, about 40km east of Hinche, are accessible by public transport. Take a *tap-tap* to either Cerca-la-Source or Los Posos. You could do this trip in half a day, but it's probably best treated as a day trip from Hinche.

ELSEWHERE IN THE CENTRAL REGION
Mirebalais is the second most important town in the central region. It sits in a valley about halfway between Hinche and Port-au-Prince and is surrounded by fertile land irrigated by the Artibonite River and several smaller rivers. The town has a post office, a Teleco office and a small hotel (Hotel St Nicolas).

One of Haiti's biggest festivals takes place on July 15 at **Ville Bonheur**, a few miles east of Mirebalais. It was here, in 1884, that a vision of the Virgin Mary is said to have appeared in a palm tree. Every year thousands of pilgrims converge on a small church in the town to celebrate this event. Meanwhile, 3km away voodoo baptismal rites are being held under the waterfalls of **Saut d'Eau**. These falls are 30m high and plunge into a series of shallow pools.

You can get to Ville Bonheur from Mirebalais. Saut d'Eau is within walking distance of Ville Bonheur.

About an hour north of Mirebalais, just past the small hamlet of Domond, the road skirts around the edge of **Lake Péligre**. This 16km² body of fresh water was created when the **Péligre Dam** (also visible from the road) was built in the 1950s. This in turn was the site of Haiti's first hydroelectric plant, which was completed in 1971.

Hispaniolan parrot

Part Three

Dominican Republic

Lignum vitae

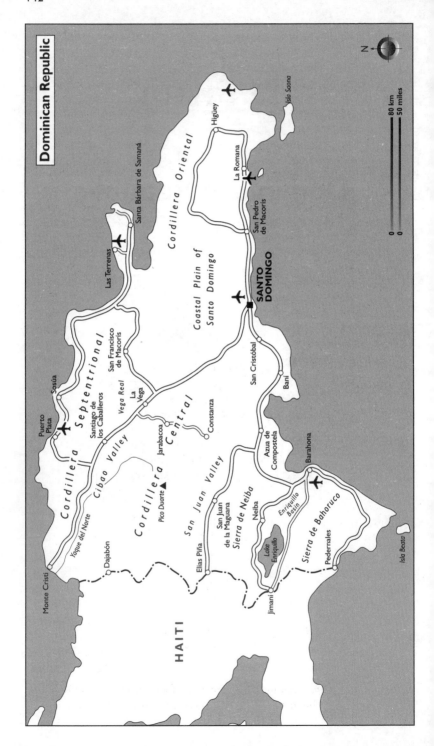

Dominican Republic: Background

GEOGRAPHY
Size and location
The Dominican Republic occupies the eastern two-thirds of Hispaniola. At 48,921km² it is the second largest country in the Caribbean, about the same size as the US states of Vermont and New Hampshire combined. The Dominican coastline stretches for 1,633km and is bordered by the Caribbean Sea to the south and the Atlantic Ocean to the north. Apart from Haiti, the Dominican Republic's closest neighbour is Puerto Rico, which lies to the east across a deep stretch of water called the Mona Passage.

Topography
Highlands
Like Haiti, a large proportion of the Dominican Republic (about 80%) is mountainous, but unlike Haiti, much of the country's four main mountain ranges continue to enjoy forest cover, relatively fertile soils and a degree of agricultural production. The most northerly of these ranges is the **Cordillera Septentrional**, which extends from the coastal town of Monte Cristi near the Haitian border to the Samaná Peninsula in the east, running parallel to the Atlantic coast. The highest range in the Dominican Republic – indeed, in the whole of the West Indies – is the **Cordillera Central**. Connected to the Massif du Nord in Haiti, it gradually bends southwards and finishes near the town of Azua de Compostela on the Caribbean coast. The Cordillera Central is home to the West Indies' highest peak, Pico Duarte (3,175m). In the southwest corner of the country, south of the Cordillera Central, there are two largely dry and rocky ranges. The more northerly of the two is the **Sierra de Neiba**, while in the south the **Sierra de Baoruco** is a continuation of the Massif de la Selle in Haiti. The other main highland area, the **Cordillera Oriental**, is lower than the other mountain ranges and would perhaps be more accurately described as a series of rolling hills extending west along the Atlantic coast, parallel to the southern shore of Samaná Bay and disappearing in the foothills of the Cordillera Central.

Highland valleys
With mountain ranges running parallel to each other, the Dominican Republic boasts a number of highland valleys. Variously described as the 'bread basket' or 'food basket' of the Dominican Republic and a 'paradise' by Christopher

Columbus, the **Cibao Valley** is the most fertile area in the country. Almost everything is grown either here or in the **Vega Real** (Royal Meadow), another fertile valley at the eastern end of the Cibao. Rather less productive is the semi-arid **San Juan Valley**, south of the Cordillera Central and extending westward into Haiti, where it becomes the Central Plateau. Still more barren is the **Neiba Valley**, tucked between the Sierra de Neiba and the Sierra de Baoruco. This valley is also known as the Cul-de-Sac, but to avoid confusion with the Cul-de-Sac Plain in Haiti, and because I think it gives a better idea of what this land is like, I'm going to take the lead of the geologists and call this area the **Enriquillo Basin**. Although it lies only 85km to the southwest of Pico Duarte, Lake Enriquillo lies 40m below sea level and is the lowest point in the West Indies. Much of the rest of the land in the Enriquillo Basin is also below sea level, resulting in a hot, arid, desert-like environment.

Lowlands

The coastal plain of **Santo Domingo** is the largest and most economically important of the lowland areas in the Dominican Republic. Stretching north and east of Santo Domingo, it covers the area left by the Cordillera Oriental and extends as far as the Atlantic Ocean. West of Santo Domingo its width is reduced to 10km as it hugs the coast, finishing at the mouth of the Ocoa River. A few other small coastal plains can be found around the towns of Puerto Plata and Azua, as well as around Samaná Bay and the Pedernales peninsula in the southwest.

Islands

The two largest off-shore islands are **Saona**, which lies off the southeastern coast and **Beata**, off the Pedernales peninsula.

Rivers and lakes

Four major rivers drain the numerous highland areas of the Dominican Republic. The **Yaque del Norte** carries excess water down from the Cibao Valley and empties into Monte Cristi Bay. Likewise, the **Yuna River** serves the Vega Real and empties into Samaná Bay. Drainage of the San Juan Valley is provided by the **Yaque del Sur**, which empties into the Caribbean, and the **Artibonite River**, which crosses the border into Haiti. Although the Artibonite is the largest river in Hispaniola, in the Dominican Republic the Yaque del Norte is the longest and most important.

Other than Lake Enriquillo, the Dominican Republic is not blessed with many natural lakes; the only other one of any size is **Laguna del Rincón** in the Enriquillo Basin.

CLIMATE

Local differences in climate are predictable in a country where the highest point is 3,175m above sea level and the lowest is 40m below sea level. On average, however, the temperature hovers in the high 20s°C throughout the year. This is the case on the coastal plain of Santo Domingo, the north coast and the lowland areas of the Cibao Valley. Climatic variations are most pronounced in the Cordillera Central, where the average temperature in the town of Constanza, for instance, is 16°C, as well as in the desert regions of the southwest, where temperatures can rise above 40°C.

The wettest period is generally from May to November. This is certainly when Santo Domingo receives most of its rain. However, on the north coast around Puerto Plata, the wettest months tend to be from October to April. The nice thing about the rainy seasons in the Dominican Republic is that the showers rarely last long (usually about an hour) and you can almost set your watch by them (in Santo Domingo they usually come in the early evening).

HISTORY
Spanish Hispaniola
In 1697 the Spanish ceded the western third of Hispaniola to France, and over the next 100 years Saint Domingue, or Haiti, was the most prosperous colony in the world. Sugar and coffee production boomed and the expression 'rich as a Saint-Domingan' was a common phrase on the streets of Paris. Meanwhile, Spanish Hispaniola (still known as Santo Domingo, but later to become the Dominican Republic) stagnated. Trade was almost non-existent and a good proportion of the meagre 6,000 population consisted of slaves and freemen. Santo Domingo was going nowhere fast; and in 1795 Spain ceded the remaining two-thirds of Hispaniola to France.

Haitian occupation and Dominican liberation
The French, however, were unable to occupy the eastern part of Hispaniola. They had their hands full in Saint Domingue, where a popular slaves' revolt lead by Toussaint Louverture threatened to overthrow French rule in the colony (see page 37). This left a vacuum, which was filled by Louverture himself when he invaded Santo Domingo in 1800. The English, who were keen to break the grip that France now enjoyed over the whole of Hispaniola, supported Louverture, but events did not quite work out as they had hoped. Louverture announced the emancipation of the slaves in Santo Domingo and soon after was captured by Napoleon's army and shipped off to France. For the next few years the French were left to establish a certain degree of order and prosperity in Santo Domingo, much to the chagrin of the English, who willingly supported a rebellion in 1808 by Spaniards and Creoles, led by a man called Sánchez Ramírez. This rebellion was successful, and in 1809 Spanish rule was restored in Santo Domingo, but the Spaniards simply continued where they had left off in 1795. Inept and indifferent government earned this period of Spanish rule the title *España Boba* (Silly Spain), and their failure to restore any semblance of order in the colony prompted the Creole people, lead by José Núñez de Cáceres, to declare their independence in November 1821. They sought union with Simón Bolívar's new republic in South America, but he was in no position to help the rebels.

In February 1822, just a few months after Spanish rule had ended, the Haitians invaded the eastern part of Hispaniola for the second time, and under

President Jean-Pierre Boyer, Haiti ruled the entire island until his assassination in 1844. Although the slaves in Santo Domingo were liberated during this period, the Haitian occupation is remembered for its abuses. Haitians held the highest offices, universities and businesses were closed, ties with the Catholic Church were severed and the population decreased dramatically.

It was in this climate that, on July 16 1838, a young man named Juan Pablo Duarte founded *La Trinitaria*, a secret society dedicated to the overthrow of the Haitians and the declaration of independence. He was joined by a few other Spanish-speaking Creoles, most notably Francisco del Rosario Sánchez and Ramón Matías Mella who, along with Duarte, are known as the 'Founding Fathers' of the Nation. After a long struggle, during which Duarte was forced to flee to Venezuela, the independence of the Dominican Republic was declared on February 27 1844. The Haitians were driven out of Santo Domingo and Duarte returned from exile expecting to be the first president of the Dominican Republic. This was not to be. Instead, it was Pedro Santana, the crude but charismatic leader of the armies that had ousted the Haitians, who marched into Santo Domingo and declared himself president in July 1844. For the remainder of the century, the Dominican Republic would be ruled be a succession of dictators and embezzlers, collectively described as 'men on horseback'. Duarte, meanwhile, was exiled by Santana and never saw Santo Domingo again. He died in Caracas in 1876.

'Men on horseback'

The Dominican Republic's first decades as an independent nation were dominated by two very different men with the same ultimate objective: absolute power. Pedro Santana and Buenventura Báez alternated the presidency between them, neither one having much regard for the interests of the nation. Pedro Santana was, in essence, a fighting man, who loved power for power's sake. What he lacked in brains he made up for in charisma and his abilities as a leader. He spent the next 16 years repelling invasion attempts by Haiti's mad ruler, Faustin Solouque, and swapping the presidency with Buenventura Báez. Báez, unlike Santana, was an educated man from a wealthy family. His great weakness was money and he used his power primarily to line his own pocket. Between 1849 and 1878 Báez was president on no less than five different occasions.

In 1861 Santana (who then held the presidency) returned the Dominican Republic to Spanish rule to protect against further attacks by Haiti. Spain agreed, but only if the country was restored as an overseas province. While the return of the Spaniards succeeded in deterring Haitian attacks, it was widely resented by the Dominicans. The final straw was when a system of forced labour for public projects was imposed on the people. This sparked a revolt in 1863 and by March 1865 Spain had left the Dominican Republic without having put up much of a fight.

The priority now was to get the country back on its feet after years of war and mismanagement. Báez, who was once again the president, needed funds quickly, and in 1869 he secured a massive loan from an American land-speculating company. At the same time he sought to annex the Dominican Republic to the United States. As far-fetched as it sounded, the US president, Ulysses S Grant, was actually in favour of the idea. However, when the Senate got wind of the loan Báez had arranged, they refused to ratify the plan. Nevertheless, American influence in the Dominican Republic was growing, and it would continue to grow during the dictatorship of Ulises Heureaux from 1882 to 1899.

Heureaux, the first black president of the Dominican Republic, will be remembered as a tyrant. Having distinguished himself as a soldier in the revolt against Spanish rule in the 1860s, when he became president in 1882 he immediately exiled his former leader, General Luperón. It was thus made very clear from the outset that Heureaux intended to rule alone and without competition, although he did occasionally select a puppet president while he continued to direct the government. If further confirmation were needed that Heureaux was the latest, and perhaps the greatest, in a line of Dominican dictators, it came in 1887 when he unilaterally removed the constitutional barrier against re-election. Opposition, however, was muted due to the vast network of spies and assassins Heureaux had created, as well as the relative prosperity the country enjoyed during his rule. Roads and railways were built, production rose, trade and agriculture were encouraged and sugar became the country's chief export. The downside to all this (apart from the suppressive regime) was that the Dominican Republic now owed more money to creditors in Europe and the United States than it could ever hope to repay. Heureaux was assassinated in 1899 by a young man named Ramon Cáceres, who became the interim president.

American influence and occupation

The situation in the Dominican Republic worried the Americans, who had a number of important bases in the Caribbean as well as the Panama Canal. Since Heureaux's assassination, the political situation had become chaotic, with several different factions jostling for power, the main ones being the Horacistas lead by Horacio Vásquez, and the Jiménistas lead by Juan Isidro Jiménez. Presidents came and went with startling regularity, some lasting only a matter of months, and in the mean time, administration and law and order deteriorated, and the debt repayments fell seriously in arrears. The United States feared that the patience of the Republic's European creditors would not hold out for much longer, tempting them to use force to collect the unpaid debts.

This fear led to what became known as the 'Roosevelt Corollary' to the Monroe Doctrine, which had warned European powers not to intervene in the Americas. Devised by President Theodore Roosevelt, it sought to prevent conditions in the Caribbean that might provoke intervention. In January 1905 it was agreed that the Americans would take over the administration of the country's customs revenues. The Dominican government would receive 45% of the receipts, while the rest would be used to pay debts. For a while this arrangement worked well and the debts were gradually repaid, but, true to form, political instability soon returned when Ramon Cáceres, who had become president in 1905, was assassinated in 1911. The struggle for power resumed and in 1914, after US pressure, elections were held. The two main contenders were Horacio Vásquez and Juan Isidro Jiménez. Jiménez won, but he was never able to augment his power and resigned in 1916.

At this point the country was in total confusion. American fears about the effect this would have on the Panama Canal and debt repayments deepened. President Wilson made the decision to intervene and assume complete control of the Dominican Republic, and in November 1916 a force of US Marines led by Captain Harry S Knapp arrived in Santo Domingo, barely a year after American forces had invaded Haiti.

The period of US occupation lasted from 1916 to 1924 and had its successes. A certain degree of fiscal order was restored and programmes to improve roads, schools, communications and sanitary conditions were initiated. However, as in Haiti, the marines abused their power. Exploitation, censorship and American atrocities led to opposition, particularly in the eastern provinces where local *gavilleros* (guerillas) openly opposed the Americans in towns like El Seibo and San Pedro de Macorís.

By the early 1920s the Americans had had enough and were starting to contemplate their departure. A provisional president was appointed in October 1922 and elections were arranged for March 1924. Horacio Vásquez, long-time head of the *Horacistas* won. Four months later the Americans had left.

The era of Trujillo

There are numerous similarities between General Rafael Leonidas Trujillo Molina and Haiti's modern-day monster, Dr François Duvalier. Their early career choices, however, could not have been more different. While Papa Doc prepared for dictatorship caring for people in the clinics of rural Haiti, Trujillo took a more conventional route and joined the army. In 1918 he entered the *Guardia Nacional*, the constabulary created by the US occupation, and took to it like a duck to water. By 1927, Trujillo had risen to become head of the national army. He had taken advantage of the relatively peaceful years of the Vásquez presidency to quietly establish his power base and in 1930 he was ready for the National Palace.

Elections had been scheduled for May 1930, but President Vásquez had a track record for bending the rules – in 1927 he had prolonged his term from four to six years – and now he was seeking re-election, contrary to the constitution. A small band of men in the Cibao were convinced that the election would be unfair and declared a revolution in February. As they marched on Santo Domingo, all eyes were on the army. Trujillo did nothing. The rebels walked into the capital, Vásquez fled, and the rebel leader, Rafael Estrella Ureña, was declared provisional president. In return for his inaction, Trujillo would be a candidate in the May election.

The army campaigned on their commander's behalf by intimidating voters and eliminating political opponents. On the day of the election only about

25% of the electorate turned out to vote. Trujillo announced his election as president with 95% of the vote and was inaugurated on August 16 1930. Shortly after, he requested congress to issue a proclamation announcing the commencement of the 'Era of Trujillo'.

Aided by the strong-arm tactics of the army and the thuggery of his secret police, The 42, it was doubtful whether Trujillo needed the excuse of a hurricane in 1930 that nearly levelled Santo Domingo to assume emergency powers (which he never relinquished). In fact, for the next 31 years Trujillo was not so much dictator as feudal lord, establishing state monopolies over any enterprise worth monopolising. During his regime, sugar, tobacco, milk, beef, airlines, shipping, newspapers and the lottery were all controlled by Trujillo and his family. All political parties became one – The Dominican – which was dedicated to glorifying Trujillo. Not that he did a bad job of that himself. Santo Domingo was renamed Ciudad Trujillo; Pico Duarte became Pico Trujillo; and billboards all over the country gave praise to 'God and Trujillo'.

There were many crimes committed against the people during the Trujillo regime, but probably the worst occurred in October 1937. It was directed, ironically, not at Trujillo's own people, but at the long-suffering Haitian community that laboured on the Dominican sugar plantations. Although the Haitians were tolerated because of the shortage of Dominican labour, their continuing infiltration in the border areas caused resentment and fears of 'Haitianisation'. Haiti, after all, was the old enemy. The last straw was the execution in Haiti of Trujillo's most important undercover agents. On October 2, thousands of Haitians were rounded-up in the border areas and the western Cibao and slaughtered. Most were decapitated to give the impression that the killings were the result of a spontaneous uprising by an enraged Dominican peasantry. Exact figures are hard to come by, but it is estimated that between 15,000 and 20,000 Haitians perished at the hands of Trujillo. International condemnation of the massacre was muted and the $750,000 compensation (later reduced to $525,000) that Trujillo paid to the Haitian government was no more than a slap on the wrist.

Yet, despite his tyranny, many commentators believe that Trujillo could have won a free election, although he never risked one. It is true that the self-styled 'Benefactor' brought considerable material progress to the Dominican Republic. The firm order imposed by the dictatorship augured well for businesses, as did the clearance of the country's foreign debt in 1947. The community at large also benefited from general improvements in the peasant economy, the establishment of pension plans, new roads, hospitals, schools, housing projects and improved sanitary conditions. All this led Joaquím Balaguer, one of the four puppet presidents during Trujillo's regime, to write that 'before 1930 the Dominican nation was protected by Providence, afterwards by Trujillo'.

On the international stage, Trujillo also enjoyed a generally good reputation. The Dominican Republic became a charter member of the United Nations and the Organisation of American States (OAS); a boundary dispute with Haiti going back to 1844 was settled in 1935; and, for the Americans,

Trujillo was the proverbial 'bulwark' against communism in the Caribbean.

However, by the late 1950s patience with Trujillo and his abuses was waning, and opposition from Dominicans was also becoming more vocal. One such dissident was Jesús de Galíndez, an exile in New York, whose book *The Era of Trujillo – Dominican Dictator* openly criticised the regime. He was promptly kidnapped, flown back to the Dominican Republic and murdered. In June 1959 hundreds of Dominican dissidents were flown from Cuba and dropped in the Cordillera Central in an attempt at invasion. It was suppressed within weeks by Trujillo's forces, but a trend had been set. Not only were Dominicans now unafraid to challenge Trujillo, but this opposition was being backed by foreigners. In 1959 Fidel Castro had supported the dissident invasion attempt and the Venezuelan president, Rómulo Betancourt, was frequently linked to individual dissidents who plotted against Trujillo. Betancourt was a continual thorn in the side of someone who was used to getting his own way. In June 1960 Trujillo finally lost his patience and ordered his agents to kill the Venezuelan president. Although the assassination attempt failed, Trujillo had gone one step too far. The OAS severed diplomatic relations and imposed economic sanctions, while the Americans closed their embassy in Santo Domingo. Meanwhile, the CIA supplied weapons to groups dedicated to ousting Trujillo.

On May 30 1961, Trujillo was being driven from Santo Domingo to his hometown of San Cristóbal. A group of armed men forced him to stop on the highway, surrounded his car and, as Trujillo staggered out brandishing his revolver, gunned him down. The Era of Trujillo had ended.

Brief democracy

The puppet president in control at the time of Trujillo's death was Joaquín Balaguer. He was in a tricky position. On the one hand he realised the need to liberalise the government after 31 years of dictatorship, but on the other he had to be careful not to upset the *Trujillistas* who continued to run the army. Perhaps his most significant action before being ousted by a military coup in 1962 was to allow the formation of the leftist Dominican Revolutionary Party (PRD).

The PRD was the first organised political party in the Dominican Republic, founded in 1939 by one of the few outspoken critics of the Trujillo regime, an intellectual named Juan Bosch. The PRD's programme of economic reform and social policies won support across the board, and Bosch proved to be a charismatic leader and great orator who struck a cord with the rural classes, businessmen and intellectuals. In December 1962, when the ruling military council succumbed to US pressure and held elections, Bosch and the PRD won by a landslide. At last, the Dominican Republic had the first democratically elected government in its history.

It didn't last long. After seven months in power, Bosch was overthrown by the military and forced into exile. When it was elected, the PRD seemed to be all things to all people, but in government it was impossible to please everyone, particularly those with an interest in maintaining the status quo. For instance, a new constitution introduced in April 1963 had upset the church because it was too secular, the industrialists because it favoured the worker and the military because it limited their power. The Americans were also suspicious of another leftist and potentially communist government in the Caribbean after the recent emergence of Castro in Cuba.

However, there was no constructive alternative to replace Bosch. Instead, the various conservative factions fought among themselves, while the PRD plotted to restore their leader as president. On April 24 1965, the PRD moved against the military, which, despite US backing, was on the verge of defeat by April 28. President Lyndon Johnson, fearing 'another Cuba', made the decision to send US marines to suppress the revolution and prevent Bosch's return, and for the second time in its history, the Dominican Republic came under US occupation. This time it lasted just long enough for the Americans to defeat the PRD and schedule new elections. Meanwhile, during all the excitement, Joaquín Balaguer had quietly returned from exile in the United States.

Balaguer and others

In the 1966 elections, Balaguer stood as a moderate conservative against Bosch, who had been allowed to return from exile in Puerto Rico. The two election campaigns could not have been more different. Balaguer spent heavily on a high-profile campaign, while Bosch, fearful of his safety, did not make a single public appearance. Balaguer won, but Bosch alleged electoral fraud, and the PRD boycotted the next two elections in 1970 and 1974. In their absence Balaguer enjoyed 12 consecutive years as president.

As secretary of education under Trujillo, Balaguer had established free universities and expanded educational and library facilities. This was a precursor to the massive public-works programme that characterised his presidency. He built roads, bridges, dams, schools, housing projects, sports complexes and tourist facilities, amassing a debt of $1.8 billion as he went. He got away with it for a while, as the economy was in reasonable shape and the United States Congress readily granted aid. However, as he entered his third term in 1974, unemployment and inflation were running dangerously high, while world sugar prices were falling dangerously low. Good old-fashioned political repression and violence, directed principally at the leftists and students, also marred Balaguer's second and third terms. In this climate, with opposition growing, he sought re-election in 1978.

The main contender was a wealthy cattle rancher, Antonio Guzmán, the chosen candidate of the revitalised PRD. During the Balaguer years, the PRD had boycotted the elections, complaining of fraud and Juan Bosch had broken away to form the Party of Dominican Liberation (PLD). Now Guzmán promised to cut back Balaguer's public-works programme and tackle the deteriorating economic situation. With the best of intentions he took over as president in 1978, and although he did manage to make the country self-sufficient in rice and beans for the first time in its history, the dice was loaded against him. The huge debt inherited from Balaguer, falling sugar prices, increasing oil prices, inflation, strikes and the devastation caused by Hurricane David in 1979 all combined to persuade Guzmán not to stand for re-election in 1982. His successor as leader of the PRD, Salvador Blanco, was elected president in May, and shortly afterwards Guzmán committed suicide.

Blanco too inherited a poisoned chalice. The economy continued to sag under the national debt (which had now risen to $4 billion) and he was forced to look abroad for help. He secured a loan from the International Monetary Fund, but in return a rigorous austerity programme was imposed. The currency was devalued, budget cuts were introduced and oil prices were raised. The net effect of all this was rioting and strikes in 1984 and 1985. By 1986 it was clear that neither Blanco nor the PRD would get another chance to solve the country's problems.

In a narrowly contested election between two old foes – Balaguer and Bosch – Balaguer took over yet again. Now nearly 80 years old and going blind, he continued where he had left off in 1978. More roads, hospitals and housing projects were built and the country's debt and inflation figures steadily began to rise. His most famous project was probably the Columbus Lighthouse, which cost millions to build in 1992 (he had defeated Bosch again in 1990 elections). Balaguer's last hurrah was in 1994 when he won his final presidential election. The economic situation had not radically improved and he was now 86 and completely blind – but the alternatives were even less appealing. Juan Bosch had lost his sparkle and upset a lot of influential groups, such as the church, while José Francisco Peña Gomez, the PRD candidate, had Haitian origins and was not completely trusted. Moreover, it was often alleged, probably with some justification, that Balaguer's election victories were due in part to irregularities at the ballot box.

In fact, Balaguer tried to seek re-election in 1996, but was barred from standing. The old dog had had his day. Nevertheless, his preferred candidate, Leonel Fernández, narrowly defeated Peña Gomez to become the Republic's first new president in ten years. The problems he inherited, however, were nothing new – debt, unemployment, corruption, electricity shortages and Haitian immigration. These remain the contemporary problems of the Dominican Republic, although Dominican politics is now a multi-party and largely democratic affair. Elections have taken place every four years since the American intervention in 1966 and the people can, and do, protest in the streets without fearing for their lives.

ECONOMY

Apart from tourism, the Dominican Republic's economy is heavily based on **agriculture**. Sugar is by far the most important commodity, accounting for about half of the country's exports. Sugarcane plantations are found all over the eastern provinces and the coastal plains around Santo Domingo. Coffee, cacao and tobacco – produced extensively in the Cibao Valley – are other important export crops, and while rice, tomatoes, root vegetables, bananas and other tropical fruits are also exported, most of them are retained for domestic consumption. This means the Dominican Republic is one of the few countries in the Caribbean that enjoys self-sufficiency in most of the basic foods. However, this particular piece of independence is not the general rule as far as the Dominican economy is concerned. In fact, there is an over-dependence on sugar and tourism, which in turn ties the country's revenue to unpredictable fluctuations in world sugar prices and tourist trends. This has led to recent attempts to diversify the economy.

Dominican **industry**, still dominated by sugar processing, is slowly diversifying into other areas. Light industries manufacturing clothes, electronic equipment, furniture and leather goods are emerging, along with smaller concerns producing traditional consumer goods like soup, candles, rope and cigars. During the Balaguer years, duty-free industrial zones with tax concessions and cheap, union-free labour were created in most provincial towns to attract multinational companies to the Dominican Republic. Mining is another area of diversification. The country has considerable mineral deposits – including one of the best sources of amber in the Western Hemisphere – but only a few are developed commercially. These include gold, silver, bauxite, nickel and salt, which is extracted from extensive deposits near Lake Enriquillo and by evaporating seawater at Monte Cristi. There are also high hopes for the future discovery of oil off the coast of Azua de Compostela.

The bulk of the Dominican Republic's **trade** is with the United States. Most of the imported foodstuffs and manufactured goods are American or Venezuelan, while the United States and Puerto Rico buy two-thirds of Dominican exports. Sugar exports leave primarily from the ports of Santo Domingo, San Pedro de Macorís and La Romana, while coffee, cacao and tobacco depart from Puerto Plata.

PEOPLE

Approximately 8 million people live in the Dominican Republic. The most populous areas of the country are Santo Domingo and the part of the Cibao Valley stretching from Santiago in the west to San Francisco de Macorís in the east. About 75% of the population are mulatto or *mestizo*, 15% are white (or light-skinned) and 10% are black. This makes the Dominican Republic one of the few countries in the Caribbean where the majority is not black. Moreover, of all the countries in the West Indies – and perhaps the whole of the Americas – Dominican culture has remained closest to its Spanish origins.

Indeed, throughout history it has been a preoccupation of the mulatto majority to deny their African roots and be as white as possible. The overriding reason for this is practical rather than ideological. When the Spanish ruled in Hispaniola, it was a fact of life that the lighter you were in colour, the better your life would be. The slaves were black; the ruling class was white; and the position of those in-between depended on the shade of their skin. Sadly, nothing has changed since these primitive times. Even today, Dominicans are reluctant to call themselves mulattos. If they have a light-enough skin and features that are not too Negroid, then to all intents and purposes they are white.

As in Haiti, there is the rich elite and the poor majority. The former typically come from Santo Domingo and Santiago, occupy themselves with the affairs of government and international business, send their children to school in Europe and lead traditional, conservative lives. The latter are often illiterate, unemployed and almost invariably poor. Most work on the land as *campesinos* (peasants); the lucky ones own small plots of land, while the remainder try to find work as wage labourers. The Dominican Republic also has a growing middle class, a by-product of the country's respectable economic and business activity since the 1970s. This group is neither rich nor poor, but they are ambitious, upwardly mobile and politically active.

Haitian immigrants

Much of the Dominican Republic's black minority is of Haitian descent. Moreover, each year thousands of migrant Haitian workers cross the border to work in the cane fields, doing the work that the Dominicans refuse to do, and for a fraction of the wages. Nevertheless, the attitude towards the Haitian immigrants is, at best, suspicious. These two countries are traditional enemies (see *History* on page 145) and the presence of so many Haitians on Dominican soil has led to paranoid fears of an invasion 'through the back door'. It also doesn't help that the Haitians are black and Dominican culture leans so much in the other direction. This was the rationale (if such a barbaric act can have a rationale) behind the massacre of some 20,000 Haitian cane cutters in October 1937. Trujillo, who ordered the killings, feared that the Haitians were darkening the Dominican people. If racism exists in Dominican society today, the Haitians bear the brunt of it.

LANGUAGE

The official language, and the language spoken by the overwhelming majority of Dominicans, is Spanish. It is perhaps appropriate in a country whose culture includes the fastest music in the world that it should also speak Spanish at break-neck speed. But the Spanish spoken here is relatively close to its Castillian origins, with virtually no dialects and, apart from the speed, no great barriers to communication for the Spanish-speaker. There is, however, one idiosyncrasy that should be mentioned. The Dominicans have a tendency to omit the letter 's' from words. Some useful expressions in Spanish can be found in Appendix 1.

RELIGION

Roman Catholicism is the official religion of the Dominican Republic and about three-quarters of its population are Catholic, but the Church is not the all-pervading force it is in Haiti. There is certainly no shortage of churches and convents, but many of them seem quiet compared to those in Haiti. The Church had its heyday during the Trujillo years when it was wealthy and powerful under the self-proclaimed Benefactor of the Church. However, since then its influence has declined, and today one of the Church's chief functions is social work. Catholic Relief Services (CARITAS) work in rural areas with the poor, while other organs of the Church manage schools, hospitals and other social services.

Protestants make up a small percentage of the population, although their numbers have been growing in recent years, and the several immigrant communities in the Dominican Republic have brought with them a smattering of other religions. There are small groups of Jews, Muslims, Mormons and even Buddhists, while the significant number of Dominicans of Haitian descent means that voodoo, especially in the countryside, is still practised.

MERENGUE

Most Dominicans like to believe that *merengue* originated in 1844, the year that the country was founded. According to legend, soldiers in the War of Independence came up with the first verse of *merengue* to satirise the cowardice of Tomás Torres, a soldier who had left his post during the Battle of Talanquera.

> Thomas fled with the flag,
> Thomas fled from Talanquera;
> If it had been I, I wouldn't have fled:
> Thomas fled with the flag.

This explanation is much more palatable than the other theory that Dominican *merengue* derives from Haitian *méringue*. To admit this would be to admit African and Haitian influences on their culture, something the Dominicans are often reluctant to do. Whatever you believe, one thing is clear: there is a strong link between *merengue* and the national identity.

Caribbean *merengue* was already well established in countries like Colombia, Venezuela, Puerto Rico and Haiti before it came to the Dominican Republic. It was essentially a fusion between European *contredanse* (derived from the English country-dance) and local African elements, and had its first airing in the ballrooms of the Dominican Republic's elite in the 19th century. It was received with shock and distaste by the intellectuals, who couldn't come to terms with its provocative movements and close contact between couples – as opposed to the more sedate group dances to which they were accustomed. Meanwhile, *merengue* flourished in the rural areas and had become an integral part of life for most Dominicans by the beginning of the 20th century.

At this time Santiago was the focal point for the development of *merengue*, or more specifically *merengue típico cibaeño* (Cibao folk *merengue*). This music was typically sung with a tight, nasal technique to the accompaniment of an accordion, a *güira* (a scraped calabash), a *tombora* (a two-headed drum made from a hollowed log) and sometimes a wind instrument. The lyrics could refer to issues of everyday life or serious political questions; either way they adopted a witty tone and were sometimes made up on the spot. The greatest composers of *merengues* in this era were Ñico Lora and Toña Abreu.

Prior to the US invasion in 1916, the elite had shunned *merengue típico*, but during the US occupation it was seized on by the Cibao elite and used as the symbol of Dominican national identity in a propaganda campaign against the Americans. Lora's *La Protesta* was typical of the many nationalist *merengues* of the time:

We'll attack them with machetes, we'll make them leave [repeat];
The Americans, the intruders [repeat].

With power and courage, we'll make them leave [repeat];
The Americans, the abusers [repeat].

Carvajal said that Americans [repeat]
Cannot rule the land of Duarte [repeat].

The status of *merengue* had changed almost overnight. From providing a social commentary on life in the villages of the Cibao, it had become the voice box of a nation. When Trujillo came to power in 1930, it became the voice box of a dictator. During the election campaign he used Ñico Lora and Toña Abreu to sing *merengues* extolling his virtues and criticising his opponents; and for the next 31 years most of the *merengues* that were produced had Trujillo as their main subject. Nevertheless, while this period lacked creativity, many agree that *merengue* made great advances during the Trujillo years. *Merengue típico* was adopted as a national symbol and imposed on the rest of the nation; *merengue* bands started to appear in the capital and gradually typical *merengue* was influenced by other types of music, principally jazz. In this way the saxophone became an important feature of a new **dance-band style** of *merengue*. People appreciated the aesthetics of Trujilloist *merengue* rather than its politics. By the end of the Trujillo era there were essentially two types of *merengue*: the accordion-based *merengue típico*, still popular in the countryside, and the saxophone-based big-band *merengue*, which was easy to dance to and all the rage with the urban elite.

The death of Trujillo brought tremendous relief and optimism to the nation, which was reflected in its music. It lost its inhibitions and, freed from its former restrictions, began to express the mood of the people. Dynamic young singers like Johnny Ventura, Féliz del Rosario and Rafael Solano sang *merengues* with a happier and more liberated sound, and at this time the *merengue* became a truly popular music, leading some to call it pop *merengue*. Ventura speeded up the music and incorporated elements of salsa and rock, and, noting the increasing popularity of American disco music in the Dominican Republic, began to use the bass drum. As a result he became the prominent *merenguero* during the 1960s.

Wilfrido Vargas took over in the 1970s and continued the trends set by Ventura. He used an even faster tempo and borrowed more outside elements (for example, synthesisers from Haitian *compas*) resulting in a new rhythm called *el maco* (the toad). This employed a two-beat pulse similar to disco music, as opposed to the traditional four beats of *merengue típico*. Los Hermanos Rosario are a popular contemporary group that came to the fore in the 1980s using the *el maco* rhythm. A practice known as *fusilamiento* (assassination) also became popular, basing *merengues* on foreign hits. Vargas, for instance, drew on Haitian and Colombian music, while others liked to spice up Latin-American and Spanish *baladas*.

In the 1980s Juan Luis Guerra came on to the scene. In 1990 his *Bachata rosa* sold 3½ million copies worldwide and he went on to win a US Grammy

Award in 1992. For the first time, *merengue* had achieved international acclaim. Guerra's style was more intellectual and sentimental than most, but at the same time people loved to dance to it. He continued the trend of using a variety of other musical influences, including *típico* and *maco* rhythms, African rhythms, flamenco, bebop and funk. However, the biggest influence on Guerra's music was jazz. The literary sophistication of his text was another of his trademarks. He wanted to make people think and dance at the same time, giving rise to the expression '*el merengue dual*' (dual *merengue*).

As pop *merengue* continues to grow in popularity and is mass-marketed in the Dominican Republic and abroad, the argument about its roots has arisen once again. Some feel that Dominican culture is intrinsically African and that pop *merengue* has moved too far away from these roots, but to counter this, new groups have formed to emphasise and represent Afro-Dominican music. Nevertheless, the popular sound on the streets continues to be the fast pulse and stuttering momentum of pop *merengue*. You'll hear it everywhere.

Bachata

While *merengue* blazed a trail through the Dominican mainstream in the 1970s, the country's other native music, *bachata*, was arguably the choice of the Dominican majority. Bachata is associated with the countryside and distinguished by its use of guitars and electric bass. It is not fast and flashy like *merengue*, but down-to-earth and honest. Street language is used to describe ironically the trials and tribulations of peasant life and the vocal quality is tight and nasal.

Bachata entered the Dominican mainstream through *merengue* singers like Juan Luis Guerra who started to include it in their repertoires. Nowadays, *bachata* singers like Antonio Cruz and Raulin Rodriguez are just as popular as their *merengue* counterparts.

LITERATURE

The best Dominican literature tends to have a political theme. This has been the case since colonial times when the Dominican friar Bartolomé de Las Casas wrote his *Apologética Historia de las Indias*, in which he condemned the brutality of the Spanish and spoke up for the Taino Indians.

Many consider Felíx Maria de Monte to be the founding father of modern Dominican literature. He came on the scene in the mid-19th century with his patriotic poetry, and was joined by others who used their writing to deliver a political message. Salomé Ureña argued for an improvement in conditions for women, while Manuel de Jesús Galván celebrated the 'noble savage' in his novel *Enriquillo*. In more recent times, the former president, Juan Bosch, was an outspoken critic of Trujillo and produced many of his best essays, novels and short stories during the Trujillo years.

Other famous Dominican writers to look for (on street signs if not in bookshops) are Gastón Fernando Deligne, Frederico Garcia Godoy and Frederico Bermudez. All of them wrote at around the turn of the century and, once again, picked up on various political themes current at the time.

SPORT

Baseball is to Dominicans what soccer is to Haitians, and from October to January the Dominican season is in full swing. The six main teams and their towns are: Tiger Licey (Santo Domingo), Leones Escogido (Santo Domingo), Estrellas Orientales (San Pedro de Macorís), Aquidas Cibaeñas (Santiago), Gigantes del Norte (San Francisco de Macorís) and Azucareros del Este (La Romana). When deciding which team to support, bear in mind that Tiger Licey have been Caribbean champions no fewer than nine times. In the Dominican off-season, the attention switches to the major leagues in North America, where a number of Dominican players play for the big teams. In the 1998 season, Sammy Sosa, a former shoeshine boy from San Pedro de Macorís, who now plays for the Chicago Cubs, broke a 37-year-old record for the number of home runs scored in a season.

Basketball is probably the second favourite sport, although it's some way behind baseball in terms of popularity. **Cockfighting** persists in the Dominican Republic as it does in Haiti.

FOOD AND DRINK
Traditional dishes

Typical Dominican cuisine, advertised everywhere as *comida criolla*, is fine if you like plenty of starchy and fried food. *La bandera* (the flag) is the name given to the standard Dominican dish of white rice, red beans, stewed meat, salad and *tostones* (fried green plantains). If a restaurant has any food at all, it will have *la bandera* in some form or another. The national dish is *sancocho*, an all-inclusive meat and vegetable stew, which could contain anything from pork to tripe and sweet potatoes to cassava. *Sancocho prieto*, a black stew, is made with seven different types of meat.

Rice is a staple food in the Dominican Republic and the *platano verde* (green plantain) is ubiquitous. *Moro* is beans mixed with rice, while *mangú* is a purée of green plantains fried with onions, popular for breakfast or as an antidote for 'mal del turista' (diarrhoea). *Mofongo* is a variation of *mangú*, often made with plenty of garlic.

Chicken is without doubt the most popular meat in the Dominican Republic. It can be stewed or grilled, but the Dominicans really like it fried. *Pollo frito* (fried chicken) is sold everywhere, as is *chicharron de pollo* (more refined, bite-sized pieces of fried chicken) and *arroz con pollo* (chicken mixed with rice). Other popular meats include pork, goat and tripe. *Mondongo* is the slightly more exotic Dominican name for stewed tripe. *Locrio* derives from the Spanish *paella* and consists of rice mixed with vegetables and any one or all of the available meats.

Seafood features heavily in the Dominican kitchen and is usually prepared with plenty of salt. Look out for *chillo* (red snapper), *mero* (sea-bass) and *lambi* (conch). Obviously, the seafood is particularly good in some of the Republic's coastal towns. Samaná, for instance, is well known for its fish cooked in coconut milk, while in Barahona you can try *carite*, a saltwater fish local to the region.

Fast food

Most of the food sold on the streets is fried. *Chicharrón* (not to be confused with *chicharrón de pollo*) is pork crackling, fried in pieces the size of your fist. *Yaniqueque* is a simple flour pancake fried in a deep pan of oil. This vies with the *quipe* (an oval-shaped meatball mixed with flour) for numerical superiority on many Dominican food stands. *Pastelitos* and *empanadas* are pockets of pastry filled with minced meat, ham, cheese, or vegetables, sold on the street and in cafés and restaurants as snacks. The sandwich is another popular snack food, although some varieties – the *cubano*, for instance, which is crammed with chicken, pork and cheese – make satisfactory meals. Then, of course, there is *pollo frito*, which is available everywhere for breakfast, lunch and dinner.

Fruits and vegetables

Pineapples, mangoes, papayas, melons, oranges and bananas all thrive in the Dominican Republic, along with some more unusual tropical fruits like the *zapote* (a brown fruit shaped like an avocado). In the cooler climate of the Cordillera Central, apples, pears and strawberries are grown. These, however, are considered exotic fruits and cost more.

Green plantains, sweet potatoes and *yuca* (cassava) provide much of the starch necessary for a good Dominican meal. Green vegetables are used quite a lot in the mountains where they are locally produced, but not much elsewhere. The *tayota* is a light green vegetable that looks and tastes a bit like a cucumber. Along with the pumpkin, it sometimes ends up in a *salcocho*.

Desserts

Dulces are arguably the most popular Dominican sweet. *Dulce de leche* is a mixture of milk and sugar, which produces a soft, very sweet candy. *Leche con guayaba* is the same thing with guava, *leche con coco* is with coconut, *leche con naranja* is with orange and so on. *Arroz con dulce* (rice pudding) is a traditional Dominican dessert, while *habichuela con dulce* is made from beans, milk, sugar and spices and is especially popular at Lent. Other than this, ice-cream is the major Dominican indulgence. Sometimes it's a little too soft for my liking, but in general the standard is high. Bon Helados are one of the best ice-cream chains and can be found in practically every town in the country.

Drink

The abundance of fresh fruit in the Dominican Republic is good news for juice lovers. In addition to the standard *jugos* (pineapple, papaya, melon, oranges etc), you can also enjoy slightly more unusual flavours such as strawberry and *chinola* (passion fruit). If natural juices are unavailable, cartons of very sweet orange juice, mango juice and fruit punch provide a reasonable alternative. Brands to look out for include Bon, Tampico and Rico (who also produce flavoured milk drinks). These juices are very popular for breakfast, as is *extracto de malta*, a malt extract drink. Malta Morena and Malta India are two of the more common names. A full range of sodas, including local brands such as Country Club, Chubby and Red Rock, is also available. Bottled water is as common here as it is in Europe or North America. Crystal, Atlantico and Constanza are good choices, but there are many others.

The Dominican Republic produces some of the best coffee in the world. Unlike Haitian Blue, however, the best stuff is not reserved exclusively for export. Street vendors sell *café negro* (black coffee) in tiny plastic cups loaded with sugar. Alternatively, you can have *café con leche* (coffee steamed with milk), or a more tropical *café con limón* (black coffee with grated lime peel). The initial taste is a little sharp, but the aftertaste is very pleasant. If you are thinking of buying some Dominican coffee to take home with you, Café Santo Domingo is certainly one of the best. ·

Moving on to the harder stuff, rum and beer predominate. Barceló, Bermudez and Brugal are the three companies competing for the hearts and minds of the Republic's rum drinkers. All of them produce white rum, dark rum and premium labels that are good, but not quite as good as Haitian Barbancourt. Dominican beer is well regarded and perfectly drinkable. Presidente is the main brand, while Quisqueya is another. Of course, along with the local drinks, imported beer and liquor is widely available.

Dominican Republic: Practicalities

RED TAPE AND IMMIGRATION
General requirements
Provided that you abide by a few simple rules, you should not encounter any great problems entering or leaving the Dominican Republic.

Officially, a ticket out of the country is required, although evidence of one is rarely demanded. Even so, since the only place you can travel to by land is Haiti, there is not really much point buying an open-jaw ticket (better to explore Haiti, then return to the Dominican Republic for your flight home). Moreover, given the relative expense of air tickets in Hispaniola, it makes more sense to buy a return ticket anyway.

Citizens of the UK, Ireland, France, Holland, Belgium, Germany, Austria, Switzerland, Italy, Spain, Norway, Sweden and most other European countries can stay for up to 90 days in the Dominican Republic with a valid passport and a Tourist Card. The same is true for citizens of Australia, Canada and the United States. The Americans, in fact, can enter the country with a passport or some other proof of citizenship (but I would always opt for the passport). The **Tourist Card** costs US$10 and is issued without fuss at Dominican consulates abroad or at the airport upon arrival. You can also get them at the border posts, but there you should be more prepared for unannounced changes and ad-hoc bureaucracy. When you leave the country, no matter whether you fly out or cross the land border, you'll be required to pay a US$10 departure tax. This money is due in US dollars, so make sure you save some for the purpose.

If 90 days is not enough, you can call the General Director of Immigration (tel: 685 2535) for an extension. For general enquiries relating to immigration, contact the Consular Department of Chancery (tel: 535 6280 ext 264).

Embassies and consulates
Dominican representation abroad
Belgium: 160a Avenue Louise, 1050 Brussels; tel: 02 646 0840
Canada: 2080 rue Crescent, Montreal, Quebec H36 2B8; tel: 514 499 1918
France: 2 route Georges Beilles, 75016 Paris; tel: 01 40 50 64 97
Germany: Bergstrasse 87, 5300 Bonn; tel: 228 364 956
Haiti: Avenue Pan-Americaine, Pétion-Ville; tel: 509 57 3697
Italy: Via Domenico Cheline 10, 00197 Rome; tel: 06 807 4665
Spain: Calle Principe de Vergara 36, Madrid; tel: 01 431 5321

Sweden: Sibi-Llegatan 13, 11442 Stockholm; tel: 08 667 4611
UK: 139 Inverness Terrace, London, W2; (consulate) tel: 0171 727 6214; (embassy) tel: 0171 727 6285
USA: 1715 22nd Street, NW, Washington DC, 20008; tel: 202 332 6280

Foreign representation in Santo Domingo
Belgium: 504 Avenida Abraham Lincoln; tel: 562 1661
Canada: 30 Avenida Máximo Gómez; tel: 685 1136
France: 353 Avenida George Washington; tel: 689 2161
Germany: Calle Lope de Vega and R Sánchez; tel: 565 8811
Haiti: 33 Calle Juan Sánchez Ramirez; tel: 686 5778
Holland: Mayor Enrique Valverde; tel: 565 5240
Spain: 1205 Avenida Independencia; tel: 535 1615
UK: 233 Avenida 27 de Febrero; tel: 472 7111
USA: Calle César Nicolás Penson; tel: 221 2171

GETTING THERE AND AWAY
By air
There are international airports serving the following Dominican towns: Santo Domingo, Puerto Plata, Punta Cana, Santiago and La Romana. The vast majority of flights arrive at either the Las Americas International Airport in the south, or the General Gregorio Luperón International Airport in the north. Some of the charters from Europe and North America arrive at the Punta Cana International Airport in the east.

As far as the price of a ticket is concerned, it's hard to say. Much will depend on the time you go (not only the date, but also the time of day), when you buy your ticket, and whether you can take advantage of any special fares on offer. As a very general guide, you might pay US$700 from Europe and US$400 from the United Sates on a scheduled airline, sometimes a lot less on a charter.

The list of travel agents in the *Appendix* might give you some idea where to start looking for an elusive cheap ticket. If you find a charter flight at an irresistibly low price, but are planning to stay on the island for some time, you could buy it and only use the outward portion. Of course, then you'll need to buy your return ticket in the Dominican Republic. The cheapest fares – especially if you have an International Student Identity Card (ISIC) – are from **ODTE** (Oficina Dominicana para el fomento del Turismo Educativo), the best-known student travel agency in the Dominican Republic. They have offices in Santo Domingo (tel: 686 3333), Santiago (tel: 971 2829), La Romana (tel: 550 8636) and San Francisco de Macorís (tel: 588 1171).

Europe
You can reach the Dominican Republic from a bewildering number of cities in Europe. In the UK the charters monopolise the market. Try Britannia, Monarch, Leisure International or Airtours. You can usually get a flight from London (Gatwick), Manchester, Birmingham and even Bangor to Santo Domingo, Puerto Plata or Punta Cana. Note that with a charter flight you cannot stay very

long. It depends on the tour company and the price of your ticket, but the usual length of stay is two weeks. However, in low season you might pick up a ticket for £99, which somewhat makes up for the time restriction.

Many cities in western Europe have flights to the Dominican Republic. Of the scheduled airlines, Air France flies daily from Paris to Santo Domingo, Iberia flies from Madrid and Alitalia from Rome. Several companies operate from German cities like Dusseldorf, Cologne, Frankfurt, Stuttgart and Munich. These include LTU and Condor. Martinair has flights to Santo Domingo and Puerto Plata from Amsterdam, and City Bird, the Belgian charter company, flies from Brussels. Other European cities currently with flights to the Dominican Republic are Zurich, Milan and Vienna.

North America

American Airlines are often the first choice when travelling to Hispaniola from the United States. They have daily flights to Santo Domingo and Puerto Plata from New York (JFK Airport) and Miami, as well as a service to La Romana (for Casa de Campo). Alternatives from New York include TWA and Continental (from Newark Airport), while from Miami you could try your luck with Air Atlantic, a Dominican airline. APA International Air (tel: 1 800 693 0007) also have flights from Miami to Santo Domingo during the summer, starting around June. Not many people arrive in the Dominican Republic at the Cibao International Airport in Santiago. Nevertheless, Lynx Air International has two flights a week from Fort Lauderdale in Florida.

The Dominican Republic is also accessible from Canada, mainly with the charter airlines. Royal Air flies to Puerto Plata from Halifax and Toronto, while Air Transit goes from Mirabel.

Caribbean and Latin America

See Chapter 21, *Onward Travel* for details of travel to and from the Caribbean and Latin America.

By sea

To my knowledge there are no dedicated passenger ships to the Dominican Republic. This means that you can either charter a yacht or arrange a berth on a cargo vessel. Alternatively, you can take a cruise (see Chapter 3, *Cruise Ship Passengers*). As for yachts and cargo vessels, try places like Miami, Fort Lauderdale and New York, but expect to pay a lot.

By land

If you look at a map of Hispaniola, there seem to be four possible border crossings between Haiti and the Dominican Republic. Working from north to south they are: Quanaminthe–Dajabón; Belladère–Elias Piña; Malpasse–Jimaní; and Anse-à-Pitres–Pedernales. In practice you can only enter the Dominican Republic legally at Dajabón and Jimaní. The crossing at Pedernales is closed, while the one at Elias Piña is open, but there are no police to stamp your passport. You might be tempted to pass through with the minimum of hassle at Elias Piña, but a passport with no entry stamp will cause you problems when you want to leave the country, and anyway the other two crossings present few problems.

There is no through bus from Haiti to the Dominican Republic crossing the border at Dajabón. Unless you are on an organised excursion from Puerto Plata, in which case transport will be provided, you must take a combination of *tap-taps* and *gua-guas*. See the relevant sections in the guide for advice on how to cross the border at Dajabón (page 207) and onward travel. You can, of course, cross the border at Jimaní in the same way. Alternatively, you can take the *Terra Bus* that runs six days a week between Port-au-Prince and Santo Domingo via Jimaní. This luxurious service takes six hours and costs US$45 single and US$75 return. For precise departure times see Chapter 5, page 63.

Travel insurance companies
Club Direct: 0800 074 4558
Columbus direct: 0171 375 0011; web: www.colombusdirect.co.uk

GETTING AROUND
By air
Distances are not really great enough in the Dominican Republic to merit a vast network of internal flights. Having said this, you can fly with **Air Santo Domingo** to a few destinations from Santo Domingo's Herrera Airport. These include Puerto Plata, Santiago, La Romana, Punta Cana and El Portillo. Look under the relevant town's *Getting there and away* section for the times of these flights.

By road
One positive thing that came from the US occupation and the subsequent Trujillo dictatorship was perhaps the best road network in the Caribbean. In stark contrast to Haiti, you can get almost anywhere in the Dominican Republic on good, paved roads. Autopista Duarte is the country's principal highway, linking Santo Domingo in the south with Monte Cristi in the north and passing through the Republic's second city, Santiago de los Caballeros. In addition, two main highways serve the capital – the Las Américas Highway, stretching along the coast east of Santo Domingo to La Romana, and the Sánchez Highway running west to Elias Piñas on the Haitian border.

Bus companies
Several bus companies operate comfortable, air-conditioned coaches to various destinations at scheduled times. They are generally fast, reliable and cheap. **Caribe Tours** is arguably the best and certainly offers the most comprehensive service. **Metro** competes with Caribe Tours in price and comfort, but only serves the north and northeast. **Terra Bus**, meanwhile, does the Santo Domingo–Santiago run in addition to its service to Port-au-

Prince. There are also a number of regional companies, for example **Transporte del Cibao** in Santiago and **Expresso Vegano**, which offers services to Santo Domingo from La Vega.

Gua-guas

'*Gua-gua*' is, in fact, the generic word for all types of bus in the Dominican Republic. In practice, however, the term is rarely used to describe those belonging to Caribe Tours and Metro. Instead, *gua-guas* are the multitude of minibuses and minivans that travel the roads of the Dominican Republic. Unlike the scheduled buses, *gua-guas* leave when they are full from various points in town. They are slightly cheaper than buses and can be quite comfortable, although this is not the norm. The great thing about the *gua-guas* is that they go virtually everywhere. Admittedly, you might have to take several to get to a remote town on the southwest coast, but at least it's possible.

Taxis

It would be unthinkable to take a taxi from London to Manchester or Los Angeles to San Francisco, but in the Dominican Republic taking a taxi from one end of the country to the other is a legitimate option, although expensive. Fares to different destinations are pretty standard and are advertised on boards at the airports and outside the larger hotels. The price quoted is for the car and not per person, so if there's a group of you, it might be worth considering.

Hiring a car

Hiring a car is also an option, but the buses are so good that you can certainly see the country quite well without one. The minimum age for hiring a car in the Dominican Republic is 25, and you must have a credit card. Small cars start at around US$50 a day, while 4WD (which is not necessary on Dominican roads) is about US$20 more. The most convenient place to go is either the Las Americas or Gregorio Luperón International airports. Alternatively, the larger hire companies have offices in Santo Domingo:

Avis: Avenida Abraham Lincoln/Sarasota; tel: 535 7191
Budget: Avenida J F Kennedy/Lope de Vega; tel: 567 0175
Hertz: 454 Avenida Independencia; tel: 221 5333
National: Avenida Abraham Lincoln/J F Kennedy; tel: 562 1444
Nelly: 139 Avenida José Contreras; tel: 535 8800
Thrifty: Avenida José María Heredia; tel: 686 0133

(Note that if you have an ISIC card you can get a 10% discount at any Nelly Rent-A-Car office in the country.)

Hitchhiking

The necessity of hitchhiking is somewhat reduced by *gua-guas*, which go almost everywhere. If you want to hitchhike just for the fun of it, expect to pay for most of your rides. How much is up to you and the driver.

Around town

Públicos, carros and *motoconchos* (as well as taxis) provide the means of getting around the larger Dominican towns. You'll probably use them most in Santo Domingo where the distances between some of the major attractions can be quite long.

Like the *gua-guas*, **públicos** are usually minibuses, although probably in a slightly worse condition. They run along fixed routes, often venturing out to the suburbs, they can get quite cramped and the charge is nominal.

Carros are basically shared taxis. They are most popular in Santo Domingo where they run up and down the main avenidas, picking up and dropping off passengers as they go. Most of the *carros* in the capital are small Nissans and Datsuns, and tight profit margins mean that the driver cannot waste space. The car is full when there are three people in front (including the driver) and four in the back. Until that number has been reached, don't get too comfortable.

It seems that everyone who owns a motorcycle in the Dominican Republic hires it out as a **motoconcho.** These are basically motorcycle taxis. Unless you're in Samaná, where small carriages are attached to the bikes, you sit on the back and hold on for dear life. The drivers can be a little pushy at times, but of all the ways of getting around town – and to places of interest just outside town – the *motoconcho* is the way to go. Unlike the *públicos* and *carros*, the price is up to you to negotiate.

ACCOMMODATION

Many people think that because the Dominican Republic is in the Caribbean, the accommodation must be expensive. Of course, if you choose to stay at a luxury resort, you can expect to pay as much as you would in the Bahamas, Puerto Rico, Jamaica or any other Caribbean island where tourism is big. But one of the great attractions of this country is its cheap accommodation. In the Bahamas you rarely find anywhere for less than US$100 a night; in the Dominican Republic you can get a room for US$10. What's more, these budget options are often quite comfortable and, most importantly, safe.

Most of the rooms at the **resort hotels** are sold in packages that include all meals, drinks and entertainment. These are known as all-inclusive holidays and the majority of tourists who visit the Dominican Republic are on this kind of deal. If this is what you want, you should book it up with a tour operator before you leave as it's not always possible (and certainly not cheap) to turn up at a resort and pay for a room by the night.

Away from the all-inclusive resorts there are plenty of **tourist hotels** to choose from. These generally have all the amenities of the resorts, but are slightly less regimented. (For instance, you don't have to wear a fluorescent wristband!) Even so, they can still be quite expensive, although you save by not paying for your meals up front. Most towns, even the commercial ones with little tourist traffic, have at least one hotel in this category.

The reservoir of other accommodation is of greatest interest to the independent traveller. These places generally cost less than US$25 per night, although it's a little misleading to call all of them **budget hotels**. In fact, some of them have all the facilities of the tourist hotels – air conditioning, cable TV, telephones in rooms, hot water etc – but are smaller and perhaps slightly rougher around the edges. But if you can tolerate the odd piece of peeling wallpaper or an incongruous painting on the wall, these places provide an affordable and comfortable alternative to the larger hotels. The price starts to fall if you can make do without air conditioning and the various other luxuries mentioned above. When you have reached the US$10 waterline (anything much below this is going to be very basic) you'll probably be getting a box-like room without a view, but with a fan, a bathroom, a clean towel and a bar of soap.

Most of the tourist towns have a fair selection of **apart-hotels**. These are designed primarily for the longer-term visitor. The rooms are often like small apartments, with a sleeping and living area as well as a small kitchen. The price usually depends on how long you stay.

Camping is not at all popular in the Dominican Republic. In fact, unless you're hiking in the national parks, there will be little or no opportunity to camp. The same applies to youth hostels.

Taxes
You will normally only have to worry about hotel tax at the larger, more expensive places. I suppose that it applies everywhere, but at the smaller, budget hotels it rarely crops up. In any case, for your information it currently stands at 23% (5% room tax, 8% sales tax and 10% service charge). Restaurants, meanwhile, charge 8% sales tax and a 10% service charge.

TOURIST INFORMATION
Make the most of the Dominican tourist offices abroad, since there are not many of them in the country itself. Admittedly, the type of information provided is not really targeted at the independent traveller, but it might be useful as an introduction.

Dominican tourist offices abroad
Belgium 160 avenue Louise, Brussels 1050; tel: 22 646 0840
Canada 2080 rue Crescent, Montreal, H3G2B8 Quebec; tel: 514 499 1918;
35 Church Street, Unit 50, Market Square, Toronto, M5E1T3 Ontario; tel: 416 361 2126
France 11 Rue Boudreau, Paris 75009; tel: 01 43 12 91 91
Germany 17 Hochstrasse D-60313, Frankfurt; tel: 69 91397878
Italy 25 Piazza Castello, 20121 Milan; tel: 02 805 7781
Spain 13 Juan Hurtado de Mendoza, Apt. 305, 28036 Madrid; tel: 01 350 9483
UK 18–20 Hancourt Building, High Holborn, London; tel: 0171 242 7778 (for Tourist Guides tel: 0891 600260)

USA 1501 Broadway, Suite 410, New York, NY; tel: 212 575 4966/
toll free 1 888 374 6361; 2355 Salzedo Street, Suite 307, Coral Gables, FL;
tel: 305 444 4592/toll free 1 888 358 9594; 561 West Diversey Parkway, Suite 214,
Chicago, IL; tel: 773 529 1336/toll free 1 888 303 1336

Public holidays

Christmas Day, New Year's Day and Good Friday are all public holidays and not much will be open on any of them. The **carnival** usually takes place sometime in February, in common with the rest of the Caribbean and Latin America. Also expect most businesses to be closed on the other Dominican holidays, either on the date itself or the closest Monday or Friday.

January 1	New Year's Day
January 6	Epiphany
January 21	Nuestra Señora de la Altagracia (Our Lady of Altagracia)
January 26	Juan Pablo Duarte's birthday
February 27	Independence Day
March/April	Easter
May 1	Labour Day
August 16	Dominican Restoration Day
September 24	Nuestra Señora de las Mercedes (Our Lady of Mercedes)
November 6	Constitution Day
December 25	Christmas Day

Adventure tourism

In Haiti, *tourisme d'aventure* (adventure tourism) is taken to mean ecotourism in all its aspects. I use the term here to describe the many outdoor activities on offer in the Dominican Republic. Of course, it's all ecotourism because it all relates to the environment, but the emphasis here is on the adventure. For instance, in the Cordillera Central you can go white-water rafting and canyoning – a combination of hiking, climbing, swimming and abseiling down waterfalls. Bird watching and caving are popular in the Los Haïtises National Park, while whale watching attracts visitors to the Samaná Peninsula from January to March. Hiking, mountain biking and horseback riding are all well-established activities in the mountains, while there are many good places around the coast for scuba diving and snorkelling. All in all, the Dominican Republic is an adventure playground, with dozens of adventure companies competing for your custom.

Due to the element of danger in some of these activities you should exercise caution when deciding which company to go with. For scuba diving, the school should be PADI approved; and adventure guides trained in accordance with IAGA (International Adventure Guide Association) guidelines is a definite plus. The guide's ability to speak English, or some language you understand, and the quality of the equipment are other considerations. Bearing these criteria in mind, I would recommend Get Wet and Iguana Mama, two of the largest adventure companies.

Get Wet (tel: 586 1170) is based in Puerto Plata, although none of their activities take place there. They have a base camp in Jarabacoa, from where rafting and canyoning trips are organised. You can also go caving in Los Haïtises and cascading (abseiling down waterfalls) in El Limon on the Samaná Peninsula. All of these activities last for the day and cost in the region of US$65 to US$100. Longer programmes, described as 'adventure weeks', can also be arranged.

Iguana Mama (tel: 571 0908), based in Cabarete, specialises in mountain-bike adventures. You can take short trips in the countryside around Cabarete, or longer ones lasting several days up in the Cordillera Central. If you prefer hiking, they have itineraries that include climbing Pico Duarte and the Caribbean's two other highest mountains, La Pelona and La Rucilla. For those with money to burn, the Samaná Nature Week might be of interest – it combines mountain biking with horseback riding, hiking, scuba diving and whale watching at a cost of US$1,495.

There are, of course, adventure companies and tour operators offering similar activities and excursions to the country's national parks, so shop around. One particularly good one for organised tours to the national parks is **Ecoturista** (tel: 221 4104).

Organised tours to Haiti

I am reluctant to recommend an organised tour to Haiti, but if you only have a limited amount of time on the island (charter flights usually require that you return home in two weeks), it's better than nothing. The side trip to Haiti is becoming increasingly popular and more tour operators in the Dominican Republic are running them. The most comprehensive tour lasts about a week and takes in the Citadelle La Ferrière, Sans-Souci Palace, Cap-Haïtien, the Côte des Arcadins, Port-au-Prince, Pétion-Ville and Kenscoff. **GO Caribic** (tel: 586 4075) is one of the largest tour operators in this field, but also try **Omni Tours** (tel: 565 6591), **Coco Tours** (tel: 586 1311) and **Metro Tours** (tel: 544 4580).

COMMUNICATIONS AND MEDIA
Post

The Dominican post office (INPOSDOM) has offices in most towns. Business hours vary slightly, but they are generally open from about 08.00 to 17.00, Monday to Friday (there might be a siesta in the afternoon) and 08.00 to 12.00 on Saturday. Current postal rates are RD$10 for a postcard or small letter to Europe, RD$5 for the same to the United States and Canada. In some towns there are private post offices offering an efficient but slightly more expensive service.

Telephone

The country code for the Dominican Republic is 809. The largest telephone company is the excellent **Codetel**, which has offices all over the country. They are generally open from 08.00 to 22.00. The Dominican Republic's telecommunications system is one of the most sophisticated in Latin America and direct dialling is possible to most places in the world. Expect to pay between RD$17 and RD$21 a minute to Europe and about RD$8 to the United States. Bear in mind that it's a little cheaper on Sundays and Codetel offers a 25% discount to ISIC card holders. You can also send faxes at the same rates and many offices have computers with internet access. There are several alternatives to Codetel, so shop around for the best prices. Other companies to look out for include **Tricom**, **Turitel** and **All America**. For national calls, the telephone companies are still your best bet. Just walk in, dial your number and pay when you've finished talking. Local calls cost RD$1 and can be made from the call boxes in the street or the large 1950s-style phones you see in shops and restaurants. To use these phones, dial your number, insert a RD$1 coin when prompted to do so, then push the button on the phone when you are connected. If you don't complete this final step, you'll get an engaged tone.

Media

There is a large selection of Spanish-language newspapers in the Dominican Republic. The best is the venerable *Listín Diario*, established in 1889, and every bit as good as the broadsheets you can buy in London or New York. Trailing in its wake, but still good, are *Hoy* and *El Siglo*. *Ultima Hora*, *El Nacional* and *La Noticia* come out in the afternoons. The good news for English speakers is that British, European and especially American newspapers and magazines are widely available. The bad news is that the only Dominican newspaper in English is *The Santo Domingo News*, which is largely aimed at tourists with little in the way of substantial news.

MONEY

The Dominican *peso* (RD$) comes in notes of 5, 10, 20, 50, 100, 500 and 1,000, as well as a small gold coin worth 1 peso. There are 100 *centavos* to the *peso* and they come in coins of 1, 5, 10, 25 and 50. The Dominican currency is one of the more stable in Latin America and the exchange rate has been hovering at around RD$14 for US$1 and RD$22 for GB£1 for some time now.

Exchanging money

There are no uniform banking hours in the Dominican Republic, but generally most banks open at about 08.00 and are closed by 15.00. Some of the larger ones are Banco de Reservas, Banco Nacional de Credito and Banco Popular Dominicano. Changing US dollars or travellers' cheques is an uncomplicated procedure. There are no commission charges and you get the rate advertised. Changing other major European currencies is also easy, although you should try to carry travellers' cheques in US dollars. The receipt you get when you exchange money entitles you to reconvert up to 30% of the original amount exchanged when you leave the country, so keep hold of it.

There are also *casa de cambios* in most tourist towns. They change travellers' cheques and cash without discrimination and usually at as good a rate as the banks. Credit cards or debit cards can be used in the numerous ATM machines and to pay for goods and services over the counter.

Don't bother with the black market – such as it is. Money-changers will approach you with a roll of notes offering to change *pesos* for US dollars at a rate roughly comparable to the banks. This is illegal, and since the benefit to you is negligible, it is really not worth the risk.

HEALTH AND SAFETY
Doctors and pharmacies
In cases of emergency dial 911 for an ambulance. At other times, you should have no trouble finding a doctor who speaks English. I have given the names and telephone numbers of a few clinics in some of the larger towns in the relevant *Tourist information* sections. Otherwise, my advice is to go to the Codetel office and scour the excellent and up-to-date Dominican telephone directory for doctors and other medical services. Pharmacies are abundant and have all the pills, potions and lotions you could want.

Security and the tourist police
Apart from the usual petty crime associated with tourism, the Dominican Republic poses no great security worries. Women travellers should have no reservations about travelling around the Dominican Republic on their own. It strikes me that the machismo in the Dominican culture is more bravado than anything else. In addition to the national police, the **Policía Turística** (tourist police) maintain a high profile around the country. They deal with problems specifically related to tourism and can be contacted toll free on **1 200 3500**.

172

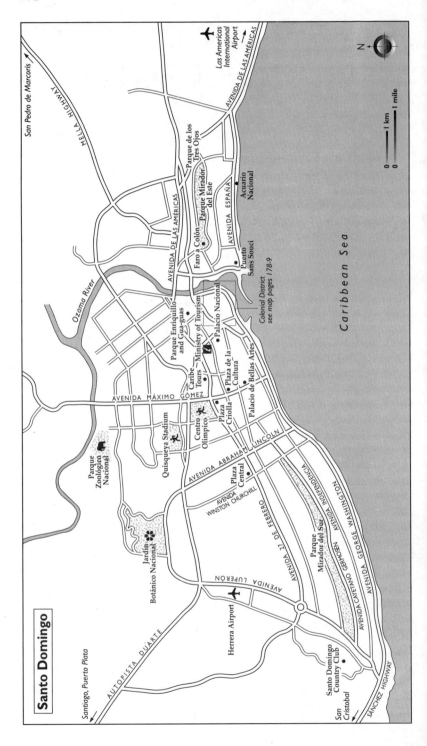

Santo Domingo

Santiago, Puerto Plata

San Pedro de Marcoris

MELLA HIGHWAY

AUTOPISTA DUARTE

Ozama River

AVENIDA DE LAS AMÉRICAS

Las Americas International Airport

AVENIDA DE LAS AMÉRICAS

N

0   1 km
0   1 mile

Caribbean Sea

Parque de los Tres Ojos

Parque Mirador del Este

Actuario Nacional

AVENIDA ESPAÑA

Faro a Colon

Puerto Sans Souci

Colonial District
see map pages 178-9

Parque Enriquillo and Gua-guas

Ministry of Tourism

Palacio Nacional

Caribe Tours

Plaza de la Cultura

Palacio de Bellas Artes

AVENIDA MÁXIMO GÓMEZ

Quisqueya Stadium

Centro Olimpico

Plaza Criolla

Parque Zoologica Nacional

Jardín Botánico Nacional

AVENIDA ABRAHAM LINCOLN

Plaza Central

AVENIDA WINSTON CHURCHILL

AVENIDA 27 DE FEBRERO

Parque Mirador del Sur

AVENIDA INDEPENDENCIA

AVENIDA CAYETANO GERMOSEN

AVENIDA GEORGE WASHINGTON

AVENIDA LUPERÓN

Herrera Airport

Santo Domingo Country Club

San Cristobal

SANCHEZ HIGHWAY

Santo Domingo

Most Dominicans simply refer to Santo Domingo as 'La Capital'. It is, after all, one of the largest cities in the West Indies, dwarfing other towns in the Dominican Republic and leading many to draw comparisons with places like Miami. Indeed, Santo Domingo has the shopping malls, cinemas, fast-food chains, theatres, museums and flashy hotels to rival any North American city. It also has the Colonial District – 3.5km² of some of the most striking and important colonial architecture in the world. It is this contrast between the old and the new which makes Santo Domingo such an interesting place to visit.

These days the population of Santo Domingo is hovering around the 3 million mark. The city sprawls across an area of more than 400km², stretching east and west of the Ozama River and from the Caribbean Sea in the south to the vast coastal plain in the north. Quite an increase since 1496 when Santo Domingo was a small settlement called Nueva Isabela on the east bank of the Ozama River.

Legend has it that Santo Domingo owes its existence to a young Spanish conquistador and the love of an Indian queen. Apparently, the conquistador – a man named Miguel Diaz – fled La Isabela to escape punishment for having wounded another settler in a duel. He headed south and settled on the banks of the Ozama River. The ruler of this part of the island was a queen known as Catalina who, for some reason, fell in love with Diaz. Fearing that her love would be unrequited, Catalina told Diaz about huge gold reserves on the banks of the Haina River. For his part, Diaz hightailed it back to La Isabela and swapped this information for a pardon for his past crimes from Bartolomé Columbus, Christopher's brother. In 1496 Bartolomé moved the Spanish garrison from La Isabela to Nueva Isabela, renaming it Santo Domingo before it was destroyed by a hurricane.

In 1502 the new governor of the colony, Nicolás de Ovando, decided to rebuild the town. It was relocated on the west bank of the Ozama River, the buildings were constructed in stone (as opposed to the wood of the original settlement) and the streets were laid out in a grid pattern, thus improving mobility and making it easier to defend. In 1508 Santo Domingo received its royal charter and became the first city in the New World. For the next 25 years or so it was also the undisputed capital of the New World, but when huge gold reserves were discovered in Mexico and Peru, attention moved away and by the end of the 16th century it had become a comparative backwater.

Nonetheless, it remained the capital of the colony and, since 1844, the capital of the Dominican Republic. Its modern-day expansion began when Trujillo came to power. He renamed the city Ciudad Trujillo in 1936 and started to transform it into a capital worthy of such a great leader. During this period famous landmarks like the Malecón and the National Palace were built and the population started to grow. When Trujillo was assasinated in 1961, the city became known once again as Santo Domingo and continued to expand – demographically, geographically and economically – to what it is today.

ORIENTATION
Most people arrive in Santo Domingo from either the Las Américas International Airport or the north of the country.

Traffic from the airport approaches Santo Domingo from the east along the Las Américas Highway. This road crosses the Ozama River at the Duarte bridge, at which point it becomes Avenida 27 de Febrero, one of the principal roads running east and west through the city. Virtually all *gua-guas* entering the capital from the east cross the Duarte Bridge, or the adjacent Mella Bridge, and terminate at Parque Enriquillo on Avenida Duarte, which stretches from north to south and ends in the heart of the Colonial District. This can be considered the downtown part of Santo Domingo where the department stores and prostitutes are found.

The other main roads that finish on the edge of the Colonial District, at Parque Independencia, all run from east to west. Avenida Independencia and Avenida Bolívar pass through the residential area of Gazcue, while Avenida George Washington (or The Malecón) is the coastal road where many of the expensive hotels are situated. Apart from Avenida Duarte, the principal roads running north and south through the city are Avenida Máximo Gómez (for the Plaza de la Cultura), Avenida Abraham Lincoln and Avenida Winston Churchill (for the Plaza Central).

Traffic from the north enters Santo Domingo on Autopista Duarte, which becomes Avenida John F Kennedy at Herrera Airport in the west of the city. *Gua-guas* terminate at different places, but few stray far from the intersection of Avenida 27 de Febrero and Avenida Duarte. The larger bus companies, meanwhile, all have stations at various points along Avenida 27 de Febrero.

GETTING THERE AND AWAY
By air
The internal flights operated by Air Santo Domingo all leave from **Herrera Airport** (tel: 567 3900) in the west of the city. There are six flights a day to Punta Plata, five to Punta Cana, three to Santiago and La Romana, and one to Barahona and El Portillo. The fares for all of these flights are around US$50 one way.

Las Américas International Airport

The majority of foreign visitors to the Dominican Republic arrive in Santo Domingo, or rather 20km east of Santo Domingo at the Las Americas International Airport (tel: 549 0450). The airport terminal is modest by London or New York standards, but large enough to have most of the facilities that make your life easier. There are two banks open until late in the evening, ATM machines, a post office (08.00-16.00), a Codetel Office (07.00–22.00), car-hire companies, taxis and a variety of restaurants and gift shops. The tourist information office is in Immigration.

Unfortunately, there is no officially recognised airport bus. Occasionally a *gua-gua* on its way from Boca Chica to the capital will pass by the airport terminal, but don't count on it. The surest way to catch a bus is to either walk, or take a *motoconcho* to the main road a couple of kilometres from the airport. Here, every other vehicle is a *gua-gua* going to Santo Domingo. Taxis, on the other hand, are not in short supply – expect to pay about RD\$200 to Parque Independencia or RD\$150 to Boca Chica.

Getting to the airport from Santo Domingo involves catching a *gua-gua* bound for Boca Chica. The airport turning is roughly halfway between the two towns, just after you pass the tollbooth on the Las Américas Highway.

By road

The two major bus companies, Caribe Tours and Metro, have terminals on Avenida 27 de Febrero. **Caribe Tours** (tel: 221 4422), on the corner of Avenida 27 de Febrero and Leopoldo Navarro near the Gran Hotel Lina, is closer to the Colonial District. In addition to frequent services to Santiago, Puerto Plata and Sosua, they also go to Río San Juan and Samaná five times a day (RD\$75) and Barahona three times a day (RD\$60). **Metro** (tel: 566 7126) is further west along Avenida 27 de Febrero at the Plaza Central. Destinations from here include various towns in the Cibao Valley (Santiago, La Vega, Moca and San Francisco de Macorís), Puerto Plata and Samaná. Between Caribe Tours and Metro at the Plaza Criolla, the impressive **Terra Bus** (tel: 472 1080) make several runs a day to Santiago.

The bus companies do not serve many destinations, especially in the east and west of the country, but this shortfall is filled by the *gua-guas*. Most of Santo Domingo's *gua-guas* leave from, or not far from, Parque Enriquillo, in the centre of downtown on Avenida Duarte between Avenida México and Calle Paris. The various destinations and departure points are as follows:

- For Santiago, Puerto Plata and other destinations north (served by Transporte del Cibao) and Higuey, go to Parque Enriquillo itself.
- For San Pedro de Macorís and La Romana, go to Calle Ravello, just off Parque Enriquillo.
- For Boca Chica, go two blocks north of Parque Enriquillo.
- For Barahona, La Descubierta (Lake Enriquillo), Jimaní (the Dominican border), San Juan de la Maguana and Elias Piña, go to the intersection of avenidas Duarte and 27 de Febrero, which is a few blocks north of Parque Enriquillo next to Hotel Caribeño.

You can catch *gua-guas* to San Cristóbal, Baní and Azua de Compostela from the vicinity of Parque Enriquillo, but they also leave regularly from Parque Independencia, which is much more convenient if you're staying in the Colonial District.

As an aid to planning your travels around the Dominican Republic, using Santo Domingo as a base, a rough indication of journey times and prices of *gua-guas* follows:

Barahona 3 hours, RD$45
Boca Chica 30 minutes, RD$12
Higuey 2½ hours, RD$45
Jimaní 4½ hours, RD$70
Puerto Plata 4 hours, RD$55
La Romana 1½ hours, RD$30
San Cristóbal 45 minutes, RD$12
San Pedro de Macorís 1 hour, RD$25
Santiago 3 hours, RD$35

GETTING AROUND

Santo Domingo is the Caribbean's largest metropolis. It occupies an area of about 400km² and some of the roads mentioned above are very long indeed. Avenida 27 de Febrero, for instance, meanders through the city for about 15km before it joins Autopista Duarte. This means that at some point you'll probably have to use the capital's hectic public transport system.

The most convenient (and expensive) way to get from A to B is by **taxi**. You can tell the driver exactly where you want to go and he'll take you there directly without picking up other passengers.

Taxis should not be confused with *carros* – cars that run along certain routes, picking up and dropping off passengers as they go. The driver of a *carro* will languidly hang his arm out of the window in the general direction he is going. Usually a *carro* will stick to one main road. The normal fare is RD$2 and slightly more for longer trips and rides after dark.

A motley selection of buses and vans – collectively called *públicos* – also ply the streets of Santo Domingo. They cost about the same as the *carros*, but their routes tend to be longer and more complex. If you're based in the Colonial District, Parque Independencia is the place to go for *públicos* and *carros* to almost anywhere in the city and its suburbs.

WHERE TO STAY
The Colonial District

The atmosphere of the Colonial District both during the day and at night is so special that you should try to stay there for at least some of your time in Santo Domingo. Fortunately, a reasonable range of hotels is available.

The best is **Hotel Palacio** (tel: 682 4730) on Calle Duarte, where rooms are US$50 for one person and fractionally more for two, but the old adage that 'you get what you pay for' certainly applies. The deep brown mahogany furniture and beams across the ceilings give the rooms a very distinguished feel, as well as a wonderful smell. You could be in the Alcázar for all the paintings of kings, princes and dukes on the walls and the iron chandeliers hanging from the ceilings. I doubt, however, that Don Diego had air conditioning, cable TV and a refrigerator stocked with soft drinks and packets of potato chips. A pretty courtyard in the middle of the hotel completes the overall effect. Not far from the Palacio, on Calle General Luperón, is its main competitor, **Hostal Nicolás Nader** (tel: 687 7887). This too has a gorgeous colonial feel, plenty of wooden furniture and a pretty courtyard. The ten rooms cost about the same as those at the Palacio. The house itself is the birthplace of the Dominican tyrant, Ulises Heureaux (see page 147). **Hostal Nicolás de Ovando** is another historical building converted into a hotel. At the time of writing, however, it was closed for refurbishment. It is expected to reopen around April 1999.

Hotel David's (tel: 685 9121), on Calle Arzobispo Nouel between Calle Santome and Calle Espaillat, has more-or-less the same facilities as the Palacio and Nicolás Nader, but is tatty and overpriced at RD$500 for a single and RD$550 for a double. The German-run **Hotel Anacaona** (tel: 688 6888) is near Conde Gate on Calle Palo Hincado, and rooms cost RD$275 for a single or double. **Hotel Aida** (tel: 685 7692), just off El Conde on Calle Espaillat, offers pretty much the same deal. **Pensione Gené** is at 505 El Conde. Look for a small blue canopy over the door with 'El Rincon del Cassette' written on it in white. Despite being at the noisy end of El Conde; the four or five rooms in this house are surprisingly quiet. They cost RD$200, which is as good as you'll get in this part of the Colonial District. **Hotel Independencia** (tel: 686 1663), on Calle Arzobispo Nouel in Parque Independencia, is another option. Rooms with fan start at RD$206. For longer stays, or if you desire a kitchen in your room, you might consider **Aparta Hotel La Arcada** (tel: 686 7456) on Calle Arzobispo Meriño.

If none of these places are suitable, go to Calle Benito González, one block north of Avenida Mella, where you're sure to find somewhere with cheap prices and a rough sort of charm. Working west to east along Calle Benito González the first place is **El Prestige Hotel** (tel: 686 0000), next to the market. It has cheap prices (RD$75), but no charm. **Hotel Don Max** (tel: 688 4299) is better. You can get a room with air-conditioning, TV and hot water for RD$250, or a room the size of a shoe box in the basement for RD$100. The manager is very friendly, speaks a little English and tries hard to please. The sign for **Hotel Lana del Norte** (tel: 685 3385) can be seen from anywhere along Calle Benito González. The rooms, while functional, are perhaps not comfortable enough to persuade you to follow the advice given by the hotel on their business cards to 'make this your second home'. After the Lana del Norte you start to approach the downtown part of Santo Domingo – the area on and around Avenida Duarte – where the general quality of the accommodation takes a nose-dive. I wouldn't like to recommend any of the hotels in this area, all of which have hourly room rates and mirrors instead of fans on the ceiling. However, you can choose from **Hotel Radiante** (tel: 688

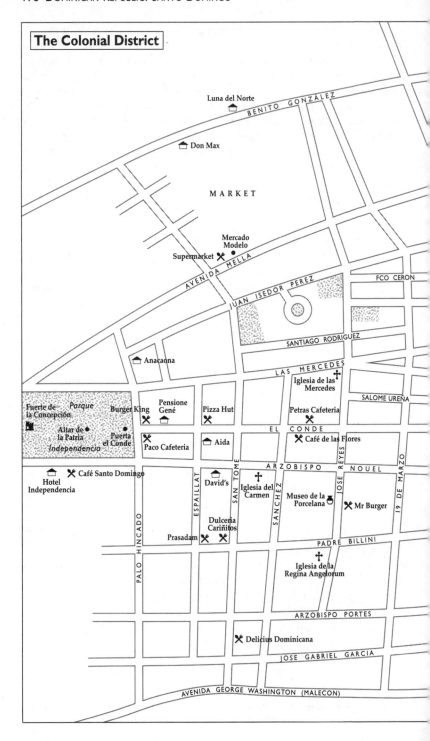

The Colonial District

Luna del Norte

BENITO GONZÁLEZ

Don Max

MARKET

Mercado Modelo

Supermarket

AVENIDA MELLA

JUAN ISEDOR PEREZ

FCO CERON

SANTIAGO RODRIGUEZ

Anacaona

LAS MERCEDES

Iglesia de las Mercedes

SALOME UREÑA

Fuerte de la Concepción

Parque

Burger King

Pensione Gené

Pizza Hut

Petras Cafeteria

Altar de la Patria

Puerta el Conde

EL CONDE

Independencia

Paco Cafeteria

Aida

Café de las Flores

JOSE REYES

Hotel Independencia

Café Santo Domingo

ESPAILLAT

David's

SAN TOME

ARZOBISPO

NOUEL

19 DE MARZO

Iglesia del Carmen

SANCHEZ

Museo de la Porcelana

Mr Burger

PALO HINCADO

Dulcería Cariñitos

Prasadam

PADRE BILLINI

Iglesia de la Regina Angelorum

ARZOBISPO PORTES

Delicius Dominicana

JOSE GABRIEL GARCIA

AVENIDA GEORGE WASHINGTON (MALECON)

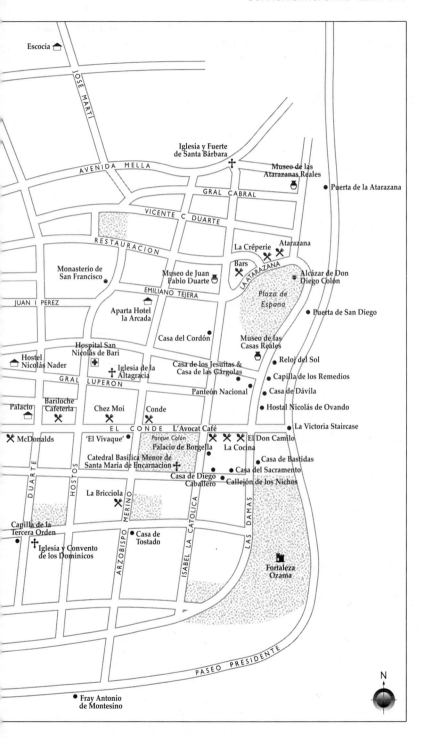

Escocia

JOSE MARTI

AVENIDA MELLA

Iglesia y Fuerte
de Santa Bárbara

Museo de las
Atarazanas Reales

Puerta de la Atarazana

GRAL CABRAL

VICENTE C DUARTE

RESTAURACION

La Crêperie   Atarazana

Monasterio de
San Francisco

Museo de Juan
Pablo Duarte

Bars

LA ATARAZANA

Alcázar de Don
Diego Colón

EMILIANO TEJERA

JUAN I PEREZ

Aparta Hotel
la Arcada

Plaza de
España

Puerta de San Diego

Casa del Cordón

Museo de las
Casas Reales

Hospital San
Nicolás de Bari

Hostel
Nicolás Nader

Iglesia de la
Altagracia

Reloj del Sol

Casa de los Jesuítas &
Casa de las Gárgolas

Capilla de los Remedios

GRAL   LUPERON

Panteón Nacional

Casa de Dávila

Palacio

Bariloche
Cafetería

Chez Moi

Conde

Hostal Nicolás de Ovando

EL   CONDE   L'Avocat Café

La Victoria Staircase

McDonalds

'El Vivaque'

Parque Colón

El Don Camilo

Palacio de Borgella

La Cocina

Catedral Basílica Menor de
Santa María de Encarnación

Casa de Bastidas

Casa de Diego
Caballero

Casa del Sacramento

La Bricciola

Callejón de los Nichos

DUARTE

HOSTOS

MERINO

ISABEL LA CATOLICA

LAS DAMAS

Capilla de la
Tercera Orden

ARZOBISPO

Casa de
Tostado

Iglesia y Convento
de los Dominicos

Fortaleza
Ozama

PASEO PRESIDENTE

N

Fray Antonio
de Montesino

9054), **Hotel Oriental, Hotel Nuevo Tres Gigantes** and **Hotel Escocia** (tel: 685 4338). I have to admit that Hotel Escocia is one notch above the rest. This large, green building just off Calle Benito González on Calle José Martí is how a brothel should be run. A computer system monitors how long each room has been occupied and staff in red waistcoats rush about delivering cold drinks and fistfuls of condoms to rooms. As an example of Dominican organisation and efficiency, not always that easy to find, Hotel Escocia might be worth a try. Rooms for the night start at RD$225.

The Malecón and Gazcue

If for some reason you don't want to stay in the Colonial District, what are the other options? There are one or two hotels in the downtown area near Parque Enriquillo (the best is **Hotel Caribeño**) and no doubt many more in various impractical locations throughout the city. However, the two best areas for accommodation other than the Colonial District are the Malecón and Gazcue.

The Malecón

The Malecón, also known as Avenida George Washington, has always been famous for its luxury hotels. This reputation is upheld today by establishments such as the **Meliá Santo Domingo** (tel: 221 6666), the **Renaissance Jaragua** (tel: 221 2222) and the **V Centenario Intercontinental** (tel: 221 0000). These are all first-class hotels charging in excess of US$100 a night. In a slightly lower league, but still good, is the **Hotel Napolitano** (tel: 687 1131), which is the first of the big hotels as you walk down the Malecón from the Colonial District. Rooms are US$65 and perhaps worth considering if there are two of you.

Hotels with more realistic prices are sandwiched between the expensive ones. **Maison Gautreauz** (tel: 687 4856) is on Calle Féliz Mariano Lluberes, a quiet, tree-lined street by the side of Hotel V Centenario Intercontinental. They have a selection of rooms that can accommodate up to five people (RD$800), and various extras such as free coffee and a baby-sitting service. **Apart-Hotel Sea View** (tel: 221 4420), opposite the entrance to Hotel Napolitano, is really for longer stays. They have rooms for RD$350 and apartments for RD$650. **Hotel La Llave del Mar** (tel: 682 5961) is the only place along the Malecón that could be described as a budget hotel. It is just south of the Colonial District and rooms with air-conditioning and hot water start at RD$200. You can get a view of the sea if you pay more.

Gazcue

Gazcue is a shady residential district bounded to the south by the Malecón. There is nothing to see here in particular, but it can be a pleasant and convenient area to base yourself. There is good access to the Colonial District, to the east of Gazcue, and the Plaza de la Cultura is at the western end.

As a general rule, the closer you are to Parque Independencia the cheaper the hotels. This is borne out by the first couple of hotels you encounter on Avenida Independencia, the busy road that cuts through the heart of Gazcue.

Above Beach at Confresi,
Dominican Republic (PB)

Below Playa Dorada, near Puerto
Plata, Dominican Republic (PB)

Above and Right
Cigar factory, Moca,
Dominican Republic (RV)

Below Charcoal seller,
Pétion-Ville, Haiti (RV)

Above Sans Souci Palace,
Milot, Haiti (RV)

Left Fort Picolet,
Cap-Haïtien, Haiti (RV)

Below The *Marron Inconnu*
(Unknown Slave),
Port-au-Prince, Haiti (RV)

Above Village houses in the Dominican Republic (PB)

Right Afternoon nap, Saint-Marc, Haiti (RV)

Below Children at Petite Rivière de l'Artibonite, Haiti (RV)

Hotel Rafael (tel: 685 0084) is 'under new management' and they have their work cut out trying to sell their best rooms with TV for RD$250. The RD$175 rooms with bathroom are better value. **Hotel Antillas** (tel: 686 8383) is not under new management, but it should be. The rooms (RD$175) are basic and the staff unfriendly.

Hotel Bolívar (tel: 685 2200) is also near Parque Independencia, but this time on Gazcue's other main road, Avenida Bolívar. This hotel doubles as a school for prospective hotel managers, although it wasn't clear during my stay whether the students were the staff or not. Rooms cost RD$350 and are air-conditioned. **Hotel Cervantes** (tel: 686 8161), on Calle Cervantes, is a three star, business-oriented hotel. All of their rooms are over RD$500 and satisfactory. Continuing west, there are two hotels of a similar standard on Calle Danae – **Hotel Guest House La Grand Mansion** (tel: 682 2033) and **Hotel La Residence** (tel: 412 7298), both with air-conditioned double rooms for about RD$300.

Back on Avenida Independencia (this time behind the big hotels on the Malecón) **Hotel La Casona Dorada** (tel: 221 3535), at number 255, is expensive and rather pretentious. Rooms are RD$500 and up; and there was extensive building work going on while I was there. **Hotel Duque de Wellington** (tel: 682 4525) at 304 Avenida Independencia is better. While still a little overpriced at RD$475 for a single and RD$525 for a double, this is one of the more intimate hotels in Gazcue and worth considering.

Finally, **Hotel Colonial** is opposite the Palacio de Belles Artes on Avenida Máximo Gómez. This road marks the dividing line between Gazcue and Ciudad Universitaria, the student quarter. The Colonial is apparently a three-star hotel, but it has seen better days. Think twice before shelling out at least US$50 for a tatty room here, because you could certainly get more for your money elsewhere.

WHERE TO EAT
The Colonial District
There are all sorts of restaurants, cafés and fast-food outlets packed into the 3½km² of the Colonial District. The really swanky places are generally in Santo Domingo, but you can eat well within the walls of the old city.

Restaurant Don Roberto is at Hostal Nicolás Nader. The food is good and occasionally the Algerian manageress rustles up a couscous – surely unique in the Dominican Republic. Hotel Palacio, meanwhile, has **Restaurant Black and Light**, which also reflects the hotel manager's nationality by specialising in German cuisine. Elsewhere, Italian food is a speciality (and especially expensive) at one of the Colonial District's smartest resturants, **La Bricciola**, on Calle Arzobispo Meriño. **Restaurante Atarazana** on La Atarazana is another up-market option, with an international menu offering a good range of steaks.

Most of the top places for Dominican food are near Parque Colón. There are three restaurants on the quietest stretch of El Conde between Calle Isabel La Católica and Calle Las Damas – **L'Avocat Café Restaurant**, **La Cocina**

Restaurant and **El Don Camilo Bar Restaurant**. All have similar menus, prices and even décor. The Creole food in general isn't bad, even if the prices are a little steep. All three have tables and chairs outside. The venerable **Restaurant Conde** is on the corner of Parque Colón. This striking building with its four, huge, wooden doors in the shape of arches was allegedly Santo Domingo's first restaurant. Disappointingly, someone down the line has made it look like an American diner and the staff are rather curt. Nevertheless, you can eat quite well here from perhaps the largest menu in the Dominican Republic. There must be about 150 different dishes, ranging from the humble *chicharrón de pollo* at RD$50 to the regal lobster thermidor at RD$285. The small **Chez Moi Bar Restaurant** is nearby on El Conde, offering rather expensive international cuisine.

The other eateries on El Conde tend to be of the café and fast-food variety. The best of the cafés could well be the **Paco Cafeteria** on the corner of Parque Independencia. This is an excellent place for people-watching over a *café negro*, which is served fresh and strong. They don't do a bad *cubano* sandwich either. The **Bariloche Cafeteria**, between Calle Duarte and Calle Hostos, is the place to go for a lunchtime dose of *comida criolla*. They have about ten different meal combinations all for between RD$35 and RD$40. Other cafés along El Conde include **Petras Cafeteria** and **Café de las Flores**, while in Parque Independencia (Calle Arzobisopo Nouel), **Café Santo Domingo** has good *comida criolla*. Most of the above serve hamburgers, pizzas, sandwiches and ice-creams, competing with the likes of McDonalds, Burger King and Pizza Hut for the top spot on El Conde.

Off the main thoroughfare, one or two small Dominican places might be of interest to the fast-food junkie. **Mr Burger** is on Calle Jose Reyes between Calle Arzobisopo Nouel and Calle Padre Billini. This is fast food with a family atmosphere. Pop in and meet 'Mr Cheese Burger', 'Mr Bacon Burger', 'Mr Chilli Burger' and the other gentlemen on the menu. Less gimmicky, but certainly no less popular, is **Delicius Dominicana** on Calle Santome near the Malecón. This is nothing more than a hole in the wall, out of which stream piping hot *empanadas* and *pastelitos* to the expectant masses.

Also in the Colonial District are several **ice-cream** places on El Conde, a large **market** on Avenida Mella and some good **bakeries**. The **Prasadam** on Calle Padre Billini between Calle Santome and Calle Espaillat, for example, is a small shop selling freshly baked brown bread and other health-food products. Next door, **Dulceria Cariñitos** is a great place for *dulces*. For an early-morning or mid-afternoon crêpe try **La Crêperie** on La Atarazana. The largest supermarket in the area is **Nacional** on Avenida Mella by the market.

The Malecón and Gazcue
The Malecón
All of the big hotels on the Malecón have restaurants serving both Dominican and international cuisine. **Restaurant La Canasta** at the Meliá Santo Domingo Hotel and **Restaurant Latino** at the Renaissance Jaragua Hotel

specialise in native food. The menus are not vast, but the dishes are carefully selected and well prepared. These two hotels also have international restaurants – **Restaurant Antoine** at the Santo Domingo and the **Manhattan Grill** at the Jaragua – serving French cuisine and steaks respectively. **El Vesuvio**, 521 Avenida George Washington, is one of the better-known restaurants in Santo Domingo, gaining its reputation as an Italian/Mediterranean restaurant, but it also does good Dominican and international dishes. If you can't get a table at El Vesuvio, try **El Vesuvio II** at 17 Avenida Tiradentes.

If you fancy some seafood, two restaurants south of the Colonial District might be worth a try. **Restaurant La Barca** is not as plush as some of the restaurants on the Malecón, but it does have one or two imaginative conch dishes and tables with views of the sea. **Restaurant La Llave del Mar** is an antidote to the refined sophistication that characterises the Malecón and its restaurants. This is not to say that the stuffed turtles, sharks, crocodiles and fish on the walls, and the glass-top tables with re-creations of the seabed beneath them, are tacky; they are just different. Note that only seafood is served here. There are several other restaurants along the Malecón, but you might be disappointed if you're looking for a really cheap place to eat.

Gazcue

If nothing on the Malecón takes your fancy, go one block north to Avenida Independencia where there are some other options. The best and probably the cheapest is **Café Villar**, not far from Hotel Duque de Wellington at No 304. This is an informal place serving a comprehensive range of *comida criolla*. The food is displayed behind a counter, but don't let this put you off – it looks and tastes great. For dessert you must try a cream cake at the excellent bakery, **Villa Hermanos**, which shares the premises with Café Villar. Nearby, **Restaurant El Fogón** is a reasonable Italian restaurant next to Hotel Duque de Wellington. Of the other restaurants on Avenida Independencia, try **Restaurant Estrella** for Chinese food and **Restaurant El Conuco** for some of the more unusual Dominican dishes like *sancocho prieto*, with seven different meats. Both of these are behind the Renaissance Jaragua Hotel. **Restaurant La Mezquita** serves *cocina españa* (Spanish food) and **Restaurant Cantábrico** specialises in seafood. The Cantábrico is one of the more expensive restaurants in Santo Domingo, notwithstanding its claim as 'El Rey de los Mariscos' (King of Seafood).

Elswhere in Gazcue, **Paco's Bananas Bar Restaurant**, on Calle Danae, is convenient if you're staying at either of the two hotels on this street. They have steaks, pastas and a few Dominican dishes. **O'Hara's Place**, on the same street, is a bar more than a restaurant, and a shrine to *Gone With The Wind* more than a bar. It is stuffed with memorabilia from the film, and the walls are plastered with contributions from the many fans who have visited O'Hara's over the years. **Restaurant El Dragon**, is a nice, simple place on Avenida Bolívar near Parque Independencia, while **Café Havana**, a Cuban restaurant, is more up-market. Both of these are convenient if you're staying at Hotel

Bolívar or Hotel Cervantes. **La Reina de España** is on the same street as Hotel Cervantes. This is one of Santo Domingo's more exclusive establishments, specialising in Spanish and international food.

At the western end of Gazcue, on Avenida Máximo Gómez, there are a number of fast-food restaurants (**McDonalds, Burger King, Wendy's, Domino's Pizza, Pollo Victorina**) and a big **Nacional Supermarket**.

Elsewhere

The restaurants in the Colonial District, Gazcue and the Malecón represent a fraction of what's on offer in Santo Domingo. Elsewhere, you can find some interesting places, although often they take some time to get to. **Mesón de la Cava** is at the eastern end of the Parque Mirador del Sur. While the Dominican food is quite good, people really come to eat in a cave 15m deep. There is also live music and a nightclub nearby. **Mesón de Castilla** is something of an institution in Santo Domingo as it has been around for a long time and still churns out popular Spanish cooking. There is an excellent restaurant at Puerto Sans Soucí called **Restaurant Bucanero** which, unlike the other facilities at Sans Soucí, is open all the time. It overlooks the harbour and specialises in seafood. You'll be pushing the boat out a bit if you decide to come to this place, so you might as well try one of their adventurous, and usually delicious, entrées. For *mofongo* enthusiasts, or would-be enthusiasts, **Casa del Mofongo** on Avenida 27 de Febrero is the place to indulge.

Santo Domingo has a Chinatown around Calle Beniti González and Avenida Duarte. None of the restaurants in this area are very expensive and they have similar menus. **Restaurante Canton** is probably the most expensive by virtue of its air-conditioning, while **Restaurante Hong Kong** is arguably the best value. There are several others, so shop around.

NIGHTLIFE

The place to go for bars in the Colonial District is the Plaza de España. There are several on the square itself opposite the Alcázar de Colón, all with tables outside and a similar selection of drinks. It probably fluctuates daily, but during my visit **Bar Mesón Museo de Jamon** seemed to be the most popular. This could have been due to the live flamenco dancing in the evenings. **Café Montesinos** and **Drake's Pub**, which has a small library of English books, are good alternatives. **Café Concierto** is next to Plaza de España on La Atarazana. An arty crowd gathers here to munch on *picaderos* and *empanadas* and stare at a wall of TV screens. Until about 23.00, much of the nightlife in the Colonial District is on El Conde. Most of the cafés sell beer and the street is usually teeming with young Dominicans out for an ice-cream, a slice of pizza or to spend a few *pesos* in the amusement arcades. This is not at the cutting edge of Santo Domingo's nightlife, but it can be fun to watch.

For more hard-core entertainment, you should venture out of the Colonial District. Depending on how much money you have, the discos and casinos on the Malecón might be of some appeal. You could try the Mélia Santo Domingo's **Omni Disco**, the Renaissance Jaragua's **Jubilee Disco**, or the **Discoteca Napolitano** at Hotel Napolitano, which also has a piano bar. All these hotels, along with a few others in the city, have casinos. Outside of the big hotels there are plenty of other places to have a drink and a dance on the Malecón. **Bella Blu** is one of the larger and livelier establishments, and on Avenida Independencia there's the **Vertigo**, **Opus** and **Jet Set**. They all play *merengue* at a healthy volume and there might be live music at the Jet Set, occasionally featuring some of the biggest names on the Dominican hit parade. Perhaps the most famous disco in Santo Domingo is the **Guácara Taína** in the Mirador del Sur district. Hundreds of people come here every night to enjoy unrelenting *merengue* in an underground cave. The cover charge is higher than elsewhere, but this doesn't seem to put anybody off. **Café Atlantico**, at the intersection of Avenida Máximo Gómez and Avenida Abraham Lincoln, is slightly more sedate, but no less trendy.

ENTERTAINMENT

The **Teatro Nacional** in the Plaza de la Cultura is one of the top national theatres in the world. If you fancy an evening of ballet, opera, theatre, music or dance, tickets cost anything from RD$100 to RD$500. The box office (tel: 682 7255) is open from 09.30 to 18.30 and is located at the entrance to the theatre. Just down the road, the **Palacio de Bellas Artes** also has cultural and artistic events.

There is an overwhelming number of cinemas in Santo Domingo. Probably the most convenient is **Cinema Centro** on the Malecón near the intersection with Avenida Máximo Gómez. It's only about a 20-minute walk from the Colonial District and they show recent films with Spanish subtitles for RD$35. The cinemas at the Plaza Central are further out on Avenida 27 de Febrero at the intersection with Avenida Winston Churchill. They have the best selection of all the latest films, once again shown with Spanish subtitles. **Palacio del Cine** is reputed to be the best, but **Cine Broadway** and **Cine Manzana**, both in the plaza itself, are just as good. Tickets cost RD$40.

If you happen to be in Santo Domingo during the baseball season (October to January), you might like to see a game. They are played at the **Quisqueya Stadium** in the north of the city, although getting tickets is often difficult due to the popularity of the sport. It's easier to get into the **Centro Olimpico**, south of the Quisqueya Stadium, where you can take in some amateur gymnastics and basketball. The **Santo Domingo Country Club** is east of the city. You can play golf here – at a price.

TOURIST INFORMATION

Obviously, in such a large and modern city there are going to be many places where you can find the various facilities that make your life on the road easier. I have only mentioned a few, concentrating on the areas where you are likely to be.

Tourist office

The Ministry of Tourism is on the corner of Avenida México and Avenida 30 de Marzo. This is not really a tourist office, but you can get what brochures are available, which effectively means the *Gia Turística* (*Tourist Guide*), a magazine published each year with general information about the country in Spanish, English and German. There is also a small tourist information office in the Colonial District on Calle Isabel La Católica on the eastern side of Parque Colón. The service is friendly enough, but don't expect much in the way of information.

Communications and media

There are **post offices** far from the centre at the Centro de los Héroes, Hotel El Embajador and Ciudad Nueva. There is also a small one at Puerto Sans Souci, but it's only open when a cruise ship is in town. By far the most useful post office for visitors is in the Colonial District next to the tourist information office in Parque Colón. The **Codetel** office is on El Conde between calles Duarte and Hostos, but there are numerous other places where you can make international calls in the city. There are also plenty of public telephones for local calls.

One thing that you might consider taking in Santo Domingo is a **language course**. Two of the better ones are run by Universidad APEC (tel: 698 0021) and Universidad Iberoamericana (tel: 689 4111).

Money

Banks are a dime a dozen in Santo Domingo. The best places to go in the Colonial District are Calle Isabel La Católica or Avenida Mella, where there are branches of Banco de Reservas, Banco Nacional de Credito and Banco Popular. The address of the **American Express Travel Service** (where you can also have post sent) is: Banco Dominicano del Progresso, 3 Avenida John F Kennedy, PO Box 1329; tel: 563 3233; fax: 563 2446.

Health and safety

If you need a **doctor**, you could try the following clinics, all of which appear in the government tourist literature and so, I imagine, are reasonably competent: Centro Médico UCE (tel: 221 0171); Clínica Abreu (tel: 688 4411); Clínica Gómez Patiño (tel: 685 9131); Clínica Corazones Unidos (tel: 567 4421).

The **police** maintain a presence in Parque Colón around the clock. The Colonial District is also on the beat of the **tourist police**, who are identifiable by their white shirts and navy blue trousers. The police station is on Avenida Bolívar in Gazcue.

THE COLONIAL DISTRICT

The fact that Santo Domingo is the oldest city in the New World is enough to secure its status as a major tourist attraction: 'Santo Domingo – cradle of America', as the brochures proclaim, and the remarkable Colonial District guarantees that this is not just more empty rhetoric. Even the most exacting tourist expecting to see houses as they were in Columbus' time or, failing that, at least some good ruins and museums, would have to admit that the Colonial District is something special.

The main thoroughfare is El Conde – a pedestrian street lined with shops and cafés that runs east to west through the heart of the old city. (The street is named after the Count of Peñalba who repelled an English attack of the city in 1655.) Parque Colon is at the eastern end of El Conde, while Parque Independencia is at the western end.

The Colonial District is best seen on foot and I have suggested two walking tours (with map), using El Conde as my point of reference, to help give you an overview of this sightseer's paradise (see Chapter 3, *Cruise-Ship Passengers*).

PLAZA DE LA CULTURA

If you still crave culture after the Colonial District, head into the heart of Santo Domingo where you'll find some of the best museums in the West Indies. The bulk of the good ones are concentrated in the Plaza de la Cultura on Avenida Máximo Gómez between Avenida Bolívar and Avenida México. As the name would suggest, the Plaza de la Cultura is concerned with all things that relate to Dominican culture. Within the large park there is the **Biblioteca Nacional** (National Library) and the **Teatro Nacional** (National Theatre), which is reputed to be in the world's top ten. There are also four excellent museums:

Museo del Hombre Dominicano (Museum of the Dominican People)
Open 10.00-17.00 (closed Monday). RD$10.
This museum comprehensively covers the development of the Dominican people from as early as the first Indian migrations a few thousand years before Christ. It contains numerous Taino artefacts, information on the earlier Indian people in Hispaniola and coverage of the period of colonisation.

Museo Nacional de Historia y Geografía (National History and Geography Museum)
Open 09.30-17.00 (closed Monday). Free.
This museum focuses on the more recent history of the Dominican Republic, primarily from 1822 to the assassination of Trujillo in 1961. The life and times of the Dominican dictator are given ample coverage – one of the more interesting exhibits is the 1956 Oldsmobile, replete with bullet holes, used by Trujillo's assassins on May 30 1961.

Museo Nacional de Historia Natural (Natural History Museum)
Open 10.00-17.00 (closed Monday). RD$10.
Exhibits here cover the whole of natural history: ecosystems, geology, the solar system and flora and fauna indigenous to the island.

Museo de Arte Moderno (Modern Art Museum)
Open 09.00-17.00. RD$20.
Given the amount of art displayed on the streets of both the Dominican Republic and Haiti, it feels somewhat alien to see it hanging up in an art gallery. This is especially

the case with primitive art, which I think looks a bit odd in cold, sterile and pretentious galleries. Nevertheless, the Museum of Modern Art does contain some important works by the most significant Dominican artists of the last 150 years. Of particular note are the murals by José Vela Zanetti, the Spanish artist who also painted the murals in the United Nations building in New York.

Two other museums, not in the Plaza de la Cultura, are worth a visit. The **Museo de Trujillo** (Store 7, Plaza Criolla) has a small selection of the dictator's personal belongings, and the **Museo de Arte Pre-Hispánico** (279 Avenida San Martín, near the intersection with Avenida Máximo Gómez) displays pre-Columbian artefacts.

OTHER THINGS TO SEE
Palacio Nacional
The National Palace is not far from Parque Independencia. Go west along Avenida Bolívar and turn right at Calle Dr Delgado. This neo-classical building, commissioned by Trujillo and designed by the Italian architect, Guido D'Alessandro, is inspired by the Pantheon in Athens. This becomes obvious when you see its huge dome measuring 34m in height and 18m in diameter. It is difficult to get inside the National Palace, but if you manage it the rooms are furnished in baroque and Renaissance styles. The centrepiece of the palace is a room, half the size of a football pitch, containing no less than 44 caryatids (female figures used as pillars).

Palacio de Bellas Artes
The Palace of Fine Arts is another impressive neo-classical building once owned by Trujillo, whose taste in architecture certainly leaned towards the grandiose. It houses the Theatre of Fine Arts, the National Ballet, the National Choir and several schools of music, dance and drama. It is next to the Plaza de la Cultura on Avenida Máximo Gómez.

Faro a Colón
The Faro a Colón (or Columbus Lighthouse) is a huge monument dedicated to Christopher Columbus and his discovery of the Americas. It is in the eastern part of Santo Domingo, across the Ozama River, in the same place where the city was founded in 1496.

The decision to build the Columbus Lighthouse in Santo Domingo was taken in 1923 at the Fifth International American Conference. A worldwide competition to design the lighthouse was won by Joseph Gleave, a 23-year-old architect student from England with no previous design experience. Nearly 70 years later, on October 6 1992, after delays caused by lack of funds and the outbreak of World War II, the Columbus Lighthouse was finally inaugurated. Built in the shape of a cross, it looks a bit like a communist architect's interpretation of the Sphinx in Egypt. The gardens surrounding the Faro, however, are lovely. The lighthouse produces a beacon of light which takes the form of a huge, white cross in the night sky. Inside there are

21 rooms containing museums, exhibition halls and a library, all connected in some way or another to Columbus. As you enter the lighthouse you'll see a marble tomb allegedly containing his mortal remains. (A church in Seville, Spain, where the explorer's remains were initially taken following his death, claims that they are still there.) The Faro a Colón is open from 10.00 to 17.00 and entrance costs RD$15.

While you are in the neighbourhood of the Faro a Colón you should take a look at the **Parque de los Tres Ojos** (Three Eyes Park), at the eastern end of **Parque Mirador del Este**. Inside the park is a large cavern containing three *cenotes* (deep, underground water reservoirs) of varying depths, each with a different type of water (fresh, salt and sulphur). This gives them all a different appearance, which is where the 'three eyes' comes from. There is also a fourth *cenote*, the depth of which is unknown, resembling the crater of a volcano. The Parque de los Tres Ojos is open from 08.30 to 17.30 and entrance costs RD$10.

Acuario Nacional
Remaining on the eastern side of the Ozama River, the National Aquarium is south of Parque Mirador del Este on Avenida España. It contains the usual tropical fish and sharks, which surround an underwater glass tunnel on all sides. Opening times are 09.30 to 18.00 (closed Monday), but plan your visit to miss the school groups.

Also on Avenida España, a kilometre or two before you reach the National Aquarium, is **Puerto Sans Souci**, where the cruise ships dock. There is a tourist information office, a bank, a post office, a Codetel office and a selection of gift shops, but they only open when a ship is in town.

Jardín Botánico Nacional
The National Botanical Gardens are on Avenida República Colombia, in the northeastern corner of the city, just about as far as you can get from the hotels in the Colonial District, Gazcue and along the Malecón. Nevertheless, they are well worth the time it takes to get to them (a taxi might be your best bet).

Named after the first Dominican botanist, Dr Rafael M Moscoso, and founded in 1976, the National Botanical Gardens consists of over 2 million m² of gardens and forests far removed from the city life a short distance away. Santo Domingo is busy, exciting and sometimes a little stressful, so coming up here can be reinvigorating. The gardens have plant collections, grouped into categories that include ferns, palms, exotic and endemic plants and orchids. There is also an ecological museum. You can see all this in 30 minutes on a small train, but wouldn't you rather walk?

The Botanical Gardens are open from 09.00 to 17.00 (closed Monday) and admission costs RD$10. The train ride and entrance to the museum are extra.

Parque Zoológico Nacional
It would make sense to combine a visit to the Botanical Gardens with the National Zoological Park, which is east of the Botanical Gardens on Paseo de

los Reyes Católicos. At 1½ million m², this is one of the largest zoos in Latin America and you get the impression that the animals have been given as much space as possible in which to roam around. Whether you visit the zoo on foot or take the short train ride on offer, look out for the Hispaniolan parrots, pink flamingoes and several other species native to the island.

The Zoological Park is open from 09.00 to 17.30 (closed Monday) and costs RD$15. Once again, the train costs a little extra.

The East

The region east of Santo Domingo is a mixture of sugar towns, luxury tourist resorts and national parks. Access to many of these is along the Las Américas Highway, which starts in Santo Domingo and runs along the Caribbean coast.

BOCA CHICA

The first stop along the Las Américas Highway is Boca Chica, 30km from Santo Domingo and just a few minutes from the airport. In the 1920s, Dominican high society chose this stretch of beach as their favourite vacation spot, making Boca Chica synonymous with style and exclusivity. Juan Bautista Vicini, a big-shot in the local sugar industry, was responsible for much of the town's early tourist development, which included the building of a yacht club and several large hotels, the first being Hotel Hamaca Beach. In the 1970s the rise of Puerto Plata and Playa Dorada on the north coast stole some of Boca Chica's thunder, and today only the most sentimental would describe it as exclusive. The town itself is the usual collection of bars, gift shops and tourist tack. Hotel Hamaca Beach has inevitably become an all-inclusive resort, along with much of the other accommodation. Fortunately, the beach remains an attractive proposition. Protected by a reef on its outer limit, the bay is calm and shallow (rarely deeper than 1.5m), with a sandy, rockless bottom. It has often been called 'the largest swimming pool in the Caribbean'.

The cheaper hotels tend to be between the beach and the Las Americas Highway. **Hotel Tropical Lost Paradise** (tel: 523 4424), on Calle Juan Bautista Vicini, is something of an institution in Boca Chica. It advertises 90 rooms, all priced at RD$150 with a fan, a bathroom and a bed, and you won't find anything cheaper in town. Other reasonable places away from the beach include **Hotel Magic Tropical** (tel: 523 4254) and the **Mango Hotel** (tel: 523 5333), with rooms for around US$20. Nearer the beach is **Hotel Pequeña Suiza** (tel: 523 4619) on Calle Duarte, **Hotel Villa Michell** (tel: 236 0238) on Avenida San Rafael, and the **Don Paco Guest House** (tel: 523 4816) on the main square, all with rooms for under US$20.

The **post office** is on Calle Duarte, as is the **Codetel** office. **Banks** can be found on Calle Duarte (Banco Popular Dominicana) and Calle Juan Bautista Vicini (Banco de Reservas), while **Western Union** is opposite the post office.

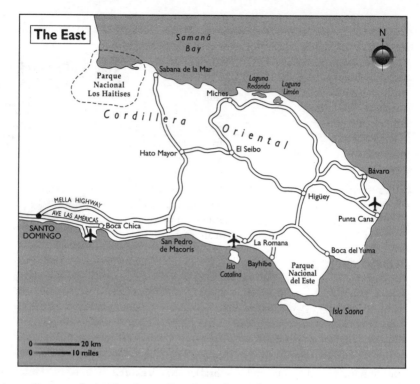

Gua-guas leave for Santo Domingo from the main square. It takes 30 minutes and costs RD$12 for an express with air conditioning, slightly less for a slower service with the windows down. To go in the other direction, towards Juan Dolio and San Pedro de Marcorís, you have to walk to the Las Américas Highway.

Costa Caribe

As you begin to approach San Pedro de Macorís there is a gradual proliferation of hotel signs by the side of the highway. This is the area known as Costa Caribe (or Playa del Este) – a collection of beaches dedicated to the country's package-tourist traffic. From west to east the beaches are Playa Caribe (also known as Embassy Beach after the US diplomats who used to go there in the 1970s), Playa Guayacanes, Playa Juan Dolio and Playa Villas del Mar. As in Boca Chica, the nearer you get to the beach the more expensive the hotels become.

SAN PEDRO DE MACORÍS

San Pedro de Macorís is a sugar-mill town 75km from Santo Domingo. As far as sights are concerned, the **Iglesia San Pedro**, built in the English Gothic style, is worth a look; and the **Malecón** affords panoramic and often quite dramatic views of the coast. If you happen to be here on June 29, the **All Saints' Festival** features native dancing derived from the traditions of the *cocolos*, immigrant workers who were brought over from the Leeward and Windward islands in the 1920s. The dances come in different styles – for example 'the savage dance' and 'the dance of Father Winter' – and are performed by *guloyas*. Traditionally, the *guloyas* are showered with coins and given bottles of rum as they go past.

The *cocolos* were brought over during a period known as the 'Dance of the Millions', when sugar prices had reached their peak and San Pedro de Macorís was booming. Immigrants from Europe and the Middle East had settled in the town and Pan-American seaplanes from New York landed regularly on the waters of the Higuamo River to offload rich Americans who wanted a piece of San Pedro's action. At about the same time, the town was providing *gavilleros* (local guerillas) to fight against the US occupation; during the Trujillo years opposition and criticism was more outspoken in San Pedro than anywhere else in the country. These days the town is known more for its politics and baseball (several natives play in the American major leagues) than for its sugar production.

The number of hotels in San Pedro is limited. **Hotel Macorix** (tel: 529 2100) on the Malecón is the best. It caters for businessmen more than anyone else, has a pool and two restaurants and is good value at RD$600 with breakfast. In town, **Hotel Royal** (tel: 529 7105) is just off the Las Americas Highway on Calle Ramon de Castillo near the market. They have rooms with air conditioning, TV and bathroom for RD$250.

Neither the **post office** (Calle Duarte), **Codetel** (Avenida Independencia), the **banks** (Avenida General Cabral), nor **Western Union** (Avenida Independencia) are very far from Parque Duarte, the town's main square.

Since San Pedro is halfway between Santo Domingo and La Romana, it has plenty of *gua-guas* going in either direction. Look for the several stops along the Las Américas Highway. A convenient one to Santo Domingo is opposite Calle Ramon Castillo, the street with the market and Hotel Royal. Alternatively, just flag down a *gua-gua* going in your direction: west for the capital; east for La Romana.

LA ROMANA

La Romana, another sugar-mill town, is 55km from San Pedro de Macorís. This is the economic and administrative centre of the southeastern region, and while Casa de Campo takes care of the tourists, La Romana gets on with processing sugarcane. There is little of interest in the town itself and few visitors stay for very long.

This accounts for the scarcity of hotels. The majority of them are on the highway before you enter town. Try **Hotel El Rancho** (tel: 556 2717), **Hotel Frano** (tel: 550 4744) and possibly the best, **Hotel Olimpo** (tel: 550 7646).

The restaurant situation is slightly better. **Pollo Rodriguez** does tasty *pollo frito* and huge plates of beans and rice, while the **Trigo de Oro** bakery is popular with *gringos* staying at Casa de Campo.

The **post office** is on Calle Castillo Marquez, while **Codetel**, the **banks** and **Western Union** can be found on or around the main square.

Gua-guas for Santo Domingo and Higuey leave from the main square. For Bayahibe, the small coastal town on the perimeter of Parque Nacional del Este, walk down Avenida Libertad until you get to the railway track which is still used to carry sugarcane to the mills down by the port. A small minibus leaves for Bayahibe when full. The trip takes less than an hour and costs RD$15. The **La Romana International Airport** is primarily for the tourist traffic to Casa de Campo. American Eagle, amongst others, fly there from Miami.

Casa de Campo

Like San Pedro de Macorís, La Romana prospered in the first half of the century when sugar prices were high. However, when sugar prices fell in the 1970s Gulf and Western, which had taken over the Central Romana Mill in the 1960s, sought to diversify its business. It invested millions of dollars to turn the internationally famous Hotel La Romana into an exclusive 2,800-hectare resort on the outskirts of town – Casa de Campo.

These days the brochures describe it as 'The Caribbean's Most Complete Resort': and with two golf courses, a tennis centre, watersports, a shooting complex, horseback riding and even polo, it just might be. There are basically two types of accommodation: expensive and very expensive. In the former category elaborate rooms called *casitas* are well over US$100 a night. They have all mod-cons including cable TV, refrigerator, mini-bar, coffee machine, hair dryer etc. Alternatively you can rent out a villa, with or without butler and maid, for well over US$200 a night.

All this makes Casa de Campo somewhat unsuitable for the independent traveller, but if you want to find out more, telephone 523 3333 in the Dominican Republic or 1 800 877 3643 in the United States. The best way to get there from La Romana is by *motoconcho*, either from the main square or, better still, Avenida Libertad. Expect to pay about RD$15.

Altos de Chavón

Altos de Chavón was constructed in 1976 by Gulf and Western to add a splash of culture to the country-club lifestyle at Casa de Campo. A 'thinking man's Disney World', Altos de Chavón is a replica 16th-century Italian village with a church blessed by the pope and a 4,000-seat Greek amphitheatre. This is one of the biggest and most obvious tourist traps in the country, but is still certainly worth a visit.

The unique thing about Altos de Chavón is that over the years it has developed a real character of its own. Since 1982, when a School of Design was established here, the imitation 16th-century village has become a living and breathing town with a raison d'être beyond simply being an 'attraction' for the tourists at Casa de Campo. The Church of St Stanislaus in the main square is used for graduation ceremonies, while behind Disco Genesis, the university residence houses students pursuing courses in fine art, and interior and graphic design.

Of course, Altos de Chavón is still largely for the tourists and the town is full of restaurants (all of them expensive and serving pretty unimaginative international food) and gift shops. Apart from the town itself, which is actually not tacky at all, you could take a peek inside the **Museo Arqueológico Regional**. For Taino artefacts and history, this small, well-presented museum is second only to the Museum of Dominican People in Santo Domingo (see page 187). Also, unlike most museums in the Dominican Republic, this one has good explanations of the exhibits in English. There is no admission fee and it closes on Mondays. Along with the museum, the other highlight is the view of the River Chavón where scenes from the films Apocalypse Now and King Kong were shot. Enquire at Casa de Campo if you want to take a boat trip down the river.

There are two options for getting to Altos de Chavón. Either you can take a *motoconcho* from La Romana (approximately RD$25), or you can take a *motoconcho* to Casa de Campo (RD$15), then catch the free bus that shuttles between the resort and Altos de Chavón. To return to La Romana, you should take the Casa de Campo shuttle, which leaves at half-hourly intervals from outside the Administration Office.

BAYAHIBE AND PARQUE NACIONAL DEL ESTE
After La Romana, the main highway continues east, crosses the River Chavón, then starts to veer inland towards Higuey. Just after the river, another smaller road sticks to the coast and leads eventually to Bayahibe and the entrance to Parque Nacional del Este.

Bayahibe
You can just imagine what Bayahibe will look like in a few years' time. Its one existing street, with a few modest *cabañas*, a couple of restaurants and a *colmado* is surely too good for the developers to resist, and indeed the all-inclusive resorts are already encroaching on the town – Casa del Mar at one end, Club Dominicus at the other. Given that Bayahibe is also at the entrance to the Parque Nacional del Este, its days as a quiet fishing village seem numbered. Nonetheless, at the moment tourism has not completely taken over and the fishing village-feel just about dominates, despite the looming presence of the Casa del Mar at the end of the beach.

Where to stay
Cabañas are the order of the day in Bayahibe and the *gua-gua* from La Romana will leave you in the thick of them. There is not a lot to choose between them, as all generally have two beds, a bathroom and a fan and cost somewhere in the region of RD$250. One of the better and friendlier ones is **Cabañas Trip Town** (tel: 707 3640) which is clean and spacious, although it can be a bit noisy if you get a *cabaña* next to the generator. Other options include **Cabañas El Tamarindo** (tel: 330 2815), **Cabañas P&P** (tel: 550 0170), **Cabañas Niñas** and **Cabañas Maura Güilamo**. **El Oasis** (tel: 476 8790), down a side street near the Scubafin Dive Centre, is a variation on the *cabaña* theme. For RD$200 you get a simple room with a shared bathroom, but there is also a common room where you can read books and listen to CDs. You get better

accommodation for the same price at the *cabañas*, but you might like El Oasis for its more personal feel. **Hotel Bayahibe** (tel: 707 3684) is the one proper hotel in town. Rooms range from RD$200 to 300 and are all quite comfortable and very often full of divers.

Where to eat
Restaurant Bayahibe has the prime location in town, at the end of the main street with a view of the sea. By virtue of this fact it can probably claim to be the most popular restaurant, although the food, like the accommodation, is pretty similar wherever you go. Try the **Café de la Tuna** next to the Bayahibe for barbecue, pizza and some interesting pasta dishes. **Restaurant La Bahia**, meanwhile, is actually on the beach. You can also make international calls from the Tricom office which is located here. Right in the heart of the *cabaña* district – namely in the middle of the street where the *gua-guas* for La Romana depart – **Colmado Betty** has a wide range of provisions. A pick-up truck with mangoes, bananas and other fruit loaded in the back often parks opposite Colmado Betty to sell its wares.

Parque Nacional del Este
Draw a line between Bayahibe and the village of Boca del Yuma on the western side of the peninsula and all the land below it, including the island of Saona, comprises the Parque Nacional del Este. The total area is 420km², none of which is populated. The mainland section of the park is a series of limestone terraces formed about a million years ago – which is quite recent in the great scheme of things – and the terrain is generally flat and dry and the climate hot. There are no rivers, streams or brooks due to the high porosity of the soil, and most of the park is covered with subtropical humid forest, dry forest and transitional forest (a mixture of tropical and deciduous forest). The principal attractions on the mainland are the caves on the western side around Guaraguao not far from Bayahibe, which contain pre-Columbian pictographs (drawings) and petrographs (rock carvings). The coastline is well known for the diversity of its coral formations and there are a number of excellent dive sites, particularly along the western stretch of coastline, which also has one or two beaches with calm and clear waters. The eastern side is characterised more by steep cliffs which drop straight into the ocean. On the southern tip of the peninsula, at Calderas Bay, there are saltwater lagoons and mangrove swamps where herons, pelicans and other birdlife can be spotted. Opposite the bay across the Catuano Channel lies the island of Saona.

Isla Saona
Saona is 25km long and 5km wide and has two tiny settlements, Mano Juan and Punta Gorda, both on the coast and boasting a total population of not much more than 300. The island's original Taino name was Adamanay, but this was changed to Saona when the Europeans arrived in the late 15th century. You can swim at Mano Juan and Punta Catuano, where the beaches are white and the water very blue. The other areas visited by the public are the

Laguna de los Flamencos (Flamingo Lagoon), the Laguna Canto de la Playa and the caves of Cutabanamá near Punta Catuano.

Flora and fauna

The main species of plant found in the park are Hispaniolan mahogany, coconut palm, wild olive, holywood, sea grape, *gumbo-limbo*, *copey* and *zamia*. Many of these are deciduous trees of Caribbean origin.

The Parque Nacional del Este is best known for its birdlife, particularly on Saona, where many species breed in the mangrove swamps and lagoons around the island. In fact, there are some 112 bird species in the park, eight of which are endemic to the island. Amongst others, these include the endangered white-crowned pigeon, the Hispaniolan parrot, the American frigate bird, the barn owl, the stygian owl, the plain pigeon, the red-footed booby and the brown pelican. Flamingos can also been seen on Saona.

Mammals are not as abundant as the birdlife, as is the case all over Hispaniola. Although the chances of a sighting are rare, since these are nocturnal creatures as well as endangered species, there is the possibility of seeing either a *soledonon* (with a small body and long snout) or a *hutia* (a bit like a gerbil), both of which are endemic to Hispaniola. Around the coastal areas you have a slightly better chance of seeing a West Indian Manatee or a bottlenose dolphin – two endangered marine mammals. There are also two species of sea turtle and, along with the various snakes and reptiles, you might see large rhinoceros iguanas on the mainland.

Getting there and away

There are two entrances to the mainland section of the park. The **western entrance** is just beyond Bayahibe – take the marked turn-off just before you enter Bayahibe and continue for a few kilometres until you reach the ranger cabin at Guaraguao. The trail here leads to the nearby caves. The **eastern entrance** is just past the village of Boca del Yuma. This trail follows the coast and is the longer of the two. Apart from these two trails, access to the rest of the park is difficult and a boat is usually needed to get to most places on the coast.

The same is obviously true for the island of Saona. The easiest place to hire boats is at Bayahibe, while the huge catamarans that take over the beach in the evenings are used to ferry tourists to and from Saona. The tourists arrive by coach from the large resorts, so it might not be possible to just show up and get on one of these catamarans. The alternative is to hire a *lancha*, a small boat with an outboard motor, which only really makes sense if there is a group of you, since fishermen hire the whole boat. My enquiries solicited a quote of RD$1,400 for a boat that could probably carry about eight people. There is a small cabin nearby that sells permits for visits to Saona (RD$15).

HIGÜEY

On the face of it Higüey doesn't seem to merit more than a few lines in a tourist guide. True, it is the most important religious site in the country and the capital of the largest province in the country (La Altagracia), but the

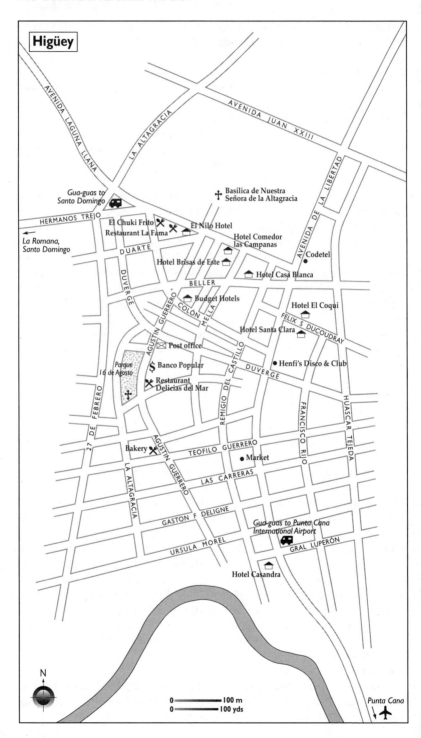

Higüey

AVENIDA LAGUNA LLANA

LA ALTAGRACIA

AVENIDA JUAN XXIII

AVENIDA DE LA LIBERTAD

Gua-guas to
Santo Domingo

Basilica de Nuestra
Señora de la Altagracia

HERMANOS TREJO

La Romana,
Santo Domingo

El Chuki Frito
Restaurant La Fama

El Nilo Hotel

Hotel Comedor
las Campanas

Codetel

DUARTE

Hotel Brisas de Este

Hotel Casa Blanca

DUVERGE

BELLER

AGUSTIN GUERRERO

COLON

Budget Hotels

Hotel El Coqui

MELLA

FELIX S DUCOUDRAY

Hotel Santa Clara

Post office

REMIGIO DEL CASTILLO

DUVERGE

Parque
16 de Agosto

Banco Popular

Henfi's Disco & Club

Restaurant
Delicias del Mar

FRANCISCO RIJO

HUASCAR TEJEDA

27 DE FEBRERO

AGUSTIN GUERRERO

Bakery

TEOFILO GUERRERO

Market

LA ALTAGRACIA

LAS CARRERAS

GASTON F DELIGNE

Gua-guas to Punta Cana
International Airport

URSULA MOREL

GRAL LUPERON

Hotel Casandra

N

0 — 100 m
0 — 100 yds

Punta Cana

cathedral isn't that beautiful and there are no beaches, mountains or ruins nearby. Nevertheless, this is a pleasant town, well worth a day or two of your time. If you arrive late at night at Punta Cana Airport, as some of the charters do, Higuey might be your first taste of the Dominican Republic. For these reasons it gets a decent coverage here.

Getting there and away
Gua-guas to La Romana, Santo Domingo and all points west, including places like El Seibo and Hato Mayor, leave from Avenida Hermanos Trejo near the basilica. Count on about 2½ hours to the capital at a cost of about RD$45.

The other main station is at the end of Avenida de la Libertad opposite the Shell service station. This is where *gua-guas* leave for Punta Cana, Punta Cana Airport and Bávaro. It takes about 45 minutes to the airport, another 15 to Punta Cana, and costs RD$20.

Punta Cana International Airport
Although this is a relatively small airport, it receives a fair amount of traffic as it serves the resort hotels at Punta Cana and Bávaro. Most of the flights are charters, but with cheap flight-only deals, this could be an important airport for the independent traveller.

Facilities are limited to a bank (Banco Gerencial & Fiduciaro), an ATM machine, an Air Santo Domingo and a Nelly-Rent-a-Car office and a few public phone boxes.

Transport from the airport is not too complicated, provided that you arrive at a reasonable hour in the day. For *gua-guas* to Higüey, from where you can make connections to La Romana and Santo Domingo, walk out of the car park to the main road and wait for one to pass, although unfortunately they stop running at about 18.00. This is frustrating, since many charter flights seem to land later on in the evening. In this case, I would budget on taking a taxi to Higüey, staying there for the night, then proceeding to your chosen destination the next morning. The current taxi fare to Higüey is RD$700. This is expensive, but not quite as bad as the RD$1,800 it costs to Santo Domingo or the RD$4,000 to Puerto Plata.

Where to stay
Accommodation with a reasonable price and degree of comfort is not hard to find. The **El Nilo Hotel** (tel: 554 5742) has the prime location directly opposite the basilica, although you might be disappointed to discover that you can't see it from your room. Rooms with air conditioning and TV cost RD$250. The other hotel overlooking the basilica is the **Hotel Comedor Las Campanas** (tel: 554 2675) on Calle Meller, which is half the price of the El Nilo. This time there is a view from the hotel balcony, but you have to crane your neck around some trees to see the basilica. Walk down Calle Meller and you come to Calle Beller. On the corner of these two streets, **Hotel Brisas de Este** (tel: 554 2312) looks bigger and better than it is. Even so, it does have rooms with all the essentials for RD$150 and the staff are very friendly. A few

doors away, **Hotel Casa Blanca** (tel: 554 6121) is smaller, but has similar rooms for a similar price. Calle Colon (the next street down from Calle Beller) is full of cheap hotels, such as **Hotel Elena Nuñez** (tel: 554 3245) and **Hotel El Tamarindo** (tel: 554 1931), the two best. Both have rooms with fan and bathroom starting at a very reasonable RD$125. **Hotel Don Juan** (tel: 554 2863) offers a similar thing, but it struck me as slightly colder and less personal than the other two. Bear in mind that room rates are lower if you arrive in the evening as opposed to the morning. **Hotel Colon** (tel: 554 4686) is no doubt the cheapest place in Higuey at RD$75. Naturally, the accommodation is spartan and there is a communal bathroom.

All of the places mentioned so far are not too far from the basilica and the *gua-gua* stop for Santo Domingo. If, however, you arrive by *gua-gua* from Punta Cana Airport, you'll be left some way from the centre, at the end of Avenida de la Libertad. **Hotel Casandra** is opposite the station and is quite adequate to tide you over until the morning. Alternatively, walk up Avenida de la Libertad for six blocks and turn right down Calle Felix S Ducoudray. The very chic, cream and pink building is **Hotel Santa Clara** (tel: 554 2040), with equally chic rooms for RD$200 or 350. Opposite, **Hotel Frog**, also known as Hotel El Coqui (tel: 554 5482), is cheaper at RD$150.

Where to eat

The best place for restaurants is Avenida Hermanos Trejo, the road in front of the basilica. The pick of the bunch is **Restaurant La Fama**, which has a full range of meat and fish dishes at reasonable prices with air conditioning thrown in for good measure. Either side of La Fama there are two good fast-food places, **El Chuki Frito** to the right, a well-run little café selling *comida criolla*, with chicken's feet the speciality, and **Restaurant El Nilo** to the left. For seafood, in addition to La Fama you could try the simple and unpretentious **Restaurant Delicias del Mar** on Parque 16 de Agosto. A little further down, on Calle Agustin Guerrero, there is a good bakery selling fresh bread and all sorts of cakes and sponges.

Nightlife and entertainment

There are a few discos and bars in town. Some of them – like **Henfi's Disco and Club** and the **El Mariachi Piano Bar**, both on Avenida de la Libertad – seem to be quite up-market. Others – like **Disco Tuko** next to the market and **Disco Don Juan** on Calle Colon – are less so. **La Roca Discoteca** and the neon-lighted **Sports Bar 40 40** are both in front of the basilica.

Tourist information

The **post office** is on Calle Agustin Guerrero just past Calle Durverge. **Codetel** has an office on Avenida de la Libertad in front of the basilica, as does **Turitel** (which might have cheaper rates to Europe and North America). Probably the most convenient place to go for **banks** is Parque 16 de Agosto where there is a Banco Popular and a Baninter. The **Western Union** office is a few blocks from the centre of town on Calle José A Santana.

Orientation and what to see

Use the **Basilica de Nuestra Señora de la Altagracia** as your point of reference. If you arrive from the west, you'll be dropped almost directly in front of it, in the centre of town. If you arrive from Punta Cana Airport, you'll have to walk up Avenida de la Libertad to reach the basilica. The church itself was built in 1952 on the site where the Virgin Mary apparently appeared during a battle between the Spaniards and the Tainos, allowing Columbus and his men to fend off the Indians. Nowadays, pilgrims come to Higüey on January 21 and August 16 to pay their respects to La Altagracia (the Virgin of the Highest Grace) who became the patron saint of the Dominican Republic in 1922. The basilica is 60m high and shaped like a pair of praying hands. It looks good in the sun, but when it's overcast it can look a bit gloomy – more Transylvanian than Caribbean. Higüey does have a town square, which is a few blocks from the basilica along Calle Agustin Guerrero. **Parque 16 de Agosto** also has a church, but it's a rather tumbledown affair and hardly competes with the basilica for attention. The **market** is off Avenida de la Libertad before you get to the gua-guas for Punta Cana.

Punta Cana and Bávaro beaches

These beaches are some 15 minutes from the airport (turn left when you get to the main road). They have white sands, placid waters, plenty of coconut palms and are the domain of the luxury resorts. Nothing here costs much under US$100 and a lot is over US$200. Reservations should be made with a tour operator in your home country.

PARQUE NACIONAL LOS HAÏTISES

Los Haïtises National Park has two distinct regions: the 208km² of mangrove forest and swamp along the coast on the southern side of Samaná Bay; and the rest of the area known as Los Haïtises that stretches from the town of Sabana de la Mar in the east to Sánchez in the north, accounting for a sizeable chunk of over 1,000km² of the northeast of the country. The inland portion of the park is characterised by thousands of *mogotes* (limestone hillocks), 2–300m in height and covered with tropical humid forest. Opportunities to see the park on foot are limited, and most tours are by boat exploring the coastline west of Sabana de la Mar.

The littoral route

Thanks to the numerous reefs, cays, lagoons and mangrove swamps along the park's coastline, plenty of flora and fauna is on display. There are also several caves, some with Taino drawings and rock carvings. The one most geared to visitors is **Cueva de Willy** in the Bay of San Lorenzo. **Cueva de la Arena**, **Cueva de la Linea** and **Cueva del Ferrocarril** are all nearby, while **Cueva de San Gabriel** is further west along the coast. Getting to the caves in the Bay of San Lorenzo involves taking a boat from Sabana de la Mar to the Bambú Pier in Caño Hondo. From here it's another 10 minutes by boat to the caves.

Most of the larger travel agencies run tours to the Los Haïtises National Park. Doing it independently is tricky because of the lack of inland trails and your dependence on a boat. In Sabana de la Mar visit the national parks office (tel: 556 733) at 54 Avenida Los Héroes for information, and head for the pier to look for a boat.

Flora and fauna

Although the quality of the soil in the park is generally poor because of the coral rock absorbing most of the surface fresh water, there is still a variety of vegetation, thanks to the abnormally high rainfall (about 2,000mm a year). The most common trees are West Indian cedar, Hispaniolan mahogany, copey, American muskwood and silk-cotton trees. In the mangrove swamps, red and white mangroves are common.

The swampy areas along the coast are ideal breeding grounds for a wide range of birdlife. The most common species are the American frigate bird, brown pelican, little blue heron and barn owl. The Hispaniolan parakeet is a rarer sight.

The park's mammal life consists of the indigenous *solenodon* and *hutia* (see also page 8).

LAGUNAS REDONDA Y LIMÓN

These two muddy, shallow lagoons, surrounded by dense mangrove and home to a wealth of birdlife, are due east of the Los Haïtises National Park. Independent travellers have their work cut out getting to these lagoons. The nearest town is **Miches**, accessible from Sabana de la Mar or Higüey via El Seibo, but the lagoons themselves are still 17km (Redondo) and 27km (Limón) away. If you want to visit this scientific reserve, the easiest way is on an organised tour.

The North Coast

The north coast has a bit of everything. There are plenty of good beaches, a fair helping of historical sites, a national park, a scientific reserve, one of best places in the world for windsurfing and a busy international airport. Puerto Plata is the main town in the region, approximately halfway along the coast between the Samaná Peninsula to the east and the town of Monte Cristi and the Haitian border to the west.

MONTE CRISTI

Not many tourists make it out to this flat, dry region in the northwestern corner of the Dominican Republic. However, for those contemplating crossing the Haitian border at Dajabón, this town is a logical stopping-off point. It also has some excellent reefs for diving and one of the largest national parks in the country.

Founded in 1506, the fortunes of Monte Cristi have been similar to those of Puerto Plata further along the coast. In the early days it prospered due to a fine, natural harbour, and Columbus considered establishing Monte Cristi as the first settlement in the New World before deciding on La Isabela. The arrival of pirates on the north coast led to the abandonment of the town by order of the Spanish king in 1605-6; and it only started to be re-settled in the 18th century, when immigrants from Germany, Italy, Spain and England made Monti Cristi their home. They brought with them the Victorian-style architecture that characterises the town today – note, for instance, the clocktower in the main square.

Monte Cristi had its heyday at the turn of the century, when its port was used to export large quantities of agricultural products and precious wood to Europe. Nowadays, most of the exporting is done at the nearby port of Manzanillo and Monte Cristi's main industries are fishing, cattle rearing and farming melons.

Orientation

Although I use the expression 'downtown' to describe the part of Monte Cristi that is not by the sea, there is, in fact, no real downtown. Monte Cristi is a grid of streets, some busier than others, but with no particular place standing out as the centre of town. The main thoroughfare is Calle Duarte, a shopping street by day and the place to go for loud bars and street food at night. Going east, Calle Duarte

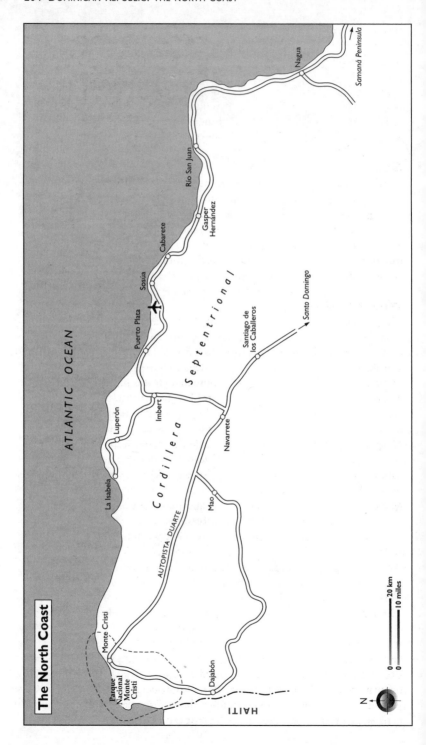

The North Coast

eventually becomes Autopista Duarte, which continues all the way to Santo Domingo. Going west, you come to the town's main square, but unlike many in the Dominican Republic, it is rarely very crowded. There is a **cathedral**, and the peculiar **clocktower** in the middle of the square is the emblem of Monte Cristi. Turn right off the main square and go down Calle San Fernando to get to the beach. You can either walk (about 15 minutes) or take a *motoconcho*. At the end of Calle San Fernando, the town's beach hotels are to the left and the road to El Morro, the mountain overlooking Monte Cristi, is to the right.

Getting there and away

Caribe Tours have a small office on the corner of Calle Rodriguez Camargo and Calle Mella. There are services to Santo Domingo (four times a day), Santiago and Dajabón. For Puerto Plata, change at Santiago. Count on about four hours to Santo Domingo (RD$80) and one hour to either Dajabón or Santiago (RD$35). The *gua-guas* serve the same destinations as Caribe Tours for about RD$5 less. They leave from the corner of Calle Duarte and Calle Benito Moncion.

Where to stay

Most of the tourists who come to Monte Cristi stay by the beach. Walk or take a *motoconcho* along Calle San Fernando and turn left. The first place you come to is the **Aparta-Hotel Cayo Arena** (tel: 579 3145), the best accommodation available. The self-catering apartments sleep four people and most have views of the sea. They cost US$80 (slightly more in high season), which is reasonable if you divide it by four. Next door, **Hotel Los Jardins** (tel: 579 2091) has four rooms with refrigerators for RD$400. In the downtown area, there are more hotels, although none of them are aimed specifically at tourists. The **Don Gaspar Hotel**, at the intersection of Calle Rodriguez Camargo and Calle Pte Jimenez, is the most expensive, with clean, functional rooms with a fan and bathroom costing RD$200. There is also a good restaurant downstairs and a disco. The **Chic Hotel** (tel: 579 2316) is a cheaper alternative on Calle Benito Moncion. It also has a good restaurant and rooms start at RD$110, with free coffee in the morning. Cheaper still is **Hotel Boss** (tel: 579 3236) opposite the cinema on Calle Juan de la Cruz Alvarez. Singles are RD$100 and doubles RD$125. **Mike's Hotel** (tel: 579 3095) is at 86 Calle Colón, halfway between downtown and the coast. RD$100 gets you a basic straw-thatched *cabaña*.

Where to eat

This region is known for goat meat. Wild oregano is a regular part of the goat's diet up here, giving its meat a distinctive taste and removing the necessity for seasoning. Goat is on the menu at the **Don Gaspar** and the **Chic Hotel**, the two best restaurants in town. The Chic Hotel places a lot of emphasis on presentation (the waiters wear black tie and the food always looks delicious), making it a popular choice with the high society of Monte Cristi. **Comedor Adela**, on Calle Juan de la Cruz Alvarez, is less concerned about image, and the chicken and rice is good, filling stuff. The **Sky Rock Bistrot** is on Calle San Fernando between

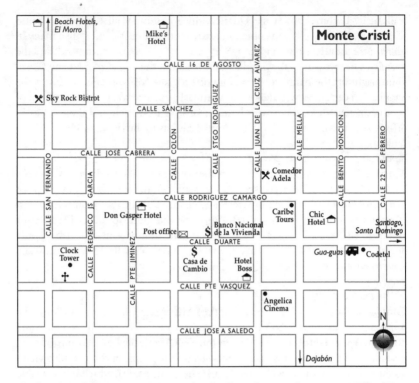

the beach and downtown. It is run by the Frenchman who manages Hotel Los Jardins and the menu is French- and Creole-based. Alternatively, there are many hamburger and hot-dog stalls on Calle Duarte after dark; and several bar-restaurants at the end of Calle San Fernando by the sea.

Tourist information

Go to Comedor Adela for a makeshift **tourist information office** run by a local Dominican. He'll probably be unavailable when you visit, but there are a few interesting articles relating to the local area in the restaurant. The **post office** and **Codetel** are both on Calle Duarte, along with the town's **bank** (Banco Nacional de la Vivienda). Since they don't change travellers' cheques, you might be better off going to the *casa de cambio* over the road where the rate is also better. Caribe Tours is another place where you can change money.

Parque Nacional Monte Cristi

The Monte Cristi National Park is one of the largest in the Dominican Republic. It covers an area of 560km² and extends from the Haitian border to the north coast of the Dominican Republic. Within its boundaries lie offshore keys, mangrove swamps, lagoons and the **El Morro** mountain, can be reached by following the coastal road east. The national park office is a couple of kilometres out of town at its foot, but offers limited practical help to the visitor (more often than not there is nobody there). Although there are no marked trails, it is relatively easy to explore El Morro on foot. Many different species of plants and flowers are found here, including one called *sabia montecristini*, which is unique to El Morro.

Access to the rest of the park is more difficult. An organised tour might be your best bet if you want to see the coastal areas, while some of the hotels in Monte Cristi run excursions to the nearby islands.

The **Cayos Siete Hermanos** (Seven Brothers' Keys) lie a few kilometres off the coast. There are many reefs around these keys, providing a good site for scuba diving. **Isla Cabrita** is just off the mainland, with a nice beach and a lighthouse. A good place to enquire about excursions to these islands is the Aparta-Hotel Cayo Arena, whose owner speaks excellent English and is very knowledgeable about the area.

The beaches around Monte Cristi are rather nondescript. The best are **Playa El Morro**, on the other side of the mountain, and **Playa Costa Verde**, 1km past Hotel Los Jardins. There is good diving and snorkelling due to the double reefs along this stretch of coast. If you look out to sea, you'll notice the waves breaking on the second reef about 400m out. Once again, the Cayo Arena can arrange trips out to the reef.

DAJABÓN AND THE HAITIAN BORDER

As border towns go, Dajabón is quite user-friendly. Compared to Quanaminthe, the first town on the Haitian side, it is also the height of luxury. If you get stuck here – for I wouldn't recommend a planned stay – it doesn't have to be too uncomfortable. **Hotel Elárimas**, just off the main square near the cathedral, is reasonable value at RD$100; and there are a few cafés and ice-cream parlours on Calle Dulce De Js Senfleur, two blocks past the main square away from the border. You can also find several banks here and *gua-guas* to Monte Cristi, Santiago and Santo Domingo leave from the arch at the end of the road. The **Haitian Consulate**, meanwhile, is on the road leading up to the border checkpoint.

The crossing itself can be a little confusing. Regardless of whether you're entering or leaving the country, your passport gets taken by the same official who checks it, stamps it, then posts it through a hole in the wall. It lands on the desk of another official responsible for collecting the US$10 exit tax. Therefore, if you're entering the Dominican Republic, make this quite clear to the exit tax collector, otherwise you might be asked to pay the US$10. Another word of warning: make sure that your passport has been stamped with the correct date. Mine was stamped a year earlier than my actual departure, an error repeated at Port-au-Prince International Airport when I arrived in Haiti. The border post at Dajabón is open from 08.00 to 17.00 every day.

PUERTO PLATA

When Columbus first reached the Bay of Puerto Plata on January 11 1493, he observed how the mountains shone like silver when covered with mist. Later, in 1496, Bartolomé Colon remembered his brother's observation when he founded Puerto Plata (Silver Port).

In the early days the prognosis for Puerto Plata looked good. It was a well-protected harbour in a good strategic position and a popular port of call for Spanish galleons making the voyage between Europe and the New World. However, as Spanish control in Hispaniola receded, pirates and buccaneers took over the north coast, and in 1606 the Spanish king ordered the destruction of Puerto Plata to save it from anarchy. For the best part of the next 150 years Puerto Plata lay in the doldrums, until, in 1746, immigrants from the Canary Islands started to arrive, injecting new life into the town. The first sugarcane in Hispaniola was planted in Puerto Plata and the port was used to export coffee, cacao, corn and tobacco produced in the Cibao Valley. Nowadays, Puerto Plata still handles about 12% of the country's export trade. However, since the development of Playa Dorada in the 1970s, tourism has grown to be the mainstay of the town's economy.

Orientation

The thing to remember about Puerto Plata is that there are two distinct areas: downtown and the Malecón. Most, if not all of the budget hotels are located downtown, along with the banks, public buildings and bus stations. The Malecón is the coastal road that stretches from the downtown area to Long Beach, a couple of kilometres to the east. It starts as Avenida General Luperón and then becomes Avenida Circunvalacion Norte as it nears Long Beach. If you continue to follow the Malecón past Long Beach, it bends away from the coast and eventually links up with Avenida Circunvalacion Sur, the main highway to Sosúa, which skirts round the southern edge of town.

Getting there and away
By air
Air Santo Domingo has four flights a day to Santo Domingo: two in the morning and two in the afternoon. A single costs US$54. Apart from this there is one flight to El Portillo on the Samaná Peninsula, two flights to La Romana and one direct flight to Punta Cana. All of them leave early in the morning and cost between US$49 and 59.

General Gregorio Luperón International Airport
This is the Dominican Republic's second airport (tel: 586 0313) situated about 18km from Puerto Plata. While at times it can get quite busy, it's never as hectic as Las Américas International Airport. The basic facilities include Banco de Reservas, open seven days a week, where you can change travellers' cheques; a post office and a Codetel office, open from 08.00 to 18.00; car-hire companies, fast-food restaurants and gift shops, which are clustered together at one end of the terminal.

The advertised taxi fare between Puerto Plata and the airport is RD$225 for up to six people. *Gua-guas* and *carros*, meanwhile, cost RD$10. To catch them you must walk from the airport terminal to the main road about ten minutes away. Flag them down as they pass. You can also go in the other direction to

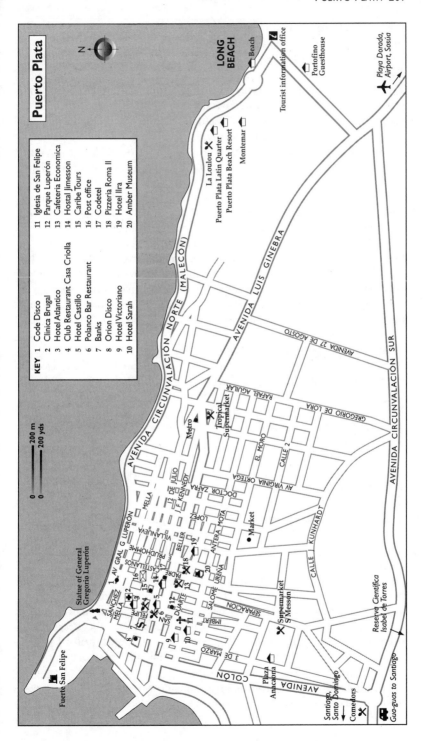

Puerto Plata

N

KEY
1 Code Disco
2 Clínica Brugal
3 Hotel Atlántico
4 Club Restaurant Casa Criolla
5 Hotel Castillo
6 Polanco Bar Restaurant
7 Banks
8 Orion Disco
9 Hotel Victoriano
10 Hotel Sarah
11 Iglesia de San Felipe
12 Parque Luperón
13 Cafetería Economica
14 Hostal Jimesson
15 Caribe Tours
16 Post office
17 Codetel
18 Pizzería Roma II
19 Hotel Ilra
20 Amber Museum

0 ——— 200 m
0 ——— 200 yds

Fuerte San Felipe

Statue of General
Gregorio Luperón

AVENIDA CIRCUNVALACIÓN NORTE (MALECÓN)

LONG
BEACH

Beach

Tourist information office

Portofino Guesthouse

La Loulou
Puerto Plata Latin Quarter
Puerto Plata Beach Resort
Montemar

Playa Dorada,
Airport, Sosúa

AVENIDA LUIS GINEBRA

AVENIDA 27 DE AGOSTO

GREGORIO DE LORA

AVENIDA CIRCUNVALACIÓN SUR

Metro

Tropical
Supermarket

RAFAEL AGUILAR

EL MORO

CALLE 2

DOCTOR ZAFRA

AV VIRGINIA ORTEGA

CALLE 1 KUNHARDT

Market

SEPARACIÓN

Supermarket
S Messon

Reserva Científica
Isabel de Torres

3 DE JULIO
J.F. KENNEDY
LÓPEZ
ANTERA MOTA
URIÑA
SALOMÉ
IMBERT

MELLA
VILLANUEVA
PRUDHOMME
BELLER
PADRE
CASTELLANOS
SÁNCHEZ
MELLA
SAN FELIPE
DUARTE
3 DE MARZO

COLÓN

AVENIDA

Plaza
Anacaona

Santiago,
Santo Domingo

Conelors

Gua-guas to Santiago

Sosúa and Cabarete. Puerto Plata is right, the other destinations are left. *Gua-guas* and *carros* leave for the airport from the main square in Puerto Plata.

By road

The two largest bus companies, **Caribe Tours** and **Metro**, both have terminals in Puerto Plata. Caribe Tours is in the heart of downtown, on Calle 12 de Julio, and operate an almost hourly service to Santo Domingo, which costs RD$80 and takes about four hours. Their other main destination is Sosúa, but it's easier and cheaper to take a *gua-gua*. Metro is more inconveniently located at the eastern end of Calle Beller, and they charge RD$85 to Santo Domingo and RD$40 for Santiago.

The choice of *gua-guas* to the more far-flung destinations is rather limited. You can get to Santiago (one hour, RD$20) or Navarette on *gua-guas* that leave from the roundabout at the end of Calle 30 de Marzo and Calle Colón, or you can go east along the coast as far as Río San Juan from the main sqaure. Note that many tourists use the *gua-guas* that run along the coast, passing places like Playa Dorada, Sosúa and Cabarete. As a result, blatant overcharging is common. Bear in mind that it generally costs RD$5 for every town or major dropping-off point (like Playa Dorada or the airport) that you pass. Therefore, Sosúa should not cost more than RD$15, Cabarete RD$20 and Río San Juan RD$25 or 30.

Where to stay

Away from the resort hotels, which are concentrated in Playa Dorada, Costambar and Cofresí, there is a good selection of hotels in Puerto Plata to suit all budgets. If you are looking for a resort hotel, the **Puerto Plata Beach Resort** (tel: 586 2423) is on the Malecón. It has all the usual facilities including a casino and a small beach (Cote Atlantica). **Hotel Montemar** (tel: 586 2800) is another large hotel on the Malecón opposite Long Beach.

Also on the Malecón, but in the affordable price range, **Hotel Puerto Plata Latin Quarter** (tel: 586 2770) has comfortable rooms for US$25. The staff are very helpful and the hotel itself is well situated, halfway along the Malecón between downtown and Long Beach. If you want to stay closer to Long Beach than downtown, there are several options. Apart from the Puerto Plata Beach Resort and Hotel Montemar there is the **Portofino Guest House** (tel: 586 2858), on Avenida Long Beach between the beach and the main road to Sosúa, which has recently opened and charges RD$400 for a room. They also have a restaurant. The **Beach Hotel** (tel: 586 2551), on the same road, although the coastal part, is a budget hotel offering simple rooms with fan and bathroom for RD$160 (air conditioning is slightly more). Unlike many budget hotels, which tend to be small and poky, the Beach Hotel stretches for half the length of the beach and has 80 rooms, which I have to admit are small and poky. Nevertheless, this is the one cheap option on this side of Puerto Plata, so make the most of it.

The choice of hotels is much greater in the downtown area. The one with the most character has to be **Hostal Jimesson** (tel: 586 5131) on Calle John F Kennedy. You might walk past this green, wooden house thinking that it's an antique shop, as old gramophones and clocks clutter the front room, giving it a somewhat Victorian feel. The rooms have a similar atmosphere and are large and quite sophisticated, although not particularly modern. A single or a double costs RD$300. Few other places have quite the same character, but you can get some good deals. From the outside **Hotel Victoriano** (tel: 586 9752), on Calle San Felipe, does look quite Victorian, but inside the rooms are like prison cells. Having said this, you get air conditioning, cable TV and a bathroom for RD$200 (RD$150 without the air conditioning). On the parallel street, Calle Imbert, **Hotel Sarah** (tel: 586 4834) offers very simple rooms with TV for RD$100, and the owner is very proud of the fact that he speaks some English. In the same area, on Calle 30 de Marzo, **Hotel Martin** and **Casa de Huespedes El España**, a distinctive bright red and yellow wooden house, also have rooms for RD$100. **Hotel Plaza Anacaona** (tel: 586 1201) is further up on Calle 30 de Marzo towards the main highway. Run by a German, this place is clean, quiet and has a nice garden shaded by trees. Rooms cost around RD$300. Returning back to the heart of downtown, not that anywhere is really very far from the centre, **Hotel Atlantico** (tel: 586 2503) is on Calle 12 de Julio next to Caribe Tours. Singles start at RD$150. Also near Caribe Tours, on Calle José del Carmen Ariza, is **Hotel Castillo**, which, although by no means the best of the budget hotels (rooms here are RD$100), is geared towards the backpacker; and Sam's Bar and Grill downstairs is an acknowledged meeting place for like-minded travellers. Finally, not far from the Amber Museum on Calle Villa Nueva, **Hotel Ilra** (tel: 586 2337) has uninspiring rooms for RD$130 (single) and RD$200 (double).

Where to eat

As a major tourist town, you would expect Puerto Plata to have its share of restaurants serving international cuisine, and you won't be disappointed. On the main square the **Central Restaurant** and the **Girasol Café** serve burgers, pizzas and other such dishes. The Central is the better of the two. **Sam's Bar and Grill** on Calle José del Carmen is obviously aimed at the backpacker. The menu features meatloaf, meatballs and some pretty large American-style breakfasts; there are American newspapers, a book exchange, a dart board and a bulletin board, which is also a good source of information about what's going on in Puerto Plata.

The best of the numerous pizzerias in Puerto Plata could be **Pizzeria Roma II** on the corner of Calle Beller and Calle Prud'Homme, although the establishments along the Malecón might have something to say about that. **Jinv's** is one of the better ones. The Malecón is home to many restaurants serving pretty much the same thing, but **Jardins Suizo**, specialising in fondues, is slightly different, as is **La LouLou**, next to Hotel Puerto Plata Latin Quarter, which is an open-air restaurant serving food and drink out of a giant baseball. On Long Beach most of the bars also have restaurants, but nothing really stands out.

For Dominican food, concentrate your search in the downtown area. **Café Sito** is down an alley beside the Canadian Consulate on Calle San Felipe. The *comida criolla* seems authentic enough and there is a cosy atmosphere. **Club Restaurant Casa Criolla**, on Calle 12 de Julio next to Caribe Tours, is less intimate, with loud music, billiard tables and a restaurant serving standard Dominican fare. You get a similar deal at the **Polanco Bar Restaurant** on Calle John F Kennedy between Calle Imbert and José del Carmen. They have a happy hour from 15.00 to 19.00 where you can get two drinks for the price of one. **Cafeteria Economica**, on Calle Beller between Calle Separación and Padre Castellanos, is small, clean and quite cute, with more Dominicans than tourists here, even though the burgers and sandwiches are hardly native. There are plenty of *comedors* (small, native restaurants) at the end of Calle 30 de Marzo where the *gua-guas* leave for Santiago. This is where you can get the most authentic *comida criolla* – the stuff that either lines your stomach or clears it out.

Puerto Plata is not a mecca of fine dining, and the best restaurants tend to be at Playa Dorada, where most of the tourists are on all-inclusive packages that include meals. However, if you feel like treating yourself, you are quite welcome to visit the restaurants as an outsider. For Chinese, try the **Jade Garden** at Villas Doradas; for Tex-Mex and American, there's **Panchos**, also at Villas Doradas; and Dominican and other Caribbean dishes are on offer at the **Caribbean Grill** at Playa Naco. There are many others and they are all expensive.

There are two very good supermarkets in Puerto Plata. Walk along Calle Separación towards the main highway for **Supermarket S Messon**, while the **Tropical Supermarket** is at the end of Calle Beller opposite the Metro bus terminal.

Playa Dorada Plaza is the shopping mall at Playa Dorada. There are several places to eat here, including a **Pizza Hut**, and live Latin-American music in the foyer.

Nightlife and entertainment

There is no shortage of bars at **Long Beach**. They start next to the Beach Hotel and follow the bend in the road towards the main highway to Sosúa. It's hard to recommend any one in particular because they're all so similar. The best thing to do is hop from one to another until you find one you like. Don't worry too much about getting back to your downtown hotel at the end of the evening, since there are plenty of *motoconchos* that zip up and down the Malecón at all hours.

Some very big discos dominate the nightlife in the downtown area. You won't forget a visit to the **Code Disco**, on the Malecón between Calle Separación and José del Carmen – the complete Dominican disco experience. Two winding staircases lead up to the entrance, the crowd is young and trendy, the dance floor is always heaving and the music is loud. The **Orion Disco**, on the corner of Calle 12 de Julio and Calle 30 de Marzo, is of a similar size and standard, but the cover charge is a very reasonable RD$10. You can play **billiards** in several of the bars near the main square, and in the square itself there is sometimes **live music** on public and religious holidays.

Cinema Roma is on Calle Beller opposite Codetel. They have screenings at 17.00 and 20.30 and tickets are RD$35.

The **beaches** in Puerto Plata are not as good as those at Playa Dorada, Costambar and Confresí. The stretch of sand at Long Beach is reasonable, but it seems to be used more for walking and horse-riding than sunbathing. There is nothing preventing you from using the Cote Atlantica Beach in front of the Playa Dorada Beach Resort, which is more suitable for sunbathing. Wherever you choose, note that there is a lot of reef around Puerto Plata.

Tourist information
There is a **tourist information office** on the Malecón at No 20, by the watchtower on Long Beach. The **post office** is on the corner of Calle 12 de Julio and Calle Separación. **Codetel** is on Calle Beller, but a cheaper alternative could be **All America**, which is on Calle John F Kennedy just after Calle José del Carmen.

Banks are not hard to find. Banco de Reservas, Banco National de Credit and several others are on Calle John F Kennedy, and many have ATM machines that take Visa and Mastercard.

There are English-speaking **doctors** at Clinica Brugal (tel: 586 2519), on Calle José del Carmen, open 24 hours a day. Another option in an emergency is the Playa Dorada Medical Care Centre (tel: 320 2222), although strictly speaking it's only for those staying at Playa Dorada.

Foreign consulates
Due to the high number of tourists on the north coast, several countries have some form of diplomatic representation in Puerta Plata:

British Honorary Consul (David Salem) 51 Calle Beller; tel: 586 4244
Canadian Consulate 29 Calle San Felipe; tel: 586 5761
German Consulate 51 Calle Beller; tel: 586 4249
Italian Consulate 59 Calle Duarte; tel: 320 7601
US Consulate 55 Calle 12 de Julio; tel: 686 3143

What to see
Start your sightseeing tour in the main square, **Parque Luperón**. The art-deco **Iglesia de San Felipe** is interesting, as are the several **Victorian gingerbread houses** around the main square. The **Fuerte San Felipe** (San Felipe Fortress) is at the western end of the Malecón on a small peninsula next to the port. It was built in 1540 and remains the sole reminder of Puerto Plata's colonial past. There is not a great deal to see inside – just a small museum and the cell in which Juan Pablo Duarte was briefly held at one point. It is open from 09.00 to 17.30 and costs RD$10. In front of the fortress is a **statue of General Gregorio Luperón**, and more recently, a plaque commemorating the 68 victims of a German plane crash off the coast on February 6 1996. The **Amber Museum**, on Calle Duarte, is an attractive white house built in neo-Classical style, and contains an interesting collection of amber deposits with spiders, termites, cockroaches, beetles, crickets and various other things trapped inside. There is also a shop selling amber jewellery and other ornaments. Opening

hours are 09.00 to 18.00 Monday to Saturday and admission costs RD$30. This might seem a little steep for such a small museum, but bear in mind that 5% of the entrance fee is donated to local charities.

The market is on Calle Villa Nueva, not far from the Amber Museum, but as markets go, this one is rather characterless. There are plenty of gift shops, but not a great deal of activity. Everyone seems to be waiting for the busloads of tourists to arrive. Finally, the **Brugal rum distillery** is just out of town on the highway to Sosúa. It is open to the public and impromptu tours can be arranged.

Excursions from Puerto Plata
Beaches
Playa Dorada is no more than 5km east of Puerto Plata. You can get there easily on *gua-guas* from Parque Luperón (it should not cost more than RD$5). Playa Dorada is a village of five-star hotels built around a golf course and a good stretch of beach. Despite the explosion of resorts on the south and east coasts, Playa Dorada remains the most popular package-tour destination in the Dominican Republic. The hotels sell all-inclusive holidays through foreign tour companies and it's unusual, although not impossible, to get a room if you just show up unannounced. Having said this, there's nothing stopping you using the beach, restaurants and shops in the village.

There are two other good beaches a few kilometres west of Puerto Plata. Go to the end of Calle 30 de Marzo and catch a *gua-gua* bound for Imbert. The first beach is about 2km down the road at **Costambar**. Like Playa Dorada, but on a lesser scale, Costambar has hotels, restaurants, shops and a long stretch of beach. Further down the road is **Cofresí**, which is smaller and slightly more exclusive than Costambar.

Reserva Científica Isabel de Torres
The highest of the mountains behind Puerta Plata is **Isabel de Torres**. On a clear day, when mist doesn't shroud the 800m peak, you should be able to see **Cristo Redentor** (Christ the Saviour), a statue of Christ with outstretched arms not dissimilar to the one at Río de Janeiro. The most popular way of getting to the top of Isabel de Torres always used to be by cable car, but this service has not operated for some time now and it's uncertain when, if ever, it will resume. The alternative route up the mountain is by road. Go to the entrance to the cable-car ride (about 1km west along the highway towards Imbert) and you should find *motoconchos* waiting to make the ascent. It's a long way up, so don't expect to get there for nothing. RD$100 seems to be the going rate. At the top there is the statue, botanical gardens, a few shops and a fort built by Trujillo in 1942 when the Dominican Republic declared war on Germany.

La Isabela
There is not a great deal to see at La Isabela Archaeological Park. It does, of course, have huge historical significance as the first European settlement in the

New World, but the archaeological excavations are disappointing. The site is divided into three zones: two civilian zones and a military zone known as El Castillo. It is here that excavations have revealed the outlines of what experts claim were Columbus' house, the church where the first mass in the New World was held, and an observation tower used by the Great Admiral to gaze at the stars.

There is no easy way to get to La Isabela. The most direct route is to take a *gua-gua* to Imbert (catch them at the end of Calle 30 de Marzo), then another to Luperón. From here you can get a *motoconcho* to La Isabela. Count on this journey taking about two hours in total. An alternative is to book yourself on a day-trip organised by a tour company in Puerto Plata.

SOSÚA

In the 1980s Sosúa started to turn into the overcrowded and rather tacky tourist town it is today. Up until then it was notable for its cheeses and sausages; in the 1930s it was nothing more than a village living off the local banana crop.

In 1938, Trujillo agreed to take a quota of the thousands of Jews trying to escape Hitler. This could have been because the dictator was eager to tone down his international reputation as a fascist or because he wanted to 'whiten out' the Dominican population after years of Haitian immigration. Whatever the reason, in 1940 a handful of Jews arrived in the Dominican Republic and settled in Sosúa, where an area of fertile land had been set aside for the establishment of an agricultural community. However, the Jews that came were intellectuals, businessmen and artists, who were unused to working the land. Instead, they formed cooperatives, improved cattle-raising techniques and established dairy- and food-processing industries. Thus, Sosúa became a major producer of meat and diary products like ham, sausage, butter and cheese. Meanwhile, a synagogue had been built (which is still in use today) and the small Jewish community had married Dominicans and settled in the town. These days you still see some of the old Jewish houses, but like the Victorian gingerbread architecture in Puerto Plata, they are rare.

Orientation

The small, crescent-shaped beach in Sosúa separates the two very distinct neighbourhoods of El Batey (on the east) and Los Charamicos (on the west). If you arrive in Sosúa on a Caribe Tours bus, you'll be left in Los Charamicos. This is the poorer part of town, where the tourist infrastructure is less developed and budget accommodation can be found. The *gua-guas* that run along the north coast can either drop you in Los Charamicos or a little further along the main road in El Batey, where most of the tourist amenities are centred. If you're staying in one neighbourhood and want to get to the other, you can walk along the main road or the beach.

Apart from Sosúa Beach, which is compact and over-used, other beaches in the vicinity include **La Playita** and **Playa Chiquita**, east of town.

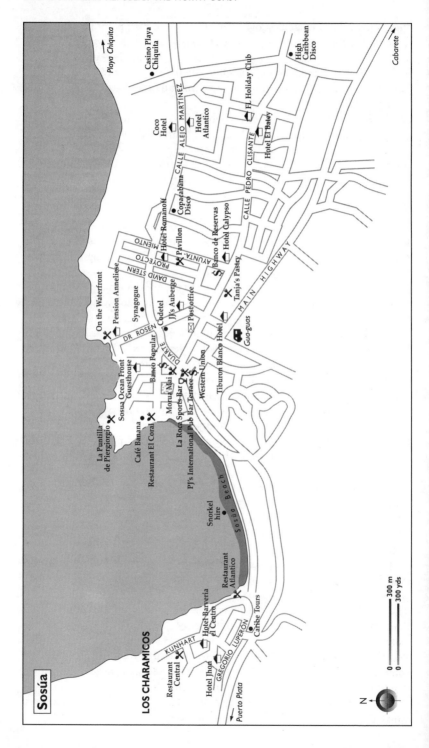

Sosúa

Playa Chiquita

Casino Playa Chiquita

High Caribbean Disco

Cabarete

CALLE ALEJO MARTINEZ

Coco Hotel

Hotel Atlantico

FL Holiday Club

Hotel El Batey

CALLE PEDRO CLISANTE

Copacabana Disco

Hotel Romanoff

Banco de Reservas

Hotel Calypso

PROYECTO

AYUNTA-

MIENTO

DAVID STERN

Pavillon

Pension Anneliese

Tanja's Pastry

On the Waterfront

Synagogue

JJ's Auberge

Postoffice

MAIN HIGHWAY

DR ROSEN

Codetel

Western Union

DUARTE

Tiburon Blanco Hotel

Guaguas

Banco Popular

Sosua Ocean Front Guesthouse

Morua Mai

La Roca Sports Bar

PJ's International Pub Bar Terrace

La Puntilla de Piergiorgio

Café Banana

Restaurant El Coral

Snorkel hire

Sosúa Beach

Restaurant Atlantico

LOS CHARAMICOS

KUNHART

Restaurant Central

Hotel Jhon

Hotel Barreria el Centro

GREGORIO LUPERÓN

Caribe Tours

Puerto Plata

N

0   300 m
0   300 yds

Getting there and away

Caribe Tours and **Transporte del Cibao** both have terminals in Los Charamicos on the main highway. These companies are most useful for travel to Santo Domingo, Santiago and Samaná, all of which are served by one or the other. For travel between towns on the north coast, use the *gua-guas* that pass along the main highway at regular intervals. It takes about 45 minutes to Puerto Plata, 1½ hours to Río San Juan.

Where to stay
El Batey

Hotels in El Batey, the larger and more developed of Sosúa's two halves, fall into two categories: the all-inclusive hotels along the coast, and the downtown hotels. Prices at the all-inclusives are the same as elsewhere in the Dominican Republic, and the downtown hotels are rarely under US$25, although remember that this is usually for the room, so it's not too bad if you can share with someone.

The **Sosúa Ocean Front Guest House**, also known as **Koch's Ocean Front Guest House** (tel: 571 2284), has several bungalows set in a beautiful, tranquil garden leading to the sea. They have hot water, air conditioning, a kitchen and mosquito nets, all for US$25: certainly one of the best buys in Sosúa. **Pension Anneliese** (tel: 571 2208) is nearby at the end of Calle Dr Rosen and has ten quiet rooms for US$25.

As you walk down Calle Dr Rosen away from the coast it becomes less and less calm, and by the time you reach **JJ's Auberge** (tel: 571 2569) you are in the heart of Sosúa's downtown. There are six rooms at JJ's, with prices starting at US$20 and fluctuating slightly according to the season. If all the rooms are full, J J O'Connell – the talkative American owner – will put you next door in a Jewish couple's former house. Staying on Calle Dr Rosen, the **Tiburon Blanco Hotel** (tel: 343 1097), almost at the intersection with the main highway, is cheaper than most in El Batey, with rooms going for RD$220 or 150 for longer stays. You get a fan and bathroom, but no other frills are attached. A similar deal is available at **Hotel Calypso** on Calle Ayuntamiento. On the same street, **Hotel Romanoff** (tel: 571 3242) has US$20 rooms in low season, US$25 in high season.

There are two good, mid-range hotels charging US$20 on Calle Alejo Martínez. **Hotel Atlantico** (tel: 571 2367) has comfortable rooms with cable TV and a pool, as does the **Coco Hotel** (tel: 571 2184) opposite. You might feel a bit out of the way of things here, but you're not really that far from the centre of town and it does have the advantage of being quiet.

A few blocks south of these two hotels, on Calle Pedro Clisante, the **FL Holiday Club** (tel: 571 1847) has definite character. It's owned by a Russian who speaks good English and is very proud of his hotel and in particular the pool, the largest in Sosúa. The rooms are also spacious and cost US$25 or 30. Over the road, **Hotel El Batey** (tel: 571 2910) is the same price and quite satisfactory.

Los Charamicos

The Los Charamicos neighbourhood is not only for those on a shoestring budget. In many ways I prefer this part of Sosúa. While tourism has completely taken over in El Batey, Los Charamicos seems in comparison almost too Dominican. There is a heart and soul here that I couldn't find in El Batey. Unfortunately, there are hotels in El Batey that I couldn't find here. Go to Calle Kunhart for the cheapest hotels in Sosúa – and possibly the whole of the Dominican Republic. **Hotel Barveria El Centro** (tel: 571 2551) has recently been renovated and is excellent value at RD$50 for rooms with a fan and bathroom. **Hotel Los Hermanitos** and **Hotel Estephany** (tel: 571 2292) have similar prices, but they can't compete with the Baveria El Centro for value for money. The most expensive hotel in Los Charamicos is probably **Hotel Jhon** (tel: 571 1731), one block from Calle Kunhart, where rooms come with a fan (RD$175) or air conditioning (RD$200).

Where to eat

There are restaurants to suit all tastes and budgets in Sosúa. Some of the smartest ones are by the sea with terraces overlooking the ocean. For instance, **La Puntilla de Piergiorgio** serves expensive Italian food, **Restaurant El Coral** specialises in seafood and **On the Waterfront** has Caribbean and European dishes. They are all quite good, but you really come for the view and atmosphere.

The **Pavillon**, on Calle Ayuntamiento, is one of the best downtown restaurants, with a good choice of international cuisine – steaks are particularly recommended. Next to the Pavillon, the **Big Squeeze Juice Bar** is a good pit-stop when you need cooling down. **Pizzeria Il Malino** is on the same street and **Bologna Pizzeria** is around the corner on Calle Alejo Martínez. If you want pizza but can't be bothered to go and get it, **Mama Mia Pizzeria** (tel: 571 3394) will deliver it for you.

Tanja's Pastry, on Calle Pedro Clisante opposite Calle David Salem, is a good place for breakfast or a light lunch. It's Swiss-run, which you can tell from its immaculately clean counters and cakes, pastries and quiches which look almost too good to eat.

The area around Calle Pedro Clisante and Calle Duarte is where much of the tourist eating takes place. **PJ's International Pub Bar Terrace** is always popular, offering sandwiches, burgers, pizzas and some Dominican dishes at reasonable prices. The **Morua Mai Restaurant** is more elegant than PJ's and just as popular. It has tables outside and serves mainly European food and pizzas.

While Sosúa is not the best place in the Dominican Republic for *comida criolla*, it certainly exists. Not surprisingly, Los Charamicos is the best place to start looking. There is a restaurant at **Hotel Barveria El Centro**, and **Restaurant Central**, further along Calle Kunhart, is good and cheap. **Restaurant Atlantico** is more like the tourist restaurants in El Batey, but the menu is large and predominantly Dominican. It also has a terrace overlooking Sosúa Beach and the sea. Naturally, there are many street vendors in Los Charamicos selling *pollo frito* and other peoples' favourites.

Along Sosúa Beach the food is generally uninspiring. The two best places, both serving a full complement of Dominican dishes, could be **Restaurant Dominico Español** and **Restaurant Dominico Cubano**. In El Batey itself, try **Los Coquitos** on Calle Pedro Clisante near the FL Holiday Club for cheap *comida criolla*. This place is very popular at lunchtime.

Nightlife

Sosúa Beach is lined with bars. Some are popular with Germans, others attract an English-speaking crowd, still more are full of Dominicans, and some are empty. If this is your scene, you should select your favourite by trial and error. In the centre of town **La Roca Sports Bar** (next to PJ's) has a big-screen satellite TV, billiard and snooker tables, dart boards and some excellent cocktails. Try 'Sex on the Beach' with a 'Zombie'. There is another sports bar on Calle Ayuntamiento called **Eddy's Sports Bar**.

For dancing, Sosúa has some big and well-publicised discos. The **High Caribbean Disco**, at the end of Calle Pedro Clisante, wouldn't look out of place in Essex, with its Wet T-shirt Competitions and swimming pool by the side of the dance floor. On Friday nights there's a live band and God knows what else! The large, white building on Calle Alejo Martínez is the **Copacabana Disco**, which describes itself as 'simply the best'. If 'best' means loudest, they certainly have a claim.

Turn right off Calle Alejo Martínez and you come to the stretch of coast where Sosúa's all-inclusive hotels are gathered. There is the usual range of nightlife on offer here. If you're at a loose end at 3 o'clock in the morning, you could see what's going on at **Café Banana**, which is open until 07.00, or the **Casino Playa Chiquita**, at the eastern end of Calle Alejo Martínez.

Tourist information

In the absence of an official **tourist information office**, a German lady dispenses information from an office on Calle Pedro Clisante next to Tanya's Pastry. You can visit in person or telephone 571 3797.

The town's **post office** is the privately run EPS Post Office on Calle Pedro Clisante. They are open every day except Sunday. The **Codetel** office is at the intersection of Calle Dr Rosen and Calle Alejo Martínez.

The **banks** are dotted around town. Banco de Reservas is on Calle Pedro Clisante, Banco Popular is near Codetel and Bancredito is on Calle Duarte. **Western Union**, meanwhile, have an office on the main road just past Calle Duarte.

Activities

Sosúa is renowned for its good diving and snorkelling. You can rent snorkelling equipment by the hour (RD$50) or by the day (RD$200) on Sosúa Beach. The numerous diving centres all offer a similar type of thing: standard dives, night dives, wreck dives and free lessons in the pool. **Eurodive H²O** (tel: 571 1093) and the **Hippocampo Dive Centre** (tel: 519 1788) both have offices on the beach, while the **Aquario Diving Centre** (tel: 571 2868) is at Hotel Larimar.

CABARETE

About 5km east of Sosúa, a short stretch of the highway is lined on either side with hotels, bars, restaurants and windsurfing shops: this is Cabarete. In the 1980s it was just another small fishing village on the north coast, with several huts on the beach but nothing much more – except, that is, for some of the finest windsurfing conditions in the world.

A small band of Canadian and European surfers were the first to discover Cabarete; some are still there today to tell stories about the former Cabarete. In 1988 the town hosted the Windsurfing World Cup and its future was secured. Hotels, restaurants and four more world cups were to follow.

Today, life in Cabarete continues to revolve around windsurfing. The highlight of the year is **Cabarete Race Week**, usually held sometime in June, which is generally considered to be the windiest month. It features many of the world's best surfers, as well as windsurfing clinics, exhibitions and the odd beach party. If you're a beginner, the best time to windsurf is from April to December in the mornings, when the winds are lighter. The winds are most consistent and strongest from late spring to the end of summer, and in winter the sea can get a bit choppy, making conditions more suitable for the intermediate or expert surfer.

There is no shortage of places to rent windsurfing equipment and invest in a few lessons. Most of them are on the beach. Try **Carib Bic Centre** (tel: 571 0640), **Fanatic Board Centre** (tel: 571 0861), or **Vela/Spinout** (tel: 571 0805). Budget on about US$50 to rent the equipment for a day or to take an hour-long lesson. Weekly rentals go for around US$250, while windsurfing packages, including equipment and lessons for a week, are in the US$500 range.

Getting there and away

Gua-guas running between Puerto Plata and Río San Juan pass through Cabarete. Simply flag one down on the main road. Overcharging is common on this route and you should establish the price before getting in. Remember, the general rule is RD$5 for every town or major stopping-off point you pass.

Where to stay

Most of Cabarete's hotels are along the main street, but there are two notable exceptions in ProCab, a residential area beside the lagoon. The first is **Ali's Apartments** (tel: 571 0568), offering large apartments with kitchens and hot water. You can hire bikes and discounts are available for longer stays. Prices start at about US$20. **Hotel Residencia Dominicana** (tel: 571 0890), opposite Ali's Apartments, is equally good. The US$15-rooms are good value and they also rent bikes and have access to the ProCab tennis courts over the road.

The entrance to ProCab is at the eastern end of town known as La Punta, where the cheaper accommodation tends to be found, although none of it is really in the budget category. Having said this, you can get a shared room at **Hotel El Pequeño Refugio** (tel: 571 0770) for US$10. Ask for a room in the pink house on the beach. Naturally it's usually full of young surfing types. Opposite ProCab, the **Caribe Surf Hotel** (tel: 571 0788) has reasonable rooms starting from US$22. They can also arrange to pick you up at the airport. **Hotel Piña del Mar** is just in front of the Caribe Surf Hotel and is slightly cheaper and more rustic.

In the centre of town, the **Banana Boat Hotel** (tel: 571 0690) and **Hotel Laguna Blu** (tel: 571-0659) cater to a younger crowd. They both have kitchens and are in the US$25-35 price range. The **Cabarete Beach Hotel** (tel: 571 0755) might look like one of the smarter hotels in town, and they do have apartments for over US$100, but they also have more modest rooms for around US$30.

At the western end of town, **Hotel Albatros** (tel: 571 0841) and **Hotel Kaoba** (tel: 571 0837) are worth considering, if only because most of the other hotels in Cabarete are more than US$50 a night.

Where to eat and drink

Between every hotel there seems to be a bar or a restaurant. Many of them offer the homogenised food you would expect in a place with so many tourists, but one or two are really quite good. **La Casa del Pescador** is certainly the best seafood restaurant in town and could be the best place to eat altogether. It's on the beach in the centre.

There are several other bars, restaurants and cafés on the beach. **Las Brisas** is the place to be on Thursday evenings, when there is a volleyball competition on the sand in front of the bar and a disco during and after it. The **Tiki Bar** and **New Wave** are also good places to go for a drink, a bite to eat and to listen to some good music. The Tiki Bar in particular often features some good live bands. The **Hola-la Café** is newer and slightly less popular than the others, but it does have the town's only cyber café.

Mi Vieja Casona, just past the entrance to ProCab, is at the lower end of the price scale. This is perhaps the only place in Cabarete where you can get authentic *comida criolla*. Their limited selection is often confined to a couple of chicken dishes that are well prepared and different from the usual fare on offer. The most outstanding eatery in Cabarete is **Panaderia Dick**. This small bakery serves excellent croissants and pastries and strong Dominican coffee. Get there early in the morning if you want to sit down, as it gets quite hectic at around 08.00.

Many of the hotels also have restaurants. One of the better ones is at **Hotel Kaoba**, which offers fondue on an all-you-can-eat basis.

In the absence of a street market, there are several supermarkets along the main road. The cheapest is **Supermercado Judith**, next to ProCab. Self-catering is something you might consider in Cabarete, since so much of the accommodation comes with kitchens and cooking facilities. If you do decide to cook for yourself and you like fish, **El Mercado del Mar** is a fishmonger with one of the most extensive selections of local fish on the north coast. It's next to Hotel Kaoba.

Tourist information

Cabarete is not lacking in amenities for the tourist. Although there's no state **post office**, a couple of private ones offer an efficient, but slightly more expensive alternative. Choose from the EPS Post Office or Planet Foto, which also sells film, English-language newspapers and has a noticeboard advertising local events. The cheapest **telephone** shop is TeleCabarete.

There is one **bank** in Cabarete, the Banco Gerencial & Fiducario, which is open from 08.00 to 16.30 and changes travellers' cheques.

The largest **pharmacy** in town is the San Raphael, opposite the Cabarete Beach Hotel. There is a small clinic behind this pharmacy, but if you need a **doctor**, I would go to the SERVI-MED (tel: 571 0964), which is in the same building as the EPS Post Office.

Activities

Cabarete is more than just a windsurfer's paradise. While it's not the ideal place to come for sunbathing or sightseeing, if more active pursuits interest you, Cabarete is hard to beat. Apart from windsurfing, there are excellent waves for conventional surfing at **Playa Encuentro**, 7km down the road towards Sosúa. You can also arrange to go on hiking, biking and horse-riding tours from Cabarete. **Iguana Mama** (tel: 571 0908), one of the largest adventure tour operators in the Dominican Republic, is based in Cabarete. In addition to their full-scale tours in the Samaná Peninsula and the Cordillera Central (see Chapter 13, page 169) they run half-day biking trips to the villages around Cabarete and the Cibao Valley and hikes up Mount Isabela de Torres. For horseback riding, **Adventure Riding Park** has a ranch 25km from Cabarete. Go to Hotel Residencia Dominicana if you want to find out more about the various tours and packages on offer.

'Hispaniola.com'

At the risk of doing myself out of a job, I feel that I must recommend this web site to anyone contemplating a visit to Cabarete. It has detailed information on practically every hotel in town, including some virtual-reality tours of the rooms, and you can make reservations over the internet. The web site also contains information about other activities in Cabarete, daily wind reports for the surfers and even a Spanish/English phrasebook with pronunciations.

RÍO SAN JUAN

Fishing and tourism fight for supremacy in Río San Juan. At the moment the contest is finely poised, giving the town a nice mixture of native authenticity and enough tourist facilities to be comfortable.

Fishing is very important to Río San Juan and the town's fishermen catch a substantial amount of the region's fish. Walk along Calle Sánchez and you'll see the *pescaderos* (named, for some reason, with girl's names) selling the daily catch. The fishing boats leave from the bay at the end of the street, sometimes staying out for as long as 15 days in the deep waters of the Banco de Plata.

Meanwhile, the **tourists** come to Río San Juan, not to see the fishing boats (although this is my favourite part of town), but to take a boat tour around the **Gri-Gri Lagoon** – a maze of mangrove swamps with clear waters, unusual rock formations and tall trees where egrets and vultures congregate in the evening. The lagoon is at the end of Calle Duarte, the town's main street, which is also where the boat tours depart. It costs RD$400 for two to six people or RD$200 for one person. For this price you get a tour of the lagoon, have a look at the **Cuevas de las Golondrinas** (Swallow Caves) and stop for a swim at **Playa Caletón**.

The beaches in Río San Juan are unfortunately nothing to write home about. To get to the best one, turn right at Hotel Bahía Blanca and walk along the path next to the Gri-Gri Lagoon. Diving courses are run by the excellent **Gri-Gri Divers** (tel: 589 2671). This outfit is more ecologically aware than most and are very strict about things like standing on and handling coral. Moreover, they run good courses and offer an hour's free snorkel hire to guests at Hotel Bahía Blanca.

Getting there and away

Walk up Calle Duarte and eventually you'll come to the main highway. Here you can catch *gua-guas* to Puerto Plata and the towns en route, Nagua (for the Samaná Peninsula) and Santo Domingo. Caribe Tours also pass through several times a day on their way to either the Samaná Peninsula or Santo Domingo.

Where to stay

The best place in Río San Juan is **Hotel Bahía Blanca** (tel: 589 2563). It has comfortable rooms ranging from RD$200-350 and a good restaurant; it can arrange tours of the lagoon and other places of interest, and there is the most stunning view overlooking the bay and the Atlantic Ocean. The other hotels in town seem to pale in comparison. **Hotel Río San Juan** (tel: 589 2211), on Calle Duarte, is about the same price, but even with air conditioning it's not such good value. **Hotel Santa Clara** (tel: 589 2286) on Calle Padre Billini, **Hotel D'Angélica** on Calle Dr Virgillo Garcia and **Hotel Comedor San Martin** on Calle Duarte are all budget hotels. The San Martin is the cheapest and most rustic at RD$75, while the D'Angélica, with its fully-furnished rooms overflowing with cuddly toys, is the best.

Where to eat

The buffet breakfast at **Restaurante Bahía Blanca** is worth a try – if not for the bacon, eggs, fresh fruit and excellent coffee, then for the aforementioned view. They also serve good food in the evenings, much of it with plenty of garlic. There are one or two international restaurants in town like **Restaurant Petit** on Calle Ruffino Belbuena and **Cheo's Café Bar** on Calle Padre Billini, but the best places are the ones selling no-nonsense *comida criolla* along Calle Duarte. Choose from **Restaurant Yanichelle**, **Restaurant San José** and arguably the most popular, **La Casona Delicatessen**.

Tourist information

The **post office**, **Codetel**, **Tricom**, the town's one **bank** (Banco Metropolitano) and **Western Union** are all on Calle Duarte. Throw in a few **pharmacies** and the only thing that isn't on the main street is the **police station**, which is on Calle Lorenzo Adames in the town square.

ON TO THE SAMANÁ PENINSULA

Caribe Tours have direct services to the town of Santa Bárbara de Samaná on the south coast of the peninsula. However, if you want to get anywhere else, you should go by *gua-gua*.

From Río San Juan, catch a *gua-gua* to **Nagua** (one hour, RD$25). From Nagua catch another to **Sánchez** (45 minutes, RD$20), but note that in Nagua you'll have to take a *motoconcho* to get to the departure point for Sánchez, which is at the other end of town from where the *gua-gua* from Río San Juan will leave you. At Sánchez, which is actually the capital of the Samaná Peninsula, you have a choice. Either you can continue along the main highway to Santa Bárbara de Samaná, or you can cross the mountains to Las Terranas on the north coast of the peninsula.

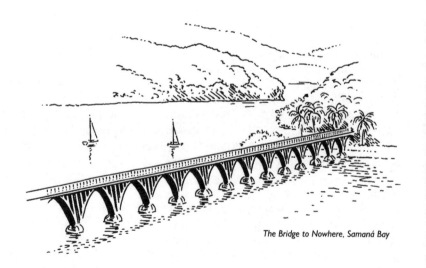

The Bridge to Nowhere, Samaná Bay

The Samaná Peninsula

The north coast continues for another 50km or so along the Samaná Peninsula. However, while the mainland part of the coast is relatively built up, the peninsula has few towns and is thinly populated. Much of the land area is taken up by mountains that run along the spine of the peninsula, which means that all the towns are situated along the coast. Sánchez is the region's capital and the gateway to the peninsula. However, from the visitor's point of view, Las Terrenas on the north coast and Santa Bárbara de Samaná on the shores of Samaná Bay are of most interest: the former for its beaches, the latter for its humpback whales.

SANTA BÁRBARA DE SAMANÁ

Santa Bárbara de Samaná, or just Samaná, is rather a nondescript town with no real centre and nothing much to see – a legacy perhaps of the fire that destroyed the town in 1946. The busiest time is during the whale-watching season. But since this is only two or three months of the year, you can generally count on Samaná being dead quiet or quite dead, depending on your mood and generosity at the time.

Getting there and away
By sea
There is a **ferry service** from Samaná to the town of Sabana de la Mar on the southern side of the bay. Boats leave from the dock at 09.00, 11.00 and 16.00 and the one-way fare is RD$35.

By road
Caribe Tours is on the Malecón opposite the dock. They make about five runs a day to Santo Domingo and also go to Puerto Plata (3½ hours, RD$70). **Metro** is next to Caribe Tours and only go to Santo Domingo, via Nagua and San Francisco de Macorís. A cheaper option than Caribe Tours to Puerto Plata is a company called **Papagayo Express**. They have one bus a day that leaves at 14.00 and costs RD$50. Their office is on the road leading into town near Hotel King.

Where to stay and eat
The best hotel in town is the **Tropical Lodge Hotel** (tel: 538 2480) at the eastern end of the Malecón. It is wonderfully quiet, has great views of the bay and

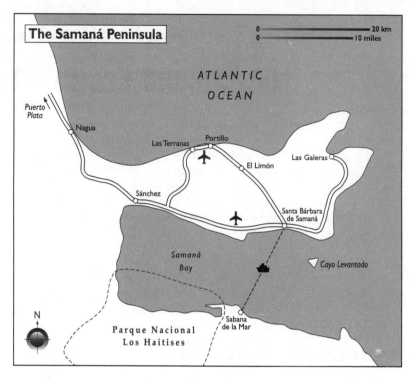

costs RD$500 with air conditioning, RD$450 without. There are three hotels near the clocktower in the centre of town (in as much as it has a centre). **Guest House Kiko** (tel: 538 2565) is the best value, friendliest and most basic. It has rooms with fan and bathroom for RD$150 and is up the hill leading off from the left of the clocktower. I didn't think much of **Hotel Docia** (RD$200) and **Hotel Nilka** (RD$250), both of which are left of the clocktower. There are some more budget options on the road leading into town. The most noticeable is **Hotel King** (tel: 538 2353), with its pink, spiral staircase leading up to rooms that go for RD$150 (single) and RD$200 (double). You could also try the **Plaza Taino Hotel** (tel: 538 2894). **Hotel Fotuna**, next to Hotel King, is a little too basic.

Restaurants and bars line either side of the Malecón. The one selling the most authentic Dominican cuisine could be **Restaurant Camilo's** or **Restaurant El Bucanero** next to Samaná dock. The multicoloured **Café de Paris** serves pizzas, small breakfasts, cocktails and sundaes.

What to see

The one interesting thing to see in Samaná is the **Bridge to Nowhere**. It stretches out into Samaná Bay, only to disappear in a clump of trees on a small islet called Cayo Vigia. In the absence of any good mainland beaches near Samaná, the offshore island of **Cayo Levantado** has become too popular for its own good. You can get get there from Samaná dock for a price (not so bad if there's a group of you), or from a small village 8km east of Samaná called

HUMPBACK WHALES: THE GREAT PERFORMERS

I imagine that getting up close to any whale is a humbling experience. Watching the humpbacks can also be an exhilarating one. These natural-born performers have more moves than Fred Astaire, and a song or two included in their repertoire. When you are out whale-watching, look for some of the following moves:

- *Breaching:* This is the pretentious word for the great jumps frequently performed by humpbacks. The most breaches observed in one period was 130 in 75 minutes and they come in a variety of styles. The most common is when the whale emerges from the surface on its side, twists around and lands on its back, although the less elegant belly flop is also popular.
- *Tail slash:* Humpbacks have large tails and they often like to lift them above the surface and crash them back down on the water.
- *Flippering:* Along the same lines as tail slashing, this time the whale floats on the surface, turns on its axis and beats the water with its long flippers.
- *Spyhop:* This is when the humpback raises just its head above the water in a fashion not dissimilar to a submarine periscope.
- *Rolling:* The whale lies on the surface and rolls through 360°.
- *Logging:* The whale just floats on the surface as if dead.

You might not be able to hear them, but male humpbacks on breeding grounds will almost invariably be singing a song. These songs – a series of plaintive moans, snores and groans – can be heard by other whales up to 30km away. All humpbacks within the same region sing broadly the same song, which changes and evolves slightly over time. So why do they sing, sometimes for many hours without stopping? Since the songs are only heard during the winter, it probably has something to do with reproduction. Perhaps the males are announcing that they are ready for romance, or are trying to attract a mate. When a female does show some interest, the male stops singing and escorts her for about 15 minutes, during which time mating might take place. Meanwhile, other singing males might pursue the courting couple, trying to oust the original escort from his position close to the female. They normally succeed after a few hours of aggressive jostling, mate with the female, then lose interest and return to their songs.

Las Flechas which, incidentally, was the site of the first battle between the Europeans and the native Indians on January 13 1493.

Whale-watching

Between mid-January and mid-March, over 10,000 humpback whales migrate from their feeding grounds in the Northern Atlantic to reproduce in the warm, shallow waters off the north coast of the Dominican Republic, and in Samaná Bay. The Canadian lady who runs **Whale Samaná** (tel: 538 2494), the best of the several whale-watching tour operators on the peninsula, likes to describe Dominican waters at this time as a 'large singles' bar circuit'. During the season (January 15 to March 15) Whale Samaná have two tours a day, each lasting between three and four hours and costing RD$450. I recommend this outfit, which was established in 1984 and was one of the first of its kind in Samaná. They know what they're talking about, they have an obvious passion for humpback whales and their approach to whale watching in general stikes me as being very responsible and ecologically aware.

Samaná Bay whale-watching regulations

Some say that whale watching is intrusive and disruptive. Others argue that it is an educational and responsible alternative to whaling. Whatever your own opinion, it might be useful to know that whale watching in the Samaná Bay is strictly regulated. These regulations, mutually agreed by Samaná boat owners, conservation groups and the Dominican Navy, are as follows:

- Vessels must stay at least 80m from a whale group that includes a calf, and 50m from adult whales.
- When a vessel reaches the regulated distance, it must put its engine in neutral and wait.
- A vessel may not stay with a whale or a group of whales for more than 30 minutes.
- After passing Cayo Levantado, the velocity of the whale-watching vessels should not be more than 5 knots. If a vessel encounters whales further into the Bay (before Cayo Levantado), it must immediately lower its velocity to 5 knots.
- No vessel will permit passengers to swim with the whales.

LAS TERRENAS

When Antoine, a celebrated French singer, arrived in Las Terrenas, it didn't take long before he was crooning songs celebrating his arrival in 'paradise', which referred to two of the best beaches in the Dominican Republic. At the end of the town's main thoroughfare you have two options – right for **El Portillo Beach** or left **Playa Bonita**. Both of these beaches have plenty of sand, calm waters and incredible sunsets. El Portillo is the larger of the two. A sandy road runs parallel to the beach and ends up in **El Limón**. A few kilometres from here there is a waterfall called **Salto de Caloda** which, at 30m high, is certainly worth a look.

Getting there and away
By air

Air Santo Domingo fly to El Portillo Airport, 6km from Las Terrenas. The flight to Santo Domingo leaves at 09.20 and costs US$49 one way. For the same price and at a similar time you can fly to Puerto Plata, while the two flights to Punta Cana leave at 17.45 and cost slightly more.

By road

All *gua-guas* going south across the mountains are bound for Sánchez. The ride is a spectacular one with stunning views at times of the Samaná coastline. For this reason, you might consider the less fashionable seats in the back of the pick-up trucks that normally make the journey. It takes 45 minutes and costs about RD$25. The one other destination served is El Limón. Once again, pick-up trucks ply this route along the sandy, coastal road running east from Las Terrenas.

Where to stay

The majority of the hotels in Las Terrenas – and there is no shortage of them – are on the beach. There are a few resort-type hotels, but most are moderate tourist hotels, *cabañas* or guesthouses. Starting on Playa Bonita and working from east to west, **Hotel Diny** (tel: 240 6113) appears to be the first possibility. A garden separates the hotel from the beach, there is a restaurant and rooms start at RD$130, which is as cheap as you'll get in this part of Las Terrenas. The restaurant **Casa Papon** has a couple of rooms for RD$350 which are literally on the beach, just a few metres from the sea. Outside of the resorts, **Hotel Tropic Banana** (tel: 240 6110) is one of the most expensive and best hotels in Las Terrenas. It is French-run – as the games of *pétanque* (like bowls) in the front garden suggest – and the 28 rooms are all very comfortable. Singles go for US$50 and doubles for US$70. Breakfast is included and a small reduction in price can be expected during low season. There is a side road next to the well-fortified Caco Beach Resort, down which you can find a couple of cheaper hotels. The **L'Aubergine Hotel** (tel: 240 6167) and the **Finchen Hotel** (tel: 240 6241) both cost about RD$200: the former has a good restaurant serving tasty pizza, while the latter will pick you up from El Portillo Airport. The **Las Cayenas Hotel** (tel: 240 6070) is almost at the end of Playa Bonita. Rates are high at RD$400 for a room with a fan, but the atmosphere is very relaxed and the hotel itself, built in the colonial style, is quite attractive.

There is as good a choice of accommodation on the other side of town along El Portillo Beach. **Viejo Villa** has rooms with kitchens for RD$300, while rates at the **Papagayo** (tel: 240 6131) and **Las Palmeras** (tel: 707 7263) start at RD$250. The best places, however, are about 20m back from the beach. **Casa Robinson** (tel: 240 6496) has a few bungalows set in lush gardens for RD$350 (RD$450 with kitchen), while those at the French-run **Casas del Mar** are elegantly decorated in art-deco style and cost RD$380.

Las Terrenas, like every other town in the Dominican Republic, has its rock-bottom, last-resort hotel for the truly impoverished or stingy. Walk up the main street until you see the sign for the **Sabana Real** (tel: 240 6240 and ask for Papi) and continue down a side path for about 100m. Eventually you'll see a collection of small, white, concrete boxes in the middle of nowhere, each available for rent at RD$75 a night. In fact, I had no reservations staying here. Although the rooms are basic, they are also surprisingly functional, with electricity, water, a fan and a bathroom; and being so isolated, it's very quiet.

Where to eat

Generally speaking, the more pricey restaurants aimed specifically at the tourists are on the beach, while the less glamorous options are along the main street. Having said this, however, the best and most Dominican restaurant I found was in the middle of the Pueblos de los Pescadores – a cluster of *cabañas* on Playa Bonita consisting mainly of restaurants. **Salta P'atras** is the bright yellow one in the middle. It has a small menu with good Dominican food at very reasonable prices. You could also try **Casa Papon** or **Casa Salsa**, but these, and the others in the Pueblos de los Pescadores, are more expensive and less native in their style of cuisine than the Salta P'atras.

Along El Portillo Beach, the restaurants have a similar theme: pizzas, pasta, steaks and other dishes chosen so as not to offend the international palate. Try the very new **Restaurante Las Palmeras**, **Restaurant La Capannina** or **Casa Pepa** for Spanish food. Also note that most of the hotels in Las Terrenas have restaurants.

The number of *comedors* you see on the main street increases the further you walk out of town. Two good ones, near enough to the beach to be convenient, are **Comedor Suny** and **Comedor Economica El Zapote**. Both are clean and serve fish, chicken and *chuletas*. The El Zapote also has good fruit juices. About ten minutes further down the street, **Supermercado Ti Billy** has a good, albeit expensive, selection of groceries.

Tourist information

There is apparently a government **tourist office** at the end of the main street before you turn left or right for the beaches. Its advertised opening hours are 08.30 to 13.30 and 14.30 to 17.00. If this place is closed or unhelpful, you could try Sunshine Tours (tel: 240 6164) – a travel agency that also dispenses local tourist information and sells maps. There are several other facilities at this end of the main street, including **Codetel**, a **bank** (Banco del Progresso) and an ATM machine. The **Western Union** is ten minutes up the same road going out of town. There is a **Planet Foto** for film and stamps on Playa Bonita in the Pueblo de los Pescadores, and the **police station** is nearby.

Activities

There are five diving centres in Las Terrenas and there seems to be little to choose between them. **Tropical Diving Center** (tel: 240 6110) is next to the Hotel Tropic Banana and **Popy Divers** (tel: 240 6187) is part of the Kanesh Beach Hotel. You can hire windsurfs and snorkelling gear at **Sunshine** on Playa Bonita, while **Rancho Las Terrenas**, also next to Hotel Tropic Banana, offers horseback riding.

The Cibao Valley

The valley that lies between the mountain ranges of the Cordillera Central and the Cordillera Septentrional is called the Cibao. When Columbus discovered Hispaniola, he pinned great hopes on the gold reserves in the Cibao Valley, and although he was ultimately disappointed with what was extracted from the mines, he found he had discovered the most fertile and productive part of the island. Irrigated by the Yaque de Norte River, the Cibao Valley – described as the 'bread basket' of the Dominican Republic – provides the country with most of its agricultural produce. Moreover, it has always been a politically and culturally important region, and a large proportion of the country's population live in the Cibao towns of San Francisco de Macorís and Santiago de los Caballeros.

SANTIAGO DE LOS CABALLEROS

I arrived in Santiago by bus and decided to walk from the Caribe Tours terminal to the centre of town. Half an hour later I was still trudging down the same road, lined with auto-dealerships on one side and car-repair shops on the other. 'I'm not going to like this town' I thought. Fortunately, I was wrong. Santiago is the Dominican Republic's second city and the commercial hub of its most economically important region, the Cibao Valley, so naturally it's going to be large, sprawling and not always very attractive. However, judge Santiago not while you're walking into town, but when you finally get there. I wouldn't describe it as beautiful, but Santiago does have one of the prettiest town squares around, a fair amount to see and a deceptively relaxed pace of life.

Like other towns in Hispaniola, Santiago was rebuilt after an earthquake levelled the town in 1562. Before this watershed it was little more than a fort, constructed in 1494, on the orders of Columbus, to protect the vast gold reserves that were thought to exist in the region. After the earthquake, the town was rebuilt on its present site on the banks of the River Yaque del Norte and was to become the economic, political and cultural centre of the country. These days it plays second fiddle to Santo Domingo in terms of politics, but remains the centre of the Republic's important tobacco and coffee industries, a major producer of rum – and also a city of culture. For instance, *merengue*

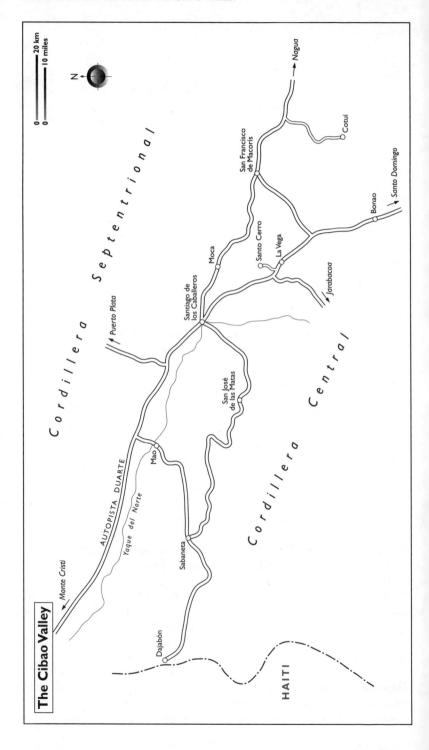

The Cibao Valley

music has its origins here and the carnival in Santiago is reputed to be the most authentic in the country.

Orientation

Once you get to the centre of Santiago from either the terminals of the main bus companies or the airport, both of which are in the northern part of the city, finding your way around is not difficult. The main thoroughfare is Calle del Sol and the heart of the city is Parque Duarte, which is more or less in the middle of Calle del Sol. Due south of the park is the River Yaque del Norte; west is the market and the commercial part of town; east there are shopping streets leading up to the Monument to the Heroes of the Restoration; and north there are more shopping streets leading up to Avenida 27 de Febrero for the bus terminals and the airport.

Getting there and away

By air

Air Santo Domingo has services to and from Santiago's **Cibao International Airport** on the northern outskirts of the city. The one flight a day to Santo Domingo leaves at 09.55 and costs US$49 (one way), while the flight to Punta Cana leaves at 17.15 and costs US$89. To get into town from the airport, jump in one of the *carros* that regularly go up and down Avenida Bartolomé Colon. Alternatively, it's about a 20-minute walk.

By road

Santiago is easy to get to from almost anywhere in the country. Bus companies like **Caribe Tours**, **Metro** and **Terra Bus** all have regular sevices to Santo Domingo (two to three hours, RD$60-70). The first two are based some way from the centre of town on Avenida 27 de Febrero, and unless you want to walk for about an hour, you should take a *motoconcho* from the station. Terra Bus, on the other hand, is more conveniently situated, opposite the Monument to the Heroes of the Restoration. Caribe Tours also serve a wide range of other destinations including Puerto Plata, Sosúa and Monte Cristi. For destinations in the south, go to Santo Domingo and make your connections there.

Gua-guas are most useful if you want to go to other towns in the Cibao Valley or the nearby mountains. They seem to leave for La Vega (45 minutes, RD$10) from almost anywhere in the city. One of the best places is in the Mercado Yaque on the corner of Avenida Valerio and Calle B Scauts. This is also where pick-up trucks leave for the mountain town of San José de las Matas. The other main *gua-gua* stop is on Calle 30 de Marzo, opposite Calle Salvador Cucurullo. Here you can catch *gua-guas* to Mao, Puerto Plata and Moca (one hour, RD$15-20).

Where to stay

The two most expensive hotels in Santiago have little character and are aimed at the businessman rather than the tourist. Santiago is not, after all, a

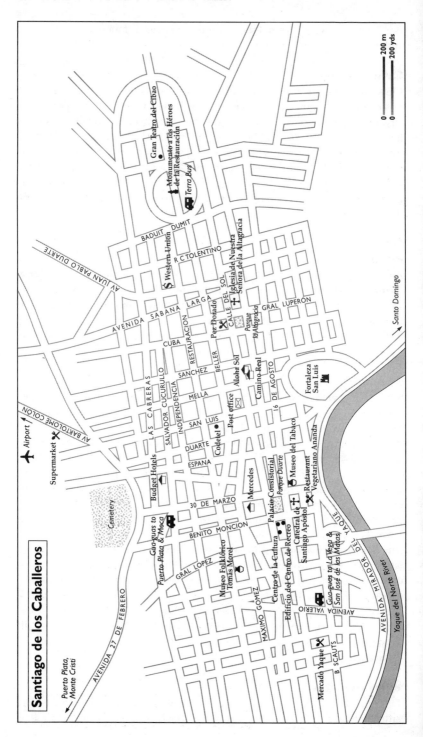

Santiago de los Caballeros

Puerto Plata, Monte Cristi

Airport

Supermarket

Cemetery

AVENIDA 27 DE FEBRERO

AV BARTOLOME COLON

AV JUAN PABLO DUARTE

Gran Teatro del Cibao

Monumento a los Héroes de la Restauración

Terra Bus

BADUIT DUMIT

Western-Unión

R C TOLENTINO

Iglesia de Nuestra Señora de la Altagracia

AVENIDA SABANA LARGA

CALLE DEL SOL

GRAL LUPERÓN

Parque la Altagracia

Por Dorado

Aloha Sol

Camino Real

CUBA

RESTAURACIÓN

LAS CABRERAS

SALVADOR CUCURULLO

INDEPENDENCIA

SANCHEZ

MELLA

SAN LUIS

DUARTE

ESPAÑA

30 DE MARZO

BELLER

Post office

Codetel

16 DE AGOSTO

Fortaleza San Luis

Santo Domingo

Museo del Tabaco

Restaurant Vegetariano Ananda

Mercedes

Parque Duarte

Palacio Consistorial

Guaguas to Puerto Plata & Moca

Budget Hotels

BENITO MONCION

GRAL LOPEZ

Museo Folklórico Tomás Morel

Centro de la Cultura

Edificio del Centro de Recreo

MAXIMO GOMEZ

Catedral de Santiago Apóstol

Guaguas to La Vega & San José de las Matas

AVENIDA VALERIO

AVENIDA MIRADOR

Mercado Yaque

B SCAUTS

Yaque del Norte River

200 m
200 yds

fully-fledged tourist town. **Hotel Aloha Sol** (tel: 583 0090) on Calle del Sol and **Hotel Camino Real** (tel: 581 7000), round the corner on Calle Mella, both charge about RD$750 for a single. If you want a double, opt for the Camino Real, which charges RD$800, as opposed to nearly RD$1,000 at the Aloha Sol.

Santiago's most venerable hotel is **Hotel Mercedes** (tel: 583 1171) on Calle 30 de Marzo, a 1920s vintage with mahogany banisters, high ceilings and the proverbial 'colonial feel'. The smarter rooms with air-conditioning and TV go for RD$380, while the budget option with a fan but no bathroom is less than half the price. Apart from the Mercedes, the other cheap hotels are along Calle Salvador Cucurullo. There is hardly anything to choose between them, both in terms of price and quality, so go for the one that you like. In my case this was **Hotel Colonial** (tel: 247 3122), with its white, mock-Victorian mansion and friendly staff. But you might prefer **Hotel Monterey** (tel: 582 4558) or **Hotel Dorado** (tel: 582 7563), all of which charge between about RD$125 and RD$250 for rooms, depending on what you want in them. **Hotel Lima** (tel: 582 0620), on the corner of the same street, is not as good as the others. The rooms cost RD$90 and are slightly more basic, but still OK.

Where to eat

The two most expensive hotels in Santiago also have restaurants. **Restaurant D'Manon** at Hotel Aloha Sol is known for its meat dishes (rabbit is a speciality), while **Restaurant Vista Mar**, on the top floor of Hotel Camino Real, is known for its good views. The D'Manon is the better of the two. **Restaurant Pez Dorado** on Parque La Altagracia competes with the hotels in the price and quality league. The menu is crowded with steak, seafood and Chinese dishes, but it's not cheap.

Some of the less expensive hotels have restaurants, cafés, or simply serve meals at lunchtime. For example, the **Sunset Cafeteria** at Hotel Mercedes has several set menus including *la bandera* (rice, beans, meat and salad) for RD$35, while **Hotel Colonial** serves huge dishes of chicken and rice for lunch. Elsewhere in town there are several places where you can eat pizza, hamburgers and other fast food. In a small side street to the left of the cathedral steps there's something completely different – a vegetarian restaurant in the Dominican Republic. It's called **Restaurant Vegetariano Ananda** and they also offer yoga sessions after your meal. I knew there had to be a catch!

Fruit vendors line Calle 30 de Marzo and abound in the **Mercado Yaque**, which is at the western end of town around Calle 16 de Agosto. There is an extremely large supermarket called **Super Pollo** on the airport road (Avenida Bartolomé Colon) within easy walking distance of the town centre.

Nightlife and entertainment

There is a good bar along Calle 16 de Agosto. It has **'Rompe el Molde'** written on a sign over the door, but this is an advertisement and not its real name. You'll know the one I mean if you pass by at about 18.30 and see half of Santiago drinking beer wrapped in brown paper bags after work. The **Frunafol Café** on Calle del Sol is another popular place, especially before and after performances at the nearby Centro Cultura. The most interesting drinking spot has to be the **Talanca Bar du Jazz** on the corner of Calle Restauración and Tolentino. Photographs of the Beatles, the Stones and Bob Marley adorn the walls, and jazz rather than the usual *merengue* is played. However, the fascinating thing about the Talanca is the huge tree which literally splits the bar in half and threatens to suffocate it with its branches.

The best nightclubs within walking distance of the centre are probably on Calle del Sol next to the Monument to the Heroes of the Restoration. Look for the building with the green roof, which is apparently the largest disco in Santiago. Otherwise, **Disco Boulevard** provides the usual Dominican disco experience: loud and flamboyant. The **Imagenes Disco** is at Hotel Camino Real. It occasionally has live bands and you have to be dressed smartly to get in.

The **Gran Teatro del Cibao** (tel: 582 7901) is also next to the Monument to the Heroes. Call the box office to find out what's on during your visit. Dominican theatre is usually staged and tickets are not often under RD$100. If you have no luck at the theatre, the **Centro Cultura** frequently has dance, music and drama performances that all tend to show off the cultural richness of the Cibao region. Pass by and look at the billboards outside for upcoming events.

Tourist information

The **post office** is on Calle del Sol; the main **Codetel** office is next to the Monument to the Heroes of the Restoration (a smaller, more central one is on Calle San Luis); the **banks** are at various points along Calle del Sol (Scotiabank is nearest to Parque Duarte); and **Western Union** has an office on Avenida Duarte between Calle Independencia and Restauración.

Santiago is famous for its **merengue** (see Chapter 12, page 155) and this is as good a town as any to stock up on cassettes. There are one or two unpretentious places along Calle Salvador Cucurullo (the budget hotel street) with extensive selections for very reasonable prices. A particularly good one is Mundo 30, next to Hotel Dorado.

What to see

Many of the sights to see in Santiago are around **Parque Duarte**, or not far from it. The park itself, however, is *the* highlight. On one of the busiest shopping streets in the country, this tree-lined plaza is a real sanctuary, and because of the trees, the park enjoys almost complete shade all through the day. There's also a lovely bandstand in the middle. On the edge of the park, **horse-drawn carriages** can be hired for one-hour tours of the city at a cost of RD$150.

The **Catedral de Santiago Apóstol** (Cathedral of St James the Apostle) is on the eastern side of the park. It was built in the 19th century in a mixture of styles, mainly neo-Classic and Gothic; the stained-glass windows are by the Dominican artist, Rincón Mora, and the tomb of the Dominican tyrant Ulises Heureaux is inside. The cathedral forms part of the 'cultural' portion of the park. Next to it is the **Edificio del Centro de Recreo** (Recreational Centre), formerly an exclusive gentlemen's club, but now just somewhere for its members to play billiards and drink a glass of rum away from the general noise. Nearby is the **Palacio Consistorial**, the 19th-century town hall, within which is the **Museo de la Villa de Santiago**, which charts the history of the town since it was founded, although it had been closed for some time when I visited. The **Centro de la Cultura** (Cultural Centre) is around the corner on Calle del Sol. They regularly have evenings of dance, music, theatre and even ballet, most of which has a strong Cibao influence. Back on Parque Duarte, the **Museo del Tabaco** (Tobacco Museum), on the corner of Calle 30 de Marzo and 16 de Agosto, is open from 09.00 to 17.00 (with a siesta from 12.00 to 14.00). Entrance is free, although you should sign the visitors' book and leave a contribution.

Parque Duarte is not the only square in town. The other, **Parque La Altagracia**, is on Calle del Sol between Calle Luperón and Larga. This is nowhere near as nice as Duarte (there are no trees for a start) and its only attraction is the **Iglesia de Nuestra Señora de La Altagracia** (Church of Our Lady of Highest Grace) – Santiago's Catholic church. This is about halfway between Parque Duarte and the most prominent landmark in town, the **Monumento a los Héroes de la Restauración**. Elevated slighty above the downtown area, this 67m-high marble monument commemorates those who fought in 1865 for the restoration of independent government after years of Spanish rule. You can walk to the top where you get good views of Santiago and the rest of the Cibao Valley, and there is a museum halfway up with maps, photographs and models describing the War of Restoration and its heroes.

There is another museum to the west of Parque Duarte on Calle Restauración where it intersects with Calle Gral Lopez. The **Museo Folklórico Tomás Morel** has a collection of masks and costumes tradititionally worn at **carnival** in the Cibao. Entrance is free (leave a contribution), but opening times are erratic. Santiago is famous for its carnival during the months of February and August. The main figures you'll see at these celebrations are the *lechones* (pigs), who wear masks and costumes similar to the ones at the Folklore Museum and are supposed to represent the devil.

Excursions from Santiago de los Caballeros
Moca and the cigar factories
Moca is about one hour east of Santiago in the heart of the coffee and tobacco growing area of the Cibao Valley. According to the tourist brochures, Moca is famous for its 'coffee, beautiful women and brave men'. The town's name is also derived from 'mosca', the Spanish word for fly, and there are an awful lot of them about. The two main things to see in Moca are

BUYING AND SMOKING DOMINICAN CIGARS

Cigars are taken very seriously in the Dominican Republic and their quality can often be as good, or better, than Cuban cigars. Here are a few tips on buying and smoking Dominican cigars.

The major cigar manufacturers in the Dominican Republic are Arturo Fuente, Leon Jimenes, Matasa, General, Consolidated and Davidoff. Along with some well-established smaller operations, these manufacturers provide cigar companies with high-quality Dominican brands such as Arturo Fuente, H Upmann, Romeo y Julieta, La Gloria Cubana and Ultimate Dominican. Arguably the finest Dominican cigar is the Fuente Opus X.

It is rare to find a gift shop that doesn't stock a range of cigars – long ones, short ones, fat ones and thin ones. However, exercise caution when buying from these shops, or at least be aware that the quality of their cigars might fall short of expectations. It is not uncommon to find inferior cigars with top-brand labels attached to them; and cigars displayed on the beach under the burning sun are obviously not going to be as good as those stored at controlled temperatures in a posh cigar shop in Santo Domingo.

Before purchasing a cigar, go through a basic quality-control check. Firstly, look at it. A good hand-made cigar is straight with a nicely rounded top and a flat end. The wrapper – the outside leaf which gives the cigar its distinctive look – accounts for 1% of the cigar, 90% of the taste. Inspect the veins of the wrapper carefully. They should be unbroken. Secondly, feel the cigar. It should be solid. A soft cigar probably doesn't have enough tobacco in it, making it loose and causing it to burn too fast. On the other hand, if a cigar is too firm it probably has too much tobacco and won't draw. A good indication of quality is the length of time the ash remains on the cigar before dropping off.

Once you have bought your cigar, a whole new set of rules apply to smoking it. Light it slowly with a cedarwood match, as lighters can give it a gassy taste. Rotate the end under the flame so that the whole of the cigar is well lit. This will ensure that it burns at a constant heat. To maintain this constant heat, avoid knocking the ash off the cigar. How much of the cigar you smoke is a controversial issue. It seems that ultimately the choice is up to you. Finally, before smoking your cigar – even if you have a Fuente Opus X – take the label off. You are now part of a club where all members are equal!

the **Iglesia del Sagrado Corazón de Jesus** and the **Monumento a los Héros del Tiranicido**. The Church of the Sacred Heart of Jesus has a large tower which you can climb; and the Monument to the Heroes of the Tyrannicide was erected in the centre of town to celebrate the death of the tyrant Ulises Heureaux who was assassinated here on July 25 1899 (see page 147).

There are many **cigar factories** in and around Moca where you can see how tobacco is dried, blended, rolled and wrapped to make some of the finest cigars in the world. Securing a visit is often simply a question of turning up and asking politely to be shown around. Slightly more formal tours can be arranged at some of the larger factories in Santiago. The most convenient one to get to is **Compañia Anónima Tabacalera** (tel: 582 3151), which is at the end of Calle Duarte opposite the Fortaleza San Luis. Call them and ask to speak to Germán Matías or Cesar Jimenez in the Public Relations Department. **E Leon Jimenez** (tel: 241 1111), one of the largest cigar manufacturers in the Dominican Republic, who also make Marlboro cigarettes, are on 56 Avenida 27 de Febrero on the northern outskirts of the city.

San José de las Matas and the mountains
Although I suggest a visit to San José de las Matas as an excursion from Santiago, the town is so relaxing, the air so fresh and the countryside so beautiful, that you can quite easily spend a few days here. Fortunately, the two hotels in town are comfortable and excellent value. Try the **Oasis Hotel** (tel: 578 8298) on the main square or **Hotel Los Samanes** (tel: 578 8316) on the road leading into town. Both have clean rooms for under RD$200 and good restaurants.

It doesn't take long before San José gives way to the gently undulating foothills of the Cordillera Central. Walk out of town towards the hills for about 20 minutes and you'll come to **Los Piños**, a large park designed for tourists, with pine trees and plenty of open space – ideal for a picnic perhaps. **Hotel la Mansion** is in the park's grounds, but it has not been open since November 1997 (although there are rumours that it might make a comeback at the end of 1998).

LA VEGA
It is hard to recommend the town of La Vega as a place to stay for very long. Unless you arrive in February during **carnival**, when it's one of the most colourful places in the country, you'll probably use La Vega as a gateway to the mountains of the Cordillera Central. If you want to or have to stop here, the small town of Santo Cerro and the ruins of La Vega Vieja are worth seeing.

Orientation and what to see
The main square in La Vega is called **Parque Duarte**. Calle Independencia and Calle Restauracion intersect at Parque Duarte. The former is the principal shopping street, while the latter is the road leading into town from places like Jarabacoa and Santo Cerro. Three blocks down from Parque Duarte, Calle Restauración intersects with Calle Nuez de Caceres, the street with many of La Vega's hotels and the **mercado municipal** (main market).

The main sight in La Vega is probably the **Catedral de la Concepción de La Vega**. Built in 1992, it looks a bit like Battersea Power Station in London. Another interesting piece of architecture is the **Fire Station** at the end of Calle Independencia.

Getting there and away
Caribe Tours and **Metro** have terminals on Autopista Duarte, not too far from town. Walk along Calle Duarte or Caceres until you get to Avenida Rivas, then continue along Rivas for about ten minutes and you'll come to a fork in the road – Autopista Duarte is to the right. Caribe Tours has services to Santo Domingo, Santiago, Puerto Plata, Sosúa, Monte Cristi and Dajabón. Metro goes to Santo Domingo and Moca. **Expresso Vegano**, a regional carrier, provides a more convenient and slightly cheaper alternative to Santo Domingo. They leave from the town's main square next to the cathedral and their frequent runs to the capital take about two hours and cost RD$35. They also have a terminal on Autopista Duarte.

Gua-guas leave from different places, according to where you want to go. For Santo Domingo the departure point is opposite Expresso Vegano on Autopista Duarte (two hours, RD$30); for Santiago it's opposite the Texaco service station on Calle Restauracion (45 minutes, RD$10) and for Jarabacoa it's next to the Texaco service station (45 minutes, RD$15). If you have problems getting to any of these stops, *motoconchos* are easy to find in the main square and everywhere.

Where to stay
The hotels in La Vega are best described as functional. The pick of the bunch could be **Hotel Posada Pegasus** (tel: 573 8613) on Calle Beller, a quiet street off the main hotel area, Calle Nuez de Caceres, which has rooms with TV, air conditioning and hot water for RD$200. Rooms without the 'frills' are RD$125. Here you'll also find **Hotel Astral** (tel: 573 3535) with rooms that range from RD$200-450. Better value is the **Hotel Familiar San Pedro** (tel: 573 2844) on the other side of the road, where even rooms with air conditioning cost only RD$150. Next door is **Hotel Santa Clara** (tel: 573 6909), La Vega's most basic lodging. For RD$60 you get somewhere to shelter you from the rain at night. There are also two hotels on Calle Padre Billini. One block from Parque Duarte is **Casa de Huéspedes El Paraiso de Don Julio** (tel: 573 6659). The location is good, but the RD$175 rooms are rather dark and stuffy. **Hotel Olimpico** is further up on the same road and past Avenida Imbert. This is another budget hotel, half a notch up from Hotel Santa Clara, where rooms cost RD$100.

Where to eat
The restaurant situation in La Vega is dire. Unappetising cafés surround Parque Duarte, the most up-market being **Plaza's Café** which has tables outside and menus for about RD$25. For quick *comida criolla* in a different

setting try **De Cache 1**, another café near the post office on Calle Meller. **Pollo Real** (one of the many Dominican versions of Kentucky Fried Chicken) has an outlet on Calle Restauracion, as do **Helado Bon**, serving ice-cream. On the same street, next to the cathedral, **Pizza Torres** purport to serve pizza.

Despite the abundance of fruit and vegetables produced in the fertile valley around La Vega, little of it seems to be sold on the streets. Instead, you have to trek down to the **mercado municipal** for fresh food. There are one or two medium-sized **supermarkets** in town, as well as a **bakery** on Calle Duarte, the road running parallel to Calle Nuez de Caceres.

Entertainment and nightlife
The **cinema** is opposite Parque Duarte on Calle Restauracion. Relatively recent films are shown in Spanish. For discos and other nightspots, you'll have to venture out to Autopista Duarte. Is it worth the trouble?

Tourist information
The **post office** (open 08.00 to 16.00 Monday to Friday; 08.00 to 12.00, Saturday) and the **police station** are opposite each other on Calle Meller, three blocks or so from Parque Duarte. **Codetel** is in the main square, as is the competing **Tricom**. Most of the main **banks** have branches in La Vega – Banco de Reservas is just off Parque Duarte, while Banco Nacional de Credito is on Calle Independencia – and there is a **Western Union** office on Calle Duarte. There is also a **Planet Foto** for film developing and postal services on Calle Restauración, not far from where the *gua-guas* leave for Santiago and Jarabacoa.

SANTO CERRO AND LA VEGA VIEJA
Santo Cerro is one of those romantic places you go to because of what has happened in the past. Legend has it that on March 25 1495, Christopher Columbus planted a cross on Santo Cerro, which means 'Holy Hill', during a fierce battle with the Tainos. When the Indians tried to pull it down, the Virgin Mary appeared behind the cross. This apparition frightened the Tainos and Columbus seized the opportunity to win the battle. The site where Columbus is supposed to have planted the cross, the Santo Hoyo de la Cruz (Holy Hole of the Cross) is preserved in the **Iglesia Las Mercedes**, one of the prettiest churches in the Dominican Republic. As you enter the church grounds there is a tree surrounded by a fence on your right, which is apparently a descendant of the medlar tree, which provided the wood for Columbus' cross. Whether you believe this story or not, the views of the Cibao Valley from Santo Cerro are worth the trip.

Looking down from the Iglesia Las Mercedes you can see the ruins of **La Vega Vieja** (Old La Vega). Before an earthquake levelled the town in 1562, La Vega enjoyed all the riches that went with sugar-cane production and the discovery of gold. Columbus even built a fort to protect the town from the Tainos. The New World's first coin mint was founded in La Vega, as well as the island's first brothel and archbishopric. The ruins at **La Vega Vieja Archaeological Park** are mainly of the fort.

Getting to Santo Cerro and La Vega Vieja is problematic if you don't have your own transport. Infrequent *carros* leave from Calle Restauración in La Vega to make the 5km trip up to Santo Cerro. They are just as infrequent going the other way. The fare is RD$5. Alternatively, if the price is right, you might persuade a *motoconcho* to take you.

The Cordillera Central

The Cordillera Central is the highest region in the West Indies and most of it is protected by two of the country's largest national parks. The few towns in the region are situated in the foothills around the perimeters of the national parks.

JARABACOA

Jarabacoa is a town for outdoor types. Whether you're after a relatively sedate excursion to one of the nearby waterfalls, a more strenuous hike in the mountains, or a demanding canyoning adventure, Jarabacoa is the place to come. The town also provides access to Cienaga, the most popular departure point for the climb up Pico Duarte.

Getting there and away

Caribe Tours, with services to Santo Domingo, is on Avenida Independencia at the entrance to town. *Gua-guas* to La Vega leave from the same place. For onward travel into the mountains of the Cordillera Central, go to the other end of town. *Gua-guas* and sometimes *carros* to Constanza leave from the Shell service station on Avenida Carmen. For Manabao, the last town before La Ciénaga, walk down Avenida Carmen, cross the small bridge and take the first turning on your left. This is the road to Manabao and *gua-guas* depart sporadically.

Where to stay

Most of the tourists who come to Jarabacoa only stay for the day. They arrive by bus from the resorts (largely on the north coast), do some form of activity like rafting or canyoning, and are whisked back to the beach in time for the sunset. As a result, there are few hotels here, but if you stand in the main square with your back to the church and look straight ahead, you'll find one on the second floor of the large, white building in front of you. The whole complex is called **Plaza Ortiz** (tel: 574 6191) and there is also a bar with billiard tables on the first floor and a disco (Galaxia Disco) in the basement. The rooms are spacious and have large windows, but otherwise are quite characterless. Ask for one overlooking the square. It seems that the RD$200 is negotiable. The **Hogar Hotel Ligia Piña** (tel: 574 2739) is on Calle Mella. The prices are about the same as the Plaza Ortiz, but the rooms are dingier and

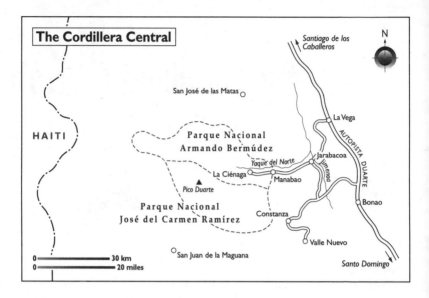

more depressing. **Hotel Jarabacoa** (tel: 574 2610) on Calle Durverge is another option at a modest RD$100.

This is the sum total of the downtown hotels. The others are on the roads leading out of town. Walk for about ten minutes along the road to Constanza and you'll reach **Hotel Pinar Dorado** (tel: 574 2820), a tourist hotel where nothing costs much under RD$500. There is a swimming pool, a nice garden and a cafeteria-style restaurant. Further along the road, the **Rancho Baiguate Hotel and Resort** – another tourist hotel in the RD$500-plus range – is at the end of a side road to your left. In between these two you can find the cheaper **Hotel Holly Day In** (tel: 574 2778) for RD$100 and the unfinished **Hotel California** (tel: 330 4350) for RD$200. About 2km along Avenida de la Confluencia (quite far from downtown) **Hotel El Triunfo** has unspectacular accommodation for RD$200 if you arrive in the morning or RD$100 if you arrive in the evening. The **Jarabacoa River Resort** (tel: 574 2772) is almost at Parque Confluencia itself. It has a small pool and overpriced, box-like rooms.

Where to eat

While hotels in Jarabacoa are few and far between, restaurants are thick on the ground. Starting in the main square, the **Don Luis Restaurant** and **Restaurant del Parque** are both good – the del Parque just edging it by virtue of its lovely terrace overlooking the park. The **El Rancho Restaurant**, next to Caribe Tours on Avenida Independencia, has a good selection of dishes, my favourite being the 'juicy rice with chicken'. The **Brasilia Restaurant**, on Calle Mario Nelson Galan, is very intimate, but the choice when you actually try to order something from their extensive menu is really quite pathetic. Hearty *la bandera* meals are served at lunchtime along Avenida Libertad at the **Johanna Restaurant** and the slightly cosier **El Mogote**

Restaurant. In the evening, along Calle Mario Nelson Galan, a number of stalls sell *pollo frito* and slices of pizza, strategically placed near the entrance to the Galaxia Disco.

There are one or two **supermarkets** on Avenida Independencia. Supermercado Tony on the corner of Calle Colón proudly advertises that English is spoken inside, making it a good place to get local information as well as your groceries. There is a **bakery** – not the best you'll find, but adequate nonetheless – on Avenida Libertad, and the **mercado municipal** is next to Plaza Ortiz on Calle Mario Nelson Galan.

Tourist information

There is a very friendly **tourist information office** (tel: 574 2772) next to Caribe Tours on Avenida Independencia which does its best to help. Ask for one of their maps giving an overview of the attractions near Jarabacoa. **Banks** are found either on the main square (Banco Nacional de Credito), one block from the main square (Banco de Reservas), or on Avenida Independencia (Banco Popular). **Western Union** is just off Avenida Independencia on Calle P Herrea. For camera film and other sundry items, **Planet Foto** is opposite Banco Nacional de Credito. The **police station** is on Avenida Independencia and the **tourist police** are next door.

Orientation and what to see

Jarabacoa is a pleasant, albeit unspectacular town, 30km southwest of La Vega at an altitude of 500m. Apart from a pretty main square, the town itself has little to recommend it. In fact, if you're expecteing a quaint little mountain town, you might be disappointed. However, in its defence, it has spectacular surrounding nature.

Most people approach Jarabacoa from La Vega. Just before you reach the town centre, a road leads off to the right and passes through rolling hills for about 5km until it reaches the hamlet of El Salto, on the banks of River Jimenoa. This is where you can find **Salto de Jimenoa**, one of the two waterfalls near Jarabacoa. The entry gate is next to the hydro-electric power station and to get to the falls you must walk across a series of footbridges. The appearance of a restaurant, lifeguards and lockers immediately sets the tone. The waterfall plunges into a large pool, which is popular for swimming and can get quite crowded. Admission costs RD$10 and to get there from Jarabacoa you'll probably have to take a *motoconcho* (about RD$20). There is allegedly a (yellow) *gua-gua* that leaves for El Salto from behind the tourist office, but I never saw it.

The other waterfall, **Salto de Baiguate**, is within walking distance of the town centre – although it will take about an hour. Walk along the road to Constanza, pass Hotel Pinar Dorado and turn right when you see the sign for Salto de Baiguate. It takes another 40 minutes or so from the turn-off to the waterfall. Baiguate is smaller than Jimenoa, but its location, in a ravine with mountains on either side, makes it the prettier of the two. There is a small pool for swimming and a modest strip of sand for drying off.

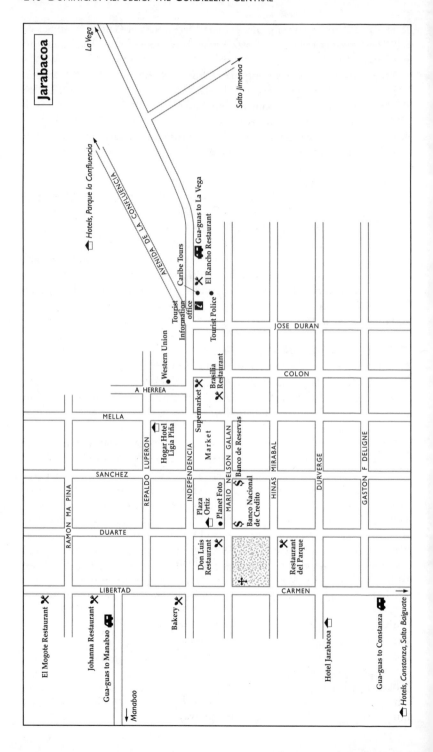

The really popular place for swimming, though, is **Parque La Confluencia** at the end of Avenida de la Confluencia, about 5km from Jarabacoa. The park itself – a few benches and trees beside River Jimenoa – is not the most beautiful in the world, but the *balneario* (spa), created by the rushing waters of the river, attract visitors from as far away as Santo Domingo. At peak times (weekends and school holidays) the park really gets too crowded to be enjoyable. The best time to visit is in the evenings just before it closes at around 18.00. While *motoconchos* will gladly take you out to the park, you might not find one so easily to take you back to Jarabacoa. This is especially true in the evening, so be prepared to walk.

Activities
I have already mentioned **Get Wet** (tel: 574 6689) in Chapter 13. They are one of the best adventure tour companies around and they have a base camp in Jarabacoa, opposite Hotel Pinar Dorado, just off the road to Constanza. Their two main activities in Jarabacoa are canyoning and river rafting. If you can only afford to do one, opt for the canyoning, which is a more unique and challenging experience.

PARQUE NACIONALES ARMANDO BERMÚDEZ AND JOSÉ DEL CARMEN RAMÍREZ
These two parks occupy almost the whole of the central mountain area: Armando Bermúdez covers 766 km^2 in the north and José Ramírez 764 km^2 in the south. The four highest peaks in the Antilles – Pico Duarte (3,175m), La Pelona (3,087m), La Rucilla (3,049m) and Pico Yaque (2,760m) – are situated within the parks' boundaries. The other outstanding feature is the rivers, with 12 of the country's most important rising within the limits of the two parks.

Flora and fauna
With average temperatures between 12 and 21°C and rainfall exceeding 2,500mm in most areas, the vegetation is classified largely as subtropical humid mountain forest or rainforest. The flora changes according to the altitude. In the lower regions West Indian cedar, mountain wild olive, copey, matchwood, juniper and wild tamarind are common, and the higher you go the more palms, ferns and pines you'll see. In the highest parts (2,000–3,175m) Creolean pine is abundant.

There is a diverse birdlife in the parks, including Hispaniolan parrots, woodpeckers and trogons, palm chats, white-necked crows, green-tailed warblers, Antillean siskins, ruddy quail doves and mourning doves. The terrestrial fauna is less rich. The indigenous *hutia* and the introduced wild boar can be found in the more remote and inaccessible areas.

Climbing Pico Duarte
Climbing the tallest mountain in the West Indies will take three days. You must first get to La Ciénaga, the gateway to the Armando Bermúdez

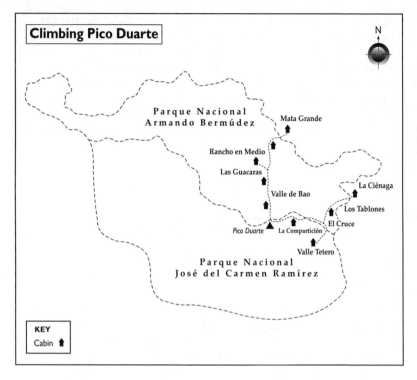

National Park. Take a *gua-gua* from Jarabacoa to Manabao, then another to La Ciénaga. The summit of Pico Duarte is 23km from La Ciénaga. If you haven't already done so in Santo Domingo, you should buy a permit to enter the park and fix a price for a guide – both mandatory reqirements for those wanting to climb Pico Duarte. Stock up on food and water in Jarabacoa.

Along the trail itself are several rudimentary cabins with cooking facilities in which you can spend the night (bring a sleeping bag). Alternatively, camping with a tent is permitted. About halfway along the route a side trail leads to Valle Teatro, a mountain valley with grass meadows and a cabin in situ, but note that this diversion will add another day to the hike.

Once you have scaled Pico Duarte's 3,175m and enjoyed views of the Caribbean Sea, the Cibao Valley and Lake Enriquillo, you can either retrace your steps to La Ciénaga or continue across the park to the entrance at Mata Grande. The distance between Pico Duarte and Mata Grande is 45km, which will take you another three days to cover. Once again, cabins are available en route.

Of course, you might prefer to climb Pico Duarte on a trek organised by an adventure company. **Get Wet** and **Iguana Mama** come highly recommended (see Chapter 13 on page 169). You could also try **Rancho Baiguate** (tel: 574 6890) at the hotel of the same name in Jarabacoa (see page 244).

CONSTANZA

Apples, pears, peaches, strawberries, raspberries and kiwis are not automatically associated with the Caribbean, yet they all grow in Constanza, which is also famous for its fresh flowers. Situated in the southeast of the Cordillera Central, Constanza is situated at a height of 1,200m and has a cooler climate than most other places in the Dominican Republic (the average yearly temperature is 16°C). In fact, in the nearby **Reserva Científica Valle Nuevo** – a plateau in the geographical centre of Hispaniola – temperatures occasionally drop to freezing and alpine vegetation seen nowhere else in the Caribbean can be found.

Getting there and away

The *gua-guas* that leave from next to the busts and heads of Duarte, Mella and Sánchez (the Monument to the Heroes of the Restoration) go to Jarabacoa and Bonao. You could make a connection at Bonao for Santo Domingo, but a better way to get to the capital is with a bus company called **Linea Cobra** (tel: 539 2415). Either call them or pass by 37 Calle Sánchez to put your name down for the daily 05.00 departure to Santo Domingo. Tell them which hotel you're staying at and the bus picks you up in the morning.

Where to stay

You might be slightly dubious if I told you that the best hotel in the centre of Constanza costs only RD$60, but **Hotel Reyes Rodriguez**, a large, pink building four blocks from the main square on Calle Gratereaux, charges exactly this for rooms with a fan, bathroom and even hot water, which is a consideration up in the mountains. Other good value establishments include **Hotel Uda Baez**, just off Calle Luperón on Calle Rufino Espinosa, and **Hotel Margarita** (tel: 539 2943) on Calle Luperón. Rooms cost RD$75 at both places. At the Uda Baez you get a bathroom attached, while at the Margarita mosquito nets are provided. The rest of the hotels in Constanza are either on or just off Calle Luperón. **Hotel California** is on it, and was preparing for its grand opening when I was there – it seems to have potential. **Hotel Mi Casa** (tel: 539 2764) is on Calle Sánchez – a comfortable room with two beds costs RD$200. **Hotel Brisas del Valle**, meanwhile, is on Calle Gratereaux, between Luperón and the main square, and might be the worst of a very good bunch.

   Hotel Mi Cabana (tel: 539 2930) is Constanza's only tourist hotel. It has all the facilities – tennis courts, swimming pool, restaurant etc – but it's a long way from the centre of town, just in front of the Nueva Suiza (see page 250). I have to say that it felt almost as deserted.

Where to eat

Lorenzo's, on Calle Luperón, is the best place to eat. The food is well presented and tasty, the service excellent, and the after-dinner coffee out of the top drawer. One notch down from Lorenzo's, but still quite good, are **Restaurant La Montana** on the main square and the **Restaurant Mi Casa** at the hotel of the same name. My earlier comments about the potential of the soon-to-be-opened

Hotel California were based on my experience at the **Restaurant California**, which had started business in time for my visit. Like Lorenzo's, a lot of care is taken over the presentation of the food and the prices are quite reasonable. For something a little different, try **Pollo Loco**, a little place past Lorenzo's on Calle Luperón, with chicken roasting on a spit outside. This is a good alternative to the standard fried chicken – and the smell is irresistible.

A number of **fruit stands** can be found at the entrance to town next to the Monument to the Heroes of the Restoration.

Tourist information

The **post office** is on the main square, while **Codetel** and the main **banks** (Banco National de Credito and Baninter) are on Calle Luperón. **Western Union** has an office on Calle Sánchez opposite a sports shop selling camping equipment.

Orientation and what to see

Many of the hotels, restaurants and other facilities useful to the visitor are on the town's main street, Calle Luperón. Almost all of them are north of the main square, **Parque Duarte**, whose distinguishing feature is its Japanese garden. In the 1950s Trujillo allowed Japanese and Hungarian farmers to come to Constanza. The Hungarians were promptly sent away when they showed a reluctance to work, but the Japanese developed an industry which provided the whole country with most of its temperate fruit and vegetables. The Japanese remain in Constanza today, and although you don't see them milling around in the streets, Parque Duarte is a reminder of their presence.

The other things to see are along the road to San José de Ocao, which also leads to the Valle Nuevo Scientific Reserve. The **Nueva Suiza** is about a ten-minute walk from Constanza. In former times this was a successful government-run hotel, built by Trujillo, but today you have to slip through a gap in the barbed-wire fence to stroll around the hotel's grounds, which have been deserted for over three years. The views of Constanza and the surrounding valley are excellent, even if the hotel itself is in a sorry state, with a slightly spooky atmosphere.

A further 2km along the road it forks left and right. Take the left turning for another 10km or so and you'll arrive at a waterfall called Agua Blanca (White Water). There are three tiers to the waterfall and it falls into an icy cold pool. You'll need your own transport to get to Agua Blanca, unless you can persuade a *motoconcho* to make the trip.

Just before the turning for the Nueva Suiza, call in at the **Jardin Exotico** (there is a sign), where a great variety of plants and flowers can be bought or just admired. Wander around the gardens with the owner, who will be delighted to describe in Spanish all the different species. He has, amongst others, roses, hyacinths, marigolds, aniseed, bougainvillea, hibiscus, mint and cinnamon.

The Southwest

The Carretera Sánchez (Sánchez Highway) starts in Santo Domingo as Avenida George Washington and continues all the way to Elias Piña on the Haitian border. Just after the town of Azua de Compostela, you have the option of veering south towards Barahona: the gateway to the hot, dry and arid Enriquillo Basin and Pedernales Peninsula.

As a tourist attraction in its own right, the Sánchez Highway was where Trujillo was held up on his way to San Cristóbal and gunned down on May 30 1961 (see also page 148).

SAN CRISTÓBAL

Only San Cristóbal's connections with General Rafael Leonidas Trujillo make it worth visiting. It is a noisy, unattractive town, 30km along the Sánchez Highway, but fortunately less than an hour away from Santo Domingo, so you don't have to stay overnight to take in its sights. They can be covered quite easily in a day trip from the capital. In any case, you won't find many hotels in San Cristóbal. The best of the very few in town, **Hotel San Cristóbal**, was closed when I was there. Whether or not it has reopened should be academic if you take my advice and avoid staying overnight.

Most of the sights in and around San Cristóbal have something to do with Trujillo, who was born here in 1892. For a start, the **Iglesia de San Cristóbal**, a pretty, yellow church on the town's main square – not to be confused with Parque Colón, where Codetel and several banks are situated – houses the tomb of the Great Benefactor. His actual body, however, is in France. Across from the church there is a monument where the house in which he was born once stood. Two of Trujillo's country houses are just outside San Cristóbal. **Castillo del Cerro** (Cerro Palace) is on a hill overlooking the town and was used to hold dances and other public functions. There is a museum there now, devoted to Trujillo and his life. For living purposes, the less conspicuous – and therefore less vulnerable – **Casa de Caoba** (Mahogany House) was preferred. On the same road is **La Toma**, a series of shallow pools that served as Trujillo's private bathing spot. Now they are open to the public seven days a week. *Motoconchos* are probably the best way of getting to Castillo del Cerro, Casa de Caoba and La Toma. Finally, back in the centre of town, on the corner of Parque Colón, the **ayuntamiento** (city

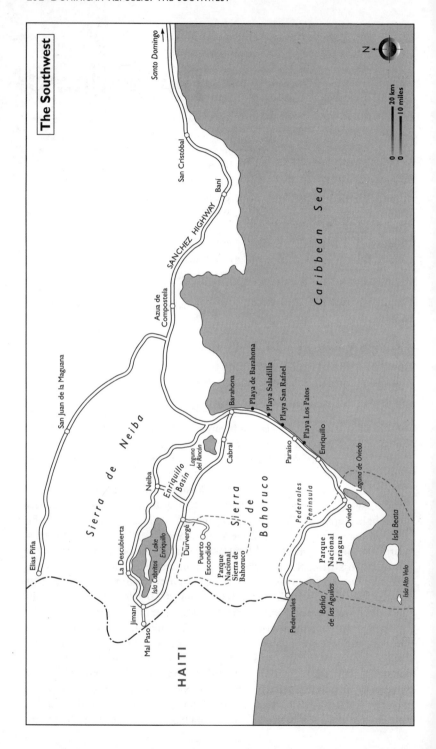

hall) is where the first Constitution of the Dominican Republic was signed on November 6 1844.

BANÍ

Every now and then you come across a town with an idiosyncrasy that defies all logical explanation. Baní is one such town. Its little foible is its cleanliness. For some reason the streets are spotless, not just by Dominican standards, but by any standards. Indeed, Baní would not look that out of place in Switzerland or Japan. The litter-free environment renders **Parque Cabral**, the town's main square, one of the prettiest in the country. The church, **Iglesia Nuestra Señora de Regla**, is also quite pleasing; and there's a **municipal museum** (open 07.00–12.00) in the city hall on the main square. Apart from all this, look out for the **pink mangoes**, which are exclusive to this part of the Dominican Republic.

Hotel Caribani (tel: 522 3871), opposite the city hall, and **Hotel Alba** (tel: 522 3540), on Calle Meller a few blocks from Parque Cabral, are both satisfactory should you decide to stay overnight. San Cristóbal to Baní takes about 45 minutes and costs RD$10.

AZUA DE COMPOSTELA

Azua is the main town in an area where sugar cane, rice, coffee and melons are important crops. At one time it was the alternative port to Santo Domingo, but an earthquake in 1751 ended that career. Nowadays, the ruins at Puerto Viejo (Old Port), about 5km from Azua's present site, are the only tourist attraction in an otherwise forgettable town.

SAN JUAN DE LA MAGUANA

About 15km past Azua the highway forks. Continuing straight ahead leads to Barahona and the Pedernales Peninsula, but turning right, the road skirts around the southern edge of the Cordillera Central, passes through the town of San Juan de la Maguana, and ends up at the Haitian border.

San Juan de la Maguana is another agricultural town of some regional importance, but with little to detain the tourist for very long. The lone attraction – the **Corral de los Indios** – is a few kilometres north of the town, a large, stone circle with stones around the edge, which was apparently used as a meeting place for the Taino Indians.

You could continue along the Sánchez Highway for another 50km to the town of **Elias Piña** (also known as **Comendador**) on the Haitian border, but since you can't get your passport stamped here, there's not much point.

BARAHONA

Barahona is the Dominican Republic's 'big little town' and by far the most important town in the region. The port does a brisk trade in sugar cane, coffee, salt, grapes, plantains and other crops; there's an airport, and the province as a whole is considered to be the area with the greatest tourism potential in the country. All this notwithstanding, Barahona is still quiet, cozy and relaxed.

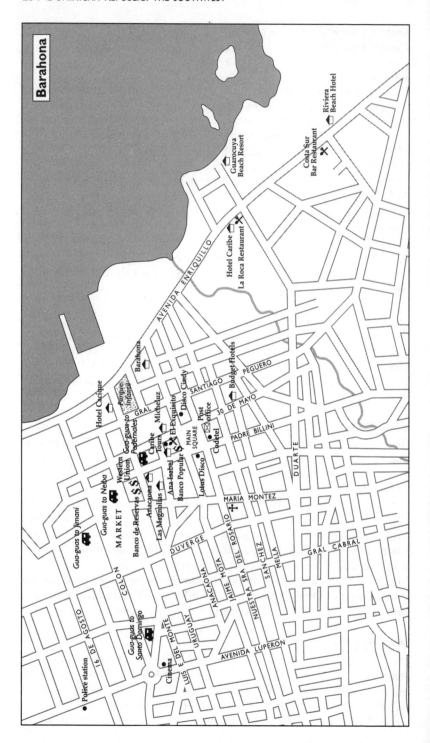

Getting there and away

Caribe Tours is on Calle Anacaona next to Hotel Ana Isabel. There are four runs a day to Santo Domingo, it takes three hours and costs RD$60. Alternatively, *gua-guas* leave for the capital at regular intervals from Calle Casandra Damiron, in a park at the entrance to town.

Gua-guas to destinations in the southwest leave from various points around the market. They are as follows:

Jimaní (for the Haitian border, La Descubierta and Lake Enriquillo): corner of Calle Maria Montez and Calle Colón (two hours, RD$40)
Neiba Calle Luis E. Del Monte (1½ hours, RD$25)
Pedernales Calle Uruguay, between Calle 30 de Mayo and Calle Padre Billini (2½ hours, RD$40)

Where to stay

For a provincial town that doesn't rely on tourism (yet), Barahona has plenty of hotels. They are mainly found in the centre of town or along Avenida Enriquillo.

There are several moderately priced downtown hotels. All of them charge about RD$300 for an air-conditioned room, slightly less for just a fan. Choose from **Hotel Las Magnolias** (tel: 524 2244), **Hotel Ana Isabel** (tel: 524 5422), **Hotel Barahona** (tel: 524 2415) and **Hotel Micheluz** (tel: 524 2358). **Hotel Anacaona** (tel: 524 5563), on Calle Uruguay, is RD$50 or so cheaper, but still quite adequate. Walk down Calle 30 de Mayo (south of the main square) for many of the budget options. You pay your money and take your chance with **Hotel Central**, **Hotel Capitolio** and **Hotel Altagracia**; but I can recommend the **Los Hijos de Dindo Hotel** (tel: 524 5510), which has rooms with a fan, bathroom and bible for RD$150. **Hotel Cacique** (tel: 524 4620) on Calle Uruguay is also cheap (RD$120).

As a general rule, you pay slightly more for the hotels on Avenida Enriquillo. The **Riviera Beach Hotel** (tel: 524 5111) has all-inclusive rates, a nice pool and a better stretch of beach than the 35-year-old **Guarocuya Beach Resort** (524 4121), which from the outside looks derelict. Inside, however, there is a tranquil, breezy feel, as well as good views of Neiba Bay. Rates are RD$460 (single), RD$578 (double) and RD$696 (triple). **Hotel Caribe** (tel: 524 4111) is opposite the Guarocuya and the best value on Avenida Enriquillo. From Monday to Friday you can get a room with air conditioning, TV, hot water and a good breakfast for RD$224 (single), RD$360 (double) or RD$520 (triple). Breakfast is not included at the weekends.

Where to eat

The best and friendliest place in the downtown area is **Restaurant El Exquisito**, on Calle 30 de Mayo, where the menu is varied and the prices reasonable. The restaurant over the road at **Hotel Micheluz** is more pretentious, while the *cabañas* at **Restaurant La Campiña** on the main square are empty too often to inspire confidence.

The quality restaurants in Barahona are along Avenida Enriquillo, and the three hotels all have good places to eat. The **El Manglar Restaurant** at the Riviera Beach Hotel is the most expensive; **Restaurant Punta Inglesa** at Hotel Caribe is good value. Also consider the **La Roca Restaurant** and the **Costa Sur Bar Restaurant**.

The **market** is on the northern side of Calle Luis E Del Monte.

Nightlife and entertainment

The most conspicuous landmark in Barahona is the flashing, blue, neon sign of the **Lotus Disco** in the main square. It is popular with the town's younger generation and the benches in the square provide the perfect vantage point from where to monitor the standard of the evening's clientele before deciding whether or not to go in yourself. If the Lotus doesn't appeal, try **Disco Cindy** just off the main square on Calle Jaime Mota. The **Costa Sur Bar Restaurant** on Avenida Enriquillo sometimes has live bands.

The **cinema**, on Avenida Luperón at the entrance to town, shows recent films with Spanish subtitles.

Tourist information

The **post office** and **Codetel** are next to each other on the main square. One of the town's **banks** is also on the square (Banco Popular), while another (Banco de Reservas) is opposite Hotel Anacaona on Calle Uruguay next to the **Western Union** office. The **police station** is on Avenida Luperón at the entrance to town.

Orientation and what to see

Barahona lies on the east coast of the peninsula, some 65km from where the Sánchez Highway splits north and south. The town itself is not hard to work out. The main thoroughfare is Calle Luis E Del Monte, which connects with the coastal road, Avenida Enriquillo. The hotels and restaurants are either in the centre of town or on Avenida Enriquillo.

The sights of Barahona are limited to the **Catedral Santa Cruz**, on Calle Maria Montez, and the **Parque Infantil Educativo y Turistico**, on Avenida Enriquillo, which has a landscaped garden in the shape of the southern half of the Dominican Republic, complete with mountains, rivers and lakes.

THE ROAD TO PEDERNALES

You can get all the way to Pedernales on the Haitian border, and to most of the towns en route from Barahona, along one of the remotest roads in the country. However, if you want to explore the two national parks split by the Pedernales road, you'll really need your own transport. Alternatively, you can go on an organised tour.

The road hugs the coast for the first 50km or so between Barahona and Enriquillo. The several beaches along this stretch have good reputations and as a general rule they get less crowded the further south you go. Going from north to south look out for Playa de Barahona, Playa Saladilla, Playa San Rafael and Playa Los Patos.

After Enriquillo, the road starts to veer inland until it reaches Oviedo, then it turns abruptly and cuts across the peninsula to Pedernales. The entrance to **Parque Nacional Jaragua** is just east of Oviedo. At 1,400km², this is the largest protected area in the Dominican Republic. It covers the southern tip of the Pedernales Peninsula and the offshore islands of Beata and Alto Velo. Within its boundaries is the 27km² **Laguna de Oviedo**, home of the country's largest flamingo population; some of the country's finest beaches (Bahía de las Aguilas on the west coast, for instance); and several caves with Taino pictographs and petrographs. The vegetation is mainly subtropical dry and thorn forest or, in layman's terms, cactus – and lots of it. As well as the flamingos, there are great egrets, green-tailed warblers, American frigate birds, little blue herons and little green herons – all of them particularly abundant in Laguna de Oviedo and on the offshore islands. The mammal life includes rhinoceros iguanas, ricord iguanas and the four marine turtles common to Hispaniola: the hawksbill, leatherback, loggerhead and green.

On the northern side of the Pedernales road lie the mountains of **Parque Nacional Sierra de Bahoruco**. (The entrance to the park is at Puerto Escondido, a few kilometres south of Durvergé, a town near Lake Enriquillo.) The park occupies an area of 800km² and is covered with Hispaniolan mahogany, Creolean pine and orchids – over 150 species. Some rare bird species, like the Hispaniolan trogon, the white-necked crow and the vervain hummingbird constitute some of the wildlife in the park.

THE ENRIQUILLO BASIN

The Enriquillo Basin is the hot, dry patch of desert in between the mountain ranges of the Sierra de Neiba and the Sierra de Baoruco. Lake Enriquillo, the largest and saltiest lake in the West Indies, dominates the Basin; the island of Cabritos dominates the lake; and crocodiles, iguanas and flamingos dominate the island. A road loops around the lake, just touching the Haitian border in the west, and linking up with the Sánchez Highway and Barahona in the east.

A few kilometres from Barahona, along the section of the loop road that runs south of Lake Enriquillo, is the small town of **Cabral**. This is the turn-off for the **Laguna de Rincón**, the largest freshwater lagoon in the Dominican Republic and home of the largest population of endemic and endangered Hispaniolan freshwater slider turtles.

Lake Enriquillo and Parque Nacional Isla Cabritos

Occupying an area of 200km² and with extremely salty water, Lake Enriquillo is probably more accurately described as a small sea. Indeed, about a million years ago it was part of a channel that linked the Bay of Neiba in the Dominican Republic with the Bay of Port-au-Prince in Haiti. Over time, sediments deposited by the River Yaque del Sur gradually closed off the mouth of the bay, thereby isolating the lake from the sea.

CHIEF ENRIQUILLO

One of the greatest pieces of Dominican literature is a book called *Enriquillo* by Manuel de Jesús Galván. It tells the story of Chief Enriquillo, perhaps the most remarkable of the Taino chieftains and the focal point of Indian resistance to Spanish oppression.

Born the son of a Taino chieftain, Enriquillo spent his early life as a slave serving the conquistadors who had killed his father. He worked hard and tried to live as constructive a life as possible under the circumstances. However, when his master, a man called Andrés de Valenzuela, tried to rape his wife, Enriquillo complained to the judges of the Royal Audience in Santo Domingo. The predictable ruling was that if the Taino slave insisted on demanding justice, he would be imprisoned.

Rather than accept this decision, Enriquillo rounded up his friends and fled to the mountains of the Sierra de Baoruco in 1519. For the next 14 years he held out against the Spanish, employing a uniquely Taino-style of resistance. In total, he foiled four attempts to capture him, on each occasion disarming his attackers and releasing them unharmed. This passive and dignified resistance earned the respect of the Spanish and in 1533 a peace treaty signed by Emperor Charles V and accepted by Enriquillo ended the rebellion. The treaty abolished slavery and guaranteed the well-being of the Taino people. Although a little too late to save Hispaniola's native Indian population, this victory immortalised Chief Enriquillo as one of the heroes of Dominican history.

There are three islands in the lake: Barbarita, Islita and Cabritos. The first two are small and rarely visited, but Cabritos – 12km long, 2km wide and ranging from 4 to 40m below sea level – is a national park.

Getting there and away

The entrance to Lake Enriquillo and Parque Nacional Isla Cabritos is about 2km east of La Descubierta. *Gua-guas* run direct to La Descubierta from Santo Domingo, but if you're coming from Barahona, you must change in either Neiba (the cheaper option) or Jimaní.

Access to the lake costs RD$10, payable at the entrance, and you can walk along its shores and swim in a small freshwater pool. You must pay a further RD$50 for a permit if you want to go across to Cabritos. There are two boats a day leaving at 07.30 and 08.30. In theory it costs RD$80 per person, but the boats will only leave if they have ten people. What most people do is arrive at the entrance at bit before the time of departure and get together with others wanting to make the trip.

Flora and fauna

With temperatures rising to 50°C and low annual rainfall, the vegetation is dominated by several species of cacti. There are endemic species like the *neobottia* tree cactus, as well as other varieties including *cayuco*, *cholla* cactus.

Most people visit Cabritos to see one of the largest American crocodɪ. populations in the world. These impressive creatures are best viewed in the early morning or late afternoon when they come out of the water to warm up under the sun. During the day they like to escape the heat by retreating to the deeper areas of the lake (see also page 10). Other wildlife, found on the shores of the lake and the islands, include rhinoceros iguanas, ricord iguanas, pink flamingos, several types of heron and the ubiquitous, but not always that obvious, Hispaniolan parrot.

La Descubierta

This is the place to base yourself for easy access to Lake Enriquillo and the national park. The town is a tourist attraction in its own right by virtue of the *balnearios* in a shaded park off the main square. These pools would be better if they weren't so crowded, especially in the afternoons, when busloads of Dominican school children arrive.

Hotel **Iguana** (tel: 519 9086), on the road leading to the lake and to Neiba, is the pick of La Descubierta's hotels. Good, clean rooms cost only RD$100 and the family who run it are extremely warm and genuinely honoured to have you as their guests. If the Iguana is full, try **Pension Hostal Del Lago** (tel: 224 9525) or **Hotel Padre Billini** (tel: 696 0327), both of which are near the main square. **Restaurant Brahaman's** is next to the *balnearios* and has simple *comida criolla*, offers tourist information and runs excursions to Lake Enriquillo. *Gua-guas* to Santo Domingo, Neiba and Jimaní leave from the main square.

Neiba

Neiba is about an hour from La Descubierta, and its two hotels, both on the main square, qualify it as another possible base from which to visit Lake Enriquillo, although it's not as convenient or as pleasant as La Descubierta. The two hotels are **Hotel Babey** (tel: 527 3356) and **Domitorio Sun Lover**. They both cost RD$100.

JIMANÍ AND THE HAITIAN BORDER

Jimaní is a dusty, two-street town on the western edge of Lake Enriquillo, a couple of kilometres from the Haitian border. The road leading into town is Calle 27 de Febrero, where you can find a **Codetel** and **Western Union** office. At the end of Calle 27 de Febrero, Calle 19 de Marzo leads to the border post at **Mal Paso**. At the intersection of these two roads is a small hotel (RD$150 a night), a few cafés and *gua-guas* to Santo Domingo. A *motoconcho* from here to Mal Paso costs RD$10.

Immigration at Mal Paso is open from 08.00 to 19.00 every day. This is a relaxed border post and you should not encounter any great problems. Have your US$10 exit tax ready, even though you might not be asked to pay it.

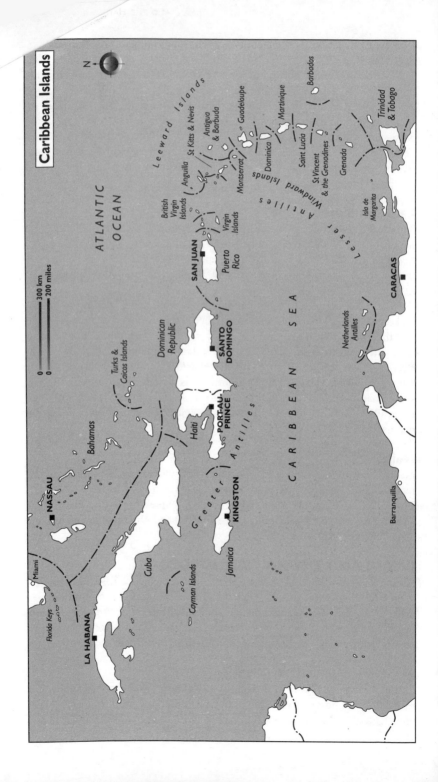

Onward Travel

Hispaniola is unique in the Caribbean in that you can get to almost anywhere in the region (by this I mean the Caribbean *and* Latin America) from either Haiti or the Dominican Republic. Of course, much will depend on your budget, since air travel and living expenses, particularly on the other Caribbean islands, are not cheap. But if you can afford it, you might like to consider incorporating Hispaniola in a grander tour of the region. This chapter is designed to give you an idea about the practical travel options from Haiti and the Dominican Republic. Other Bradt titles cover many of the onward destinations mentioned below (see page 269).

THE GREATER ANTILLES

The other islands that comprise the Greater Antilles – Cuba, Jamaica and Puerto Rico – are perhaps the most obvious choices for onward travel. Nothing can prepare you for or compete with Haiti, but Cuba is a good Hispanic foil for the Dominican Republic, as is Puerto Rico, albeit in a different way. Meanwhile, beaches, mountains and a vibrant culture can be found in Jamaica.

Of the three, **Puerto Rico** is the easiest to reach. From the Dominican Republic, American Eagle (an off-shoot of American Airlines) fly to San Juan on a daily basis from Santo Domingo, Puerto Plata, Santiago, Punta Cana and La Romana. **Cuba** is also accessible from Santo Domingo. Currently, Cubana and Lacsa (the Costa Rican airline) each operate flights to Havana, two times and three times a week respectively. **Jamaica** seems slightly harder to reach, although Tropical Airlines fly to Kingston from Port-au-Prince about three times a week, and there might be one or two seasonal charters from the Dominican Republic. There are rumours that Caribintair, who operate internal flights in Haiti, will fly to Jamaica in the near future, but nothing is yet certain.

THE LESSER ANTILLES

The islands of the Lesser Antilles provide another alternative for onward travel. **Guadeloupe** can be reached from either Port-au-Prince or Santo Domingo with Air Guadeloupe. Air France also fly there from Port-au-Prince, with the plane continuing on to **Martinique**. ALM Antillean Airlines fly to **Curaçao** from Port-au-Prince and Santo Domingo, while Aeropostal go to **Aruba** from the Dominican capital.

In addition to these islands in the Lesser Antilles, there is a glut of smaller airlines that fly to the **Bahamas** and the **Turks and Caicos Islands**, north of

Hispaniola. Many use the small international airport at Cap-Haïtien. Look for Congo Air, Techmask, Cap Air, Bahamian, Turks and Caicos Airways and Sky King, who fly to Providenciales in the Turks and Caicos from Puerto Plata.

CENTRAL AMERICA

The only country in Central America currently accessible from Hispaniola is **Panama**. Copa, the national airline, have daily flights to Panama City from Port-au-Prince and Santo Domingo, although the flights to Port-au-Prince have been the subject of recent controversy. Haiti is a notorious transit point for drugs en route from Latin America to the United States, and cocaine has been discovered on the flights from Panama. If the number of discoveries increases, there is the possibility that this service will be suspended. The situation seems more stable on Copa's flights to the Dominican Republic.

SOUTH AMERICA

The most interesting options for onward travel are in South America. The number of South American destinations served by airlines from Hispaniola is not vast, but it outstrips most other islands in the Caribbean. Moreover, once you arrive on the continent you can travel overland to the places that you want to explore.

From Haiti, you can only get to **French Guiana** – the Air France plane that goes to Guadeloupe and Martinique continues on to Cayenne. There is more choice from the Dominican Republic, with a service to **Colombia** from Santo Domingo and Puerto Plata provided by Aces, a Colombian outfit that flies to Bogotá a few times a week. You can also get to **Ecuador** and **Peru** from Santo Domingo with Iberia. This flight originates in Europe (Madrid), so you could buy a return ticket to either Quito or Lima and break your journey in Santo Domingo to travel around Hispaniola.

AIR PASSES

A good way to save some money if you're going to be doing a lot of travelling in the region is to buy an air pass. For visitors to Hispaniola, probably the best one is the **ALM Visit Caribbean Airpass**, with two obvious advantages. Firstly, ALM serves both Port-au-Prince and Santo Domingo, so you can easily treat Hispaniola as a base from where to visit other countries. Secondly, the pass includes one of the airline's two US gateways – Miami and Atlanta – which is useful if you live in the United States, or are returning to Europe from there. The other ALM Caribbean destinations are Jamaica, Puerto Rico, St. Maarten, Antigua, Trinidad and the Netherlands Antilles. The pass costs US$695 and is valid for 30 days.

Another, much cheaper option is the **BWIA Caribbean Airpass**. Also valid for 30 days, this pass only costs US$399, but they don't fly direct to Hispaniola, so you have to get to one of the countries they do serve before you can start to use the pass. These countries are Jamaica, Antigua, St Maarten, St Lucia, Barbados, Grenada, Trinidad and Tobago, Venezuela and Guyana. There is no US gateway included on this pass.

Appendix 1

LANGUAGE
Creole phrasebook
Grammar

For English speakers, Creole grammar is not all that hard to master. While the words are predominantly French, the sentence structure is rather similar to English. Another big plus is that most words – be they nouns, verbs, or adjectives – never change their form. Instead, grammatical distinctions are made by the use of 'markers': *'liv la'* means 'the book', but *'liv yo'* means 'the books'. Similarly, verbs have the same ending no matter what their tense: *'M'gen lajan'* means 'I have money' and *'M'te gen lajan'* means 'I had money'. To negate the sentence, insert *'pa'* immediately before the verb. So *'M'gen lajan'* becomes *'M'pa gen lajan'* – 'I don't have money'.

Pronunciation

a	**a**nd	*r*	at the start of a word, like the Parisian pronunciation of Paris; in the middle of a word, as in English
ch	**sh**oe		
dj	**j**ob		
e	**a**ble		
è	**e**ffort	*s*	**s**ea (never as in boy**s**)
g	**g**as (never as in gin)	*tch*	**ch**in
gn	**o**nio**n**	*u*	similar to **w**eek (lips more rounded and tense)
i	b**ee**		
j	mea**s**ure	*y*	as in English in the initial and medial positions; as in boy at the end of a word
o	sn**ow**		
ò	**ou**ght		

All other letters are pronounced as in English.

Basics

Hello	*bonjou, bonswa* (from noon onwards)	I am...	*mise...*
		Where is...?	*kote...?*
		Do you have...?	*ou gen...?*
How are you?	*kòman ou ye?*	Can you...?	*ou kapab...?*
Please	*tanpri*	Can I...?	*mikapab...?*
Thank you	*mèsi*	I want/need...	*mibezwen...*
Goodbye	*orevwa*	How much/many?	*konbyen?*
My name is...	*yo rele m...*	What time is it?	*ki lè li fè?*

Numbers

one	*youn/en/*	eleven	*onz*	twenty-two	*vennde*
	un/in	twelve	*douz*	thirty	*trant*
two	*de*	thirteen	*trèz*	forty	*karant*
three	*twa*	fourteen	*katòz*	fifty	*senkant*
four	*kat*	fifteen	*kinz*	sixty	*swasant*
five	*senk*	sixteen	*sèz*	seventy	*swasann dis*
six	*sis*	seventeen	*disèt*	eighty	*katreven*
seven	*sèt*	eighteen	*dizuit*	ninety	*katreven dis*
eight	*uit*	nineteen	*diznèf*	hundred	*san*
nine	*nèf*	twenty	*ven*	thousand	*mil*
ten	*dis*	twenty-one	*venteen*		

Days and months

Monday	*lendi*	January	*janvye*	July	*jiyè*
Tuesday	*madi*	February	*fevriye*	August	*out*
Wednesday	*mèkredi*	March	*mas*	September	*septanm*
Thursday	*jedi*	April	*avril*	October	*oktòb*
Friday	*vandredi*	May	*me*	November	*novanm*
Saturday	*samdi*	June	*jen*	December	*desanm*
Sunday	*dimanch*				

Useful words

afternoon	*apremidi*	good	*bon*	thing	*bagay*
bed	*kabann*	Haiti	*Ayiti*	today	*jodi-a*
bread	*pen*	how	*kòman*	tomorrow	*demen*
breakfast	*dejene*	hungry	*grangou*	town	*lavil*
chicken	*poul*	late	*ta*	United	
day	*jou*	man	*nèg*	States	*Ozetazuni*
dear	*cheri*	money	*lajan*	very	*trè*
diarrhoea	*djare*	morning	*matin*	water	*dlo*
early	*bonè*	passport	*paspò*	what?	*kisa?*
eat/food	*manje*	post office	*lapòs*	When?	*kilè?*
egg	*ze*	rice	*diri*	where?	*kote?*
English	*angle*	room	*chanm*	which/who?	*kilès?*
expensive	*chè*	sea	*lamè*	with	*ak*
fish	*pwason*	station	*estatyon*	woman	*fanm*
go	*ale*	street	*lari*		

Spanish phrasebook
Pronunciation

a	cat	*g*	gun (before a, o and u); conch (before e and i)
c	cut (before a, o and u); the (before e and i)	*h*	silent
ch	church	*i*	bit
e	pen	*j*	home

ll	yes	*v*	bed
ñ	onion	*y*	as in English (y on its own
o	dome		pronounced like bee)
q	cat	*z*	thick
r	as in English, but stronger		
rr	rolled r		
u	mule (silent after q and between g and e or i; pronounced like w after h and g)		

All other letters are pronounced as in English.

Basics

Hello	*hola*	Do you have…?	*tiene…?*
Good morning	*buenos dias*	Can you…?	*puede…?*
Good afternoon	*buenas tardes*	Can I…?	*puedo…?*
How are you?	*cómo está?*	I want…	*quiero*
Please	*por favor*	I need…	*necesito…*
Thank you	*gracias*	How much?	*cuánto(a)?*
Goodbye	*adiós*	What time is it?	*qué hora es?*
My name is…	*me llamo…*		
I am…	*soy/estoy…*	Do you speak English?	*Habla usted inglés?*
Where is…?	*dónde está·…?*		

Numbers

zero	*cero*	eleven	*once*	twenty-two	*veintidós*
one	*uno*	twelve	*doce*	thirty	*treinta*
two	*dos*	thirteen	*trece*	forty	*cuarenta*
three	*tres*	fourteen	*catorce*	fifty	*cincuenta*
four	*cuatro*	fifteen	*quince*	sixty	*sesenta*
five	*cinco*	sixteen	*dieciséis*	seventy	*setenta*
six	*seis*	seventeen	*diecisiete*	eighty	*ochenta*
seven	*siete*	eighteen	*dieciocho*	ninety	*noventa*
eight	*ocho*	nineteen	*diecinueve*	hundred	*cien*
nine	*nueve*	twenty	*veinte*	five hundred	*quinientos*
ten	*diez*	twenty-one	*veintiuno*	thousand	*mil*

Days and months

Monday	*lunes*	January	*enero*	July	*julio*
Tuesday	*martes*	February	*febrero*	August	*agosto*
Wednesday	*miércoles*	March	*marzo*	September	*septiembre*
Thursday	*jueves*	April	*abril*	October	*octubre*
Friday	*viernes*	May	*mayo*	November	*noviembre*
Saturday	*sábado*	June	*junio*	December	*diciembre*
Sunday	*domingo*				

Useful words

afternoon	*tarde*	go	*vamos*	today	*hoy*
bed	*cama*	good	*bueno(a)*	tomorrow	*mañana*
bread	*pan*	how	*cómo*	town	*ciudad*
breakfast	*desayuno*	hungry	*hambre*	United	*Estados*
bus stop	*parada del*	late	*tarde*	States	*Unidos*
	autobús	man	*hombre*	very	*muy*
cheap	*barato(a)*	money	*dinero*	water	*agua*
chicken	*pollo*	morning	*mañana*	what?	*qué?*
day	*día*	passport	*pasaporte*	when?	*cuándo?*
diarrhoea	*diarrea*	post office	*oficina de*	where?	*dónde?*
early	*temprano*		*correos*	which?	*cuál?*
eat	*comer*	rice	*arroz*	who?	*quién?*
egg	*huevo*	room	*habitación*	with	*con*
English	*inglés*	sea	*mar*	woman	*mujer*
expensive	*caro(a)*	street	*calle*		
fish	*pescado*	thing	*cosa*		

Appendix 2

FURTHER READING

General

Leigh-Fermor, Patrick *The Traveller's Tree: A Journey Through the Caribbean Islands* (Penguin, 1984)

Longmore, Zenga *Tap-taps to Trinidad: A Journey Through the Caribbean* (Arrow Books 1989)

Sauer, Carl *The Early Spanish Main*

Wilson, Samuel M *Hispaniola: Caribbean Chiefdoms in the Age of Columbus* (University of Alabama Press, 1990)

Haiti

Abbott, Elizabeth *Haiti: The Duvaliers and Their Legacy* (Robert Hale, 1991)

Courlander, Harold *The Drum and the Hoe: Life and Love of the Haitian People*

Duvalier, François *Memoires of a Third World Leader* (1969)

Ferguson, James *Papa Doc, Baby Doc: Haiti and the Duvaliers* (Basil Blackwell, 1987)

Gold, Herbert *Best Nightmare on Earth: A Life in Haiti* (1991)

Greene, Graham *The Comedians* (1976)

Heinl, Robert Debs et al *Written in Blood: The Story of the Haitian People 1492-1995* (University Press of America, 1996)

Leyburn, J G *The Haitian People* (Yale University Press, 1966)

Rodman, Selden *Haiti: The Black Republic* (Devin-Adair, 1984)

Roumain, Jacques *Gouverneurs de la Rosée* (Port-au-Prince, 1944)

Thomson, Ian *Bonjour Blanc: A Journey Through Haiti* (Hutchinson, 1992)

Wilentz, Amy *The Rainy Season: Haiti Since Duvalier* (Vintage, 1994)

Dominican Republic

Austerlitz, Paul *Merengue: Dominican Music and Dominican Identity* (Temple University Press, 1997)

Crassweller, Robert D *Trujillo: The Life and Times of a Caribbean Dictator* (Macmillan, 1966)

Ferguson, James *The Dominican Republic: Beyond the Lighthouse* (Latin America Bureau, 1992)

Hartlyn, Jonathan *The Struggle for Democratic Politics in the Dominican Republic* (1998)
Moya Pons, Frank *The Dominican Republic: A National History* (1994)
Ruck, Rob *The Tropic of Baseball: Baseball in the Dominican Republic* (1993)

WORLDWIDE WEB SITES
The following is a small selection of some of the more interesting and relevant web sites:

General
British Foreign Office Travel Advice: http://www.fco.gov.uk
Cheap Flights: http://www.cheapflights.co.uk (flights from the UK).
CIA World Factbook: http://www.odci.gov/cia/publications/pubs.html
Earthwatch: http://www.earthwatch.org
Electronic Embassy: http://www.embassy.org (foreign embassies in Washington DC)
EnviroWeb: http://envirolink.org
Friends of the Earth: http://www.foe.co.uk
Greenpeace International: http://www.greenpeace.org
MCI International Travellers Clinic: http://www.intmed.mcw.educ/ITC/Health.html
The Virtual Tourist: http://wings.buffalo.educ/world/
Tourism Concern: http://www.gn.apc.org/tourismconcern
US Travel Warnings: http://travel.state.gov/travel_warnings.html

Haiti and the Dominican Republic
Cabarete: http://www.hispaniola.com (accommodation, activities and much more)
Juan Luis Guerra: http://www.educ/~rvillaro/JLG/ (links to other pages on *merengue*)
The Art of Haiti: http://medalia.net/
The Studio Wah: http://www.studiowah.com (with an encyclopedia of Haitian artists)
Voodoo Information Pages: http://www.arcana.com/voodoo/

OTHER BRADT GUIDES TO LATIN AMERICA

The following is just a selection of our books for adventurous travellers. Send for a catalogue to:

Bradt Publications, 41 Nortoft Road, Chalfont St Peter, Bucks SL9 0LA, England; tel/fax: 01494 873478; email: bradtpublications@compuserve.com.

The Amazon Roger Harris and Peter Hutchison. £12.95. First edition
A complete guide to the whole Amazon region for both independent travellers and those on a package tour.

Guide to Belize Alex Bradbury. £10.95. Second edition
An informative guide to the natural beauty of Belize.

Guide to Brazil Alex Bradbury. £11.95. Second edition
Covering the nature and wildlife of Amazonia, the Pantanal, the Serra do Mar, and the northeast coast.

Backpacking in Central America Tim Burford. £10.95. First edition
From Guatemala to the Darién Gap, day walks and longer hikes in the region's protected areas.

Central and South America by Road Pam Ascanio. £12.95. First edition
The first guide to tackle head-on the problems of driving through Latin America.

Chile and Argentina: Backpacking and Hiking Tim Burford £11.95.
Fourth edition
A fully updated and expanded edition of this practical guide.

Cuba Stephen Fallon. £11.95. Second edition
A comprehensive guide to this flamboyant island

Climbing and Hiking in Ecuador Rob Rachowiecki, Mark Thurber and Betsy Wagenhauser. £12.95. Fourth edition
The definitive guide to the volcanoes, mountains and cloudforests of Ecuador, by two former residents.

Backpacking in Mexico Tim Burford. £11.95. First edition
A comprehensive and practical guide to hiking trails, volcanoes and national parks.

Peru and Bolivia: Backpacking and Trekking Hilary Bradt. £11.95.
Seventh edition
The classic guide for walkers and nature lovers.

Venezuela Hilary Dunsterville Branch. £12.95. Third edition
A guide for eco-tourists emphasising the mountains, jungles and national parks with several sections specifically on hiking.

COMPLETE LIST OF GUIDES FROM BRADT PUBLICATIONS

Africa by Road   Bob Swain/Paula Snyder   £12.95
Albania: Guide and Illustrated Journal   Peter Dawson/Andrea Dawson/Linda White   £10.95
Amazon, The   Roger Harris/Peter Hutchison   £12.95
Antarctica: A Guide to the Wildlife   Tony Soper/Dafila Scott   £12.95
Australia and New Zealand by Rail   Colin Taylor   £10.95
Belize, Guide to   Alex Bradbury   £10.95
Brazil, Guide to   Alex Bradbury   £11.95
Burma, Guide to   Nicholas Greenwood   £12.95
Cape Verde Islands   Aisling Irwin/Colum Wilson   £11.95
Central America, Backpacking in   Tim Burford   £10.95
Central and South America by Road   Pam Ascanio   £12.95
Chile and Argentina: Backpacking and Hiking   Tim Burford   £11.95
Cuba, Guide to   Stephen Fallon   £11.95
Dominica   Lennox Honychurch   £12.95 (summer 1999)
East and Southern Africa: The Backpacker's Manual   Philip Briggs   £13.95
Eastern Europe by Rail   Rob Dodson   £9.95
Ecuador, Climbing and Hiking in   Rob Rachowiecki/Mark Thurber/Betsy Wagenhauser   £12.95
Eritrea, Guide to   Edward Paice   £10.95
Estonia   Neil Taylor   £11.95
Ethiopia, Guide to   Philip Briggs   £11.95
Galapagos Wildlife   David Horwell/Pete Oxford   £14.95   (summer 1999)
Ghana, Guide to   Philip Briggs   £11.95
Greece by Rail   Zane Katsikis   £11.95
Haiti and the Dominican Republic   Ross Velton   £11.95
India by Rail   Royston Ellis   £11.95
Laos and Cambodia, Guide to   John R Jones   £10.95
Latvia   Stephen Baister/Chris Patrick   £11.95
Lebanon, Guide to   Lynda Keen   £10.95
Lithuania   Gordon McLachlan   £11.95 (spring 1999)
Madagascar, Guide to   Hilary Bradt   £12.95
Madagascar Wildlife   Hilary Bradt/Derek Schuurman/Nick Garbutt   £14.95
Malawi, Guide to   Philip Briggs   £10.95
Maldives, Guide to   Royston Ellis   £11.95
Mauritius, Rodrigues and Réunion   Royston Ellis/Derek Schuurman   £12.95
Mexico, Backpacking in   Tim Burford   £11.95
Mozambique, Guide to   Philip Briggs   £11.95
Namibia   Chris McIntyre   £12.95
North Cyprus, Guide to   Diana Darke   £9.95
Peru and Bolivia: Backpacking and Trekking   Hilary Bradt   £11.95
Philippines, Guide to   Stephen Mansfield   £12.95

Poland and Ukraine, Hiking Guide to   Tim Burford   £11.95
Romania, Hiking Guide to   Tim Burford   £10.95
Russia and Central Asia by Road   Hazel Barker   £12.95
Russia by Rail, with Belarus and Ukraine   Athol Yates   £13.95
South Africa, Guide to   Philip Briggs   £11.95
Southern Africa by Rail   Paul Ash   £11.95
Spain and Portugal by Rail   Norman Renouf   £11.95
Spitsbergen, Guide to   Andreas Umbreit   £12.95
Sri Lanka by Rail   Royston Ellis   £10.95
Switzerland by Rail   Anthony Lambert   £10.95
Tanzania, Guide to   Philip Briggs   £11.95
Uganda   Philip Briggs   £11.95
USA by Rail   John Pitt   £11.95
Venezuela   Hilary Dunsterville Branch   £12.95
Vietnam, Guide to   John R Jones   £11.95
Your Child's Health Abroad   Dr Jane Wilson-Howarth/Dr Matthew Ellis
£8.95
Zambia, Guide to   Chris McIntyre   £11.95
Zanzibar, Guide to   David Else   £11.95

Bradt Guides are available from bookshops or by mail order from:

Bradt Publications
41 Nortoft Road
Chalfont St Peter
Bucks SL9 0LA
England
Tel/fax: 01494 873478
Email: bradtpublications@compuserve.com

Please include your name, address and daytime telephone number with your order and enclose a cheque or postal order, or quote your Visa/Mastercard card number and expiry date. Postage will be charged as follows:

UK: £1.50 for one book; £2.50 for two or more books
Europe (inc Eire): £2 for one book; £4 for two or more books (airmail printed paper)
Rest of world: £4 for one book; £7 for two or more books (airmail printed paper)

Index